The Dysfunction of Ritual in Early Confucianism

OXFORD RITUAL STUDIES

Series Editors
Ronald Grimes
Ute Hüsken, University of Oslo
Eric Venbrux, Radboud University Nijmegen

THE PROBLEM OF RITUAL EFFICACY
Edited by William S. Sax, Johannes Quack, and Jan Weinhold

PERFORMING THE REFORMATION
Public Ritual in the City of Luther
Barry Stephenson

RITUAL, MEDIA, AND CONFLICT
Edited by Ronald L. Grimes, Ute Hüsken, Udo Simon, and Eric Venbrux

KNOWING BODY, MOVING MIND
Ritualizing and Learning at Two Buddhist Centers
Patricia Q. Campbell

SUBVERSIVE SPIRITUALITIES
How Rituals Enact the World
Frédérique Apffel-Marglin

NEGOTIATING RITES
Edited by Ute Hüsken and Frank Neubert

THE DANCING DEAD
Ritual and Religion among the Kapsiki/Higi of North Cameroon and Northeastern Nigeria
Walter E.A. van Beek

LOOKING FOR MARY MAGDALENE
Alternative Pilgrimage and Ritual Creativity at Catholic Shrines in France
Anna Fedele

THE DYSFUNCTION OF RITUAL IN EARLY CONFUCIANISM
Michael David Kaulana Ing

The Dysfunction of Ritual in Early Confucianism

MICHAEL DAVID KAULANA ING

OXFORD
UNIVERSITY PRESS

OXFORD
UNIVERSITY PRESS

Oxford University Press is a department of the University of Oxford.
It furthers the University's objective of excellence in research,
scholarship, and education by publishing worldwide.

Oxford New York
Auckland Cape Town Dar es Salaam Hong Kong Karachi
Kuala Lumpur Madrid Melbourne Mexico City Nairobi
New Delhi Shanghai Taipei Toronto

With offices in
Argentina Austria Brazil Chile Czech Republic France Greece
Guatemala Hungary Italy Japan Poland Portugal Singapore
South Korea Switzerland Thailand Turkey Ukraine Vietnam

Published in the United States of America by
Oxford University Press
198 Madison Avenue, New York, NY 10016

Library of Congress Cataloging-in-Publication Data
Ing, Michael David Kaulana.
The dysfunction of ritual in early Confucianism / Michael David Kaulana Ing.
p. cm.
Includes bibliographical references and index.
ISBN 978-0-19-992489-9 — ISBN 978-0-19-992491-2
1. Confucianism—Rituals. I. Title.
BL1858.I44 2012
299.5'1282—dc23
2012000910

1 3 5 7 9 8 6 4 2

Printed in the United States of America
on acid-free paper

To Sherene

Acknowledgments

I BEGAN THIS project several years ago while a graduate student at Harvard University. While there, I benefited from interacting with many wonderful scholars. In particular, Michael Puett, Tu Weiming, and John Berthrong offered their kind guidance and spurred me to deeper levels of reflection. They patiently mentored me—giving me "one corner" 一隅 of the research process while expecting me to return with the other three. My hope is that I have at least brought back one corner in the pages of this book.

Discussions with scholars such as Jonathan Schofer, Catherine Hudak Klancer, Peng Guoxiang, Misha Tadd, Sarah Queen, Jason Clower, Wai-yee Li, Bede Bidlack, Masayuki Sato, Matt Stefon, Vincent Leung, and Taylor Petrey occurred at just the right time. I am indeed thankful for their direction.

I have also benefited greatly from my colleagues here at Indiana University. Aaron Stalnaker and Bob Eno have been my biggest supporters, and Cheryl Cottine and Susan Blake have provided crucial feedback on portions of the manuscript.

Cynthia Read, the reviewers of this manuscript, and the editors at Oxford have also been invaluable. Rodney Taylor, in particular, has encouraged me to complete this project. I would also like to thank Ponte Ryūrui 品天龍涙 for providing the calligraphy that appears on the cover.

Parts of chapter 7 appeared as "The Ancients Did Not Fix Their Graves: Failure in Early Confucian Ritual" in *Philosophy East & West* 62.2 (April 2012), 223–245. I am greatful to Roger Ames and those at *Philosophy East & West* for permission to republish this piece in its present form.

Lastly, and most importantly, no one deserves my gratitude more than my family. Sherene, Kai'ava, and Lalea make every day so much more meaningful; and my mother and father, Linda Ing and David Ing, have helped in ways too numerous to count.

While this project reflects the insights of all these people, its shortcomings are my own.

Contents

Conventions

I EMPLOY THE *Pinyin* system of Romanization throughout this project except for the names of contemporary authors whose work is published under alternative forms of Romanization. If a system other than *Pinyin* was used in a quotation, I converted the terms into *Pinyin* and often added Chinese characters. I use the traditional script form of Chinese characters except when citing an article or book composed in simplified characters.

When referencing East Asian scholars, I follow the custom of referring to them with their last name first, although in the notes and bibliography I follow the guidelines set forth in the recent edition of *The Chicago Manual of Style*.

For the sake of clarity, I use single quotation marks to designate technical terms, and I use double quotation marks in their standard grammatical sense—to designate the words or terms of others. When words are italicized they are either foreign words or words I wish to stress in a given sentence.

When quoting the *Liji*, I reference the chapter and passage number from the *Liji Zhuzi Suoyin* 《禮記逐字索引》, which is part of the Chinese University of Hong Kong's Institute of Chinese Studies's Ancient Chinese Text Concordance Series (published by Taiwan Shangwu Yinshuguan 台灣商務印書館 in 1992) edited by D. C. Lau and Chen Fong Ching. In many places, I have changed the punctuation as it appears in the *Liji Zhuzi Suoyin*, and in some cases I have chosen character variants as suggested by Lau and Chen or other editions of the *Liji*. The Chinese University of Hong Kong's Ancient Chinese Texts Database (www.chant.org) also has an online version of the *Liji Zhuzi Suoyin*, which I have consulted.

The Dysfunction of Ritual in Early Confucianism

Introduction

THE "LIYUN" 禮運 chapter of the *Liji* 《禮記》 opens with the account of a time when the "Great Way" (*dadao* 大道) pervaded the world—when people treated everyone as family, and the sick, widowed, and orphaned were cared for. In this period, robbers and thieves were nonexistent, and people had no need to close the doors to their homes. The text goes on to call this period a time of "Grand Unity" (*datong* 大同).

Thereafter, however, things changed. For reasons not explained in the text, the Great Way became obscure and people began working for their own benefit rather than for the benefit of all of humanity. Fortunately, a number of "profound persons" (*junzi* 君子) appeared on the scene and devised a means by which people could still maintain a sense of unity. These people created, or further developed, a system of rituals that ordered things to the point of generating a situation that the text calls "Modest Prosperity" (*xiaokang* 小康). From the vantage point of Confucius, the figure recounting the story, these rituals were necessary in creating a prosperous world.

The social cosmology provided by the "Liyun" is significant for several reasons. Most importantly, it argues for a shift in the development of human society from a time where the world was in synchronization with the Great Way, to a time where human beings had to self-consciously rely on additional devices to regain a semblance of this proper relation. These devices, or guides, are *li* 禮, a term that I will often translate as 'ritual.' The opening passage of the "Liyun" describes these rituals as *ji* 紀, or the figurative knots that hold society together.[1] Without these knots human society would be like loose items, scattered across the world without coherent pattern, and left in a state of disorder.

It is worthy to note that the shift from one time period to the next is marked by a new need for mediation. The Great Way no longer tied society together; rather, society needed a supplementary series of knots to be bound together as before.[2] These knots, in the form of ritual, are the means by which human beings were able to attain proper unity. They constitute an additional component that was either absent or already operating subtly during the previous period. In this worldview, the Great Way is no longer immediately accessible. Human beings must work through ritual in order to realize it. Ritual, as such, serves to compensate for something lost in the transition to a world of Modest Prosperity. Yet, as we will see, the *Liji* is often uncertain about the capability of ritual, and the human beings involved in performing ritual, to succeed in mediating society with the Great Way.

The title of this chapter, "Liyun" 禮運, is open to multiple interpretations. Among the possibilities are "The Implementation of Ritual" (in other words, how or why human beings should put ritual into practice), "The Motion of Ritual" (in the sense of ritual being the means by which society is able to move and work together), or "The Movement of Ritual" (implying the coming forth, or creation, of ritual). I take the title in the latter sense, teasing out its implication to also include the movement of the social world of human beings into a situation where a ritual tradition is now necessary. Following early commentators, I view it in the sense of a change in condition (a *yunzhuan* 運轉), where, due to this break with the past, people find themselves in a significantly different state of affairs—a state of affairs characterized by both the positive and negative implications of more complex ritual performance.[3] I will say more about this view in chapter 5.

This book is set against a backdrop such as the one described in the "Liyun" chapter of the *Liji*. While the *Liji* contains a number of conflicting voices, many of which are at odds with the social cosmology of the "Liyun," a common voice can be heard recognizing that ritual can fail to create an ordered world. This voice is often merely a thin congruence of perspectives that conceals beneath it larger aspects of disagreement and discord. In other words, while other chapters of the text provide different reasons for the failure of ritual, they all explicitly or implicitly agree that ritual can in fact fail to achieve its intended aims and that this failure is cause for concern. In the pages that follow, I will engage in a close reading of the *Liji*—one that seeks to maintain a dual commitment to the diversity of perspectives presented in the text, on the one hand, and their overlapping concern for the dysfunction of ritual, on the other.[4]

The Text

The *Liji* is a collection of forty-nine texts—most of which purport to be written by Confucius's immediate disciples (ca. fifth century BCE). Some of the texts are relatively short—translating to ten or twelve sentences.

Others are much longer—translating into three hundred to four hundred sentences. A few portions of the *Liji* are liturgical—providing a kind of script for particular ritual performances. Most portions, as elaborated below, theorize *about* ritual—arguing for why ritual should be performed, rather than discussing the specific steps a ritual should follow.

Sometime before the second century CE these forty-nine texts—many of which were already associated with each other—were collected into one source known as the *Liji*. In its entirety, the *Liji* contains nearly ninety thousand Chinese characters (roughly six times as many as the *Analects*). Around the second century BCE, the *Liji* in its then current form became a part of the earliest Confucian canon known as "The Five Classics."[5] Only several centuries later were texts such as the *Analects* included in the canon. The *Liji*, in other words, is a very significant text for the tradition usually known as 'Confucianism.' In the early periods of the tradition, it was more significant in certain ways than texts such as the *Analects*, despite how well known the latter is today.

While a more complete textual history of the *Liji* is found in the appendix, I will note here that, in short, the *Liji* is a redacted text that took its received form between the first century BCE and the second century CE. Large portions of it were written previous to the Qin Dynasty (221–206 BCE); although beyond the portions found in recent archeological finds, it is difficult to pinpoint exactly which sections are from this period. The redactor(s) of the *Liji* took an active role in compiling the text by adding and combining passages, among other activities. For the purposes of this project, issues of redaction and source material will be dealt with as necessary. In other words, I will engage them when they serve to highlight or potentially overturn my line of argumentation.

By and large, I am looking at continuities between the chapters, and by implication, the continuities between the larger debates in early China. However, I do not assume continuity; rather, I remain open to the possibility that any two texts (or even chapters, and often portions of chapters) are in fact discontinuous unless proven otherwise. As with any text, there are factors besides ideological coherency at play in its composition. In the case of the *Liji*, we are largely unaware of many of these factors; and so moments of coherency will often be our own superimpression made on the text, rather than an ideological coherency intended by the author(s). Since most situations will never yield the entirety of factors going into textual composition, I imagine we should, to a certain degree, be satisfied with the realization that our work is largely our own projection.

The complexity of the *Liji*'s textual composition leads me to take figures in the text, such as Confucius, as literary rather than historical figures. In other words, for the sake of this project I examine representations of (mostly) historical figures as presented in the *Liji*. I am less concerned with discovering the "authentic" Confucius.[6] As such, I treat the text as a series of arguments situated in larger discussions of its time. In this light, when I refer to "Confucius" or other named figures, I refer to Confucius as represented in the *Liji* or other early Chinese texts.

There are a number of reasons I have chosen to work with the *Liji*. Despite its prominent position as one of The Five Classics in early China, the *Liji* has been largely neglected in Western scholarship. There are four major translations of the text, the last one completed in 1930 (compared with dozens of translations of the *Yijing* 《易經》, or *Book of Change*). The first, published by Joseph-Marie Callery in 1853, is a French translation of selections of the *Liji*, totaling a little more than half of the original text.[7] The second is James Legge's 1885 English translation of the text in its entirety.[8] In the introduction to each of these translations, the translators express their views on the importance of the *Liji*. Callery describes it as "the most exact and complete monography which the Chinese nation has been able to give of itself to the rest of the human race."[9] And Legge claims, "More may be learned about the religion of the ancient Chinese from this classic than from all the others together."[10] While these statements are largely hyperbolic, I do agree with Callery and Legge that the *Liji* provides unique insights into the religious and ethical views of early China. For a complex of reasons, however, the fervor that Legge and Callery had for the *Liji* was not passed down to future generations of Western scholars.

In the English-speaking academy there are no monographs on the *Liji*. The longest sustained study is Jeffery Riegl's dissertation—"The Four 'Tzu ssu' Chapters of the *Li chi*"—completed nearly 30 years ago.[11] Riegel's analysis is largely historiographic and philological. His research was groundbreaking in terms of introducing the English-speaking academic community to the debates surrounding the *Liji*'s textual composition, and more particularly, articulating the Zisizi 子思子 controversy to the Western academy.[12] Recent archeological finds, however, have undermined his major claim that the *Liji* was a text written by Han Dynasty court ritualists as a retrospective act of creating tradition.

The neglect of the *Liji* in the sinological community is reflected in other academic communities that engage Chinese material. The contemporary interest in Confucian ethics, and the role that ritual plays in ethics, has oddly enough not generated more interest in the *Liji*. Interpreters uniformly agree that *li* 禮 is a key component of Confucian ethics; however, several early works such as the *Liji*, the *Yili* 《儀禮》, the *Zhouli* 《周禮》, and remnants of the *Da Dai Liji* 《大戴禮記》, which total several thousand pages about *li* 禮, and a host of related terms, have been left for the most part untouched—especially in comparison to the outpouring of scholarship done on the *Mencius*, the *Xunzi*, and the *Analects*.

While the *Yili*, the *Zhouli*, and the *Da Dai Liji* are also worthy of investigation, I have chosen to work with the *Liji* because of its status as a "classic" in early Confucianism, as well as the fact that it tends to be more concerned with explaining *why* certain rituals were necessary rather than explaining *how* to perform them. A brief comparison with texts such as the *Yili* demonstrates this point. The *Yili* contains a number of what can be called 'companion chapters' to the *Liji*. For instance, the *Yili* contains chapters whose titles can be translated as "The District Drinking Ceremony" ("Xiangyinjiuli" 鄉飲酒禮), "The District Archery Ceremony" ("Xiangsheli" 鄉射禮), "The Banquet Ceremony" ("Yanli" 燕禮), and "The Capping Ceremony for Officials" ("Shiguanli" 士冠禮). Each of these chapters provides a liturgy for performing these rituals. The *Liji*, on the other hand, has related chapters entitled "The Significance of the District Drinking [Ceremony]" ("Xiangyinjiuyi" 鄉飲酒義), "The Significance of the Archery [Ceremony]" ("Sheyi" 射義), "The Significance of the Banquet [Ceremony]" ("Yanyi" 燕義), and "The Significance of the Capping [Ceremony]" ("Guanyi" 冠義). Rather than providing a script for these ceremonies, the *Liji* chapters argue for the importance of performing them. As such, the *Liji* is more suited to the purposes of this project in examining attitudes toward dysfunctional ritual.

The Argument

The general question this project addresses is—how do the authors/redactors of the *Liji* recognize, explain, and cope with dysfunctional rituals? Through an examination of this question, I demonstrate that failures in ritual were causes of acute concern for the authors of the *Liji*. More specifically, in this project I describe early Confucian attitudes toward preventable and unpreventable failures in ritual. I argue that early Confucians often found an ambiguous distinction between the two, and that this gives way to a tragic reading of ritual. This is in contrast to many contemporary interpretations of Confucian ethics, where the ritual agent is ascribed the ability to recognize a clear distinction between preventable and unpreventable failures and thereby render his process of self-cultivation invulnerable to failures beyond his control.

I will develop several terms throughout this study to substantiate this argument. While I will elaborate on these terms in the chapters that follow, it will be useful to introduce them here. **Ritual** is often a translation of the term *li* 禮. Ritual refers to codified performances that were generally thought to create a more ordered world. 'Order' in this sense can be understood as properly aligning the outer dimensions of the human body with the inner dimensions of the human psyche; properly relating various people to each other—a grown man should, for instance, be a good husband, son, father, brother, and friend; properly associating human beings in the midst of a myriad of other entities (*wu* 物) that inhabit the world including animals and spiritual forces (*guishen* 鬼神); and properly situating human society between the heavens and the earth such that all people move in conjunction with the changes in season and live in accordance with the contour of the land. In the *Liji*, order tends to be spoken of in terms of the character *zhi* 治.

The **ritual script** comprises the rules a ritual should follow.[13] These rules may be recorded in texts—portions of the *Liji* read this way—or passed down orally. In short, the script refers to the steps of a ritual believed to be prescribed by authoritative figures of ritual performance. In many instances, these steps require ritual performers to take specific actions. In other instances, these steps come in the form of general guidelines that ritual agents adapt to their circumstances. The *Liji* does not always specify the ritual script at play in a particular circumstance. For several centuries, scholars have noted that there are in fact conflicting ritual scripts in the early Confucian tradition.[14] While the precise script for a particular ritual performance is not always provided, the *Liji* tends to highlight points of tension when ritual performers deviate from the script deemed authoritative for that performance.

It is worth noting here that this study is not an ethnographic account of ritual performance or an attempt to reconstruct the ritual practices of early China. Instead, this is an interpretation of a text about ritual. As such, I primarily focus on the discourse of ritual as presented in the *Liji*, and only to a lesser degree do I focus on the historical practices discussed in the *Liji*. While I hope to demonstrate the strength of such an approach, I am also aware of its shortcomings.[15]

Dysfunction is synonymous with failure (since there is no verbal form of 'dysfunction,' I frequently use the term 'fail'). A ritual fails most explicitly when one or more the aims desired by a person involved with the ritual is not realized. The failure may be the fault of the people associated with the ritual or may be the fault of an inadequate ritual script—including inadequacies that do not account for extra-ritual agencies that may determine the outcome of the ritual (e.g., the death of one's father during a marriage ceremony threatens one's continued participation in a marriage ceremony since one has an obligation to immediately tend to the funerary rites of one's father). If people are not **competent** ritual performers—equipped with the necessary skills and knowledge to follow the ritual script—the ritual could fail. This is a common reason for the failure of ritual. Throughout this project, I call these dysfunctions **failures in competency**. On the other hand, if the ritual script is ill-suited to account for the complexities confronted by ritual agents—these difficulties may be in terms of geographic variation or other political, social, or cosmic powers exerting themselves on the event—the ritual could fail. I call these dysfunctions **failures in efficacy** since in these situations the ritual script is rendered inefficacious. One way to conceptualize a distinction between failures in competency and failures in efficacy is to speak of the former as "failures *in* ritual" (i.e., a mistake made in the performance of the ritual) and the latter as "failures *of* ritual" (i.e., the inability of the ritual script to generate its purported end).[16] While this distinction is helpful in understanding the difference between failures in competency and failures in efficacy, the demands of proper grammar make it difficult to consistently apply the distinction; and as such, I use both "failures in ritual" and "failures of ritual" interchangeably in the body of this project.

Fluent ritual agents are participants in the ritual who are able to recognize potential failures in efficacy and modify or rewrite the ritual script to avoid the failure. Confucius is often depicted as having a high degree of fluency since he is able to alter rituals in different circumstances to ensure their continued success. Fluency is developed through years of cultivating oneself by means of engaging in ritual practice.

I further divide failures in efficacy between preventable and unpreventable failures. **Preventable failures in efficacy** are those failures that a fluent ritual agent can preempt by changing the ritual script. If, for instance, the script for a sacrifice demands using ocean fish, but those participating in the sacrifice live far away from the ocean, a fluent ritual agent will recognize the possible failure and alter the script such that these people will perform the ritual effectively—perhaps by using river fish instead of ocean fish. Proper alterations are made by exercising one's sense of appropriateness, or *yi* 義. Fluent ritual agents have a highly refined sense of appropriateness.

Unpreventable failures in efficacy are failures of ritual that cannot be stopped regardless of the fluency of the ritual agent. If, for instance, the ancestral hall catches fire during a sacrifice, engulfing the hall in flames, there is nothing the fluent agent can do to prevent the failure of the sacrifice. While I will examine both preventable and unpreventable failures in efficacy, my primary concern is with attitudes toward unpreventable failures in efficacy and how the text discusses unpreventable failures in efficacy in relation to preventable failures in efficacy.

Ambiguity results from a situation where conflicting explanations of a failed ritual, when considered independently, are similarly persuasive. The *Liji* is not always clear when the failure of a ritual is the fault of the ritual performer or the fault of an inadequate ritual script. These circumstances are fundamentally ambiguous.

The ambiguity of ritual failure, in conjunction with the demands of competent ritual performance, generates a degree of **anxiety** in the figures described in the *Liji*. Their concern with proper performance and the real possibility of ritual failure functioned productively such that it allowed them to effectively respond to the complexities they faced in life.

Synthesizing these terms into an overview of this project can be done as follows: The early Confucians associated with the *Liji* were undoubtedly interested in cultivating competent ritual performers. They sought to develop ritual scripts that, when followed, inculcated the necessary skills and dispositions in ritual performers to become intuitive ritual agents. These ritual agents, of course, sometimes failed to follow the script; but a committed ritual agent would constantly seek to improve himself and minimize these failures. Early Confucians also realized that ritual scripts sometimes failed to meet the demands of varying circumstances—not everyone could, for instance, afford the lavish funerary rites dictated by the script. Ritual scripts, therefore, required alteration. Both failures in the competency of ritual performers as well as failures in the adequacy of ritual scripts are preventable in the sense that a cultivated ritual agent could perform any ritual appropriately—whether it meant following the ritual script or altering the ritual script to meet the needs of the circumstance.

Early Confucians, however, also realized that some failures of ritual were unpreventable. The death of one's parents, for instance, was a legitimate reason to cease the performance of almost any ritual—there is nothing that can be done to prevent the failure of these rituals in the face of such a significant event. Most contemporary interpreters of Confucianism, at a general level, subscribe to these views of preventable and unpreventable failures of ritual. However, the majority of these scholars believe that the cultivated ritual agent is capable of recognizing a clear distinction between preventable and unpreventable failures of ritual. The joyful ease of the refined ritual agent, in their view, is predicated on recognizing and turning away from the things that he or she has little control over, and instead turning inward to the realm that he or she does have control over—the realm of self-cultivation.

In contrast to this position, this project demonstrates that early Confucian texts can be read as arguments for ambiguity in ritual failure. If, as discussed in one text, Confucius builds a tomb for his parents unlike the tombs of antiquity, and rains fall causing the tomb to collapse, it is not immediately clear whether this failure was the result of random misfortune or the result of Confucius straying from the ritual script by building a tomb incongruent with those of antiquity. Early Confucian texts pose several of these situations and suggest that the line between preventable and unpreventable failures of ritual is not always clear. These vignettes also demonstrate that happiness and human flourishing is, to a certain extent, contingent on agencies other than the self. Relationships between oneself and other human beings, for instance, partially constitute the self and thereby leave the self permeable to the intrusion of those relations. The agencies of other people often lie beyond one's control.

Ritual performance, in this view, is a performance of risk. It entails rendering oneself vulnerable to the agency of others, and resigning oneself to the need to vary from the successful rituals of past, thereby moving into untested and uncertain territory. This theory of ritual is tragic in the sense that it explores how Confucians coped with the dissonance between an understanding of ritual where ritual served to construct an ordered world and their experience with ritual as it sometimes failed to bring about this world. This project demonstrates that the anxiety associated with notions of dissonance and vulnerability functioned 'productively.' In other words, the anxiety associated with the inevitability and ambiguity of ritual failure, as well as the anxiety associated with the contingent nature of successful ritual, generated a profoundly meaningful series of opportunities valued for their creative and therapeutic power in responding to the complex circumstances early Confucians confronted in life.

Chapter 1 provides a characterization of ritual. It examines various conceptions of *li* 禮 in the *Liji* and demonstrates that some authors of the text understood *li* 禮 in a more restrictive sense. For them, rituals were ceremonial occasions held at different times of the year or at different moments of one's life. Other authors of the text, however, understood *li* 禮 in an expansive sense—and for them, ritual became a means of properly comporting oneself even in the mundane acts of everyday life. This chapter also shows that the authors or redactors of the *Liji* were preoccupied with concepts other than *li* 禮 that served as codified performances for creating an ordered world.

In exploring the notion of order, chapter 1 describes the 'impressive' and 'expressive' functions of ritual. In its impressive sense, rituals act to shape human beings—changing the way they feel and act. Expressively, rituals serve as conduits to make manifest the refined dispositions of cultivated people. Both functions of ritual take into account notions of human "sentiment" or *qing* 情—a term that I will translate and explain as 'untaught disposition.' Training these dispositions cultivates competent and fluent ritual performers. This chapter closes, therefore, with a brief discussion of the terms 'competency' and 'fluency.'

Chapter 2, "A Typology of Dysfunction," introduces the notion of ritual failure. It explores several of the terms mentioned above—such as failures in competency and failures in efficacy—and provides examples from the *Liji* to illustrate them. This chapter serves to frame several of the issues developed in subsequent chapters, including how a fluent ritual agent 'opens the ritual script' to allow for variations in ritual practice, as well as how an open script served to legitimate the role of early Confucians in the sociopolitical structure of early China by emphasizing the need for living interpreters of the tradition. It closes by introducing the notion of unpreventable failures in efficacy.

This chapter also explores the literature on ritual failure in the field of ritual studies. It notes that in contrast to many other religious traditions, where "it is men who make mistakes, not the ritual," early Confucianism provides a tragic account of ritual where ritual is not only necessary to enable human flourishing, but is also a source of anxiety and even complicit in furthering its own contingency.[17]

In chapter 3, I discuss how the scholarly field of Confucian ethics handles the issue of ritual failure. In particular, I examine how contemporary interpreters account for modifications of a ritual script, how they describe the cultivation of appropriateness (*yi* 義), how they explain the application of appropriateness in situations of potential failure, and how they account for unpreventable failures in efficacy. My major critique of this discourse is that contemporary interpreters mishandle unpreventable failures in ritual because, in their view, a failed ritual is easily attributed to either a defect in the ritual agent's competency, in which case the ritual agent needs to focus more on cultivating himself, or to powers beyond the ritual agent's control, in which case the ritual agent should focus on those failures within his power to prevent and trust the unpreventable failures to a larger teleological plan. Since, in their view, the ritual agent can clearly recognize the difference between the two, and since unpreventable failures in ritual cannot determine the self-cultivation of the ritual agent or his happiness, there is little need to analyze unpreventable failure in terms of its ethical bearing on the ritual agent.

Chapter 4 gives a detailed analysis of preventable failures of ritual. It argues that most failures of ritual, as described in the *Liji*, are preventable if the ritual performers are competent and fluent. This chapter also introduces specific shortcomings of ritual scripts and explains how the fluent ritual agent deals with these shortcomings in order to ensure the success of ritual.

Chapter 5 provides a close reading of the account contained in the "Liyun" chapter of the *Liji*, which describes the coming forth of ritual into the world. It argues that the *Liji* constructs a narrative of dysfunctional ritual that is not simply about incompetent people making mistakes in the performance of ritual; additionally, it constructs a narrative about the inevitability of ritual failure owing to necessary changes made in the world to support the flourishing of a more complex and more interdependent human population. Ritual, in this view, must change in order to maintain its efficacy but also struggles to perfectly capture the *dao* 道, or the process of flourishing where all things in the world maximize their potential for growth and development. Other chapters of the *Liji* are also discussed in reference to this narrative. The significance of chapter 5 is that it provides a hermeneutic for understanding unpreventable failures in ritual.

In chapter 6, "Whose Fault is Failure? The Ambiguity of Impinging Agencies," I focus on ambiguities in ritual failure. In particular, I discuss two relevant ambiguities in the *Liji*. The first is an ambiguity between failures in competency and failures in efficacy. The second is an ambiguity between preventable and unpreventable failures in efficacy. Both ambiguities result from the view held by early Confucians that the success of ritual is contingent on powers beyond those in the control of the ritual performers. This chapter demonstrates that the authors of the *Liji* believed that determining where the agency of one party begins and the agency of another ends is often a difficult affair.

Chapter 7, "The Ancients Did Not Fix Their Graves," builds on the arguments of the previous three chapters by interpreting one vignette from the "Tangong Shang" 檀弓上 chapter as a preventable and then an unpreventable failure in ritual. It demonstrates that the passage can be effectively read as an argument for ambiguity in ritual failure and elaborates on a tragic theory of ritual in which the ritual agent faces the following kinds of circumstances: a dissonance between an expectation of how the world should work and an experience with how the world actually works; an inability to distinguish among the various agencies competing to shape the self; a resignation to the need to vary from the ideals of the past; an awareness of the possibility of failure when varying from these ideals; and an anxiety born of uncertainty.

In chapter 8, "Productive Anxieties and the Awfulness of Failed Ritual," I explore the anxiety associated with the uncertainty of vulnerability (i.e., the notion that ritual success is contingent on agencies beyond the control of an individual ritual agent) and the anxiety associated with the need to vary from the successful rituals of the past. This chapter seeks to explain how Confucians coped with the dissonance between an understanding of ritual where ritual served to construct an ordered world and their experience with ritual as it sometimes failed to bring about such a world. It demonstrates that the anxiety associated with notions of dissonance and vulnerability functioned 'productively.' In other words, the anxiety associated with the inevitability and ambiguity of ritual failure, as well as the anxiety associated with the contingent nature of successful ritual, generated a profoundly meaningful series of opportunities valued for their creative and therapeutic power.

Finally, the section entitled "Concluding Reflections: Toward a Tragic Theory of Ritual" situates the theory of ritual articulated in previous chapters within the field of ritual studies. It analyzes 'correspondence' and 'subjunctive' theories of ritual; and in relation to these theories, it articulates a tragic theory of ritual that enriches the study of ritual change and ritual efficacy. In short, this theory recognizes that the world ritual is meant to construct is set against the backdrop of a dysfunctional world—a world comprised of competing ritual traditions, natural disasters, and death. Ritual performers project their hope onto the dysfunctional world while recognizing the loose fit between the two. In this light, the kind of justification that ritual provides for its performance is not necessarily about the eventual triumph of the ritual world. Rather it can often justify itself by providing a kind of honesty about the world. It reframes the world such that we learn to accept that there are things we do not know, and powers that we cannot control. Ritual, as such, is an embodied confession of our own limitations. It is a way of enacting our vulnerability and coming to terms with uncertainty. While I have striven to make the material in chapters 1 through 8 accessible to those with little knowledge of China or Confucianism, those with interests primarily in ritual studies may find this section the most interesting.

My hope is to bring the richness of the *Liji* to bear on the contemporary discourses of Confucian ethics and ritual studies, but not at the expense of the text. I believe that the text should shape the questions we ask, as much as the questions we ask shape our reading of the text. Thus, if I were to provide a label for this project, I would consider it a 'discursively informed description' of the *Liji*.[18] The discourses I have in mind are those of Confucian ethics and ritual theory in early Confucianism. By 'description,' I mean a sinologically responsible reading of the text or textual passages. This is not to suggest that there is uniform consensus as to what counts as responsible Sinology, but I have strived to render my interpretations of the text viable as judged by the community of interpreters seeking to analyze early Chinese material. In other words, I see this project as according with the basic standards of literary interpretation of Chinese sources.

In short, I intend to employ what Charles Wei-hsun Fu called a "Creative Hermeneutic"—where the interpreter understands a text (or passage) according to five stages.[19] In the first stage, one engages "the superficial verbal encoding" of what is recorded.[20] This involves asking, "What *exactly* is said?" In the second stage, one explores the "full range of possible interpretations" of the passage.[21] In other words one asks, "What does this *mean*?" In the third stage, the interpreter contextualizes the passage by investigating the factors that may have influenced it (historical or otherwise)—what *could* have been said? I label the first three stages, borrowing a term from Lee Yearley, the "elaborative" phase of interpretation.[22] Here one engages in the practice of thickly describing the text. In the fourth stage, the interpreter begins to move beyond the text and speaks on behalf of it—what *should* have been said to more fully articulate its message? Last of all one asks, "What *must* be said now... to keep that message fresh, and hence relevant to the ever-changing times?"[23] These last two stages can be labeled (again borrowing from Yearley) the "emending" phase of interpretation.[24] My aim is to work between the third and fourth stages—to accurately describe the *Liji*, but also to render it intelligible to the contemporary discourses of Confucian ethics and ritual studies.

In this sense, I am writing *about* the *Liji*, but I am writing *for* the fields of ritual studies and Confucian ethics. Hence, while I use the term 'ritual' in the context of early Confucianism, I believe that what I describe is recognizable to those that work with ritual in other contexts. While I do not think constructing a universal theory of ritual is possible, I do think it is possible to construct theories of ritual that are to a large degree commensurable with each other. Since it is beyond the limits of this project to apply the theory articulated in this book to other contexts, I will leave those scholars working on other traditions the task of identifying specific points of application. At the same time, I will note areas where this Confucian theory of ritual challenges other theories of ritual and pushes the study of ritual in new directions.

The Liji *and Early Confucianism*

As stated in the title of the book, this project is an investigation into 'early Confucianism,' by which I mean the tradition represented in the *Liji*. Choosing the label 'early Confucianism' is undoubtedly fraught with the problems of being unnecessarily vague ("What does 'early' mean?") as well as counterproductive in light of the scholarship over the past two decades that takes Confucianism as little more than a construction of the Western imagination. I do not intend to completely resolve either of these issues, but it should suffice to say as far as the former challenge is concerned, the ambiguity of the label reflects a certain degree of ambiguity in the textual composition. Until about twenty years ago, the dominant academic position was that the text in its entirety was a creation of Han Dynasty court ritualists. With the discovery at Guodian in 1993 and the subsequent acquisition of the Shanghai Museum manuscripts, however, the dating of the *Liji* must be keenly reconsidered. Since the text does have portions that extend back well into the Warring States, as well as portions that likely came from the Han, labeling the text as either 'Pre-Qin' or 'Han' did not seem appropriate. In this light, I have settled on the term 'early.'

Scholars have also criticized the term 'Confucianism' in the past two decades. The most severe critique claims that Confucianism is an Orientalist designation used to reaffirm Western hegemony.[25] As far as it will be used in this study, 'Confucianism' is to a large degree a functional, rather than a substantive term. In other words, in as far as this project is concerned, I am not so much arguing for the historical existence of any particular school as much as I am using the term for the purpose of communicating with the field of scholars that recognize the issues raised by figures such as Lionel Jensen, and yet contribute to a common discussion.

At the same time, I do believe that the *Liji* became an important part of a tradition that self-consciously created boundaries, and that these boundaries served to include some within the tradition and exclude others from it. This tradition has been primarily labeled "Confucian" in the Western academy, and *Ru* 儒 in the East Asian academy. As far as the *Liji* is concerned, I view it as not simply a Confucian/*Ru* 儒 text in terms of its relationship to a long custom of scholars self-identifying as such, but also as an early Chinese text in terms of it being contextualized and situated within the debates of the time period. My reading does not assume that every part of the text must cohere with other "Confucian" material (such as the *Mencius* and the *Analects*). Indeed, I am open to the possibility that the *Liji* shares striking affinities with material not usually considered Confucian.

Conclusion

The *Liji* was certainly in dialogue with other early Chinese texts, and I have attempted to take them into account as well, however not with the same detail. In a sense, I have 'foregrounded' the *Liji*, meaning that I have not ignored other texts that may have been in conversation with it, but neither have I treated them with the same level of nuance, nor have I devoted the same amount of space to discussing them. These other texts are 'backgrounded,' therefore, in the sense that they form part of the context of the larger discourse, yet they are not the central figure in this project. They are supporting actors, so to speak, in a play where I am the director, and the *Liji* has the leading role.

I

Ritual in the Liji

Tian 天 *gave birth to all people;*
for every thing there is a norm.
In following their standard,
people are drawn to magnificent virtue.

天生烝民、有物有則。
民之秉彝、好是懿德。[1]

THE PURPOSE OF this chapter is to provide a characterization of ritual as found in the *Liji*. I use the phrase 'characterization of ritual' intentionally to reflect an array of information garnered to serve the purposes of this project, of which defining ritual constitutes only one part.[2] Indeed, several books could be written about the notion of ritual in the *Liji*. Rather than attempt to construct a comprehensive description of ritual in the text, I will focus on two questions relevant to the larger aims of this project—what is 'ritual' as far as the *Liji* can be said to be about ritual? And, what is ritual meant to accomplish? Gaining a firm understanding of these two issues will set the stage for future chapters. In short, this project as a whole is meant to follow the rather simple scheme of characterizing ritual (in chapter 1), characterizing dysfunction (in chapter 2), and then exploring attitudes toward dysfunctional ritual in chapters 3 through 8.

Broadly speaking, rituals are scripted performances enacted by human beings for the purposes of ordering the world. This 'world' is seen as being comprised of social things such male and female relationships; personal or individual things such as the untaught dispositions inherent in human beings; or nonhuman things such as rain, animals, or spiritual powers. The need for ritual implies a need for properly relating the things that make up the world to each other. 'Order' in this sense can be understood as appropriately aligning the outer dimensions of the human body with the inner dimensions of the human psyche; creating harmonious relationships between various groups of people; properly associating human beings in the midst of a myriad of other entities (*wanwu* 萬物) that inhabit the world including animals and spiritual forces (*guishen* 鬼神); and adequately situating human society between the heavens and the earth such that all people move in conjunction with the changes in season and live in accordance with the contour of the land. Rituals, therefore, serve as guides for proper relation. When human beings perform ritual, they put the things of the world in synchronization with the *dao* 道—an important, yet little discussed, concept in the *Liji* most simply understood as the process of flourishing whereby all things in the world maximize their potential for growth and development.

Human beings, in contrast to other entities in the world, have the task of performing rituals in order to create a flourishing world. While the success of ritual can often be measured by its efficacy in generating a well-ordered world, this chapter will focus on the purposes of ritual as they relate to human beings. The reason for focusing on these aspects of ritual, as opposed to others, is that human beings, according to the *Liji*, are the sole entities responsible for performing ritual. Ritual success is thereby predicated on appropriate human action; and ritual failure is often (but not always) predicated on inappropriate human action. The chapters that follow will continue to explore the role of human beings as stewards of ritual success and failure. In exploring these issues, I will often refer to those human beings intimately or remotely involved in any aspect of ritual performance as 'ritual agents.'

While there are many purposes of ritual, two primary purposes, as it relates to the individual, are to first make an 'impression' on a ritual agent such that properly performing ritual results in a cultivated self. Secondly, ritual allows for the proper 'expression' of this cultivated self. I will refer to these purposes below as the 'pressive functions of ritual.' Channeling water is a reoccurring metaphor in the *Liji* for understanding the pressive functions of ritual. Similar to the way in which a levee not only shapes the direction of water flow but also enables the flow of water, ritual both shapes the dispositions of ritual agents and allows for the expression of their dispositions.

Despite its title, the authors or redactors of the *Liji* did not take *li* 禮 as the only scripted performance meant to order the world. What this means as far as this project is concerned is that the term 'ritual' is not simply equated with the term '*li* 禮.' Other concepts such as *yue* 樂 (musical performances) and *fa* 法 (models of regulation) also provided scripted performances that served the same (or similar) purposes. The authors of the *Liji* also employed a series of metaphors for terms such as *li* 禮, *yue* 樂, and *fa* 法. These include concepts such as the carpenter's square (*ju* 矩), the compass (*gui* 規), the chalk-line (*sheng* 繩), scales and balances (*heng* 衡 and *quan* 權), gauges that measure time (*biao* 表), and levees or dikes (*fang* 坊). The past performances of the sages—not always discussed in these terms—also constituted scripts for proper performance. The *Liji* sometimes uses these terms interchangeably. In this sense, *li* 禮, as I will demonstrate below, was often understood so broadly that it incorporated any scripted performance meant to order the world. I will likewise employ the term 'ritual' in this expansive sense. As such, when I use the word 'ritual' in talking about the *Liji*, I do not necessarily have the notion of *li* 禮 in mind; and neither does it entail the appearance of the character *li* 禮 in the section of the *Liji* under discussion. Nevertheless, *li* 禮 is undoubtedly *the* central concept of the text, and was often understood by the authors of the text to encompass many of the other concepts that appear in the text. As such, I will devote a large part of this chapter to a discussion of ritual in terms of *li* 禮.

Translating *li* 禮 as ritual is of course conventional, and if taken too strictly could impoverish the notion of *li* 禮. A certain amount of 'interpretive elasticity,' therefore, is required in understanding *li* 禮 as ritual. In other words, we, as interpreters, must be willing to stretch the range of meaning we normally assign to the notion of ritual. This also requires a degree of what we can call 'interpretive overwriting,' where we replace some of our previous assumptions of what constitutes ritual with concepts that come from the notion of *li* 禮.

Ritual as Li 禮

A dominant paradigm among contemporary scholars is that in its early stages *li* 禮 referred exclusively to formal religious events held at certain times by the aristocracy of the early Zhou and possibly late Shang Dynasties (ca. eleventh–ninth centuries BCE), and was gradually broadened to include every aesthetic and/or moral performance of human beings as defined by the disciples of Confucius. Scott Cook, for instance, charts the development of *li* 禮 as follows: "a type of ceremonial vessel → the use of such a vessel → ceremonial performance in general → other types of institutions or activities that achieve a similar rank-defining function to sacrificial ceremonies → hierarchical structure in general."[3] Of note in Cook's description is the 'specific to general' development of *li* 禮. Yuri Pines takes a similar approach, adding that "Confucius was the first to add moral dimensions to this term, reinterpreting *li* 禮 as primarily ritual behavior, rather than the mere equivalent of the sociopolitical system."[4] In Pines's view, the relevance of *li* 禮 was extended until it achieved an "apotheosis" (i.e., a close association with the cosmos) in the late Warring States (ca. fourth–third centuries BCE).[5] Masayuki Sato traces the appearance of *li* 禮 from the oracle bones until Mencius. His conclusions are similar to those of Cook and Pines except that he continues to trace the expansion of *li* 禮 to include a state of mind manifest in action (as described in *Mencius*).[6] Roger Ames, perhaps, best explains the notion of *li* 禮 in an expansive sense:

> [W]e might assume that *li* 禮 do not reduce to generic, formally prescribed "rites" and "rituals," performed at stipulated times to announce relative status, and to punctuate the seasons of one's life. The *li* 禮 are more, much more.....*Li* 禮 requires the utmost attention in every detail of what one does at every moment that one is doing it, from the drama of the high court to the posture one assumes in going to sleep, from the reception of different guests to the proper way to comport oneself when alone; from how one behaves in formal dining situations to appropriate extemporaneous gestures.[7]

In Ames's view, *li* 禮 is all-encompassing and permeates the daily life. William Theodore de Bary argues that similar trends of expanding the meaning of important terms occurred throughout early Confucianism. "[T]he idea is not so much to analyze and define concepts precisely as to expand them, to make them suggestive of the widest possible range of meaning. Generally, the more crucial or central the concept, the greater the ambiguity."[8]

The *Liji*, as a text written by many authors and compiled over several centuries, presents a variety of descriptions of *li* 禮. Some of these descriptions restrict *li* 禮 to a series of ceremonial events, and other descriptions expand *li* 禮 to include the mundane actions of everyday human affairs. For the sake of convenience, arguments for limiting *li* 禮 to ceremonial occasions will be referred to as 'restrictive theories of *li* 禮'; this is because, in this view, *li* 禮 is restricted to the performance of named ceremonial circumstances distinct from everyday affairs. Arguments for understanding *li* 禮 beyond the specific occasions of ceremony will be referred to as 'expansive theories of *li* 禮.' I will investigate both theories below. The *Liji*, it can be argued, represents a transitional period where the tension between restrictive theories and expansive theories of *li* 禮 are played out and compete with each other as found in the differing voices that comprise the text.

As far as restrictive theories are concerned, the *Liji* lists a distinct number of *li* 禮 in several places. The "Jitong" 祭統 chapter, for instance, speaks of five constant principles (*jing* 經) of *li* 禮.[9] The ensuing chapter, "Jingjie" 經解, then goes on to list five specific kinds of *li* 禮—court rituals (*chaojinzhili* 朝覲之禮), envoy and inquiry rituals (*pinwenzhili* 聘問之禮), mourning and sacrificial rituals (*sangjizhili* 喪祭之禮), district drinking rituals (*xiangyinjiuzhili* 鄉飲酒之禮), and marriage rituals (*hunyinzhili* 昏姻之禮).[10] Other chapters talk about "six *li* 禮" (without listing them), or come up with eight *li* 禮—defining them as the "great body" (大體) of *li* 禮.[11] Of particular importance is the early commentator Zheng Xuan's (127–200) account of the coming forth of five kinds of *li* 禮. His commentary on the first chapter of the *Liji* explains the creation of five *li* 禮 by each of the early sages. These rituals were preserved in the *Liji* and passed down to his time.[12] Although later scholars took Zheng's gloss as general categories under which they grouped all other rituals, it is unclear whether any of these lists in their original contexts were meant to be definitive.[13]

More commonly, the *Liji* refers to two groups of *li* 禮—three hundred *jingli* 經禮 (or *liyi* 禮儀) and three thousand *quli* 曲禮 (or *weiyi* 威儀).[14] Similar groupings of three hundred and three thousand also occur in the *Da Dai Liji* 《大戴禮記》 and the *Kongzi Jiayu* 《孔子家語》, among other texts.[15] These texts are not clear on the distinction between, or the contents of, the two groups, leaving later commentators to interpret them on their own accord. Most commentators take the three hundred *jingli* 經禮 as a reference to the offices (and the ceremonies relating to those offices) discussed in the *Zhouli* 《周禮》, and the three thousand *quli* 曲禮 as a rough approximate of the rites involved in implementing the *Zhouli* (as, per their interpretation, covered in the *Yili* 《儀禮》).[16] Interestingly enough, although the *Yili* does list a number of ceremonies and explains them in great detail (most of the chapters are titled after them—although the titles were probably added long after compilation), there is likewise no claim for comprehensiveness within the text itself. Depending on how one takes these notions of three hundred and three thousand, it seems plausible, although not conclusive, that early Confucians saw a limit on the number of rituals necessary to order the world.

'Expansive' can be understood in two different, yet significant, ways. First it can refer to the possibility that *li* 禮 are events beyond ceremonial occasions. The tenth chapter of the *Analects*, which describes Confucius's everyday actions in great detail, for instance, could be read as demonstrations of *li* 禮 in both ceremonial and non-ceremonial occasions.[17] Second, 'expansive' can also refer to a performative (or 'processual') conceptualization of *li* 禮. In other words, rather than (or perhaps in addition to) referring to an event, *li* 禮 can be seen as referring to the way in which an event is performed. The "Zhongni Yanju" 仲尼燕居 chapter of the *Liji* suggests both of these expansive readings. It is worth noting that that the title of the chapter can be translated as "Confucius in Retirement," whereas the content of the chapter is about the performance of ritual. The juxtaposition of the title and content suggest that Confucius, even while at rest, was concerned with the performance of ritual. At one point in the text, Confucius's disciple, Zizhang, asks him about *li* 禮. Confucius responds,

> Do you think that preparing tables and mats, ascending and descending [the hall], making offerings, and drinking wine are necessary to call something a ritual [*li* 禮]? Do you think that dancing, holding up plumes and flutes, and playing bells and drums are necessary to call something a musical performance [*yue* 樂]? To speak, and then to perform what was spoken is ritual [*li* 禮]. To act and delight in the action is a musical performance [*yue* 樂].
>
> 爾以為必鋪儿、筵，升降，酌、獻、酬、酢，然後謂之禮乎？爾以為必行綴兆，興羽籥，作鍾鼓，然後謂之樂乎？言而履之，禮也。行而樂之，樂也。[18]

This passage makes it clear that *li* 禮 are not limited to ceremonial occasions. The author is explicit that *li* 禮 transcends the implements of ceremony and includes the performance of what it calls *yan* 言. While there is some debate as to the meaning of *yan* 言 in early China, one permissible interpretation of this phrase is that following through on one's word (i.e., the performance of what one said—*lü* 履) constitutes *li* 禮.[19] There is a clear contrast in this passage between the implements of ceremony, used only in limited circumstances, and the limitless (or at least much less limited) usage of speech. In this light, *li* 禮 are not just ceremonial moments held at predetermined times, but are a fundamental element of everyday life. Other passages in this chapter define *li* 禮 as the "order of affairs" 事之治 and explain that "whatever the profound person encounters, [he] is never not in accordance with *li* 禮" 君子無物而不在禮矣.[20] Other chapters in the *Liji* state that *li* 禮 "should not be detached from one's self for even an instant" 不可斯須去身.[21] The fact that an expansive argument needs to be made explicit within the *Liji* implies that there were competing theories that the authors of these portions of the text were arguing against. The tension, therefore, between expansive and less expansive theories of *li* 禮 plays out in the pages of the *Liji*.

The earliest etymological analysis of *li* 禮 comes from Xu Shen's 許慎 (ca. 58 CE–ca. 147 CE) *Shuowen Jiezi* 《說文解字》. Xu defines *li* 禮 as the composite of two characters, *shi* 示 and *li* 豊. *Shi* 示 he defines as an ideograph meaning "up," referring to the objects of the sky—the sun, moon, and stars—which, according to Xu Shen, were given as signs to human beings, in order that we can "observe the patterns of the heavens [and] fathom the changes of the seasons," thereby allowing us to see the times of "fortune and misfortune." In short, Xu refers to *shi* 示 as "the affairs of the spirits [above]."[22] The second character, *li* 豊, is defined as a pictograph of an instrument of ritual—a vessel with an offering placed on it. Combining these together, Xu then defines *li* 禮 as "to perform" or "to carry out (according to a certain path)."[23] It is "serving the spirits in order to obtain blessings" 禮：履也。所以事神致福也.[24] Xu's interpretation of *li* 禮 expresses much of the same tension explained above in terms of restrictive and expansive theories of *li* 禮. He defines *li* 禮 as partially a pictograph of ceremonial implements and interprets it in terms of "serving the spirits" (hinting at a restrictive theory in terms of services performed at ceremonial occasions), but at the same time he explains it along the lines of performance (hinting at an expansive theory in terms of the comportment necessary for the ceremonial event and transferable into other areas of life, as things other than ceremonies can be "performed" [*lü* 履]).[25]

The *Liji* also presents conflicting accounts of the origins of *li* 禮—sometimes describing how the cosmos serves as a source for *li* 禮 and at other times describing how human beings provide the crucial point of reference. The "Liyun" 禮運 chapter, for instance, explains,

> As for *li* 禮, it must be rooted in the Great One. [It] divides to become the heavens and the earth, rotates to become *yin* 陰 and *yang* 陽, transforms to become the four seasons, and splits to become ghosts and spirits. What it sends down is called the mandate; and its abode is in the heavens. *Li* 禮 must be rooted in the heavens. [It] moves

[down] to reach the earth, extends to [all] affairs, changes and follows the times, and assists in demarcating boundaries. When it abides in people it is called "nourishment."

是故夫禮，必本於大一，分而為天地，轉而為陰陽，變而為四時，列而為鬼神，其降曰命，其官於天也。夫禮必本於天，動而之地，列而之事，變而從時，協於分藝，其居人也曰養。[26]

The subject of the second sentence is ambiguous (as reflected in the translation). Grammatically speaking, it is open to be understood as either *li* 禮 or the Great One. Most commentators take it as the latter, and have good reason to, given that the "it" of the second half of the passage takes an active role in "sending down the mandate"—a role that would anthropomorphize or divinize *li* 禮 and thereby make this passage extremely unique in this sense.[27] This ambiguity, however, works well to demonstrate that *li* 禮 is rooted in a cosmic source and permeates the world. The "Xiangyinjiuyi" 鄉飲酒義 chapter, which contains an explanation of the district drinking ceremony, shows how the creators of this ritual used the cosmos as a model.

The significance of the district drinking ceremony is this. The designated guest represents the heavens. The designated host represents the earth. Their attendants represent the sun and moon. Three [other] guests represent the three bright stars [Venus, Jupiter, and Mars?]. When the ancients made *li* 禮 they wove it together with the heavens and the earth, tied it together with the sun and moon, and united it with the three bright stars. [It] is the root of governance and instruction.

鄉飲酒之義：立賓以象天，立主以象地，設介、僎以象日月，立三賓以象三光。古之制禮也，經之以天地，紀之以日月，參之以三光，政教之本也。[28]

In performing certain roles in the district drinking ceremony, the participants represent the heavens, the earth, the sun and moon, and three stars. The ancient sages designed this ritual such that the performers of the ceremony accord with these elements of the cosmic world. *Li* 禮, in this regard, is a ceremony for synchronization with this world. The enactment of this ceremony is a reenactment of the process of the cosmic world.

On the other hand, the *Liji* also describes how human beings served as the origin of *li* 禮. The "Yueji" 樂記 chapter, for instance, explains that,

"When the early kings constructed rituals and musical performances, they took people as their standard" 先王之制禮樂，人為之節.[29] The "Wensang" 問喪 chapter also claims that the rite of mourning for three years at the death of one's parents is "the fruit of human sentiment" 人情之實也.[30] It goes on to state that the desire to perform these mourning rites "is not sent down from the heavens or sent up from the earth; rather, it is simply [a matter] of human sentiment" 非從天降也，非從地出也，人情而已矣.[31] The most extended account of the coming forth of *li* 禮—the topic of chapter 5—details how the early sages created *li* 禮 after noticing the deplorable living conditions of early human society.[32]

The purpose of recounting various theories about the scope and origin of *li* 禮 is to demonstrate the diversity of claims made in the *Liji*. There is no clear consensus of what constitutes *li* 禮, yet the redactors of the *Liji* chose to include these contending voices all together in one text. The question remains as to why they would do this without resolving what would seem to be the central issue—namely, defining *li* 禮. One way to understand the work of the redactors of the *Liji* is to take *ji* 記, in the title of the text, to mean a kind of collection or a "recording of things one by one."[33] In other words, the aim of the redactors was not to define or to systematize *li* 禮; rather, their aim was to collect a variety of texts that claimed to deal with *li* 禮 in an effort to create a compendium that future government officials could draw from as necessary. In this light, the *Liji* is similar to other collected (and less systematic) works of the early Han Dynasty such as the *Lüshi Chunqiu* 《呂氏春秋》 and the *Huainanzi* 《淮南子》. James Legge, roughly following this line of thought, translates the title of the *Liji* as "A Collection of Treatises on the Rules of Propriety or Ceremonial Usages."[34] The *Liji*, as such, is not meant to make a sustained argument about what constitutes *li* 禮.

I would add to this that the notion of *ji* 記 in the title of the *Liji* should also be understood in terms of 'theories about' or 'reflections on' *li* 禮.[35] In other words, the text as a whole is less concerned with defining precisely what comprises *li* 禮 and more concerned with describing what *li* 禮 is meant to accomplish. A brief comparison with texts such as the *Yili* demonstrates this point. The *Yili*, as mentioned in the introduction, contains a number of 'companion chapters' to the *Liji*. For instance, the *Yili* contains chapters whose titles can be translated as "The District Drinking Ceremony" ("Xiangyinjiuli" 鄉飲酒禮), "The District Archery Ceremony" ("Xiangsheli" 鄉射禮), "The Banquet Ceremony" ("Yanli" 燕禮), and "The Capping Ceremony for Officials" ("Shiguanli" 士冠禮). Each of these chapters provides a step-by-step guide for performing these rites. The *Liji*, on the other hand, has related chapters entitled "The Significance of the District Drinking [Ceremony]" ("Xiangyinjiuyi" 鄉飲酒義), "The Significance of the Archery [Ceremony]" ("Sheyi" 射義), "The Significance of the Banquet [Ceremony]" ("Yanyi" 燕義), and "The Significance of the Capping [Ceremony]" ("Guanyi" 冠義). Rather than providing a script for these ceremonies, the *Liji* chapters argue for the importance of performing them. The opening of the "Guanyi" chapter, for instance, states:

> That which enables human beings to act as human beings is ritual and rightness [*liyi* 禮義]. Ritual and rightness begin with squaring the deportment of the body, gathering lively color in the face, and smoothly speaking one's words. When one's deportment is [fully] square, one's face is [full of] color, and one's words are [totally] fluent, ritual and rightness are complete. Then the relationship between the ruler and the minister can be squared, the relationship between fathers and sons can be more personal, and the relationship between the old and young can be harmonized. Once the relationship between the ruler and minister is squared, the relationship between fathers and sons is more personal, and the relationship between the old and young is harmonized, ritual and rightness take up permanent place. As such, one's clothing ensemble [i.e., a metaphor for the self] is complete after the capping ceremony is performed. With the ensemble complete, one's deportment is square, one's face is [full of] color, and one's words are fluent. This is why it is said that the capping ceremony is the beginning of ritual, and why the ancient sage kings emphasized it.
>
> 凡人之所以為人者，禮義也。禮義之始，在於正容體、齊顏色、順辭令。容體正，顏色齊，辭令順，而後禮義備。以正君臣、親父子、和長幼。君臣正，父子親，長幼和，而後禮義立。故冠而後服備，服備而後容體正、顏色齊、辭令順。故曰：「冠者，禮之始也。」是故古者聖王重冠。[36]

The *Liji*, in contrast to the liturgical style of the *Yili*, provides reasons why the capping ceremony should be performed rather than a script for its performance. At the same time, however, there are some chapters, such as the "Neize" 內則 chapter, that could serve as a liturgy for the performance of ritual.

While the authors of the *Liji* do not have a singular view of the purposes of *li* 禮, they do agree that *li* 禮 are of the utmost importance in creating an ordered world and that *li* 禮 are transformative practices that human beings—in distinction from other creatures of the world—must perform. My use of the term 'ritual,' throughout this project, strives to remain consistent with the aims of the *Liji* by focusing less on the specifics of what constitutes a particular rite and more on the views of the authors or redactors in terms of what these practices are meant to accomplish.

Ritual Success and the Pressive Functions of Ritual

Rituals are scripted performances that are meant to order the world. As discussed above, the notion of 'order' within the *Liji* is multifaceted—it begins with the transformation of human beings into cultivated ritual agents and is complete when all entities in the world are flourishing by moving in synchronization with the *dao* 道. Human beings, as the sole performers of ritual, play the pivotal role in this process.

Ritual, as discussed in the "Liqi" 禮器 chapter and throughout the *Liji*, acts to mold human beings into "ritualized vessels" that are able to move together fluently to bring about a flourishing world.[37] Ritual, in this sense, has a two-part purpose. First, it shapes human beings into effective ritual vessels. Second, it becomes the means by which human beings express their degree of cultivation and attempt to bring the rest of the world to order—as human beings are transformed into better human beings, they express this transformation and also transform the world around them. Often these purposes are accomplished at the same time. For instance, certain funerary rites were understood to both shape human beings into proper ritual performers and to enable human beings to shape the world around them by satisfying the spirits of the deceased. The act of offering up sacrifices at a funeral, therefore, was thought to affect both the ritual agent and the spirits that inhabit the world by means of the proper expression of reverence on the part of the ritual agent. For the sake of this project, I will differentiate these purposes and investigate them as separate kinds of 'pressive functions of ritual.' By 'pressive,' I mean to suggest that rituals, in the view of the authors of the *Liji*, act to make an 'im-pression' on the performers of the rite. They 'impress' upon the participants appropriate ways to feel, act, and think. They also serve to 'ex-press' these appropriate feelings and thoughts in actions. Ritual, in this latter sense, acts as a kind of "cultural grammar" that enables the expression of feelings and virtues that contribute to a flourishing world.[38] The sections that follow will discuss the impressive and expressive purposes of ritual.

The Impressive Functions of Ritual

Ritual shapes the untaught dispositions of human beings, or *renqing* 人情.[39] Within the *Liji* these dispositions are defined as "joy, anger, grief, fear, love, hate, and desire" 喜，怒，哀，懼，愛，惡，欲.[40] Following the "Liyun" chapter, people "are able [to experience these dispositions] without having to learn [to experience them]" 弗學而能.[41] In other words, dispositions such as joy and grief are inborn sentiments that are not acquired through a process of study. Human beings do not have to be taught to feel grief or joy. We must, however, be taught *how to* express these dispositions. Rituals are the means by which untaught dispositions are trained and are thereby properly expressed. The "Liyun" chapter continues, "The sages possessed that by which they ordered the untaught dispositions of human beings.... If not with ritual, what else would they use to order these dispositions" 聖人之所以治人七情。。。。舍禮何以治之?[42] Other chapters of the *Liji* explain that "ritual enhances untaught disposition" 禮以飾情 and that ritual serves to "moderate untaught disposition" 微情.[43]

Sentiments such as love, hate, and desire are 'untaught' in the sense that they are 'inborn' or 'natural'; but they are also 'untaught' in the more traditional sense of the word, meaning that they are 'untrained' or, more literally, "not tight"—as in "a rope that is not taut."[44]

To use another metaphor, these dispositions are 'raw' or are 'uncooked.' Raw, in this light, does not mean that these dispositions are necessarily bad. Similar to the way in which raw fish, for instance, could become part of a good meal, untrained love could happen to be expressed appropriately. These dispositions, therefore, are non-moral (or are pre-moral), meaning that they are neither inherently good nor bad. How they are expressed, however, is a moral concern. This same chapter of the *Liji* that lists these dispositions, the "Liyun" chapter, employs a metaphor that likens these raw dispositions to an uncultivated field—ritual is the means by which the field is tilled.[45] Similar to the way in which an unattended plot of land could by chance produce food fit for human consumption, untrained disposition could occasionally produce proper performance; however, cultivating the field is a much more effective means of generating the desired result, similar to the way in which training people's dispositions with ritual is more effective.

Without ritual, the dispositions of human beings tend to go out of control. Ritual, therefore, is often spoken of in terms of its ability to "restrain" (*yue* 約) or "order" (*zhi* 治) the dispositions of human beings. In particular, the notion of *zhi* 治 features prominently. More than any other term, ritual is claimed to *zhi* 治 things such as the untaught dispositions of human beings (*zhirenqing* 治人情), the body (*zhigong* 治躬), and the heart or mind of human beings (*zhixin* 治心).[46] *Zhi* 治 in the *Liji* connotes a sense of management or direction. Ritual, as such, serves to manage or direct the dispositions that are aroused in the course of life.

This line of thought progresses in the following manner. As one experiences life, and interacts with other people or things in the world, certain dispositions are inevitably aroused. The arousal of these dispositions is not problematic in itself, but if one acts on them in a non-ritualized manner, it becomes problematic. The "Zhongyong" 中庸 chapter, for instance, emphasizes this former point. It explains, "When joy, anger, grief, and happiness . . . are aroused and remain within their proper bounds, this is harmony" 喜怒哀樂之。。。發而皆中節，謂之和.[47] The idea here is that dispositions such as joy and anger, once aroused, must be expressed. They can be expressed either appropriately or inappropriately. The "Zhongni Yanju" chapter explains the notion of expressing certain human dispositions in line with ritual. It states,

> Being reverent, but not in accordance with ritual, this is called being wild. Being respectful, but not in accordance with ritual, this is called being presumptuous. Being brave, but not in accordance with ritual, this is called being unruly.
>
> 敬而不中禮，謂之野。恭而不中禮，謂之給。勇而不中禮，謂之逆。[48]

Every disposition should be manifest by means of ritual. Ritual ensures that human sentiment is expressed in its proper bounds.

The notion of *zhong* 中 features prominently in both passages above. In its verbal sense, *zhong* 中 means to "hit the mark"—as in the way in which an arrow hits its target (coincidentally, *jie* 節, which appears in the "Zhongyong" passage, also refers to a target used in archery contests). To *zhongli* 中禮 (translated above as "to accord with ritual") can also be understood in a colloquial sense, as in when an actor "nails the performance." Ritual, following a passage from the "Sannianwen" 三年問 chapter, is meant to "balance human disposition" (*chengqing* 稱情)—mitigating it when excessive and arousing it when insufficient.[49] This same chapter also explains that when ritual balances disposition it "establishes a pattern" (*liwen* 立文). In other words, ritual works to make a lasting impression on human disposition. The ideas of "hitting the mark" and "balance" are tied together in a passage from the "Zhongni Yanju" chapter, which purports to recount an exchange between Confucius and his disciple Zigong.

> Confucius said, "Zigong, you are excessive [*guo* 過], while Shang [another disciple] is deficient [*buji* 不及]....
>
> 子曰：「師，爾過；而商也不及。。。」
>
> Zigong shuffled on his mat and replied, "Dare I ask how one comes to find balance [*zhong* 中]?"
>
> 子貢越席而對曰：「敢問將何以為此中者也？」
>
> Confucius responded, "It is ritual! Ritual! Ritual is the means by which one creates a sense of balance."
>
> 子曰：「禮乎禮！夫禮所以制中也。」[50]

The ritual agent is trained to "hit the mark" or to "find the balancing point" between excess and deficiency by performing ritual. Untaught disposition becomes taught disposition through engaging in ritual practices.

In the *Shuowen*—the second century glossography mentioned above—*zhi* 治 is defined in relation to the flow of water.[51] The notion of managing water or ordering the flow of water is a prominent metaphor for ritual in the *Liji*. An entire chapter actually uses this metaphor as its central theme. The "Fangji" 坊記 chapter likens ritual unto a dike, dam, or waterway. The second passage of the chapter explains, "Ritual is rooted in the untaught dispositions of human beings—serving to pattern and refine them. [Ritual] can be thought of as a dike for people" 禮者，因人之情而為之節文，以為民坊者也.[52] This metaphor is repeated over a dozen times in this portion of the *Liji*. In these passages, *fang* 坊 is most simply translated as a "dam," "dike," or "waterway"—things used to manage the flow of water. A *fang* 坊 manages water similar to the way in which ritual manages the dispositions of people.

The character *fang* 坊 also appears in the "Jiaotesheng" 郊特牲 chapter. Commenting on this passage, Kong Yingda explains that a physical *fang*

坊 has two uses. He remarks, "*Fang* 坊 are used to collect water and are used to obstruct water" 坊者，所以畜水，亦以鄣水.[53] Here, Kong explains that *fang* 坊 can perform multiple hydraulic functions. Not only do *fang* 坊 act as dams, but they also act as channels, or waterways, that serve to collect water. Ritual, as implied in this metaphor, also performs multiple functions.[54] They do not simply "stop up" excessive sentiment, but also work to collect and channel scattered dispositions and pool them together so that they flow in the proper direction.

Fang 坊 is semantically and graphically related to *fang* 方, which some scholars suggest was originally a pictograph of a boat alongside water.[55] By the time of the *Liji*, however, *fang* 方 also acquired the meaning of "direction" or "orientation" (among other meanings). A useful way of understanding the impressive function of ritual is to view ritual as a means of reorienting people's dispositions to flow in the right direction.

The sentiments experienced at the death of a family member or friend are commonly discussed in the *Liji*. For most people, experiencing grief at the loss a family member is an overwhelming event. The sentiments of grief can lead people to take all kinds of actions in an attempt to mourn the loss. They might refrain from eating food, neglect other important responsibilities, or even maim themselves. Other people may experience little to no grief at the loss of a loved one. Hence, their mourning practices will vary little from their ordinary affairs. For the former group of people, mourning rituals provide a series of practices that allow for the controlled expression of grief. Fasting, for instance, as a part of mourning is given a specific starting point and an ending point according to the funerary rites. Fasting, therefore, gives vent to the feelings of grief, but does not permanently harm the health of the person fasting. For the latter group of people, mourning rites serve to stir their feelings of grief, giving them a form of practices that enables them to more deeply experience the loss. Returning to the home of the deceased and calling after them, for instance, is meant to cause the mourner to reexperience the loss of the relationship. In short, the sentiments of grief, manifest in mourning, are not to be excessive (*guo* 過) or insufficient (*buji* 不及).

The *Liji* as a whole tends to be more concerned with the excessive expression of human disposition. A central theme is that human beings naturally have feelings that well up within themselves as a result of encountering certain circumstances in life. Without ritual, these feelings will be directionless. They will manifest themselves in random—and likely destructive—actions. We, as human beings, must, therefore, give them proper direction.[56] Rituals are the tools for providing direction and cultivating a habituated sense of proper performance.

The "Yueji" chapter explains that "ritual is that which guides one's orientation" 禮以道其志.[57] The notion of *zhi* 志, translated in this passage as "orientation" can also be understood as "intention" or "focus." Without ritual, human beings will often orient themselves in unproductive directions. Ritual, therefore, serves to cultivate a focus in the right direction.

Rituals serve to impress upon people the proper boundaries for the expression of their dispositions. They also serve to reify other kinds of boundaries that are conducive to a harmonious world. These boundaries, according to the *Liji*, include social distinctions between male and female (*nannü zhibie* 男女之別), cosmological distinctions between light and dark (*youming zhibie* 幽明之別), and situational distinctions between fortune and misfortune (*jixiong zhibie* 吉凶之別).[58] The "Yueji" chapter actually defines ritual as "the dividing line between the heavens and the earth" 禮者天地之別也.[59] Rituals, following the "Zhongni Yanju" chapter, are a "patterning" (*li* 理) of the world.[60] They highlight the differences necessary to create a flourishing world.

Rituals train competent ritual performers. As one engages in ritual practice, one gains an understanding of the ritual script and learns how to perform ritual. A reoccurring theme in the *Liji* is that people should *zhili* 知禮—literally, they should "know ritual."[61] Competent ritual performers are those who have knowledge of the ritual script and posses the skills necessary to enact it. The issue of competency cannot be stressed enough. As people perform ritual, they are cultivated into competent ritual vessels that live their lives according to ritual and guide others in the proper performance of ritual.[62]

The impressive functions of ritual are those that shape the untaught dispositions of human beings. Rituals both stir up and restrain sentiments such as grief, joy, and anger. They pattern or make an imprint on these dispositions so that they "hit the mark," or are expressed in appropriate degrees. As these rituals are repeated, they make a lasting impression on ritual performers—ensuring that their future performances fluently follow the dictates of ritual.

The Expressive Functions of Ritual

The second pressive function of ritual is to allow for the expression of human disposition. The "Jianzhuan" 間傳 chapter relates, "When mourning for one's parents why is hemp worn? [It is because] hemp is unpleasant in appearance; and so what begins on the inside is displayed on the outside" 斬衰何以服苴？苴，惡貌也，所以首其內而見諸外也.[63] The idea in this passage is that the inner dispositions of human beings can be manifest in their outward actions. In this case wearing hemp—an unpleasant material—is an indication of the unpleasant feelings associated with the loss of one's parents. The majority of the "Jianzhuan" chapter focuses on this expressive function of ritual as it relates to the sentiments of grief expressed in mourning rites. The passage just quoted, for instance, after detailing the clothing worn by the participants concludes, "This is grief made manifest in one's bodily apparel" 此哀之發於容體者也.[64] Similar passages list the kinds of food associated with the mourning rites and explain it as "grief made manifest in food and drink" 此哀之發於飲食者也; other passages detail the amount of conversation different mourners should engage in, explaining it as "grief made manifest in language" 此哀之發於言語者也.[65] All of these passages highlight the expressive function of ritual—inner grief is demonstrated by wearing coarse clothing, eating bland food, and refraining from excessive conversation.

Throughout the *Liji*, ritual is described as a means of gauging the internal dispositions of the participants. These dispositions, the "Liyun" chapter explains, are inaccessible to others beyond oneself; however, they become manifest when one performs ritual.

> The things people strongly desire are found in the form of food, drink, and sex. The things people greatly disdain are found in the form of death, destruction, poverty, and hardship. Desire and disdain are significant features of the human heart-mind; but people conceal their heart-minds such that they cannot be penetrated or discerned. Refinement and repulsiveness both lie within the heart-mind and do not readily appear in the countenance. If one wanted to use something to discover it, how could [one] use anything else but ritual?"
>
> 飲食男女，人之大欲存焉；死亡貧苦，人之大惡存焉。故欲惡者，心之大端也。人藏其心，不可測度也；美惡皆在其心，不見其色也，欲一以窮之，舍禮何以哉？[66]

Ritual, following this passage, is a means of gauging the internal refinement or repulsiveness of people. Ritual allows the observer of ritual to peer into the heart-minds of the performers. Elegantly performed ritual reveals an elegantly arrayed internal disposition. An inelegant performance reveals the opposite. At several places, the *Liji* echoes a familiar refrain: "Observe their rituals and musical performances to know their state of order or chaos" 觀其禮樂，而治亂可知也.[67] Rituals, in this sense, are presentations of one's inner state—a discordant performance signifies inner discord, and a refined performance signifies inner refinement. At the same time, rituals are also reflective of larger degrees of societal order and chaos—a poorly performed ritual hosted by government officials is representative of a chaotic government.

It is also possible to insincerely perform ritual. This occurs when a ritual agent carries out the actions required by a ritual script, but does not possess enough of the sentiments, or the kinds of sentiments, that should accompany those actions. The *Liji* tends to assume that its readers are those who *want* to express the proper degree of sentiment.[68] As such, the text is little concerned with insincerity. In other words, the authors of the text presume that as most people go through life they will naturally experience certain sentiments and *need* to express them—when one's father dies, for instance, most people will spontaneously feel grief, and this grief must be expressed. The authors or redactors of the *Liji* also recognize that some people may not naturally have a sufficient degree of sentiment—these people may not in fact feel much grief when their father dies. In these situations, the mourning rituals are meant to arouse sentiments of grief so that the mourner experiences them in proper degree. A prerequisite of this latter group is that they in fact want to feel more sentiment then they actually do. They recognize, for instance, the right amount of grief in mourning for their father and realize that they fall short. Ritual, in these cases, spurs human sentiment to a higher degree. If the ritual agent does not spontaneously experience enough sentiment, yet recognizes that he should, but does *not want* to experience more, the ritual can fail to stir up more sentiment. This kind of ritual failure can be called a failure in sincerity. For the most part, however, the *Liji* is not concerned with failures in sincerity. It tends to assume that its audience has a certain degree of commitment to performing ritual appropriately (although they may disagree on what counts as appropriate). As such, the *Liji* spends relatively little time discussing issues of moral motivation as they fall into the category David Nivison defined as *acedia*—situations where the ritual agent may recognize what is appropriate, but not be sufficiently motivated to perform it.[69]

The expressive function of ritual is particularly important for mature ritual agents, that is, those ritual agents who, through practice, possess the knowledge and skill to competently perform ritual. To borrow an image mentioned earlier, ritual is the fruit of human disposition—it is the result of mature or ripened sentiment.[70] In other words, rituals are the natural performances of those who have cultivated appropriate dispositions. These ritual agents have spent years practicing ritual such that it "patterns" them or makes a lasting impression on them and their dispositions. When they express their dispositions, therefore, they spontaneously act in accordance with ritual. These individuals are 'fluent' in the sense that they gracefully articulate their inner state of refinement to the outer world. They navigate their way through the world with ease and smoothly move in synchronization with the *dao* 道.

Coincidentally, the modern translation of 'fluent' into Chinese is *liuli* 流利, which, when taken literally, means a kind of "sharp flow," or a situation where water moves quickly to its destination. 'Fluid' and 'fluent' in English are also etymologically related.[71] Fluid refers not only to liquid, but also to the ability of liquid to move and take various shapes. A fluid, or fluent, ritual agent is someone who moves like channeled water in expressing his dispositions. He bends where necessary and flows freely throughout the world. The "Zhongni Yanju" chapter, already quoted above, makes this very point. The opening passage contains an allusion made by Confucius in order to explain why his disciples should practice ritual.

> The Master said, "Sit, you three, and I will tell you about ritual, so that by means of ritual you will flow [*liu* 流] around the world and there will be no area that [you] will not cover."
>
> 子曰：「居！女三人者，吾語女禮，使女以禮周流無不遍也。」[72]

Ritual is the means by which the ritual agent navigates his way through the world. The idea implied by these kinds of passages is that the cultivated ritual agent is someone who is able to fluidly move in conjunction with the other things in the world. Ritual is a kind of social lubricant that enables the proper functioning of society. It also ensures that the human world moves in step with nonhuman objects and the larger cosmic world.

Fluent ritual agents, as discussed in future chapters, are also able to recognize potential failures of ritual and modify them to avoid the failure. Confucius, for instance, is portrayed as a highly fluent ritual agent, and is thereby able to alter rituals in different circumstances to ensure their continued success.

This notion of fluency in early Confucian texts is often discussed under the rubric of appropriateness (*yi* 義), timeliness (*shi* 時), and discretion (*quan* 權). In the *Liji*, the notions of ritual knowledge (*zhili* 知禮) and poise (*zhong* 中) also play this role. The "Liqi" chapter, for instance, explains that one who knows ritual, knows how to replace an animal sacrifice when that particular animal is not available; and the "Zhongyong" chapter explains that the poised agent is able to perform appropriately in almost any situation he confronts—be it situations of physical hardship, poverty, or over abundance.[73] Other passages of the *Liji* speak of circumstances where exceptions are allowed in mourning rites. These include situations such as balding women not needing to wear the mourning headpiece, the crippled not needing to perform mourning faltering, and the elderly and sick not needing to refrain from wine and meat. A passage from the "Sangfu Sizhi" 喪服四制 chapter concludes with the injunction to "use discretion when managing these circumstances" 凡此。。。以權制者也.[74] The idea suggested here is that a certain kind of discretion or deliberation—literally a "weighing"—occurs in the person of the mature ritual agent. He or she is able to determine an appropriate response to abnormal situations.

The expressive functions of ritual are those that allow for the demonstration of human disposition. Poorly performed ritual reveals uncultivated dispositions, while properly performed ritual manifests cultivated dispositions. As a ritual agent practices ritual, his dispositions are patterned such that they become more and more refined. Eventually he performs ritual naturally. This naturalness is a kind of 'fluency' where the ritual agent is able to fluidly move in synchronization with the *dao* 道 and is able to fluently express himself in various contexts. More significant for future chapters, a fluent ritual agent is able to alter ritual in circumstances of potential failure.

2

A Typology of Dysfunction

"[It] is men who make mistakes, not the ritual."[1]

THE INTRODUCTION OF this book began by describing the scene set forth in the "Liyun" 禮運 chapter where the period of "Grand Unity" (*datong* 大同) was juxtaposed with the period of "Modest Prosperity" (*xiaokang* 小康). While both of these time periods were conducive to obtaining a sense of order and harmony, the latter is marked by a need for mediation. No longer did the "Great Way" (*dadao* 大道) spontaneously pervade the world; rather, human beings required a series of rituals to realign themselves with it. These rituals acted as figurative "knots" (*ji* 紀) to bind human beings together with the Great Way.

The first chapter of this project sought to characterize these rituals. It discussed a variety of ways the *Liji* conceptualizes terms such as *li* 禮 and how these terms were employed in an effort to create a more ordered world. More specifically, it articulated both the 'impressive' and 'expressive' functions of ritual. In its impressive sense, rituals act to shape human beings—changing the way they feel and act. Expressively, rituals function as conduits to make manifest the refined dispositions of profound people. It also discussed these functions in relation to notions of 'fluency.' A primary purpose of ritual is to create fluent human beings who are sensitive to the dynamic tendencies of the social and cosmic worlds.

This chapter will pursue the notion of 'dysfunction.' It begins by recounting the study of dysfunctional ritual in ritual studies and then proceeds to build on this account by providing a typology of dysfunctions rooted in the *Liji*. Chapters 4 and 5 will elaborate on this typology, and chapter 6 will challenge it by discussing ways in which the authors of the *Liji* found the failure of ritual to be an ambiguous affair. This chapter,

chapter 2, is meant to set the stage for later chapters and, as such, discusses the major issues of later chapters in a more general manner.

Summarily speaking, dysfunctions are failures of ritual to achieve one or more of their intended aims. Rituals, borrowing from Victor Turner, are "multivocal"—meaning that they serve different purposes for different people.[2] Some purposes are more important for some people, and a single ritual can serve several purposes for the same person. Hence the same ritual may fail in some minor respect for certain people, fail in some major respect for others, and not fail at all for a third party. The question of *for whom* a ritual failed and *in what way* it failed is a complicated issue. The capping ceremony, for instance, as discussed in the *Liji*, is meant to induct the young man being capped into adulthood, as well as teach him about values such as filial piety (*xiao* 孝) and brotherly affection (*ti* 悌). For the parents involved, it also serves as a display of their wealth and status in society; and for the state it provides a means of identifying future government officials. The intention of the capping ritual, as such, is never located in a static view from nowhere. Its failure can also be occasioned with its success—the same capping ritual could succeed in situating a young man into society, yet fail to sufficiently instruct him in becoming filial. It can also succeed in providing the state with a prospective official but fail by exerting too high of an economic cost on the participant's parents. The failures discussed in this project are those expressed explicitly or implicitly by the authors or redactors of the *Liji*. While rituals, following Catherine Bell, are "embedded in a misrecognition of what it is in fact doing," my focus tends toward the emic (rather than etic) accounts of ritual as contained in the *Liji*.[3]

This chapter will introduce two kinds of dysfunctions and the ways early Confucians dealt with them. We will see that the authors of the *Liji* sought to avoid failure by emphasizing a program of ritual practice and by 'opening the ritual script' in circumstances where following the ritual script would otherwise lead to failure. This latter move allowed early Confucians to advocate the rituals of the past, while at the same time recognize the need to adapt them to contemporary circumstances. It also served to legitimate their role in the sociopolitical structure of early China—in essence claiming that sensitivity to context required more than a textual tradition; it additionally required the presence of trained Confucians to adapt the tradition to living circumstances. This chapter then concludes by emphasizing the persistence of ritual failure. In other words, despite the fact that ritual scripts could be altered to account for various circumstances, the authors of the *Liji* also believed that there were situations where failure was inevitable. This distinction between preventable and unpreventable failures in ritual will become especially important in the chapters that follow.

The Study of Failure in Ritual Studies

The study of ritual as an area of academic inquiry began over a century ago. It was not until the last fifty years, however, that a more focused attempt was made to understand ritual through the lens of failure. Clifford Geertz's 1959 article "Ritual and Social Change: A Javanese Example" is groundbreaking in this regard.[4] In it, Geertz examined the funerary rites held for a 10-year-old boy in Central Java, noting how this particular funeral "failed to work with its accustomed effectiveness."[5] While Geertz's main argument concerned the dynamic relationship between "culture" (i.e., symbols) and "social systems" (i.e., practice), he also analyzed this particular event concluding, "This disrupted funeral was in fact but a microscopic example of the broader conflicts, structural dissolutions, and attempted reintegrations which, in one form or another, are characteristic of contemporary Indonesian society."[6] For Geertz, this failed ritual became a means of noting the tensions between traditional practices and the demands of modern living. Elements of this analysis reemerge in his famous "Deep Play: Notes on the Balinese Cockfight," published in 1972.[7]

The earliest systematic study of failed ritual is Ronald Grimes's 1988 article "Infelicitous Performances and Ritual Criticism."[8] In it, Grimes creates a taxonomy of over a dozen failures, or—borrowing from J. L. Austin's speech-act theory—"infelicities" of ritual. While I only employ Grimes's taxonomy inasmuch as it is useful for addressing the issues of this project, the full taxonomy demonstrates an attempt to catalogue the various ways ritual—as a cross-cultural category of analysis—can fail. He presents an abbreviated form of this taxonomy as follows:

1. Misfire (act purported but void)
   a. Misinvocation (act disallowed)
      i. Nonplay (lack of accepted conventional procedure)
      ii. Misapplication (inappropriate persons or circumstances)
   b. Misexecutions (act vitiated)
      i. Flaw (incorrect, vague, or inexplicit formula)
      ii. Hitch (incomplete procedure)
2. Abuse (act professed but hollow)

  a. Insincerity (lack of requisite feelings, thoughts, or intentions)
  b. Breach (failure to follow through)
  c. "Gloss" (procedures used to cover up problems)
  d. "Flop" (failure to produce appropriate mood or atmosphere)
3. "Ineffectuality" (act fails to precipitate anticipated empirical change)
4. "Violation" (act effective but demeaning)
5. "Contagion" (act leaps beyond proper boundaries)
6. "Opacity" (act unrecognizable or unintelligible)
7. "Defeat" (act discredits or invalidates acts of others)
8. "Omission" (act not performed)
9. "Misframe" (genre of act misconstrued)[9]

Grimes's study is significant for highlighting the prevalence of ritual failure. He actually begins his article by noting the many failed rituals in the Hebrew Bible—a theme, according to Grimes, rarely considered in Biblical Studies. Grimes's piece is also significant in that it draws attention to how the same ritual can succeed in some ways but fail in others. He, for instance, explains, "A fertility rite may not make crops grow. Nevertheless, it can succeed socially while it fails empirically. Worship can lapse into civil ceremony and thus serve a vested political interest, thereby failing ethically. Meanwhile, it can succeed in providing symbols that nourish or comfort individuals."[10] Following this reading, rituals serve structural, functional, ethical, and symbolic purposes. A failure in one purpose does not necessarily entail the failure of other purposes. Most importantly, Grimes points out that in cases of a failed ritual, the propensity of those invested in the ritual is to blame the ritual performers rather than attributing it to some weakness in the rite itself. He adds, "They [i.e., ritual participants] will blame themselves before impugning the rite and will criticize some part of it before challenging the whole of it."[11] The idea that people are to be blamed for the failure of ritual and not the ritual script (or the non-immediate forms of power invoked in the ritual) is a dominant theme in the observations of ritual theorists.

The typology I will employ in this project is, in some regards, simpler than Grimes's taxonomy. If I were to use his terminology, however, I would say that this project pays particular attention to what he has called "flaws," "hitches," "misapplications," and "ineffectualities"—at the same time focusing on issues of preventability.[12]

The topic of ritual failure in Ritual Studies is related to the study of change in ritual scripts and ritual practice. While most religious traditions and theorists of ritual recognize that every performance of a ritual is unique, they also tend to claim that ritual scripts do not change, or are at least not supposed to change. The late Roy Rappaport, for instance, noted that ritual is a "re-enactment of that which in its very essence is invariant."[13] To change a ritual, in this light, is taken as an admission of failure on the part of the original ritual script. This theme is reiterated in Catherine Bell's chapter on ritual change in her book *Ritual: Perspectives and Dimensions.*[14] Bell notes that a "dilemma" of ritual "lies in the simple fact that rituals tend to present themselves as the unchanging, time-honored customs of an enduring community," yet this community and the scholars studying this community often recognize that these rituals have varied over time.[15] In response to this, Bell argues that most religious communities reconceptualize the nature of these variations to explain them as "limited and commonsensical arrangements necessary in particular instances" rather than "changes" to a ritual or "failures" of a ritual.[16] Relying on Barbara Meyerhoff's research, Bell points out that the invisibility of ritual's origins and the invisibility of its inventors tends to add to the authority of ritual.[17]

The Collaborative Research Centre on Dynamics of Ritual funded by the German Research Council is undoubtedly the heart of contemporary studies on ritual failure.[18] Funded through 2014, the Collaborative Research Centre has so far sponsored over thirty projects that examine different aspects of ritual change or ritual failure. Besides countless publications in German and other European languages, two collected volumes in English have emerged—*Dynamics of Changing Rituals* edited by Jens Kreinath, Constance Hartung, and Annette Deschner; and *When Rituals Go Wrong: Mistakes, Failure, and the Dynamics of Ritual* edited by Ute Hüsken.[19] Both books contain the research of dozens of scholars studying the rituals of numerous traditions across the world (both ancient and modern).

These scholars have taken up the task of creating the appropriate vocabulary to understand the dynamics of ritual. Some theorists claim, for instance, that "failure" is too strong a word to express how religious traditions account for the variation of ritual practice or the modification of ritual scripts; they instead prefer "imperfections."[20] Other scholars argue for the appropriateness of terms such as "modification," "transformation,"[21] "flaw," "mistake," "error,"[22] or "recursivity."[23] In the field of Ritual Studies there is little consensus on proper terminology.

A common point of focus for these scholars is studying how religious communities account for variations of their rituals over time, and how these communities explain situations where rituals do not result in their purported outcome. Matthais Jung, for instance, examines Catholic liturgy and explains how some clergy understand the liturgy to be comprised of certain unchangeable "divine" elements as well as elements that ought to change—the latter of which should be altered "if they have suffered from the intrusion of anything out of harmony with the inner nature of the liturgy or have become less suitable." The purpose of Catholic rites, in this view, is to "express more clearly the holy things, which they signify."[24] Unfortunately, many of these accounts (written by either scholars or practitioners) do not provide a robust explanation of how ritual agents distinguish between changeable and unchangeable elements of a ritual.

Other scholars such as Axel Michaels and Karin Polit demonstrate that many Indian traditions attribute the inability of a ritual to deliver its purported outcome to mistakes on the part of ritual performers rather than flaws in the ritual script. Polit, for instance, explains that, "Most Garhwali people believe that a properly performed ritual cannot fail... In this view, the only explanation for the failure or inefficacy of a ritual is human failure."[25] Michaels, likewise, makes the same point—succinctly stating that from the perspective of the Vedas, "it is men who make mistakes, not the ritual."[26]

A dominant theme throughout these studies is that most religious traditions maintain claims of ritual purity—their rituals neither change nor fail.[27] The challenge that these scholars have taken up, then, is to create categories of analysis that are both accurate in terms of their observations and authentic to the experiences of those they study.

The case of Confucianism, at least as portrayed in the *Liji*, is significantly different from those examined by the theorists of ritual mentioned above. Ritual performances are not only unique, but ritual scripts are meant to change. Ritual scripts, as described in the "Liqi" 禮器 chapter, are like communal wine feasts—everyone involved contributes to the feast similar to the way in which rituals are created and recreated by incorporating the best practices of past traditions.[28] Early Confucians, in this sense, are open to criticizing a given ritual script (although they may not agree on how or when to modify it). Similar to the accounts provided above, however, the authors of the *Liji* also tend to blame human beings for failures of ritual. In other words, despite the fact that they recognize the need to alter ritual scripts, those responsible for performing the ritual are also responsible for altering the script. As such, the failure of a ritual is usually described as the fault of the ritual agent for either incompetently performing the ritual script or inappropriately modifying it in a particular circumstance. This does not mean, however, that all ritual failures are preventable. As I will demonstrate below, and discuss more thoroughly in chapter 5, there are sometimes situations where regardless of how appropriate a script seems, the ritual fails to achieve its purported result.

Dysfunction in the Early Confucian Context

Early Confucians tend to describe their world as being in a state of disorder. Whether disorder was inherent in the creation of the world itself or if human beings caused the condition is not always clear; but what is clear is that human beings have the primary responsibility to overcome disorder and bring about an ordered world. Rituals are the means by which human beings achieve order. They act as guides for things in the world (both animate and inanimate) to be put in proper relation to each other. They serve to place human beings in synchronization with the *dao* 道. Failure to achieve synchronization means that either the efforts of ritual agents have fallen short or that the rituals at their disposal, for one reason or another, are incapable of providing the synchronization they were thought to provide. This early Confucian worldview is open to the possibility that both human beings and the rituals at their disposal are flawed or are vulnerable to agencies beyond the control of ritual performers. The authors of the *Liji* were deeply concerned about the possibility of ritual failure.

From a general perspective, we can speak of two kinds of failures, or dysfunctions, with regard to rituals in the *Liji*—'dysfunctions in competency' and 'dysfunctions in efficacy.' The former is agent-focused and the latter is script-focused.

The ritual script, as I use it in the context of this project, refers to the rules or steps a ritual should follow. These rules may be recorded in texts—such as the *Liji*, *Yili* 《儀禮》, or *Zhouli* 《周禮》—or passed down orally. They may be very specific prescriptions for action, or general guidelines adaptable to various circumstances. In short, the ritual script refers to the steps of a ritual believed to be prescribed by authoritative figures of ritual performance. Oftentimes these figures are depicted as having lived many centuries before the current circumstances described in the *Liji*.

One difficulty with regard to ritual scripts is the fact that the *Liji* does not always specify the ritual script at play in a particular circumstance. Additionally, scholars have noted for centuries that early Confucian texts sometimes provide conflicting ritual scripts. While the *Liji* does not always provide the precise script intended for a particular ritual performance, it usually highlights points of tension when ritual performers deviate from the script understood to be in play.

A dysfunction in competency is a failure on the part of ritual agents to properly follow a ritual script—not wearing the prescribed mourning clothes at the death of a family member, for instance. Ritual agents may not follow a script for a variety of reasons. They might lack sufficient knowledge of the script, they might lack sufficient skill in performing the script, or they might lack sufficient motivation to follow the script (among other reasons). Dysfunctions in competency occur when a ritual agent believes that he *should* follow the script, but fails to follow it. Failures in competency, while common, are for the most part preventable. In other words failures in competency can be eliminated through a more robust program of ritual training. The better trained ritual agents are, the better they will be at following the script. Since the *Liji*, for the most part, presupposes that its readers have sufficient competency to follow a ritual script, I will not discuss dysfunctions in competency with the same detail that I will discuss dysfunctions in efficacy.

A dysfunction in efficacy occurs when a ritual script is ill-suited to account for the complexities confronted by ritual agents; these difficulties may be in terms of geographic variation or other political, social, or cosmic factors exerting themselves on the event—all people are required to fast, for example, as a part of the mourning rites, but the sick and the old are incapable of fasting for the required period of time. Requiring them to follow the ritual script as it stands would endanger their lives. In these situations the *Liji* recommends that those in charge of the ritual alter the script in accordance with their own discretion (*quan* 權). The *Liji*, as a whole, is more concerned with failures in efficacy then it is with failures in competency. It tends to assume that the readers of the text (and the characters depicted in the text) have knowledge of the ritual script deemed proper for various occasions; and that they are otherwise competent to perform the ritual in line with the script. Therefore the focus of the *Liji*, with regards to ritual failure, is on recognizing situations where a script is inadequate for a particular context and on making the appropriate change. It is particularly concerned with ritual performers misinterpreting a situation and either making inappropriate changes to a ritual script or making changes to a ritual script where none should have been made.

Failures in efficacy can be further divided between preventable and unpreventable failures. Preventable failures in efficacy are those failures that a fluent ritual agent can avert by changing the ritual script. If, for instance, the script for mourning calls for condoling the surviving family shortly after their family member's passing, but some friends of the deceased arrive after this period due to having traveled a great distance, a fluent ritual agent will recognize the threat this poses to the ritual script and modify it such that some form of condolence takes place when they arrive. Unpreventable failures in efficacy are failures of ritual that cannot be stopped regardless of the fluency of the ritual agent. One way to distinguish between dysfunctions in competency and dysfunctions in efficacy is to conceptualize the former as "failures *in* ritual" (i.e., a mistake made in the performance of the ritual) and the latter as "failures *of* ritual" (i.e., the inability of the ritual script to generate its purported end).[29]

Heuristically, it is convenient to speak of these two dysfunctions as being separate; however, the reality of the situation is often far more complex. Precisely *what* failed or *who* caused the failure—ritual agents, the script, or some extra-ritual agency—is often a topic of debate within the *Liji*. The following passage illustrates a key aspect of this debate.

> When Confucius was traveling to Wei he came upon the mourning rites for a person he had previously lodged with. He went in and wept to the brink of sorrow. Upon exiting he sent [his disciple], Zigong, to unbridle two horses from his carriage and leave them for the grieving family. Zigong remarked, "You've never given horses at the mourning rites for your disciples, isn't giving them to someone that [simply] housed you quite excessive?"
>
> 孔子之衛，遇舊館人之喪，入而哭之哀。出，使子貢說驂而賻之。子貢曰：「於門人之喪，未有所說驂，說驂於舊館，無乃已重乎?」
>
> The master replied, "When I went in to pay my condolences to him, I encountered such singleness of sorrow that tears fell from my eyes. I would not like to shed so many tears, and not act on the basis of them. Go unbridle the horses [and give them to the family]."
>
> 夫子曰：「予鄉者入而哭之，遇於一哀而出涕。予惡夫涕之無從也。小子行之。」[30]

While much could be said about this passage, the point worth mentioning here involves the challenge that Zigong raises concerning Confucius's gift. The question posed by Zigong, in essence, is why does Confucius offer such an extravagant gift to the family of a casual acquaintance? From Zigong's view, the script for this situation dictates providing a less luxurious gift. Zigong, therefore, implies that Confucius has failed (or will fail) in this scenario—he has incompetently performed the gift-giving portion of the mourning rites. On this account, the failure lies within the person of Confucius. Confucius, of course, rejoins that he is following his sentiments in providing such a gift. Without re-exploring the role of sentiment in ritual performance, the relevant implication here is that Confucius does not believe that he has failed; rather, he implies that the ritual script has failed to adequately provide the guidance necessary to properly express his sentiments of sorrow. To give a lesser gift would be ineffective in expressing these sentiments. In light of the failure of the script, Confucius makes a necessary rendition.

Following Zigong's view, dysfunction lies at the hands of the agent in the situation. In Confucius's view, however, the ritual script has failed. Within the interpretive tradition of the *Liji*, these kinds of passages are rarely read as a critique of Confucius. Indeed, when pitted against his disciples it is almost always seen as him that provides the winning argument. Therefore, this passage tends to be read as a dysfunction in efficacy. The point however, adequately demonstrated by this passage, is that the line between dysfunctions in efficacy and dysfunctions in competency does not readily present itself. It often requires an added level of debate and interpretation in order to be distinguished (if at all distinguishable). Furthermore, the line is not only unclear within the internal narrative of the event itself—as evidenced by Zigong's confusion—but is also not always clear to the observers of the event, or the readers of the text; besides accepting Confucius's view on the basis of his authority, the only other reason provided in support of his position is that he is following his feelings of sorrow, a view explicitly discounted by Confucius in several other places.[31] There is no simple reading of this passage to identify it as either a dysfunction in competency or a dysfunction in efficacy. Nevertheless, both positions allude to the fact that dysfunctions in efficacy and dysfunctions in competency were real concerns.

Modifying Ritual

One way to prevent dysfunctions in efficacy is to modify the ritual script. The authors of the *Liji* were more than passively aware of this. Indeed, they often advocated altering ritual scripts. The "Yueji" 樂記 chapter states this quite succinctly: "The five emperors of antiquity lived in different times and did not pass on their musical performances [*yue* 樂] to each other. The three kings of the early dynasties lived in different ages and did not hand down their rituals [*li* 禮] to each other" 五帝殊時，不相沿樂；三王異世，不相襲禮.[32] Other portions of the *Liji* explain that "rituals follow what is fitting [for the context]" 禮從宜 and that rituals "change and follow the times" 變而從時.[33] In short, the *Liji* endorses changing ritual scripts depending on the ruling dynasty, the custom of people in different locations, the time of the year, the varying terrain of the earth, the material possessions or physical limitations of the participants, as well as a host of other things (all discussed in chapter 4). The "Liqi" chapter, perhaps written with many of these in mind, provides a working list of the kinds of rituals that the profound person must understand.

> When a profound person follows a ritual script [*li* 禮], there are those [scripts] which are [already] accurate and can be put straight into action, those which are inaccurate and must be modified, those which are individually proper for each participant, those which are followed in line with one's social position, those which are instilled and take time to develop, those which promote [worthy men] to advance in position, those which emulate [the past] and embellish it, those which emulate [the past] and simplify it, and those which are followed selectively.
>
> 君子之於禮也，有直而行也，有曲而殺也，有經而等也，有順而討也，有擶而播也，有推而進也，有放而文也，有放而不致也，有順而摭也。[34]

While there are ritual scripts that should be uniformly applied, there are also scripts that should be modified, and even scripts that should be selectively followed. The purpose of quoting this passage is to demonstrate the awareness of the authors in advocating the alteration of ritual scripts. They are mindful of the fact that to simply perform rituals as scripted could result in a failure of the ritual. Nowhere is the depiction of failure more clear than in the "Yueling" 月令 chapter, which describes the chaos that ensues by performing the rites of one month at the wrong time. It explains,

> If, in the early month of spring, the summer regulations are followed, the rain will not fall in its proper time, the [leaves on] shrubs

> and trees will wither and fall to the ground, and the people in each state will be in constant fear. If the autumn regulations are followed, there will be pestilence among the people, violent winds will rage, heavy rains will fall incessantly, and various wild shrubs will arise. If the winter regulations are followed, reservoirs will fail to hold the [increasing] water; snow and frost will be severe, and seeds will be unable to be planted.
>
> 孟春行夏令，則雨水不時，草木蚤落，國時有恐。行秋令，則其民大疫，猋風暴雨總至，藜、莠、蓬、蒿並興。行冬令，則水潦為敗，雪霜大摯，首種不入。[35]

Ritual performed at the wrong time brings about a disordered world. Ritual, in this case, must be adjusted to the times of the seasons in order to function properly. The rituals of summer, performed in spring, cause the rain to fall at the wrong time. The rituals of fall, performed in spring, bring pestilence to the people. Rituals performed without sensitivity to time, the *Liji* claims, will fail and result in a chaotic world. The issue of proper timing was often included in ritual scripts—ritual scripts could, for instance, prescribe certain performances to accord with certain seasons. On other occasions, however, sensitivity to timing was something only a living ritual agent could determine—no script could take into account the multitude of circumstances a complex world presented.

Opening the Ritual Script

What we find in many parts of the *Liji* is an attempt to incorporate an awareness of proper adaptations into the ritual script itself. For instance, the "Tangong Xia" 檀弓下 chapter recounts the following exchange between Zilu and Confucius.

> Zilu remarked, "How unfortunate are the poor. While [their parents] are alive they lack the means to provide for them. When they die they lack the means to hold the burial rites [*li* 禮] for them."
>
> 子路曰：「傷哉貧也，生無以為養，死無以為禮也。」
>
> Confucius responded, "If parents are happy eating bean stew and drinking water, their children should be considered filial. If at death,

their hands, feet, and body are clothed, and burial is performed swiftly, [even] without an outer coffin—all being determined by their material possessions—their children have properly performed the rites [*li* 禮].

孔子曰：「啜菽飲水盡其歡，斯之謂孝；斂手足形，還葬而無槨，稱其財，斯之謂禮。」[36]

Here the ritual script is adjusted to include variations in the objects used in burial rites on the basis of material wealth. Changing the implements of the rite in accordance with what the participants can afford becomes part of the rite itself. The impoverished are not expected to use the goods normally dictated by the script. Variation from the script is required in order to bring a fitting resolution to the situation. From one angle, there appears to be a dysfunction in efficacy: the ritual script calls for certain kinds of material goods to be used, but using them is beyond the means of the poor. The script fails, therefore, in that it demands the impossible (or the nearly impossible) from the participants.[37] However, the important thing to note is that the script is expanded to account for these deviations. The rite should not be performed in strict accordance with the original script.

Similar arguments are found for incorporating not only the financial considerations of participants, but also the timing of an event and the natural resources of different geographic locations. The "Liqi" chapter, for instance, explains that, "The profound person considers those who live in the mountains, but use fish and turtles in their rites, and those who live in marshes, but use deer and pigs in their rites, as people who do not 'know ritual [*zhili* 知禮]'" 居山以魚鱉為禮，居澤以鹿豕為禮，君子謂之不知禮.[38] I introduced the idea of 'knowing ritual' in the last chapter. There, I related it to the concepts of poise (*zhong* 中), appropriateness (*yi* 義), and timeliness (*shi* 時)—all discussed under the rubric of 'fluency.' One who knows ritual is able to bring about a well-ordered world in that all things within the world operate fluently with each other. As it relates to the discussion here, knowing ritual entails knowing how to modify rituals in accordance with the different contexts of the earth. The person who knows ritual realizes that the sacrifices made in various rituals depend upon the natural production of the earth in the regions where the ritual is performed.[39] More broadly speaking, one who knows ritual understands when deviations from the script are necessary. They recognize potential failures in efficacy and modify the script accordingly. Thus, a fluent person will prevent dysfunctions in efficacy by making an appropriate alteration. Following a line in the "Liyun" chapter, "The early kings were able to alter ritual in order to accord with what was appropriate" 先王能脩禮以達義.[40] Knowing ritual, in essence, means knowing how to adjust ritual scripts to include appropriate alternatives.

Alteration (changes in content) and alternation (changes in the time of performance), therefore, came to be thought of as part of the inherent makeup of ritual performance; and knowing ritual meant knowing, among other things, how to alter it. The inclusion of change into the concept of ritual, therefore, meant that ritual, in the early Confucian context, was thought of as having an 'open script.' In other words, rituals were amendable to multiple adaptations. They did not require the same performance in every context. At the same time, however, these scripts were not unlimitedly open; they were not subject to the random whimsies of the participants. Indeed, the amount of leeway in altering ritual scripts is constrained.

Put in the terms of this project, early Confucians often broadly conceptualized the ritual script such that it included a variety of alternatives. So, for instance, pigs *or* fish could be offered in sacrifice, and both were seen as operating in accordance with the same script. Opening the ritual script also entailed reconfiguring the idea of dysfunction. While dysfunctions in efficacy were openly acknowledged, and sometimes taken for granted, the failure of a ritual was seen first and foremost as either the fault of an incompetent participant or the fault of a ritual agent who was insufficiently fluent, before it was blamed on the ritual script. What this meant, in other words, was that early Confucians tended to emphasize the duty of human beings to compensate for potential failures of ritual. As such, a dysfunctional ritual tended to be seen as a failure, not of the ritual script—as the ritual script accounted for or at least accommodated alterations—but of human beings in lacking the fluency to fulfill their duty in properly altering the script.

A significant interpretive move occurs in response to the issue of altering ritual scripts—while early Confucians recognize that rituals scripts could not account for every possible complication, more often than not a dysfunctional situation is attributed to the failure of those involved with the ritual to either perform it properly, or to recognize a potential failure in efficacy and to make a necessary adaptation to the script. In other words, while a potential failure in efficacy could suggest that a script will fail regardless of the efforts of human agents, it turns out that there is often much that human beings could do, and *should* do, to prevent a dysfunction in efficacy. In short, a dysfunction in efficacy is often transformed into an issue of the ritual agent's fluency. In the case mentioned above where the poor are excluded from the funerary rites, if the ritual fails, it is not because the script was dysfunctional in that it excluded the poor from participation, but rather the ritual fails because the agent responsible for the ritual failed to change the script in accordance with the material wealth of the participants. Changes, if made appropriately, are counted as part of the script itself.

Reconceiving the ritual script to account for adaptations allowed early Confucians to employ a specialized discourse concerning ritual. This discourse essentially claimed that rituals rarely fail, all the while recognizing the necessity of altering them. In a sense, the authors of the *Liji* were aware of the real possibility of dysfunctions in efficacy, but this reconceptualization of ritual served to gloss over these dysfunctions, making failures in efficacy seem few and far between. This allowed them on the one hand to caution others not to break from the scripts of ritual, but on the other hand it also prevented ritual scripts from becoming overly rigid. As such, proponents of this position could tout a system of rituals as being nearly perfect, and thereby discount other intellectual options of the time that advocated alternatives such as the elimination of ritual altogether. In distinction from this latter view, represented in texts such as the *Zhuangzi*, the authors of the *Liji* affirmed the value of rituals and at the same time committed themselves to changing them according to the context.

From Precepts to Preceptors

Opening ritual scripts to include elements of change enabled early Confucians to shift notions of ritual authority onto themselves rather than a text or liturgy. If rituals were supposed to be context sensitive, there must be an agent present to interpret the context. Ritual in this sense could not be completely codified in a textual or oral tradition. Rather, they required a profound person, or group of profound people, to adapt them to living circumstances. To employ a contemporary expression, ritual performance required a touch of the master's hand.

One way of understanding this situation is that early Confucians attempted to assert the necessity of their role in the social structures of the time. Their argument implied that rituals passed down from previous dynasties, regardless of how effective they seemed or how reliable the texts that recorded them were, were insufficient for ordering their contemporary world. As it happens, properly employing these rituals required the presence of an interpreter or a fluent agent, that is, a Confucian. This allowed early Confucians to affirm the value of past dynasties by accounting for the seeming failures that occurred when attempting to replicate their rituals in the present. In other words, a failure of a rite from the past in the present was not the fault or the failure of the early dynasties. Indeed, they got it right. Rather, it becomes the fault and failure of the current dynasty to find and train fluent individuals to make the necessary adaptations to past ritual. In a sense, then, this was an argument for the value of the past in providing a series of effective rituals within their previous context, but at the same time it was also an argument for the need for authoritative figures who were well versed in the rituals of the past to lead the present dynasty into the future. Early Confucians positioned themselves as these authority figures. In short, this move allowed them to endorse the past, but at the same time not be bound by the past.

This move from precepts to preceptors created an added burden on early Confucians as any failure of ritual became a mark of their ineptitude. If things went wrong, blame could be laid at their hands. But at the same time it also enabled them to assert their relevancy in successive dynasties. While texts became an increasingly important element within the tradition of Confucianism, their significance was overshadowed by the significance of the interpreter, and his attempt to render the texts meaningful to contemporary concerns. This shift also meant that the primary concern of early Confucians was to cultivate competent and fluent ritual agents. As such, much of their efforts were geared toward developing competency and fluency.

The Persistence of Failure

All of this is not to say, however, that opening the ritual script completely eliminates dysfunctions in efficacy. While a successful adaptation of a ritual suggests that its previous form would have been dysfunctional in the current context, the threat of dysfunctions in efficacy still remained. Stated directly, it lay beyond even the most fluent individuals to constantly make the necessary changes to the ritual script. In other words, rituals sometimes fail and there is nothing that can be done—despite how fluent one is—to prevent it. While specific instances will be discussed in chapter 5, it will be helpful here to quote from a passage that illustrates this in general terms.

> The [various] rituals performed throughout the world [i.e., in early China] are meant to [do the following]: seek after a return to the beginning [of society?], seek after [communion with] the spirits of the world, seek out the harmonious employment [of all things in the world], seek after appropriateness, and seek after compliance. By seeking after the beginning, rituals enrich the root. By seeking after [communion with] the spirits of the world, they [encourage] respect for superior powers. By seeking to harmonize things, they establish the bonds of society. By seeking after appropriateness, they [encourage] those in high positions and those in low positions to not rebel against each other. By seeking after compliancy, they eliminate animosity. One who is able to integrate these five [uses of ritual], thereby orders the rituals of the world. *Although there will still be oddities, evil doings, and disorder, they will be few.*
>
> 天下之禮，致反始也，致鬼神也，致和用也，致義也，致讓也。致反始，以厚其本也；致鬼神，以尊上也；致物用，以立民紀也。致義，則上下不悖逆矣。致讓，以去爭也。合此五者，以治天下之禮也，雖有奇邪而不治者，則微矣。[41]

The closing line makes clear that disorder occasionally occurs regardless of one's best efforts to incorporate various kinds of ritual. Ritual, while successful for the most part, is not entirely capable of creating a world without disorder.

In this light, it is helpful to speak of two variations of failures in efficacy—one that is possible for a fluent agent to prevent and another that cannot be prevented. The former, as argued above, tends to be subsumed under the discourse of fluency. The latter, however, lay beyond the skill of the fluent agent. Borrowing a familiar refrain from the "Fangji" 坊記 chapter, regardless of how well one constructs a tradition of ritual, "people will still contravene it" 民猶踰之.[42] The significance of unpreventable dysfunctions in efficacy cannot be overstated. In short, they entail that early Confucians saw the world as a ruptured world—a place where failures in fundamental endeavors occasionally, yet necessarily, occur. In this sense, life is unpredictable, and a central challenge becomes coping with uncertainty. Chapter 8 discusses the ways in which early Confucians coped with concerns of dysfunction. It will be demonstrated there that early Confucians had anxieties about cultivating a sense of fluency as well as facing unpreventable failures in efficacy. Both of these anxieties functioned 'productively' in that they generated opportunities to vary from and reinvent tradition.

Chapters 4 and 5 more fully investigate the preventability of ritual failure. Chapter 4 explores several threats to ritual success and discusses how fluent ritual agents account for these threats by considering the material and physical limitations of ritual participants, the varying terrain of the earth, the changing times of the seasons, and the variation of culture and society throughout their conception of human history. Chapter 5 then explores the notion of unpreventable failures in ritual and demonstrates that the *Liji* constructs a narrative about the inevitability of ritual failure predicated on necessary changes made in the world to support the flourishing of a more complex and more interdependent human population. Ritual, in this view, must change in order to maintain its efficacy but also becomes a more contingent affair.

Conclusion

The purpose of this chapter was to introduce two kinds of failures in the rituals advocated by early Confucians. These were discussed as dysfunctions in competency and dysfunctions in efficacy. The former occur when people fail to correctly follow a ritual script. The latter occur when the ritual script fails to provide sufficient guidance for properly ordering the world. Early Confucians were aware of these dysfunctions and sought to avoid them. The primary means they employed to account for these failures were theories of 'competency' and 'fluency'—the latter of which calls for the cultivation of context sensitivity and knowledge of ritual such that a fluent agent is able to recognize potential failures in efficacy. Once the fluent agent is aware of a potential failure in efficacy, he adjusts the script such that it generates sufficient guidance for properly ordering the world.

Early Confucians expanded the notion of appropriate ritual performance to include a variety of renditions. 'Opening the script' in this sense meant that early Confucians could advocate the rituals of the past, while at the same time recognizing the need to adapt them to contemporary circumstances. Opening the ritual script to include variations of ritual performance also entailed a claim that living interpreters of the tradition were necessary to make appropriate adaptations. This claim served to legitimate the role of Confucians in the sociopolitical structure of early China.

This chapter also highlighted the reality of dysfunctions in efficacy. While all dysfunctions in competency are preventable, and most dysfunctions in efficacy can be offset by the fluency of a cultivated individual, there are still other 'unpreventable' dysfunctions in efficacy. The reality of unpreventable dysfunctions in efficacy entails an outlook that sees the world as vulnerable to a variety of agencies with power to determine ritual success—for even the best attempts of human beings to create an ordered world by means of ritual will still fall short and occasionally fail. How this dysfunction is coped with is the topic of chapter 8. It will be demonstrated there that early Confucians turned this concern with dysfunction into a productive anxiety that while on the one hand elicited sorrow in the face of failure, on the other provided moments of imagination and opportunities for new renditions of the received tradition.

3

Coming to Terms with Dysfunction

Confucian ethics is, in this sense, an ethics of flexibility.[1]

MOST MODERN INTERPRETERS of Confucian ethics focus on describing the process of cultivating fluent moral agents that are skilled at both following ritual scripts and altering ritual scripts in situations of potential failure. The primary emphasis of these modern scholars has been to explore the contours of fluency in ritual performance—meaning both how fluency is developed and how the fluent agent reasons through various situations. One blind spot in the contemporary discourse is the role of what I have called 'unpreventable failures in efficacy.' Many contemporary interpreters focus, on the other hand, on 'preventable failures in efficacy.' In other words, they concentrate on situations where changing the ritual script, if done appropriately, prevents the ritual from failing. As this chapter demonstrates, however, many contemporary interpreters mishandle situations where a ritual fails regardless of the changes that might be made to its script. This is to say that they mishandle unpreventable failures in ritual.

Modern scholars of Confucian ethics examine a variety of early Confucian texts—usually the *Xunzi*, *Mencius*, and/or the *Analects*—and do not present a uniform account of the purposes of ritual or of how a ritual might fail. At a general level, however, they agree on some characteristics of the process of moral development and the role that ritual plays in that process. Roughly speaking, most scholars subscribe to the following systematic characterization of these features.

According to early Confucians, human beings find themselves in constant interaction with each other as well as with other things in the world (both animate and inanimate things). As interaction occurs, certain feelings, or emotions, are inevitably aroused. People must learn to express these feelings appropriately (some argue they must even learn to have a new set of feelings—i.e., the "right" feelings for a particular situation).[2] They must develop constant dispositions, or virtues, to perform in such a way that they become like the exemplars of the past and that the world—by means of their influence—becomes a more ordered place. This process of development (or "reformation" as some claim) begins at a young age when people are taught by teachers or family members through instruments of instruction called ritual (*li* 禮).[3] They practice these rituals until they are able to perform them naturally, at which point these rituals become a means of expressing proper dispositions. As people grow and mature they develop a refined sense of how to perform these rituals in a variety of situations. Part of this process of maturation involves refining their sense of appropriateness (*yi* 義).[4] Mature moral agents become "connoisseurs" of their life situations in that they recognize subtle distinctions in their feelings and how some rituals better express these feelings than others.[5] They also recognize situations where following a ritual script is inappropriate. In these circumstances, they exercise their refined sense of appropriateness to create an exception to the rule, or they enact a "ruling on a rule."[6] In other words, they determine when the action prescribed by a ritual script should not be applied to the current situation (or they rewrite the rule/ritual to account for exceptions).[7]

In terms of dysfunctional ritual, the work of current scholars tends to build on this account by exploring how the process of "ruling" functions, with most scholarship constructing accounts of how appropriateness is "extended" (*tui* 推) from familiar to unfamiliar situations.[8] The largest point of disagreement in this narrative is the amount of flexibility given to the moral agent to disregard the norms of the past.

A closer inspection of several features of this account will provide a more nuanced look at competing positions within the scholarly field of Confucian ethics. It will also allow us to develop a deeper appreciation for the complexities of these positions and, more importantly, it will put us in a position to analyze several shortcomings as they relate to ritual failure. The five features of various scholarship discussed below include: (1) accounts of how refined moral agents resolve exigencies; (2) descriptions of how the maturation of refined moral agents serves as a process of cultivating appropriateness and transcending rules; (3) explanations of how refined moral agents exercise appropriateness and engage in analogical projection; (4) debates about the degree of flexibility moral agents have in deviating from the past; (5) accounts of how refined moral agents confront unpreventable dysfunctions in efficacy.

In discussing these five features, I will note the strengths of several approaches to ritual failure in the field of Confucian ethics. Stated succinctly, these approaches provide robust accounts of how ritual agents prevent ritual failure. I will also note the weaknesses of several approaches to ritual and ritual failure in the field of Confucian ethics. The most pointed critique I will make applies to a trend I call 'the inward turn.' This trend reads early Confucian texts as advocating a turn away from failures in efficacy and a turn toward an internal realm where the joy and cultivation of the ritual agent is invulnerable to agencies beyond his control.

Resolving Exigencies

Many scholars discuss dysfunctions in efficacy under the rubric of "exigencies." Exigencies are situations where the actions prescribed by some set of rules are in tension with the moral agent's sense of appropriateness (*yi* 義). This could be because two sets of rules are in direct conflict with each other (such as when the actions prescribed in mourning for the death of one's father conflicts with the birth rites of one's child) or because the results of following a rule would be disastrous (as in the example from *Mencius* found below). In these "hard cases," one performs in a way that seems to deviate from the rule.[9] Put in the language of this project, exigencies are circumstances where following a ritual script fails to bring about the purposes of a ritual. In other words, exigencies are dysfunctions in efficacy.

The classic case of an exigency is found in *Mencius* 4A17 where a figure named Chunyu Kun confronts Mencius about his seeming lack of success in bringing order to the kingdom. Commentators have been particularly interested in the initial problem Chunyu Kun puts to Mencius. In short, he asks Mencius to suppose that his sister-in-law were drowning. Since physical interaction between a man and his sister-in-law is limited to specific ceremonial instances, how, he asks, would Mencius respond to this predicament? Confronted by this problem, Mencius explains, "Only a wolf would let his sister-in-law drown and not aid her. For men and women not to touch when exchanging things accords with the ritual script [*li* 禮], but to extend a hand to assist one's drowning sister-in-law is an exigency [*quan* 權]" 嫂溺不援，是豺狼也。男女授受不親，禮也；嫂溺援之以手者，權也.[10] Current scholars interpret this statement in two distinct ways. Utilizing Antonio Cua's framework, one group takes a "subsumptive" position, and another group takes an "indeterminate" position.[11]

According to subsumptive readings of exigencies, variations from a rule are exceptions created by an appeal to more general rules or principles. In this reading, the rule being challenged is "subsumed" by a less specific rule. It is an "upward" process of justification where the rule in question can be altered on the basis of a 'meta' rule.[12] In the case of *Mencius* 4A17, one could argue that a sister-in-law should be saved on the basis of the principle of humaneness (*ren* 仁). This principle, at several places in the text of *Mencius*, seems to outweigh the demands of a ritual script (*li* 禮). Traditionally, most scholars have taken humaneness as the most fundamental principle of Mencius's thought. When a particular rule proposes a course of action in conflict with humaneness, one recognizes a built in exception and follows the rule in light of the more general rule. In this case, males and females should not touch *unless* their touching constitutes an act of humaneness. In this situation, the rule is not broken; rather, the "spirit" of the rule is followed.[13]

Robert Eno is representative of a scholar who takes a subsumptive position. He explains that hard cases are reconciled "through reference to second-level rules."[14] These second-level rules involve recourse to virtues such as humaneness (*ren* 仁) and appropriateness (*yi* 義). I will discuss how these virtues purportedly function below, with a particular emphasis on hard cases.

Most scholars who take a subsumptive position tend to see appropriateness as the most "basic" value of Confucianism. D. C. Lau, speaking of the *Analects*, claims that, "Although Confucius does not state it explicitly, one cannot help getting the impression that he realizes that in the last resort *yi* 義 [appropriateness] is the standard by which all acts must be judged while there is no further standard by which *yi* 義 [appropriateness] itself can be judged.... [T]he rites [*li* 禮], as rules of conduct, can, in the final analysis, only be based on *yi* 義 [appropriateness]. We can say, then, that in Confucius's moral system, although benevolence [*ren* 仁] occupies the more central position, *yi* 義 [appropriateness] is, nevertheless, more basic."[15]

Most critics of this position take an indeterminate approach to exigencies. In this reading, action in hard cases is not decided by recourse to more fundamental rules; nor do rules contain built-in exceptions. Rather, exigencies demand a judgment concerning the applicability of a rule to a situation. In the case of *Mencius* 4A17, the rule for proper interaction between men and women is not modified to account for the situation of a drowning sister-in-law. It also is not broken if a man were to save the life of his sister-in-law when she was in danger. What happens instead is that the rule is deemed irrelevant to the current situation.[16] According to this position, ritual scripts and the contexts in which ritual scripts are performed are two significantly different things. A cultivated individual is one who is able to recognize (and resolve) the tension between the script and the situation. Antonio Cua, a proponent of this position, summarizes the indeterminate approach quite well with the statement "rules do not contain their own rules of application."[17] Cua's point here is that the actions dictated by a ritual script are not self-evidently appropriate to their circumstances. One must learn to make a "ruling on the rule." Explained more clearly, Cua states, "A *ruling*, on our conception, is a decision or judgment on the relevance of rules to particular circumstances."[18] In short, an indeterminate interpretation of exigencies entails the suspension, but not the negation, of a ritual script that would otherwise determine proper action in the situation.

Indeterminate approaches to dysfunctions in efficacy are a predominate position in the field of Confucian ethics. These explanations, in contrast to subsumptive explanations, tend to be more systematic and well argued. Bryan Van Norden, in his 2007 book *Virtue Ethics and Consequentialism in Early Chinese Philosophy*, for instance, puts forth a lucid explanation of the problem of subsumptive positions. In short, he spells out the difficulty of defining these second-level rules, as they either require an endless list of exceptions in modifying the first-level rule, or they lose their generality when other sections of a Confucian text deem the second-level rule inapplicable in another situation.[19]

While those who put forth subsumptive and indeterminate approaches disagree as to how the cultivated Confucian deals with exigent situations, many of the assumptions and implications they make are the same in terms of the dysfunction of ritual. They both, for instance, presume that rituals could possibly fail and that these failures could in fact be shortcomings inherent in the ritual scripts rather than in the people involved in performing the ritual. The response from a subsumptive position might be to broaden the ritual script to account for exceptions; and the response from an indeterminate position might be to rule a script temporarily inapplicable; but in similar ways both positions reinforce the need of the moral agent to cultivate virtues to compensate for failure. The moral agent must refine a sense of appropriateness to either build an exception to the script or to render a particular script inappropriate for the occasion.

Both subsumptive and indeterminate positions, I would argue, are found in the *Liji*. As discussed in the previous chapter, a common response of the authors of the *Liji* to failures in efficacy is to broaden the ritual script to include a variety of alternatives—for instance, the poor need not use the outer coffin that the script dictates for burials; as long as things are done in accordance with their wealth, they are still properly performing the ritual. This seems to create a built-in exception and approaches a subsumptive position—outer coffins should be used *unless* the family cannot afford one.

On the other hand, passages such as the opening passage of the "Tangong Shang" 檀弓上 chapter (discussed more fully in the section on failures in fluency in chapter 4) take an indeterminate position. Here, a figure named Gongyi Zhongzi passes over the predetermined successor to his post, naming someone else on the basis that earlier figures such as Wen Wang and Weizi did the same. Gongyi Zhongzi justifies his action on the basis that he is simply following "the way of the ancients" (*guzhidao* 古之道).[20] Confucius, providing the final judgment of the situation, explains that Wen Wang and Weizi are in fact paradigms of virtue, but their actions do not constitute a permanent revision of the script. This way of the ancients, as such, does not include the precedents of Wen Wang and Weizi as permanent exceptions to the rule.

By and large, the *Liji* is not interested in the distinction between subsumptive and indeterminate exigencies employed by modern scholars (and charitably speaking, most modern scholars are also aware that the texts they study are not interested in this distinction either). Yet the application of this distinction to texts that, at least at face value, express little concern with this distinction reveals several problems with the approach of contemporary interpreters that employ it.

The major problem worthy of discussion here is the proclivity of these modern scholars to seek for a precise form of moral reasoning that resolves the tension that exigencies present. In other words, for texts that are obviously concerned with rituals and the possibility that rituals could fail, there is relatively little effort made to elucidate a form of thought that provides clear guidance on how to make exceptions or modifications to ritual scripts. Many contemporary interpreters, at least implicitly, take this to be a deficiency of the text and see it as their role to remedy this deficiency. The result is that they arrive at a "Confucius" or a "Mencius" that is in effect a sound ethicist. This, I should point out, is not to say that the project of rendering Confucianism into modern philosophical terminology is without value. The term *quan* 權, usually translated as "exigency" or "weighing," for instance, plays a significant role in many texts and is developed in several sophisticated ways throughout the history of the Confucian tradition.[21] The problem, however, is that many current interpreters presume the lack of rigorous distinctions to be either unspoken concepts in the theories of the authors, undeveloped ideas that they tease out, or their own framework of analysis asserted onto the material. While each of these approaches has its value, and I am aware that this project to some degree engages in all three, little attention is given to the possibility that early Confucians had good reasons for not employing these kinds of distinctions. Is it possible, for instance, that early Confucians were aware and unconcerned about developing a clear program of reasoning in exigent situations? Is it possible that the numerous hard cases found in Confucian texts point to not only the difficulty, but the impossibility, of resolving every exigent situation? In short, while the language employed by contemporary scholars on the topic of exigencies brings certain facets of Confucian ethics to the forefront, it also downplays other aspects, and a priori eliminates some possibilities.

In contrast to this, my suggestion is to preserve the tensions highlighted in exigent situations and remain open to the possibility that the ambiguities encountered in exigent situations could not always be resolved. Indeed, early Confucians did not always *want* to resolve ambiguity because ambiguity often served as a productive tension in their process of self-cultivation and community formation. Chapters 5 through 8 cover this in more detail.

Maturation as a Process of Cultivating Appropriateness and Transcending Rules

Where I prefer the language of fluency in discussing the process of self-cultivation, many scholars in the field of Confucian ethics employ the language of maturation. According to this view, maturation entails, among other things, acquiring the ability to alter ritual scripts or render them inapplicable to certain circumstances. The mature moral agent, having been well seasoned in the performance of ritual, no longer requires the rules a ritual script provides to put him in synchronization with the *dao* 道. In the process of ritual practice, his relationship with ritual is transformed. As he gains maturity, he reflects on, and abides by, the meaning embodied in a ritual; and he is thereby able to evaluate, criticize, or alter its performance.[22] Said another way, maturation is the process of cultivating appropriateness (*yi* 義). One who is mature is able to perform appropriately in any given circumstance—even exigent circumstances.

These scholars exert a great deal of effort in exploring the relationship between appropriateness and rituals/rules in the process of maturation. They tend to agree that as one refines a sense of appropriateness, rituals become less necessary in shaping proper feeling, thought, and action. Scholars such as Philip J. Ivanhoe liken maturation to the process of using a temporary brace to support a young plant: a mature person is like a fully grown plant in that he or she no longer needs the trellis (i.e., ritual scripts) to support his or her growth.[23] Other interpreters analogize the process of maturation with using training wheels on a bicycle: once one becomes adept at riding a bike, the training wheels can come off; and once one becomes adept at living a moral life, the need for ritual scripts can be stripped away.[24] This line of thought is best captured by Lee Yearley, who stated, "The perfected person [i.e., the mature agent] is so finely attuned both to the movements of human nature and to the particular circumstances faced that rules appear to have no obvious place."[25] Edward Slingerland describes the process of maturation as a kind of "transcendence" of rules.[26] The mature moral agent has cultivated such a high degree of appropriateness that he has moved beyond the need to rely on rules or ritual scripts for guidance in ethical deliberation.

Many of these same scholars qualify their position by explaining that while mature agents "transcend" rules or ritual scripts, they do not stop performing rituals in their daily life; rather, rituals take on a new role. Instead of functioning to shape or cultivate proper dispositions and actions, rituals become expressive of developed virtues (or dispositions). Rituals, in other words, while no longer needed to refine the cultivated person, are still required as a means for expressing their refined dispositions. Stated in the terms of this project, the function of ritual shifts from an impressive to an expressive role.

The most sophisticated account of this transition comes from Li Chenyang's theory of ritual as "cultural grammar."[27] In his reading, rituals act as a kind of rule that partially constitutes—but does not entirely determine—culture. This is similar to the way that the rules of grammar work in relation to language. Those who become fluent in a language tend to follow the rules of grammar, and the rules of grammar become part of the means by which they express their fluency. As grammar is embedded in language, so too are rituals embedded in culture; and as mastering a language cannot be achieved independent of its grammar, so too is mastering a culture intimately tied to mastering its rituals.[28] "In this account," Li argues, "society cultivates its members through *li* 禮 toward the goal of *ren* 仁 [i.e., cultural excellence], and persons of *ren* 仁 manifest their human excellence through the practice of *li* 禮."[29] As people master a language—Shakespeare is Li's preferred example—they come to not only follow the rules of grammar naturally (i.e., without a forced effort of deliberation), but they also learn how to occasionally break the rules of grammar for the sake of creative expression.[30] Mature moral agents are likewise able to deviate from the prescribed actions of ritual scripts in moments of cultural creativity, or, as described above, in exigent situations.

A summary account of these views suggests that a mature moral agent is one who develops a high degree of appropriateness by following the prescribed ritual scripts. This position also argues that once a moral agent attains high degrees of appropriateness, he no longer requires these scripts to provide guidance for proper performance. But at the same time, since rituals are an inherent part of any cultural life, rituals are not discarded from the life of the mature moral agent; instead they become expressive of refined dispositions. Part of being refined means that one can alter or disregard a ritual script on the basis of appropriateness. Roger Ames and David Hall capture this position quite well when they explain, "A person in learning and reflecting upon these ritual actions seeks in them the *yi* 義 [appropriateness] contributed by his precursors, and in so doing, stimulates, develops, and refines his own sensitivities.... As received wisdom, ritual actions are normative to the extent that they are counsel for the person living in the present, but are empirical in that what is appropriated requires one's own judgment.... This person is counseled by his tradition, but must evaluate and alter this tradition in pursuit of appropriateness."[31] They continue on to define *yi* 義 as "the capacity to originate and/or alter ritual actions."[32] Stated another way, rituals serve to properly refine the sensibility of people in need of cultivation; as learning occurs, one realizes that the rituals of the past "counsel" one in the present, meaning that they suggest but do not dictate proper action. Determining proper action requires exercising one's own judgment and depends upon one's attainment of *yi* 義 in modifying or recreating a ritual script.

Most contemporary scholars have achieved a vague level of consensus on the proper terminology to be used in discussing appropriateness in its relation to ritual. Broadly speaking, appropriateness is a "sense" that functions to determine the applicability of a rule to its context. What constitutes a sense, of course, is still a matter of debate.[33] In this light, contemporary interpreters have suggested that appropriateness (or the sense needed for determining the applicability of a ritual script to a situation) could be a variety of things including a virtue, skill,[34] habit, attitude, technique, character, competence, orientation,[35] inclination, sensibility,[36] "personal style,"[37] "sagely eye,"[38] and more. The majority of interpreters do not develop these terms to a degree that renders them useful in further explicating appropriateness, and some of them use these terms interchangeably.

The most developed account, and the one with perhaps the largest following, interprets appropriateness as a virtue. Proponents of this position include Lee Yearley, Philip J. Ivanhoe, and more recently Bryan Van Norden. All of these figures have been pivotal in bringing Confucian material into mainstream philosophical discourse by utilizing the framework of virtue ethics—a theory rooted in Aristotle and revived a few decades ago, most notably by Alasdair MacIntyre.[39] While the field of virtue ethics is by no means monolithic, virtue ethicists are differentiated from other kinds of ethicists (such as consequentialists) because of the attention they give to virtues and the role of these virtues in enabling human flourishing.[40] In contrast to alternative theories, which may or may not take into account a notion of human flourishing, virtue ethics focuses on cultivating virtues as the hallmark of the moral individual (rather than focusing on actions that generate "good" outcomes as would the consequentialist). As one would expect, virtue ethicists have elaborate accounts of what constitutes a virtue and how virtues are distinct from other capacities (such as skills).[41] Lee Yearley, for instance, in his landmark monograph *Mencius and Aquinas,* defines a virtue as "a disposition to act, desire, and feel that involves the exercise of judgment and leads to a recognizable human excellence or instance of human flourishing. Moreover, virtuous activity involves choosing virtue for itself and in light of some justifiable life plan."[42] He then proceeds to contrast virtues with "vices," as well as "counterfeits" and "semblances" of virtue. He later moves on to distinguish between virtues and skills, and virtues and habits.[43] Bryan Van Norden provides a more extended analysis, but essentially follows the same line of thought.[44]

My purpose here is not to provide a full account of virtue ethics or the ways in which virtue ethics has been employed in interpreting Confucianism.[45] Rather, my hope, here, is to highlight the way in which those who draw on the language of virtue ethics render virtue and/or happiness invulnerable to agencies beyond the individual. In this view, self-transformation, or the cultivation of virtue, while dependent on things such as the proper performance of social roles, becomes an eminently voluntary and individual affair.

Contrary to this view, human flourishing as a sign of virtue is problematic in circumstances of unpreventable failures in efficacy. This is particularly true in circumstances where the fault of the failure is not clearly attributable to any one party. If, for instance, Confucius buries his parents in a grave unlike those of antiquity, and it rains, collapsing the grave in the middle of the burial rites, it is not entirely clear whether Confucius is to blame for deviating from the ritual script or whether the collapse is the result of natural circumstances. For readers of the text, this raises questions such as the following: Is Confucius deficient in some aspect of virtue, or is the situation simply beyond his control? If the latter, then how is virtue generated in situations where human flourishing is not tenable—especially in long-term situations where flourishing is suppressed?

I will address the problems of vulnerability and preventability more below, and engage them more thoroughly in chapters 7 and 8. I should point out here, however, that other scholars working in the field of virtue ethics have responded to some of these issues—Robert Adams, for instance, articulates a "shared" notion of virtue; and Lisa Tessman makes an argument for "burdened virtues," or "virtues that have the unusual feature of being disjoined from their bearer's own flourishing."[46] Other notions of "moral regret" or "residue," developed by Bernard Williams, and "action guidance" versus "action assessment," developed by Rosalind Hursthouse, also work to alleviate parts of these problems.[47] Contemporary scholars of Confucian ethics, however, have yet to fully explore the applicability of these ideas.[48]

Exercising Appropriateness and Analogical Projection

Since many scholars argue for a particular virtue to be at work in determining the relationship between rituals and their contexts, they also provide various accounts of how this virtue functions in exigent situations. These accounts tend to be arguments about the process of moral reasoning. In short, these scholars seek to answer questions such as, how does the virtuous agent think-through hard cases? How do moral agents justify or explain their actions in light of their seeming deviation from the script?

How is the virtue of appropriateness put into action? Answers to these three questions can be understood, borrowing again from Antonio Cua, in terms of "analogical projection" and "retrospective vindication."

Analogical projection, also referred to as "analogical reasoning" or "extension," is the process of determining proper action on the basis of one's moral knowledge of past experiences (either one's own experiences or the paradigmatic experiences of others). It entails reasoning from the familiar to the less familiar, or applying what one has learned in one situation to another.[49] Cua describes the process of analogical projection as follows:

> The very notion of projection implies that the agent must be able to imagine himself in different situations relative to the past and the present. Given the evidentiary base for the items selected for projection, he imaginatively places himself in his past in surveying the present scene, thereby bridging, by analogical projection, his ethical knowledge of the past and present situation in light of a commitment to the intrinsically actuating import of *dao* 道. We have here a presupposition of a *gap* between ethical knowledge and changing circumstances in human life. An analogical projection provides, so to speak, a *mediation* of the ideal of *dao* 道 and the actual world of humanity.[50]

Summarily speaking, analogical projection involves mediating the complex moral demands of the present with the exemplary actions of the past. In other places, Cua explains that this mediation takes place through the exercise of appropriateness.[51]

Interpreters such as Cua base their theories of analogical projection on concepts such as *tui* 推 (extension), *quan* 權 (ethical deliberation), and *yi* 義 (appropriateness). Discussions about analogical projection tend to focus on whether or not the process is a form of top-down reasoning and how much of analogical projection is a cognitive versus an emotional process.

David Wong in his article "Reasons and Analogical Reasoning in Mengzi" provides a lucid description and critique of top-down reasoning, which he sees evident in the approach of scholars such as D. C. Lau.[52] Wong explains top-down reasoning as follows:

i. Case x has characteristics F, G…
ii. Case y has characteristics, F, G…
iii. x also has characteristic H.

iv. F, G . . . are H-relevant characteristics.
v. Therefore, unless there are countervailing considerations, y has characteristic H.[53]

Mencius, in Wong's view, does not utilize a process of top-down reasoning. In contrast to this, Wong proposes a "paradigm" approach involving "sprout intuitions," or the natural responses that people have as a result of their inherent dispositions. He asserts that for Mencius, "the judgment that case x has characteristic H and the judgment that y is relevantly similar in also possessing H is *prior to* the identification of any characteristics F and G that form the conditions for H similarity. That judgment is therefore prior to any general principle stating that F and G are H-relevant."[54] Stated another way, reasoning from one situation to another involves a kind of attentiveness to the natural responses of human nature. This is a "paradigm" approach in that it involves comparing our sprout reactions in one case, or paradigm, with those in another. This process of comparison does not involve any recourse to a general principle or analysis of shared characteristics; rather, what is shared is a natural reaction that is, in effect, an innate proclivity toward the right action. As such, when one confronts a perplexing situation, one immediately compares one's sprout intuitions in this case with the sprout intuitions of "baseline cases."[55] These baseline cases function as a repository of moral insight that one can draw from and depend on in determining how one should act in situations with similar sprout intuitions.[56]

Philip J. Ivanhoe argues that analogical projection is a form of emotional extension where one identifies, appreciates, and acts on the basis of good emotions rooted in human nature. In contrast with theories coming from other scholars such as Kwong-loi Shun who imply that analogical projection is a process of identifying similar cognitive reasons for moral action, Ivanhoe claims that analogical projection is about recognizing moral resonances between situations. Using the example of learning music, Ivanhoe likens analogical projection to learning to hear certain chords played by a musical instrument. After attuning one's ear to a particular chord, one becomes adept at hearing that chord in the midst of other competing sounds. Similarly, the moral exemplar is one who has learned to identify good feelings such as compassion and has the ability to identify and appreciate them in the midst of other feelings (such as the drives for food and sex).[57] The virtuous person is a virtuoso in the sense of developing a refined ability to recognize even the slightest moral inclinations in cacophonous situations and appropriately act on them. More recently, other scholars such as Bryan Van Norden have argued that both cognitive and affective elements of extension are at play during the process of moral reasoning.[58]

In Cua's terminology, analogical projections are "experiments in paradigmity."[59] In other words, they are attempts to be like the paradigmatic figures, or the sages, of the past. They are experiments in the sense that one does not merely replicate the actions of the sages. Instead, one exercises the same faculties and virtues that the sages possessed, but does so in such a way that one creates a unique "style of life." One of Cua's preferred lines to quote comes from the *Xunzi* and states, "respond to changing [circumstances] by means of appropriateness" 以義應變.[60] In Cua's reading, times change and necessitate adapting the actions of the past for the present. Doing this, however, does not entail deducing a formula where one can replace the variables of the formula and always yield an answer dictating proper action. Rather, one must, borrowing from Amy Olberding, make a "leap into idiosyncrasy."[61] In other words, one takes into account the paradigmatic experiences of the past, but one is always creating a new and personalized present. According to Cua, moral reasoning is "retrospective" and is a process of "vindication" rather than "explanation."[62]

By "retrospective vindication," Cua means that moral determinations are accounts of deliberation provided after an action has already been performed. The choices one makes are justified by recounting the reasons one chose the particular action, but the nature of this examination is meant to show that one was left with "no choice between alternatives," rather than the fact that one clearly determined "the right" course of action beforehand.[63] An important distinction for Cua is the difference between "explanation" and "vindication." The former he sees as providing a deductive account of how one arrived at a decision. The latter he sees as functioning more like legs of a stool as opposed to links of a chain in providing support for a moral decision. In this view, there may be many reasons, not necessarily dependent on each other, that provide justification for a decision. Vindication is part of an "open discourse" where the appropriateness of an action is continually subject to the evaluation of the community.[64] As such, the moral norms of a community maintain an intimate relationship with the past, but also a flexibility to adapt to the present.

The purpose of recounting various theories of analogical projection and Cua's notion of retrospective vindication is to provide a sense of the depth the current field has gone to in attempting to describe how one determines an appropriate response in exigent situations. In terms of this project, these scholars have produced highly sophisticated and nuanced accounts of how one reasons through the failure of ritual. Scholars such as Cua describe Confucianism as a tradition deeply concerned with producing moral agents who competently perform according to the guidance given by ritual scripts. They also describe it as a tradition concerned with producing mature moral agents who exercise the virtue of appropriateness by means of analogical projection in circumstances where dysfunctions in efficacy seem immanent.

In conjunction with the level of nuance in discussing issues such as analogical projection, the debate about how analogical projection allows one to vary from the rituals of the past is also a complex topic. As I discuss in the following section, the degree to which one is allowed to deviate from (or recreate) a ritual script is a matter of wide debate.

Flexibility in Deviating from the Past

While many contemporary interpreters agree that some process of analogical projection is involved in properly modifying dysfunctional rituals, they tend to disagree with respect to the amount of leeway a refined person has in deviating from the actions prescribed by a ritual script. The differing positions of contemporary scholars can be placed on a spectrum between more allowable and less allowable deviation from a ritual script. In placing their positions on this spectrum, it is worth noting that no interpreter argues for a fully allowable or unallowable theory of deviation. Even those scholars who take a less allowable position still account for passages where figures such as Confucius endorse modifying ritual. One way to conceptualize the difference between the two ends of the spectrum is in terms of creating new rituals. Positions that advocate the most allowance tend to be open to the possibility of creating new rituals. On the other hand, positions that favor less allowance tend to accept minor changes in the performance of ritual, but not accept the possibility that new rituals could be created. Stephen Wilson, an advocate of the latter position, captures this difference in his critique of Roger Ames and David Hall, both of whom argue for the possibility of creating new rituals. Wilson states, "There is, as we have seen, a certain amount of innovation we might apply to the cultural forms we inherent—minimally, this is a sensitivity to context in ritual settings—but in no way does this warrant

Hall and Ames's vocabulary of authoring and creating."[65] Wilson continues, "In this connection, it is notable that there are no examples in the *Analects* of Confucius changing a rite and only one example of his even slightly modifying one."[66]

Herbert Fingarette, one of the most influential scholars of Confucian ethics, is representative of a less allowable approach. In his reading (of the *Analects*),

> Confucius seems to take for granted, without having questioned or even become aware of his assumptions as such, that there is one *li* 禮 and that it is in harmony with a greater, cosmic *dao* 道. He assumes that this *li* 禮 is the *li* 禮 of the land in which he lives (other lands being barbarian), that the Ancients of his tradition lived this *li* 禮. He assumes that this *li* 禮, and the cosmic *dao* 道 in which it is rooted, are internally coherent and totally adequate, and that, finally, the only moral and social necessity is, therefore, to shape oneself and one's conduct in *li* 禮.[67]

In Fingarette's view, Confucius takes the rituals of his time as the rituals proper for the entire world at any time. The goal for those following Confucius, then, is to discover the rituals Confucius advocated (usually understood as the rituals of the Zhou Dynasty) and enact them precisely as Confucius advocated. Only accordance with these rituals will bring about a prosperous world.

The metaphor of a 'ritual as symphony' is a significant metaphor employed by many scholars. In Fingarette's usage of this metaphor, the vast majority of human beings are performers in the symphony, but not composers.[68] The composers were the great songwriters of the past, who composed all of the 'good' songs that could possibly be composed—leaving no new songs for others to write. As such, these songs script people's lives, and people's mission becomes one of learning their parts, practicing them, and playing them naturally. This is likened unto the early sages who created the rituals of the great dynasties—the rituals that all other dynasties should follow. In this light, there is no need to create new rituals. Instead the greatest need is to implement these rituals such that as many people as possible live in accordance with them. This position excludes the possibility of creating new rituals.

Other scholars closer to the less allowable end of the spectrum include Donald Munro and David Nivison. It is worth noting that many of these scholars read the symphony metaphor in a similar way. At the same time, however, rather than emphasizing the lack of creativity of the performer in comparison with the composer, many of them emphasize the creativity of different performers in playing the same piece of 'good' music. In other words, if people accept that the songwriters of the past already invented all the good music that could possibly be composed, this does not necessarily mean that those who come after have no opportunity for creativity. While people in effect would be left to play the music written for them, they each can still perform personal renditions of the same piece of music. This is to say that two virtuosos never play the same song the same way. They express a kind of boundless creativity within the confines of the scripted music. In terms of ritual, the sages of the past may have created every ritual possible; however, people coming after the sages still have creative moments of performing in accordance with the ritual script by carrying out their own rendition of it.

Closer to the more allowable end of the spectrum are scholars such as David Hall, Roger Ames, and Randall Peerenboom. Peerenboom in particular succinctly captures this position in the following statement: "Confucius rejects such limiting notions as rule ethics, pure procedural justice, and a normatively predetermined way. That there are no hard and fast rules means that one must respond to the particular circumstances with an open mind, with a willingness to be flexible and to join in a cooperative search for a harmonious solution."[69] While Hall and Ames may not agree with every point of Peerenboom's argument, Peerenboom captures the general tone that Confucian ethics is highly flexible.

Part of the debate between positions of more and less allowable deviation centers on the degree to which statements recounting the acts of cultivated people in Confucian texts are prescriptive. In other words, there is little consensus as to how to understand the normative import of accounts that describe the actions of figures such as Confucius. The tenth chapter of the *Analects*, for instance, which depicts the actions of Confucius in his day-to-day activities, can be read as prescriptions for the kinds of actions all other human beings should engage in, or it can be read as merely describing the activities of one man. Scholars that advocate a more allowable position tend to read these kinds of passages as descriptions with limited normative import. Amy Olberding, a student of Roger Ames, for instance, in commenting on this chapter of the *Analects* remarks, "Confucius is not a model of virtue; he is a model of a man who is virtuous. If I wish to be like Confucius, I cannot be like him."[70] In these interpretations of Confucianism, "truth and reality are ultimately personal categories, unique for each participant."[71]

Unpreventable Dysfunctions in Efficacy

A dominant paradigm of current scholars—particularly those utilizing a virtue ethics approach—focuses on the cultivation of the self and the ability of the moral agent to rectify circumstances where the rules or rituals of the past are inappropriate for the present. Within the framework of preventable failures in ritual, the efforts of these current interpreters are laudable. Early Confucians were undoubtedly concerned with becoming mature moral agents who were connoisseurs of their life situations and able to extend their proper inclinations to novel events.

Most of these interpreters acknowledge the possibility of unpreventable failures of ritual within early Confucian texts. They argue that these texts advocate a clear and recognizable distinction between preventable and unpreventable failures in ritual. According to their reading, cultivated human beings are capable of realizing when a dysfunctional situation is within their ability to prevent and when it is beyond their ability to prevent. They emphasize this ability by focusing on a notion of fate (*ming* 命) where the failures that are outside of one's control are differentiated from the failures within one's control. This is best demonstrated in Edward Slingerland's 1996 article "The Conception of *Ming* in Early Confucian Thought."[72] While Slingerland accepts that Confucians saw parts of the world as being fundamentally beyond human control, and even capable of causing rituals to fail, he discounts the role of dysfunctional ritual in moral development by means of what I will call 'the inward turn.' At one point Slingerland explains,

> The Confucian response to an apparently capricious and often inexplicable fate is thus neither an attempt to control it through supplication or prayer (an endeavor that Hume saw as the origin of all human religion) nor a type of pessimistic resignation to a meaningless life. It is, on the contrary, a realistic and mature redirection of human energy toward the sole area of life in which one does have control—the cultivation and moral improvement of one's own self—coupled with a faith in the ability of self-cultivation to pro-

duce in one an attitude of joyful acceptance of all that life may bring.[73]

The inward turn is a redirection away from the things that one cannot control, and a focusing instead on the things that one can in fact control. The result of this inward turn is a joyful acceptance of the failures that are not one's fault. In other words, joy is predicated on realizing that some dysfunctional situations are capable of being prevented, and others are not capable of being prevented. One simply does the best one possibly can in preventing the failures that are within one's sphere of control, and allays concern over the failures outside of one's control. This does not mean, though, that "negative emotions" like grief are ruled out of the process of self-cultivation; rather, as Stephen Angle notes, they are part of a "holistic" response to certain situations. Part of feeling joy, in this view, is properly expressing grief in the right contexts.[74]

Philip J. Ivanhoe utilizes the same language of "joy" and "faith" in his account of unpreventable failure. Through an analysis of passage 2B13 in *Mencius*, Ivanhoe provides nearly the same account of the inward turn. In this passage, Mencius is on his way out of the kingdom of Qi, unable to persuade its ruler to follow his teachings. While leaving Mencius is asked why he seems dissatisfied; after all, he did the best he could given the circumstances. Mencius's response is rather cryptic, but as Ivanhoe understands it, Mencius states that he is in fact satisfied. Ivanhoe explains, "*Mencius* 2B13 is a testament to Mencius's enduring faith in Heaven's plan. It illustrates his unique view of the role of 'destiny,' *ming* 命, in the life of the morally cultivated individual. There is only so much one can do. And after all that can be done has been done, one must trust in Heaven."[75] Similar to Slingerland's description, Ivanhoe's reading presumes that human beings have the ability, or at least can cultivate the ability, to recognize the difference between failures that they should have been able to prevent, and failures that are unpreventable.

In other places Ivanhoe talks about the joy that comes about from following Heaven's plan. "What makes [an action] right is that it accords with our nature and realizes Heaven's plan. The joy of a given act marks it as right, and it is this feeling that makes self-cultivation a practical possibility. This latter point is true for all ethics of self-cultivation, at least those that do not rely on some future life or other-worldly reward. Self-cultivation must in some clear and direct way produce satisfaction, for this is what allows us to improve."[76] This does not mean that the mature ritual agent is incapable of experiencing or expressing sorrow, grief, or sadness. Rather, the mature moral agent manifests these dispositions at the right time (such as a funeral) in the right way. When manifested at the right time and in the right way, these dispositions actually add to the joy of self-cultivation since their proper display is a sign of moral refinement.[77]

A combined reading of Ivanhoe's statements, in line with Slingerland's account above, suggests the following line of reasoning: When a failure of ritual seems probable, through a means of introspection, the moral agent determines whether or not this failure is preventable or unpreventable. If it is preventable, he then makes the necessary changes to the ritual. If it is unpreventable, he accepts it as something beyond his control, but eventually feels joy in that he has done everything within his power, and in the end this failure is not his fault—it is either due to the capriciousness of Heaven or part of Heaven's larger plan for human flourishing. Stated succinctly, since there is nothing the moral agent can do about the unpreventable failure of ritual, the focus of his efforts is in refining his ability to adjust those failures that are under his control to prevent.

The accounts of Ivanhoe and Slingerland recognize the possibility of unpreventable failures of ritual. Ivanhoe, it is worth noting, realizes that doubt and distress are also a part of the initial reaction to a dysfunctional situation. He explains that *Mencius* 2B13 is also "a record of Mencius talking himself out of his initial feeling of distress." He goes on to say that it "start[s] out with apparent—perhaps real—doubt and end[s] with expressions of enduring faith in Heaven."[78] The goal, according to Ivanhoe's reading of *Mencius*, is the resolution of the tension created when one's experience in the world is dissonant with one's understanding of how the world should have operated.

Mark Csikszentmihalyi and Yu Jiyuan work out a position similar to Slingerland and Ivanhoe. Csikszentmihalyi describes the cultivated person as one who eventually reaches a stage where "genuine quandaries cannot arise."[79] In Csikszentmihalyi's reading, this is not an all-powerful state of self-realization where everything is within the control of the cultivated person. Indeed, Csikszentmihalyi accepts that failures can still occur. In these situations, the cultivated person can still seem concerned with failure. However, Csikszentmihalyi goes on to explain that "situations that *appear* to be conflicts to those outside *actually* are not conflicts to the actor."[80] Put in the terms of this study, the struggle of the cultivated person to recognize the preventability of failure is only on the surface—internally he is not perplexed.

Yu makes a similar argument. In describing the view of the cultivated person as found in the *Analects*, he asserts, "This inner state [of cultivation] ... cannot be destroyed by misfortunes." Yu continues, "An excellent person enjoys peace of mind and experiences no worries, fear and inner conflict."[81]

For all four of these scholars, doubt, distress, and anxiety are overcome, or only "appear" to be real, since the moral agent is able to recognize which failures are in fact unpreventable and accept them as such. The cultivation of the ritual agent and the attendant joy of cultivation are, in the end, invulnerable to failures beyond his control.[82]

The inward turn is a dominant paradigm among contemporary interpreters.[83] In contrast to it, I claim that unpreventable failures in efficacy were causes of concern for at least some of the authors of early Confucian texts because they believed that meaningful aspects of life were vulnerable to these failures, and because they found themselves occasionally unable to recognize a clear distinction between preventable and unpreventable failures. Those that advocate the inward turn are flawed in reading all early Confucian writings as texts that seek to render human flourishing and joy invulnerable to agencies beyond the ritual agent. Their move is predicated on resolving the ambiguity between preventable and unpreventable dysfunctions in ritual.

I should also note that the accounts of scholars such as Ivanhoe and Slingerland are not necessarily misreadings of the texts—I am, of course, speaking about the *Liji*, whereas most other contemporary scholars are writing about the *Analects*, *Mencius*, or *Xunzi*, and as such I remain open to the possibility that there are significant differences between these texts. Also, there are passages in the *Liji* and in other early Confucian material that seem to argue for invulnerability. Rather, my claim is that the paradigm these scholars have chosen to interpret the texts precludes the possibility that unpreventable dysfunctions in efficacy play a role in the ethical life of early Confucians (other than, of course, learning to accept fate beyond one's control). If, following Slingerland, "the true gentleman, sustained by the internal goods of the Confucian Way, is indifferent to externalities"; or, "[t]he aspiring gentleman focuses on what is under his control (self-cultivation), and consigns the rest to fate," there is no possibility that the virtuous agent might choose a right action but be left with despair, or that he might be confronted with failure and be unable to untangle the agencies involved.[84] Rather than seeking to preserve the ambiguity and productive tension sometimes latent in a dysfunctional situation, scholars such as Slingerland seek to resolve these ambiguities. Their readings of the texts are not equipped to account for the possibility that early Confucians sometimes saw a tragic world—tragic in the sense that the line between agency and fate can be compromised—and that the "right" choice is not always obvious.

Conclusion

Taking into account the critiques mentioned in this chapter reshapes the field of Confucian ethics by situating the moral agent in a world of uncertainty, and adding a dimension of creativity that stems, not simply from the fluency of the moral agent, but also from the realization that rituals sometimes fail to create an ordered world. Rather than seeking to resolve the tension presented by a perplexing situation, the possibility of unpreventable dysfunctions in efficacy preserves the anxiety of moral decision-making by rendering the results of one's actions open to failure, and at the same time closing off the ability of the moral agent to clearly determine responsibility for the failure. While on the one hand this anxiety entails confronting a wild or bewildering world, on the other hand, it also functions therapeutically to relieve some of the burden of taking responsibility for failed attempts to recreate the tradition since failure is not always a sign that one has done the wrong thing. How early Confucians coped with dysfunctional rituals is undoubtedly part of a Confucian ethic. I will discuss this more thoroughly in the next five chapters.

This rereading of Confucian ethics challenges the inward turn by drawing attention to the anxiety associated with living in a world where failure is unpreventable. Rather than depicting a world where important distinctions between things such as a fate within one's control and a fate outside one's control can be recognized by the cultivated person, the *Liji* suggests that the discourse of distinction should be set against the backdrop of an acute concern with the difficulty and even impossibility of making some of these distinctions.

4

Preventing Dysfunction

In performing ritual, follow what is fitting.
In giving direction, follow what is customary.

禮從宜，使從俗。[1]

WHILE RITUAL CAN fail because those involved in performing a ritual are incompetent or because a ritual script is inefficacious, the majority of these failures are preventable. In other words, competent agents ensure that a ritual is performed according to its script—they are knowledgeable of, and skilled in, orchestrating the right actions, and they make sure that the right feelings are attendant in those participating in the ritual. With regards to inadequacies in the ritual script, the fluent agent recognizes the shortcomings of the script and modifies it such that it continues to provide the necessary guidance for creating an ordered world.

This chapter will investigate attitudes toward preventable failures in ritual. It begins with an account of failures in competency and examines how early Confucians strived to prevent these failures. Since the *Liji*, however, tends to presume that its readers are already competent ritual performers, I will discuss failures in competency less than failures in efficacy. The majority of this chapter, therefore, focuses on how early Confucians accounted for dysfunctions in efficacy. In doing this, I will consider several failures of the ritual script. These failures will be discussed in terms of the various situations that render the ritual script inefficacious and how early Confucians sought to alter the script in order to ensure the success of ritual. These situations include temporal and geographic variation in the contexts where rituals are performed, situations where ritual agents cannot physically perform the actions demanded by a script, novel situations the ritual script did not account for, as well as a host of other circumstances. After discussing how fluent ritual agents adapt ritual scripts in order to account for dysfunctions in efficacy, this chapter will also examine what I will call 'failures in fluency.' A failure in fluency occurs when a ritual agent misperceives or mishandles a potential dysfunction in efficacy. In other words, a failure in fluency happens when a ritual agent misidentifies a shortcoming in the ritual script and inappropriately modifies the script. Failures in fluency can be contrasted with failures in competency as the latter occur when a ritual agent recognizes that a ritual script should in fact be followed and attempts to follow it, but fails because he or she lacks the necessary skill, knowledge, or sentiment demanded by the script, whereas with failures in fluency the ritual agent does not intend to follow the script. The distinction between failures in competency and failures in fluency is mostly heuristic—it enables me to highlight several issues at stake in preventing ritual failure, but should not be taken as a distinction explicitly at work in early Confucian texts.

Dysfunctions in Competency

The authors of the *Liji* believed that people could mis-perform ritual for a number of reasons. Ritual agents might lack sufficient knowledge of the ritual script, or they might not have sufficient skill in following it. They may also possess or exhibit the wrong sentiments. These are all potential failures or dysfunctions in competency. Dysfunctions in competency focus on the agents involved with any given ritual. By emphasizing a program of ritual practice where the participants gain further 'ritual knowledge'—thereby cultivating the ability to more competently perform ritual—dysfunctions in competency are prevented.

The "Tangong Shang" 檀弓上 chapter relates a failure in competency that occurred during the mourning rites for the mother of an official named Du Qiao. It states, "The lack of an officiator in the palace during the mourning rites for Du Qiao's mother was the result of carelessness" 杜橋之母之喪，宮中無相，以為沽也.[2] While the ritual script called for an officiator, and those involved in the ceremony surely understood this, one was not present. Du Qiao's family was simply inattentive in their preparation of the mourning rites. This failure can be attributed to their lack of competence or skill in ritual performance.

The "Shaoyi" 少儀 chapter contains a critique of those who participate in ritual without understanding the implements involved in ritual. It states,

"Ignorance is when ritual clothing is on one's body, but [one] does not know the names of the pieces of clothing" 衣服在躬，而不知其名為罔.[3] Ritual can fail to transform those involved in the ritual if the ritual agents lack knowledge of the components of ritual.

Failures in competency also occur when the appropriate feelings for the circumstance do not attend the performance of the ritual. The "Tangong Xia" 檀弓下 chapter, for instance, explains that if the heart of the ruler is not sincere in the performance of ritual, the ritual will lose its ability to unify the people of the state.[4] In comparison with failures in knowledge or skill, failing to possess or exhibit the right sentiment is more commonly discussed in the *Liji*, although many of these discussions center on the issue of modifying a ritual script when it does not allow for the full expression of sentiment (and as such will be covered below in terms of fluency). Dysfunctions in competency with regard to disposition occur when ritual agents recognize that a ritual script calls for certain sentiments to be made manifest during the ritual, but these sentiments are not present.

Failures in competency with regard to sentiment can occur, for instance, if one becomes preoccupied with the practical considerations of ritual.

> Before a filial son offers up sacrifices [to his deceased parents] he is concerned with preparing all the affairs [of the sacrifice]. If the time [for sacrifice] arrives, and all the implements are arrayed and everything is prepared, [he is able to] empty himself internally; and in the proper order, [he] performs the rite.
>
> Once the temple chamber is clean, the walls and roof are repainted, and all the ritual implements are ready, the son and his wife—having fasted and washed themselves—enter the chamber wearing the sacrificial attire and carrying the sacrifices. So engrossed and sincere, they move as if unable to bear [the weight of the sacrifices], and as if they are on the brink of dropping them. [As such], are their hearts not completely full of reverence and filial piety?
>
> The filial son displays his focus by ordering the sacrificial vessels, by arranging the rite and its accompanying music, by training the ritual participants, and by [appropriately] entering the chamber carrying the sacrifices. Because of his lost abstraction of mind [while performing the ritual,] he communes with the spirits, hop-

> ing that they might partake of the sacrifices. The aim of the filial son is to express his hope that the spirits partake of the sacrifices.
>
> 孝子將祭，慮事不可以不豫，比時具物，不可以不備；虛中以治之。宮室既修，墻屋既設，百物既備。夫婦齊戒、沐浴、盛服，奉承而進之。洞洞乎，屬屬乎，如弗勝，如將失之。其孝敬之心至也與！薦其薦、俎，序其禮樂，備其百官，奉承而進之。於是諭其志意，以其慌惚以與神明交，庶或饗之。庶或饗之，孝子之志也。[5]

This lengthy passage from the "Jiyi" 祭義 chapter raises several important issues. The most relevant is the notion that attention to the implements and preparations of ritual can serve as a distraction to the proper feelings required by the ritual. The performer, in sacrificing to his deceased parents, should be engrossed and sincere even to the point of entering a "lost abstraction of mind." However, if the ritual agent's mind is focused on the procedure of the ritual, or the accoutrements necessary for the ritual, rather than his relationship with the deceased, he will not have this lost abstraction of mind; and by implication he will not commune with their spirits. The implements of ritual must become an extension of the ritual agent's aim (*zhi* 志) if he wishes to engage the spiritual forces of his ancestors; however, they should not become the focus of his aim.

Other portions of the *Liji* praise certain individuals for exhibiting the right sentiments during a ritual performance. The "Tangong Xia" chapter, for instance, states,

> Yan Ding was good at mourning. Shortly after hearing of [a family member's or friend's] death he would be morose and perplexed like [he] had searched for [them] but could not find [them]. At the coffining and funeral procession he was eager and expectant like [he] had followed [after them] but could not catch up. At the burial he was exasperated as if [he] could not get the spirit of the deceased to return, and finally gave up.
>
> 顏丁善居喪；始死，皇皇焉如有求而弗得；及殯，望望焉如有從而弗及；既葬，慨焉如不及其反而息。[6]

Yan Ding is praised as someone capable of expressing the right sentiments at the right time. Failure to express the appropriate sentiments, in the appropriate degree, at the appropriate moment, constitutes a failure in competency.

Fluency as a Means of Accounting for Dysfunctions in Efficacy

Fluency is a cultivated sense of composure allowing the ritual agent to modify (or create) a ritual script in order to bring about a successful ritual. Within the *Liji*, fluency tends to be spoken of in terms of ritual knowledge (*zhili* 知禮, literally, "knowing ritual"), appropriateness (*yi* 義), timeliness (*shi* 時), and poise (*zhong* 中). Fluency is attained by means of cultivation. In other words it must be developed. Rituals are the implements used to guide people in cultivating fluency. From infancy, people are shaped by an almost endless series of rituals meant to guide them in properly relating themselves to the larger world. Children, for instance, are instructed to behave in a way that they come to naturally demonstrate sentiments such as respect to their parents. Young adults are capped, pinned, and clothed in certain robes such that they learn how to extemporaneously situate themselves according to their respective social positions. And the older generation offers up sacrifices to their deceased parents so that the propitious spirits of the world attend their activities. The motif suggested in the title of the "Liqi" 禮器 chapter demonstrates this succinctly: humans are meant to be shaped into ritualized vessels. These vessels, or *qi* 器, become more refined as they are shaped by the performances of ritual. The process of refinement is one of maturation. As people continue to practice ritual, they mature into fluent ritual agents. Fluent individuals not only express a high degree of natural ease when performing ritual, but they also recognize when following a ritual script will not generate a desirable result. In short, they recognize that ritual scripts are sometimes dissonant with creating an ordered world. The connection between fluency and variation from ritual scripts is best illustrated in a vignette found in the "Tangong Shang" chapter. Here, a soldier has died and his son has held the necessary mourning rites. Shortly after the rites were completed, a man from the distant state of Yue, most likely a friend of the soldier, arrived wishing to offer his condolences. This situation raises the issue of how the son should respond to this visitor given that the time for condolences had already passed.

> After the completion of the mourning rites for General Wenzi, a man from Yue arrived to pay his condolences. The conductor of the rites, [the son of General Wenzi], wearing the ordinary robe and white mourning cap [worn at the completion of the rites], received

> him in the ancestral temple, where he shed tears, and mucus flowed from his nose. Observing this, Ziyou remarked, "The son of General Wenzi is indeed close to the mark. He performs a rite where there are no [stipulations concerning] rites. His performance is right on target [*zhong* 中]."
>
> 將軍文子之喪，既除喪，而後越人來弔。主人深衣、練冠，待于廟，垂涕洟。子游觀之曰：「將軍文氏之子其庶幾乎！亡於禮者之禮也，其動也中。」[7]

The notion of being "right on target" is the same character translated above as "poise." The metaphor of archery and its connection to poise were already mentioned in chapter 1. Paraphrasing that discussion, the composure needed to "hit the target" (*zhong* 中) in archery is similar to the inner composure needed to properly perform one's roles in society. When these roles conflict, the poised agent will maintain his composure and always respond appropriately. Within the context of this passage, the poised agent does not fret when encountering a situation where ritual scripts do not suggest a specific course of action. Here, the son of General Wenzi, wearing the robe appropriate for the completion of the mourning rites, lets his sorrow flow as if his father had just passed away. He performs a ritual where there is no script to suggest appropriate action. In short, his poise, or fluency, allows him to creatively adapt the norms dictating visits of condolence to his circumstance.

Other passages in the *Liji* connect the notion of appropriateness (*yi* 義) to the modification or creation of rituals. The "Liyun" 禮運 chapter, for instance, explains that "when the early kings were without ritual, they produced it by relying on [their] sense of appropriateness [*yi* 義]" 禮，雖先王未之有，可以義起也.[8] This same passage, using an analogy of planting and cultivating fruit to describe the coming forth of ritual, states that "ritual is the fruit of appropriateness" (禮也者，義之實也). The majority of contemporary scholars, as discussed in chapter 3, focus on the notion of appropriateness as the primary virtue that enables profound people to alter ritual scripts according to varying contexts.

The ability of the fluent agent to alter, supersede, or disregard a ritual script is depicted in the "Ruxing" 儒行 chapter, where the ideal Ru, or Confucian, is described as being able to "destroy the mold but still have the tiles fit together" 毀方而瓦合.[9] Similar to an artisan who no longer needs a mold to construct square tiles, the fluent individual is able to order things without the guidance of a ritual script. He is able to construct aspects of an ordered world without the tools of construction.

The purpose of quoting these passages is to demonstrate the relationship between fluency and ritual. The person who is poised, appropriated, has ritual knowledge, or, in other words, is fluent, is able to alter and even create new ritual scripts.[10]

Dysfunctions in Efficacy

Successful modifications of ritual scripts are set against a backdrop of dysfunction. In other words, a proper adaptation of a ritual implies that if performed according to its received script, the ritual would have failed. The *Liji* is replete with examples of appropriate (and inappropriate) modifications of ritual scripts. The dominant paradigm of the text is that ritual scripts often require modification (or at least temporary variation). Ritual scripts, in this sense, are 'open' such that the proper performance of ritual varies according to the circumstance. As pointed out in chapter 2, the opening of the ritual script facilitates a specialized discourse about the topic of ritual. This discourse, in short, is one that argues for the efficacy of ritual on the one hand, and for the need to alter ritual on the other. Rather than rejecting ritual as inefficacious guides for properly ordering the world, most authors of the *Liji* endorse an open notion of ritual. In other words, 'properly performing ritual' entails performing ritual by following an open script. It thereby necessitates a fluent agent to interpret the situation and identify the necessary changes. The next portion of this chapter will discuss several failures of the ritual script that require the adaptation of fluent agents. If not accounted for, these failures jeopardize the overall efficacy of ritual.

The *Liji* as a whole discusses a wide variety of failures in efficacy due to shortcomings in the ritual script. I have chosen five primary failures to explore in this chapter. This list is not exhaustive, and the *Liji* does not provide its own taxonomy of these failures. Rather, the five failures below were chosen because of their prominent occurrence throughout the text. While these selections and categorizations are my own doing, the text does express a certain amount of self-reflexivity in discussing these failures. Consider, for instance, the following passage:

> Zisi's mother died in Wei and Liu Ruo said to him, "As a descendant of a sage [i.e., Confucius] the four corners of the world will

be watching how you observe the mourning rites. You should be cautious."

子思之母死於衛，柳若謂子思曰：「子，聖人之後也，四方於子乎觀禮，子蓋慎諸。」

Zisi responded, "Why should I be cautious? I have heard that if there were an occasion for a ritual, yet the material for it is lacking, the profound person would not carry it out. And if there were the occasion for a ritual, and the material is present but the timing for it is wrong, the profound person would not carry it out. Why should I be cautious?"

子思曰：「吾何慎哉？吾聞之：有其禮，無其財，君子弗行也；有其禮，有其財，無其時，君子弗行也。吾何慎哉？」[11]

Here, Zisi mentions two reasons that a ritual would not be performed despite the fact that the occasion would call for it. While he does not use the explicit language of failure, this passage can easily be understood in those terms. Even though a situation dictates the performance of a ritual, one should not perform it if the material resources are lacking or if the timing is inappropriate. The ritual fails in the sense that the script calls for its performance, but it either cannot or should not be performed (for reasons Zisi does not entirely provide). The lack of material resources and proper timing in this case are threats to the success of ritual. I discuss both of these threats below. The significant point this passage makes is that the authors of the *Liji* were aware of many of the potential failures of their rituals and to a certain degree sought to differentiate the reasons for their failure.

Changing Times

The *Liji* is preoccupied with the relationship between the rituals of the past and those in the present. In particular, it is concerned with how the rituals of the Xia, Yin (also known as the Shang), and early Zhou dynasties function in later times. It is also concerned, perhaps even more so, with the rituals of antiquity (*gu* 古)—usually taken to mean the period before the Three Dynasties—and how those ritual scripts apply to the present.

Several chapters in the *Liji* describe Confucius's attitude toward the rituals of the Three Dynasties. These passages often provide accounts of how each dynasty performed the same ritual in a slightly different way, followed by Confucius's judgment in terms of which practice he believes those he is speaking to should follow. For instance, the "Tangong Xia" chapter recounts, "In the Yin Dynasty, they offered their condolences immediately after the burial. In the Zhou Dynasty, they waited until [the funeral procession] returned and the wailing had begun to offer their condolences. Hearing this, Confucius remarked, 'Those in the Yin were too forthright; I follow [the practice of] the Zhou'" 殷既封而弔，周反哭而弔。孔子曰：「殷已慤，吾從周」.[12] In this case, Confucius's view is clear: the practice of the Yin Dynasty, at least in the context of the Zhou Dynasty, fails for being too forthright (Confucius does not address whether it was proper in its own time). Passages such as these reveal that the rituals of the past, even if they functioned properly in the past, are not necessarily successful in the present. The "Yueji" 樂記 chapter, which is also acutely aware of the potential failures associated with implementing the ritual scripts of the past, puts this in even starker language. It explains, "The five emperors [of antiquity] lived in different times and did not pass on their musical performances [*yue* 樂] to each other. The three kings [of the Three Dynasties] lived in different ages and did not hand down their rituals to each other" 五帝殊時，不相沿樂；三王異世，不相襲禮.[13] Following this reading, the contemporary age should, at the very least, not naively accept the rituals of the past; but even more likely, they should create new rituals appropriate for the present.

In situations where the rites of the Xia and Yin dynasties are contrasted with those of the Zhou Dynasty, Confucius, more often than not, advocates the Zhou Dynasty variation of the script. However, that is not always the case. Confucius sometimes approved of the practices of the Yin and Xia dynasties, even when compared with the practices of the Zhou. The same chapter that contains the passage quoted above on condolences also recounts the following: "In the Yin Dynasty [they] waited a year to perform the *fu* 祔 sacrifice. In the Zhou Dynasty [they] performed the *fu* 祔 sacrifice immediately after [they] wailed. Confucius approved of the Yin Dynasty [practice]" 殷練而祔，周卒哭而祔。孔子善殷.[14] These kinds of passages complicate claims made by some contemporary interpreters that Confucius saw the rituals of the Zhou Dynasty as universally applicable to later times.[15] The position that interpreters such as Herbert Fingarette take argues that the rituals of the Zhou Dynasty represent the final realization of all rituals necessary to order the world. In contrast, the claim here is that some of the ritual practices of the previous dynasties were clearly superior to those in the Zhou Dynasty.

In response to the problem of what to do with the rituals of the past, the *Liji* proposes to take those rituals of the past that are efficacious in the present and combine them with the rituals of the present. The rituals performed at the death of Confucius provide such an occasion. The "Tangong Shang" chapter explains how certain ritual scripts of the Xia and Yin dynasties were combined with the scripts of the Zhou:

> Gongxi Chi was the decorator at the mourning rites for Confucius. He adorned the coffin and the cloth [displayed near the coffin], as well as the fans and cords for the carriage carrying the coffin after the manner of the Zhou. He designed the banners after the manner of the Yin. And he designed the flags with streamers of silk after the manner of the Xia.
>
> 孔子之喪，公西赤為志焉：飾棺、墻、置翣設披，周也；設崇，殷也；綢練設旐，夏也。[16]

The mourning rites held for Confucius are made up of the appropriate rituals of the past and present. Part of what makes this rite successful, according to the text, is the combination of the scripts of the Xia, Yin, and Zhou dynasties. These kinds of combinations are repeated throughout the *Liji*.[17]

Oftentimes the rituals of the Zhou Dynasty are praised for integrating the scripts of the past. The "Tangong Shang" chapter, for instance, explains how this takes place in terms of using the kinds of coffins constructed in previous dynasties.

> During the reign of the Yu Clan [i.e., in the time of Shun] they used clay coffins. During the reign of the Xia Clan they enclosed their coffins with bricks. The people of the Yin Clan used an outer and inner coffin of wood; and the people of the Zhou Clan used cloth and fans [to adorn their coffins]. The people of the Zhou Clan used the inner and outer coffin of the Yin to bury those who died soon before adulthood. They used the coffin enclosed with bricks after the manner of the Xia for those who died in their pre-teen or teenage years. They used the clay coffin of the Yu Clan for those who died as children.
>
> 有虞氏瓦棺，夏後氏塈周，殷人棺槨，周人墻置翣。周人以殷人之棺槨葬長殤，以夏後氏之塈周葬中殤、下殤，以有虞氏之瓦棺葬無服之殤。[18]

The efforts of the Zhou, in this sense, become a paradigm of effectively combining the ritual scripts of the past. The "Neize" 內則 chapter captures this more succinctly. At one point it states,

> When it comes to taking care of the elderly the Yu Clan used banquet ceremonies, the Xia Clan used dinner ceremonies, the people in the Yin Dynasty used food ceremonies, and the people of the Zhou Dynasty used a combination of these ceremonies—mending and fusing them together.
>
> 凡養老：有虞氏以燕禮，夏後氏以饗禮，殷人以食禮，周人修而兼用之。[19]

The notions of *xiu* 修 and *jian* 兼, translated here as "mend" and "fuse," appear throughout the *Liji* to convey a sense of refashioning, integration, or a fusing together of different elements into one entity. The point this passage makes is clear—the Zhou Dynasty incorporates the ritual scripts of the past into their ritual scripts.

The "Liqi" 禮器 chapter expresses a similar sentiment when, after explaining that successive dynasties adapted the ritual scripts of the previous dynasty, it concludes with the statement, "The rituals of the Zhou Dynasty are like a communal wine feast" 周禮其猶醵與.[20] What makes the wine feast communal is the fact that all of the participants contribute to purchasing the wine. Similar to this feast, the rituals of the Zhou Dynasty are made up of contributions from the past. Other chapters in the *Liji* build on this theme. The "Mingtangwei" 明堂位 chapter, for instance, is basically one long treatise on the effective combination of the rituals of the past preserved by the Zhou Dynasty in the state of Lu. The chapter concludes, "The ritual clothing, implements, and offices of the Four Dynasties [the time of Shun or the Yu Clan counted as one of the dynasties] are fused together and employed in the state of Lu" 凡四代之服、器、官，魯兼用之.[21] Indeed, common themes throughout the *Liji* are that the ritual scripts of the past are not necessarily prescriptive for the present, and that some of the scripts of the past often serve as an integral part of the effective ritual scripts of the present.[22]

Missing from this discourse on integrating the rituals of the past is an explicit claim that the rituals of the Zhou Dynasty represent the final culmination of successful rituals. In other words, the *Liji* does not state that those in the Zhou Dynasty discovered all of the appropriate rituals to practice in successive times. In short, it does not suggest an end to the history of ritual. Quite to the contrary, the texts suggests that the activities of the Zhou Dynasty present a paradigm where the proper rites for the present are an integration of those rituals of the past that will not fail in the present, in addition to newly created rituals that are relevant for the present.

Besides the rituals of the Three Dynasties, the *Liji* is also preoccupied with the rituals of antiquity—although it is not always clear as to what time period counts as antiquity. The text contains dozens of (often enigmatic) statements about modifying these ritual scripts. Some of these passages are clear rebukes of those in the present who strayed from the norms of antiquity. The "Zengzi Wen" 曾子問 chapter, for instance, contains a response of Confucius to a question about mourning for a woman that was one's caretaker as a child.

> Ziyou asked, "Is it ritually proper to mourn for one's caretaker [i.e., a concubine that helps in raising the primary wife's children] as one's own mother?"
>
> 子游問曰：「喪慈母如母，禮與？」
>
> Confucius replied, "That is not ritually proper. In antiquity boys had teachers outside the home and a caretaker inside the home. [Both of these people] educated children under the direction of the master of the house. What need is there to mourn for them? Not long ago, when Duke Zhao of Lu was young he lost his mother and [was raised by] a loving caretaker. When she died Duke Zhao could not bear it and wanted to mourn for her. One of the ministers [in his court] hearing this explained, 'According to the rites of antiquity there is no mourning for caretakers. If you mourn for her, you will go against the rites of antiquity and put the regulations of the state in disarray. If, in the end, you do this, the ministers will record your acts and pass them down to later generations. This is something you should not do!' The Duke responded, 'In antiquity the son of heaven wore the white silk cap while at leisure to mark the anniversary of his mother's passing.' Since the Duke could not bear the loss of his caretaker he wore the white silk cap to mourn for her. Mourning for one's caretaker began with Duke Zhao of Lu."

孔子曰：「非禮也。古者，男子外有傅，內有慈母，君命所使教子也，何服之有？昔者，魯昭公少喪其母，有慈母良，及其死也，公弗忍也，欲喪之，有司以聞，曰：『古之禮，慈母無服，今也君為之服，是逆古之禮而亂國法也；若終行之，則有司將書之以遺後世。無乃不可乎？』公曰：『古者天子練冠以燕居。』公弗忍也，遂練冠以喪慈母。喪慈母，自魯昭公始也。」[23]

This passage suggests that the actions of Duke Zhao were inappropriate. The script of antiquity still governed aspects of the contemporary performance of the mourning rites. There are a number of similar passages where the ritual scripts of antiquity are clearly normative for the present. On the other hand, there are fewer explicit endorsements of breaking from antiquity. One of these accounts appears in the "Tangong Xia" chapter where Confucius praises a woman named Jing Jiang as one who "knows ritual" (*zhili* 知禮).[24] This same woman, the chapter explains, changed part of the mourning rituals handed down from antiquity. "The practice of leaving the coffin covered with a cloth [while wailing] is not from antiquity. It began when Jing Jiang wailed for Mubo" 帷殯，非古也，自敬姜之哭穆伯始也.[25] When read in conjunction with Confucius's description of Jing Jiang as one who knows ritual, varying from antiquity seems to be endorsed in this passage. Other passages in the *Liji* can also be read as endorsements of varying from the ritual scripts of antiquity.[26]

The vast majority of the references to altering the scripts of antiquity are ambiguous. In other words, the value judgment of the change is unclear. These kinds of passages abound in the *Liji*. Here are, for instance, two passages from the "Tangong Shang" chapter.

In antiquity, caps were made with the seam running vertically; but now they run horizontally. As such, having the mourning cap differ from the cap worn during celebratory ceremonies is not [a practice of] antiquity.

古者，冠縮縫，今也，衡縫；故喪冠之反吉，非古也。[27]

The practice of landscaping tombs is not [a practice of] antiquity.

易墓，非古也。[28]

Whether or not the text endorses these changes is not readily apparent. The classical commentators are divided. Some commentators take certain passages as laments about the decadence of the current times and other passages as changes necessary to meet the different context of the Zhou Dynasty, while other commentators interpret the same passages in the opposite manner. The *Liji* provides little internal evidence to parse each of these passages. My suggestion, developed in chapter 6, is to read these passages (where evidence does not dictate otherwise) as descriptions of two valid ritual scripts, one in antiquity and one in the contemporary setting of the text. These passages, as such, are not necessarily value judgments about variation; rather they are statements of occurrence—in antiquity rituals were performed one way, while in later times rituals were performed in another way. Each of these performances is equally valid in its own context. At the same time, however, varying from antiquity, while necessary, is never celebrated. Leaving behind the appropriate ritual scripts of the past is an ambivalent affair.

The relationship between the rituals of the past and the rituals of the present is summed quite well by a passage in the "Liqi" chapter, which reads, "In ritual, one must return to the root and mend antiquity, not forgetting ritual's origin" 禮也者，反本修古，不忘其初者也.[29] The rituals of antiquity, the *Liji* argues, must be integrated with the demands of contemporary times; they must be reconstructed such that they form an effective, yet continuous, ritual tradition.

Material Limitations

The authors of the *Liji* were concerned that ritual would fail if those involved with ritual lacked the necessary materials to perform a rite. Fluent agents often adapted the requirements of the ritual script to account for material limitations. The story is told, for instance, about the burial of Confucius's dog:

> Confucius's dog died and he commissioned Zigong to bury it saying, "I have heard that an old curtain need not be discarded, but can be used when burying a horse. I have also heard that an old canopy need not be discarded but can be used when burying a dog. I, however, am poor and do not even have a canopy. Use my mat to bury my dog, and do not let its head fall [against the earth]."

仲尼之畜狗死，使子貢埋之，曰：「吾聞之也：敝帷不棄，為埋馬也；敝蓋不棄，為埋狗也。丘也貧，無蓋；於其封也，亦予之席，毋使其首陷焉。」[30]

Confucius, lacking the prescribed material, settles on burying his dog in his mat despite his understanding that the script calls for burying a dog in a canopy.[31] The reason he gives for using a mat is his condition of poverty. The notion of altering a ritual script on the basis of lacking the means to acquire the implements otherwise necessary for carrying it out is a common theme in the *Liji*, especially in the "Tangong" chapters. One vignette in particular expresses this in more theoretical terms:

> Ziyou inquired about the implements used in the mourning rites. The Master replied, "They depend on the resources of the family."
>
> 子游問喪具，夫子曰：「稱家之有亡。」
>
> Ziyou asked, "If it depends on their resources how [are mourning rites] to be uniform?"
>
> 子游曰：「有亡惡乎齊?」
>
> The Master replied, "Those who have sufficient resources should not go beyond what is prescribed by the ritual script. If one does not have sufficient resources, clothe the body from head to foot, bury it immediately, and use ropes to lower the coffin in the grave. Can anyone not accord with this?"
>
> 夫子曰：「有，毋過禮；苟亡矣，斂首足形，還葬，縣棺而封，人豈有非之者哉?」[32]

The relevant line here is Confucius's initial response that the implements used in funerary rites "depend on the resources of the family" 稱家之有亡. A more literal translation of this line would be to "weigh the haves and have-nots of the family," where the notion of "weighing" takes the process of using a scale as a metaphor for determining the proper course of action. While the steps involved in "weighing," or deliberation, are not entirely clear—the *Liji* actually uses this term only a handful of times—what is clear is that the act of weighing requires an agent who is skilled in the process of deliberation.[33] The fluent agent is the skillful deliberator. He knows the implements that should be used in funerary rites, but is also able to modify the script in accordance with the family's wealth.

Physical Limitations

A ritual fails when those who are supposed to perform it are physically incapable of following the script. The authors of the *Liji* were concerned with the threat this posed. They believed that fluent agents should modify ritual scripts to account for physical limitations. The "Sangfu Sizhi" 喪服四制 chapter explains that fluent ritual agents should modify the script for the mourning rites in the following manner:

> When each person and each item is ready [for the rite], but the officiator cannot speak to commence [the rite] he is assisted to rise. Once able to speak and [the rite] has commenced he uses the staff to rise. When he personally participates [in the rite], his face is colored with ash. Bald [women] do not need to wear the hemp hair cover. The crippled do not need to remove their outer clothing. The lame do not need to perform the mourning leaps. The old and sick do not need to refrain from wine and meat.

> 百官備，百物具，不言而事行者，扶而起；言而後事行者，杖而起；身自執事而後行者，面垢而已。禿者不髽，傴者不袒，跛者不踴。老病不止酒肉。[34]

The passage continues on to explain that fluent ritual agents handle these circumstances by means of discretion (*yiquan zhizheye* 以權制者也). Similar to the notion of *cheng* 稱 discussed above, they "weigh" (*quan* 權) the particulars of the situation to excuse participants with physical limitations from the performances called for by the ritual script. This passage is one of the few times the notion of *quan* 權 appears in the *Liji*. In the larger discourse of modifying rituals (or rules) in early China, *quan* 權 is a key term.[35] It tends to be grouped together with concepts such as appropriateness (*yi* 義), timeliness (*shi* 時), and other terms related to the ability of the fluent agent to alter prescribed performances. As it relates to our discussion here, the point worth mentioning is that the authors of the *Liji* recognize that rituals fail in regards to those with physical limitations unless someone with a refined sense of discretion modifies the script to ensure ritual success. Several other chapters in the *Liji* make a similar point.[36]

Varying Terrain

The varying terrain of different physical locations where the same rituals are performed also threatens the success of ritual. The *Liji* is aware that if the same ritual is not adapted in accordance with the natural productions and contour of an area, it could fail to deliver its intended result. The "Liqi" chapter, in particular, is preoccupied with ensuring that rituals are modified according to the differing environments in which they take place. One passage explains,

> Ritual should accord with the seasons of the heavens, be designed after the material of the earth, flow with spiritual forces, accord with the heart-mind of human beings, and give pattern to all things in the world. As such, the seasons of the heavens have that which it produces; the patterns of the earth have that which it deems appropriate; the faculties of human beings each have their own abilities; and each thing in the world has it advantages. If it is not produced by the heavens, or nurtured by the earth, the profound person does not use it in ritual, and the spiritual forces do not partake of it. The profound person considers those who live in the mountains, but use fish and turtles in their rites; and those who live in marshes, but use deer and pigs in their rites, as people who do not "know ritual."
>
> As such, the taxes collected by the state can be taken as a great principle in performing ritual. The differing roles in ritual depend on the size of the land [the ritual is being performed in]. The lavishness or frugality of the ritual depends on the bountifulness of the year. As such, even if a particular year is especially unproductive the people will not fear [that they will be incapable of paying their taxes, or, following the metaphor, performing ritual]. This is why those who are in a position to institute ritual operate within the bounds of prudence.
>
> 禮也者，合於天時，設於地財，順於鬼神，合於人心，理萬物者也。是故天時有生也，地理有宜也，人官有能也，物曲有利也。故天不生，地不養，君子不以為禮，鬼神弗饗也。居山以魚鱉為禮，居澤以鹿豕為禮，君子謂之不知禮。故必舉其定國之數，以

為禮之大經。禮之大倫，以地廣狹。禮之薄厚，與年之上下。是故年雖大殺，眾不匡懼。則上之制禮也節矣。[37]

This passage introduces several significant issues. The most relevant is the notion that rituals should vary according to the contexts in which they are performed. Rituals should "accord with the seasons of the heavens, and be designed after the material of the earth." Where a ritual script calls for using something foreign to a context, it should be altered such that it allows ritual performers to use implements natural to the context. Those who "know ritual" understand how to alter the script. They realize when it is appropriate to substitute fish for deer or pigs for turtles. They also know how to change ritual to correspond with the size of the place a ritual is performed in. In short, a fluent ritual agent is sensitive to the environmental settings of ritual and opens the script to these factors. This point is reiterated in several other places in the *Liji*.[38]

Unprecedented Situations

Unprecedented circumstances pose a special problem in terms of the success or failure of ritual. The *Liji* presents numerous situations that seem to call for the performance of a ritual, but no single script seems to govern how such a ritual should be performed. Confucius's death is an excellent illustration of this. Despite the fact that an elaborate system of burial rites were prescribed for those of different social positions, and a complex system of mourning rites governed how people should mourn based on their relationship with the deceased, no such prescriptions seemed to have existed for the burial of Confucius and the mourning of his disciples. While part of this uncertainty may be a retrospective attempt to argue for the uniqueness of the figure of Confucius, some of it reflects the emerging relationship between "master" and "disciple"—a relationship that apparently did not have a script dictating proper mourning practices. As such, the passages describing Confucius's death and the mourning of his disciples represent moments of uncertainty and creativity—moments where old ritual scripts are questioned and new ritual scripts are formed to facilitate new relationships. The "Tangong Shang" chapter provides a description of Confucius's disciples determining what kind of mourning clothing to wear for him.

> At the mourning rites for Confucius his disciples were perplexed about the appropriate clothing to wear. Zigong said, "Previously, when the Master mourned for Yan Yuan, he mourned as if mourning for a son but did not wear the clothing [for a father mourning for a son]. In mourning for Zilu he did the same. In mourning for the Master, we should mourn as if mourning for a father, but without the clothing."
>
> 孔子之喪，門人疑所服。子貢曰：「昔者夫子之喪顏淵，若喪子而無服；喪子路亦然。請喪夫子，若喪父而無服。」[39]

Zigong concludes on the basis of Confucius's mourning for his disciples that they should mourn for Confucius as a son mourns for his father, but without wearing the clothing that a son would normally wear when mourning for a father. This passage echoes accounts of "analogical extension" discussed in chapter 3—by analogizing from Confucius's actions his disciples determine their own. Other passages describe the creation of a unique burial mound for Confucius, and the combination of rites from the Xia, Shang, and Zhou dynasties used in his funeral.[40] Confucius's death and the mourning of his disciples depict situations where no clear ritual script governs the situation, yet without the performance of ritual the disciples of Confucius cannot properly mourn for their master.

The *Liji* contains numerous other descriptions of ritual agents rewriting a ritual script or creating a new ritual script when confronted with a novel situation. The entire "Bensang" 奔喪 chapter, for instance, is a discussion of how to "hurry [home] to perform the mourning rites" for family members.[41] It presents a series of situations where ritual agents cannot meet the demands of a ritual script since they are not physically present for portions of the mourning rites. These situations are novel in the sense that the original script did not take them into account. The original script presumed that family members would be close enough to hold all the necessary rites. Ritual agents in these new circumstances must think of ways to alter the ritual script or create a new ritual script to confront these novel situations and to ensure the success of the mourning rites for their families. Other chapters such as the "Zengzi Wen" chapter and the "Tangong" chapters highlight the occurrence of unprecedented situations.[42]

Failures in Fluency

While a fluent agent tends to recognize shortcomings in a ritual script and is capable of modifying it to ensure the continued success of ritual, the authors of the *Liji* were also aware of the difficulty of cultivating fluency. Not every one is, or will become, a fluent agent. The authors of the *Liji* realized that people would constantly fail when striving to be fluent. In particular, people tend to presume to have a greater sense of fluency then they actually have, and are thereby prone to mistake a situation where the ritual script should be followed for one that calls for altering it. In other words, people tend to change ritual scripts when they should not be modified at all. As a matter of fact, in comparison to the failures in competency listed above, attempting to change a ritual script when no such change should be made is one of the primary failures depicted in the text. The opening passage of the "Tangong Shang" chapter provides a general example of this:

> Tangong went to the mourning rites for Gongyi Zhongzi wearing the mourning headband. [Previous to his death] Zhongzi overlooked his grandson in favor of designating his son [as his successor]. [Now hearing this] Tangong remarked, "How can this be? I have never heard of such a thing." He hurried over to Zifu Bozi, who was standing to the right of the gate, and asked, "How is it that Zhongzi overlooked his grandson in favor of his son?"
>
> 公儀仲子之喪，檀弓免焉。仲子舍其孫而立其子，檀弓曰：「何居？我未之前聞也。」趨而就子服伯子於門右，曰：「仲子舍其孫而立其子，何也？」
>
> Bozi responded, "Zhongzi is simply following the way of the ancients. In those times King Wen overlooked his eldest son, Yikao, and named King Wu [as his successor]. Weizi also overlooked his grandson Tu and named Yan [as his successor]. Now, Zhongzi is doing nothing more than following the way of the ancients."
>
> 伯子曰：「仲子亦猶行古之道也。昔者文王舍伯邑考而立武王，微子舍其孫腯而立衍也；夫仲子亦猶行古之道也。」

> Ziyou asked Confucius about this, and Confucius replied, "No. He should have set up his grandson [as his successor]."
>
> 子游問諸孔子，孔子曰：「否！立孫。」[43]

Gongyi Zhongzi, rather than following the ritual script in naming his grandson as successor, chooses one of his younger sons instead. The apparent justification for this is that Gongyi Zhongzi was following the precedent of profound people such as King Wen, who passed over his eldest son in favor of his younger son, who was eventually called King Wu. In the *Liji*, and throughout early China in general, the practice of naming an illegitimate successor is often spoken of as a matter of *shi* 時, or timeliness.[44] These occasional alterations of the script come about only in rare circumstances when the times dictate such a necessity, and only at the hands of a timely, or fluent, agent. Wen passed the throne to Wu only because he realized that Wu was the only one who would overthrow the licentious Shang Dynasty and restore order to the kingdom. At work in this passage is the claim by Gongyi Zhongzi that his situation is in fact one that calls for altering or disregarding the script for naming a successor. Confucius, hearing this recounted by his disciple Ziyou, provides the final judgment: Gongyi Zhongzi should have appointed his grandson. Following Confucius's view, Gongyi Zhongzi, knowing the script relevant to the situation, failed in his attempt to replicate the exceptions of the past. Failures in fluency occur when a ritual agent understands the actions prescribed by a ritual script and misinterprets the context as one that calls for deviating from the script.

Failures in fluency tend to be of two kinds. Ritual agents sometimes modify ritual scripts to comply with their untaught dispositions—mourning longer than dictated because one is still sorrowful, for instance. Ritual agents also tend to change ritual scripts to usurp power that does not belong to them—using dancers in a musical performance that only the ruler of a territory would use, for instance, thereby claiming legitimate rule over a new territory. This latter reason, in the context of inter- and intra-state relations, has been the attention of interpreters of the *Liji* for quite some time. The idiom *libeng yuehuai* 禮崩樂壞 (literally, "the rituals have collapsed and the musical performances are ruined") captures the spirit of this discourse. The idea is that the rituals and musical performances by the time of Confucius had been manipulated to such an extent that the efficacy of the entire system had failed. The age of Confucius, and his disciples, in this view, was an age of chaos because ritual had been inappropriately modified and usurped. The time period, part of which came to be known as the "Warring States," is marked by war and chaos because of innumerable failures in fluency.

Modifying Ritual to Comply with Untaught Disposition

Failures in fluency often occur when ritual scripts are inappropriately adapted to accord with one's untaught dispositions. A passage from the "Tangong Xia" chapter provides an excellent example of this. In this passage, Zisi learns of his mother's death. Due to the premature death of his father, Zisi's mother had remarried and moved to another state.

> The mother of Zisi died in the state of Wei [after remarrying]. When Zisi heard of her death he wailed for her in his ancestral temple. When his disciples came upon him they asked, "A mother of the Shu Clan has died [i.e., her new clan], why do you wail in the ancestral temple of the Kong Clan?"
>
> 子思之母死於衛，赴於子思，子思哭於廟。門人至曰：「庶氏之母死，何為哭於孔氏之廟乎？」
>
> Zisi exclaimed, "I have gone beyond [what is right]! I have gone beyond [what is right]!" He then went into another room to wail [for her].
>
> 子思曰：「吾過矣，吾過矣。」遂哭於他室。[45]

Because Zisi's mother had remarried, the ritual script for mourning rites forbids him from mourning for her in his ancestral temple. There is little reason to believe that Zisi was unaware of this. Indeed, it appears that Zisi modified the ritual script to accord with his sentiments of sorrow. When questioned about the practice by his disciples, he quickly admitted his fault and moved to wail in another room.

A similar vignette occurs in the "Tangong Shang" chapter with one of Confucius's disciples:

> Zilu wore the mourning clothing worn for mourning one's sister. He could have removed it [because the requisite time had passed],

> but did not remove it. Confucius asked, "Why don't you remove [the mourning clothing]?"
>
> 子路有姊之喪，可以除之矣，而弗除也，孔子曰：「何弗除也？」
>
> Zilu replied, "I have few siblings, and cannot bear [the loss]."
>
> 子路曰：「吾寡兄弟而弗忍也。」
>
> Confucius responded, "The early kings fashioned ritual [precisely because] no one could bear [such a loss]." Upon hearing this, Zilu immediately removed the clothing.
>
> 孔子曰：「先王制禮，行道之人皆弗忍也。」子路聞之，遂除之。[46]

In this vignette, Zilu struggles to endure the loss of his sister and continues to mourn for her beyond the time prescribed by the ritual script. He does this on the grounds that his sorrow is particularly acute due to the fact that he has few other siblings. Confucius, however, corrects him by explaining that the early kings designed ritual with this in mind. They knew that people would find it difficult to bear the loss of a loved one, yet they determined that mourning should end at a specific time in order to allow the mourner to continue on with his or her life. Mourning rituals provide a means of coping with death, but certain rites should not continue indefinitely.

These two passages demonstrate the tendency of ritual performers to modify ritual to accord with their dispositions. In the first example, Zisi's grief leads him to wail for his mother in the wrong ancestral temple. In the second example, Zilu's grief at the loss of his sister leads him to prolong the mourning rites. From the view of the authors of the *Liji*, human sentiment—especially when strongly stirred in situations such as the death of a loved one—can serve as an inappropriate pretext for the modification of ritual. Examples of failures in fluency due to the inappropriate expression of sentiment abound throughout the *Liji*.[47]

Usurping Ritual

The authors of the *Liji* were also concerned that ritual agents would modify a ritual script in an attempt to illegitimately broaden their sphere of control.

A lengthy passage in the "Jiaotesheng" 郊特牲 chapter describes how those in government positions sometimes "usurped" (*jian* 僭) ritual in an attempt to gain more control of the state than they currently possessed:

> The feudal lords hung their musical instruments in the pattern reserved for the emperor and sacrificed a white bull, [the sacrifice reserved for the descendants of the Shang Dynasty]. They played the jade instruments [that only the emperor was supposed to play], and used red shields with gold inlay, [which were reserved for the emperor]. They wore the headdress reserved for the emperor in performing the "Da Wu" song, and rode in the grand chariot, [which only the emperor was meant to ride in]. This is how the feudal lords usurped ritual.
>
> 諸侯之宮縣，而祭以白牡，擊玉磬，朱干、設錫，冕而舞《大武》，乘大路，諸侯之僭禮也。
>
> [The officials erected] a towered gate and covered the entrance with a screen. [They built] a stand to place the wine cups on and wore purple inner robes with axes embroidered on them, [which were reserved for those in higher rank]. By these means the officials usurped ritual.
>
> 臺門而旅樹，反坫，繡黼，丹朱、中衣，大夫之僭禮也。
>
> Therefore, when the emperor was weak, the feudal lords usurped [his power]; and when the officials were strong, the feudal lords were threatened. As such, the feudal lords and officials honored each other with governmental titles, greeted each other with riches, and bribed each other with material wealth. By these means the rituals of the world fell into chaos.
>
> 故天子微，諸侯僭；大夫強，諸侯脅。於此相貴以等，相覿以貨，相賂以利，而天下之禮亂矣。[48]

Usurping ritual in the context of this passage refers to officials at various levels of government changing the ritual scripts appropriate for their position into the ritual scripts appropriate for other governmental positions. The first set of rituals performed by the feudal lords, for instance, are the rituals meant for the emperor. In performing the rituals reserved for the emperor, the feudal lords take the place of the emperor; and, at least implicitly, desire the rest of the kingdom to recognize them as emperor. The notion of "usurping" in this sense implies the illegitimate adaptation of ritual in the attempt to gain power beyond one's current social station. Interpreters take these failures in fluency as representations and causes of widespread political chaos. In short, those in charge of ritual—especially at the state level—tend to purposefully mis-perform ritual when such mis-performances are capable of bolstering their political power.

Conclusion

The purpose of this chapter was to explore the notion of preventable failures in ritual from the perspective of the *Liji*. While the authors of the text realized that rituals could fail both because those performing the rituals did not always follow the ritual script and because ritual scripts themselves were flawed, they also saw the majority of these failures as preventable. In other words, they advocated the cultivation of competent agents who were able to follow the ritual as scripted, and the cultivation of fluent agents who were able to recognize failures in the ritual script and modify the script to ensure the continued success of ritual. If one were both competent and fluent, rituals would rarely fail. However, both competency and fluency are not simple attributes to cultivate. People often fell short in following a ritual script, and they often presumed themselves to be more fluent then they actually were and thereby inappropriately modified ritual.

More specifically, failures in competency occur when ritual agents lack a content knowledge of the ritual script or the skill necessary to follow the script. They also happen when ritual agents possess or manifest the wrong sentiments.

This chapter also discussed several threats to the success of ritual in the form of failures or shortcomings of the ritual script. These threats pose opportunities for the ritual agent to exercise fluency. They also demonstrate the limits of a ritual script. In other words, the authors of the *Liji* were highly aware that rituals, if performed in every circumstance according to the ritual script, would succumb to a number of dysfunctions. These dysfunctions are due to threats such as the lack of material objects to properly perform a ritual, the physical disabilities of those involved in a ritual, the varying terrain of the earth where rituals are performed, and the changing contours of the world as human society moves from one time period to the next.

Lastly, this chapter discussed failures in fluency. These failures occur when ritual agents mis-perceive a threat to the success of ritual, and modify the ritual script in light of this mis-perception. Failures in fluency are prevented as ritual agents become connoisseurs of their various life situations and learn to recognize circumstances where deviating from the ritual script is appropriate.

The importance of this chapter is to demonstrate the degree to which the authors of the *Liji* were aware of the dysfunction of ritual. Not only do they recognize that people would often make mistakes in performing ritual, but they also realized that ritual scripts were sometimes flawed in providing guidance for the successful performance of ritual. These failures are preventable in that competent ritual agents are capable of properly following a ritual script and fluent ritual agents are capable of appropriately modifying ritual scripts. The chapters that follow will investigate attitudes toward unpreventable failures in ritual.

5

The Inevitability of Failure

If there are two simultaneous occasions for mourning, what should be done?

並有喪，如之何？[1]

THE "LIYUN" 禮運 chapter opens with a scene of a dysfunctional ritual. Confucius, after observing the sacrifice performed for the spirits of the twelfth month of the year by officials in the state of Lu, removes himself from the room the ritual was performed in and, while pacing back and forth, lets out a sigh.[2] His disciple, Ziyou, hearing this, asks Confucius what was troubling him. Confucius responds with a lengthy description of two utopian time periods in human history—one he calls Grand Unity (*datong* 大同), and the other he calls Modest Prosperity (*xiaokang* 小康).

In describing the era of Grand Unity Confucius explains,

> The Great Way moved [throughout the world]; and everything under the heavens was commonly shared. Those in positions of authority were chosen because of their abilities. Trust was emphasized, and solidarity was cultivated. As such, people did not only treat their parents as parents, nor only their children as children. The old were allowed to live their lives to the fullest. The able-bodied were employed, and the young were raised into adulthood. The widowed, the orphaned, the childless, and the sick were all cared for. Men had proper allotments of work, and women were married into good families. When crafting goods, people disdained not putting them to their full use; yet they did not need to store up [goods] for themselves. When working, people disdained not exerting themselves to the fullest; yet they did not [work] simply for themselves. As such, deceitful plans were curbed

so that they did not arise; and thieves, robbers, and malcontents did not come about. Because of this, [people] did not [even] shut the outer gate to their homes. This is what is called Grand Unity.

大道之行也，天下為公。選賢與能，講信脩睦。故人不獨親其親，不獨子其子，使老有所終，壯有所用，幼有所長，矜寡孤獨廢疾者，皆有所養。男有分，女有歸。貨惡其棄於地也，不必藏於己；力惡其不出於身也，不必為己。是故謀閉而不興，盜竊亂賊而不作，故外戶而不閉，是謂大同。[3]

The period of Grand Unity, Confucius explains, is a time when the Great Way pervaded the world. People were chosen to serve in positions of leadership according to their merit rather than their family lineage. The younger generation treated all of the older generation uniformly as their parents; and the older generation looked after all of the younger generation as their children. People had no need to close the doors to their homes since thieves were nonexistent. The sick, widowed, and orphaned were cared for. And, as summed up toward the end of the passage, people had no need to be concerned about themselves (*bubi weiji* 不必為己). What is notable here is that somewhat simple social divisions mark this period of unity—roles such as husband and wife, as well as parent and child existed; however, distinctions between older brother and younger brother, as well as parent and unrelated adult, did not exist.

Confucius then goes on to describe the era of Modest Prosperity.

The Great Way was obscured, and everything under the heavens became the property of individual families. [People] treated only their parents as parents, and only their children as children. [They] crafted goods and labored for themselves. [They] considered it ritually proper to pass down positions of authority on the basis of lineage; and considered it necessary to construct city walls and moats [to protect their towns]. [They] took ritual and rightness as their standards.

By these means [people] properly arranged the social stations of ruler and minister, deepened the relationship between fathers and sons, solidified the relationship between older brother and younger brother, harmonized the relationship between husband and wife, standardized the measurements used to build things, organized farming plots and villages, praised the brave and the wise, and worked for the betterment of themselves.

It was at this point that [people] created and employed deceitful schemes; and military weapons came about. The figures Yu, Tang, Wen, Wu, King Cheng, and the Duke of Zhou arose in the midst of all this. Of these six rulers, none were not careful to do things in accordance with ritual. They thereby proclaimed their rightness, gained the trust of others, revealed the errors [of their detractors], demonstrated benevolence, and encouraged deference. [As such, they] set a standard for all people. If there were [people] who did not accord with this, they removed [them from society] because the masses regarded [any detractors] as great harms [to society]. This is what is called Modest Prosperity.

大道既隱，天下為家，各親其親，各子其子，貨力為己。大人世及以為禮。城郭溝池以為固，禮義以為紀；以正君臣，以篤父子，以睦兄弟，以和夫婦，以設制度，以立田里，以賢勇知，以功為己。故謀用是作，而兵由此起。禹、湯、文、武、成王、周公，由此其選也。此六君子者，未有不謹於禮者也。以著其義，以考其信，著有過，刑仁講讓，示民有常。如有不由此者，在埶者去，眾以為殃，是謂小康。[4]

According to Confucius, and for reasons not explained in the text, the Great Way became obscure and people found themselves living in a different world.[5] In this new world, city walls and moats were erected to keep unfamiliar people out of the cities. Weapons and armies came into being; and successors to the throne were chosen on the basis of their lineage rather than their merit.[6] In contrast to the previous time period, people labored for themselves (*huoli weiji* 貨力為己, *yigong weiji* 以功為己) rather than for the benefit of all of humanity. Fortunately, a number of exemplary figures (*junzi* 君子) appeared on the scene and devised a means to order society. These people created, or more likely, further developed, a system of rituals that ordered things to the point of Modest Prosperity. People living in this time period, the text explains, took ritual as their standard, or *ji* 紀. As mentioned in the introduction, the character *ji* 紀 can also refer to a series of knots or threads tied together. These knots serve as a means to mark out particular lengths of rope or to bind things together. Metaphorically, they refer to an abstract notion of "standard" or "measurement." The "Liqi" 禮器 chapter of the *Liji* employs *ji* 紀 as a metaphor for ritual. It states, "In performing ritual the profound person must be vigilant. [Ritual] is the knot [*ji* 紀] of the people. If the knot loosens, the people will be scattered" 是故君子之行禮也，不可不慎也；眾之紀也，紀

散而眾亂.[7] Here, *ji* 紀 is the tie that holds society together. Without it there would be chaos. In the context of the *Liji*, ritual serves as the means to standardize or order society. As implemented by the profound people that appear in the time period the "Liyun" chapter calls Modest Prosperity, ritual serves to bind (*ji* 紀) society together with the *dao* 道.[8]

Confucius explains that he hoped that the world might again attain to the greatness of these two time periods, yet, as evident from the poor performance of the ritual just witnessed, such a desire will not be realized. Confucius does not explain how the ritual he just witnessed had failed. Generally speaking, his lament is meant to suggest, among other things, that the performance of ritual during his time period had dilapidated—suffering the variety of failures discussed in the previous chapter. The situation is particularly desperate because Lu, Confucius's home state and the location of the ritual just performed, was credited with preserving the great rituals of the past; and if the rituals performed in the state of Lu were dysfunctional, there was indeed little hope in rituals performed by the rest of the world.

This opening scene raises several relevant questions. What, for instance, caused the current state of failure? Is it possible, in the view of the text, for humanity to return to a state of Grand Unity or Modest Prosperity? If so, which state is preferred, and how should humanity work toward it? As the "Liyun" chapter unfolds we gain a complex set of answers to these questions.

After Confucius provides Ziyou with an explanation for his lament, Ziyou asks two more questions. Both concern the role of ritual. Ziyou's second question is particularly interesting as it elicits a description of the origin of ritual (*lizhichu* 禮之初). Confucius explains,

> In ancient times, before there were palaces and buildings, the early kings dwelt in caves during the winter and in nests during the summer. There was no fire so they ate grass and the fruit of the trees, and the raw flesh of birds and animals. They drank the blood of these animals and feasted on their feathers and fur. There was no hemp or silk so they wore feathers and hides. Later, sages created [things]. They harnessed the benefits of fire, they smelt metal, and they shaped clay. By means of these things they constructed platforms with roofs, as well as palaces, houses, windows, and doors. They were able to grill, roast, boil, and cook [their food]. They were also able to make various seasonings. They gained control over fibers so as to produce

hemp and silk [for clothing]. By means of these things they nourished the living and tended to the dead. They were able to serve the spirits of the world. All [ritual] follows from this beginning.

昔者先王，未有宮室，冬則居營窟，夏則居橧巢。未有火化，食草木之實、鳥獸之肉，飲其血，茹其毛。未有麻絲，衣其羽皮。後聖有作，然後修火之利，范金合土，以為臺榭、宮室、牖戶，以炮以燔，以亨以炙，以為醴酪；治其麻絲，以為布帛，以養生送死，以事鬼神上帝，皆從其朔。[9]

Ritual began with the civilization of human society. The sages noticed the condition of the world and created things such as fire to better that condition. The simple creations of weaving and cooking enabled people to serve the spirits of the world. This passage in the "Liyun" chapter continues on to describe how the foundational acts of the sages led to more sophisticated ritual implements and performances:

Now the dark wine is put in the room [where the sacrificial ceremony is performed] and the sweet wines are placed at the door. The sacrificial grains and red wines are placed in the hall and the clear liquors are placed below the hall. The sacrifices are arrayed, and the tripods and tables are readied; the small and large zither, the flutes, the musical stones, the bells, and the drums are displayed; and the words of the prayer are arranged. [All this is done] to bring the spirits down from above and to enjoin with one's ancestors; to arrange the social stations of ruler and minister; to deepen the relationship between fathers and sons; to solidify the relationship between older brother and younger brother; to properly adjust the stations of those in authority and those subservient to authority; and to provide a proper place for husband and wife. This is what is called receiving blessings from the heavens.

The prayers are then pronounced, and the dark wine is offered. The blood and fur of the sacrifices are offered up; and their uncooked meat is placed on the tables, with their bones cooked in a soup. Then floor mats are brought forth, and a hempen cloth is used to cover the sacrifices. [The ruler and his wife] are clothed in newly washed silk robes. They present the sweet wines and offer up the roasted and cooked meat of the sacrifices. They alternate making these sacrifices; and the spirits are thereby pleased. This is what is called according with the deep and arcane.

> After this, they retire from the room where the ceremony was performed and boil the remaining meat [for others to eat]; separating the meat of the dog, the pig, the cow, and the sheep into dishes—some square, some round, some made of bamboo, and some made of other wood. A prayer is offered to express the filiality of those making the sacrifices; and words of compassion are expressed by the spirits [through a person representing them]. This is what is called great fortune. All of this constitutes the grand completion of ritual.
>
> 故玄酒在室，醴、醆在戶，粢醍在堂，澄酒在下。陳其犧牲，備其鼎、俎，列其琴、瑟、管、磬、鍾、鼓，脩其祝、嘏，以降上神與其先祖。以正君臣，以篤父子，以睦兄弟，以齊上下，夫婦有所。是謂承天之祜。作其祝號，玄酒以祭，薦其血、毛，腥其俎，孰其殽，與其越席，疏布以冪，衣其澣帛，醴、醆以獻，薦其燔、炙，君與夫人交獻，以嘉魂魄，是謂合莫。然後退而合亨，體其犬豕牛羊，實其簠、簋、籩、豆、鉶羹。祝以孝告，嘏以慈告，是謂大祥。此禮之大成也。[10]

Ritual, while rooted in the basic activities of cooking, weaving, and house-building, progressed from these basic activities into more intricate practices. Ritual came to involve a variety of performers, utilizing various wines, clothing, and sacrificial vessels.

This scene depicting the coming forth of ritual is not easy to chronologically situate with the description Confucius gives of the periods of Grand Unity and Modest Prosperity. It is notable that the *Kongzi Jiayu* 《孔子家語》, which also preserves a chapter entitled "Liyun" 禮運 lacks this passage and thereby resolves some of these difficulties.[11]

One way to reconcile these accounts is to chronologically situate the passages about early humanity living in deplorable conditions before Confucius's description of the eras of Grand Unity and Modest Prosperity; and in maintaining a coherent reading of the chapter as it stands in the *Liji* we have few other options.[12] It is also worth noting that many traditional commentators read the "Liyun" as presenting one coherent account of the chronological development of ritual.[13]

In essence, this entails seeing four time periods discussed in the "Liyun"—the first is this early stage in human history when people lived in caves and nests. The second is the period of Grand Unity. Since the "Liyun" chapter does not explain how human society moved from this early period into the era of Grand Unity, we are left to suppose that the creations of the sages fostered the conditions that led to it. The third period covered in the "Liyun" is the era of Modest Prosperity, and the fourth period is the time of Confucius, a post–Modest Prosperity world. Synthesizing the narrative in this manner means that ritual comes about in the earliest stages of human civilization and continues to grow in complexity through the era of Modest Prosperity.

Comparing Grand Unity and Modest Prosperity

There are many points of comparison that can be made between the eras of Grand Unity and Modest Prosperity. I will note three of the most relevant points here. First, ritual is not mentioned in the "Liyun" until the era of Modest Prosperity, where it is described as a kind of *ji* 紀. As mentioned above, ritual serves as a figurative *ji* 紀 binding society together similar to the way a knot in rope might tie things together. Without these knots, human society would be like loose items, scattered across the world without coherent pattern and left in a state of disorder. As implemented by the six exemplary rulers that appear in the era of Modest Prosperity, ritual served to bind society together with the Great Way.[14]

By introducing the notion of ritual, the text indicates that the shift from the era of Grand Unity to the era of Modest Prosperity is marked by a new need for mediation. The Great Way no longer bound society together; rather, society needed a supplementary series of knots to be bound together as before.[15] These knots, in the form of ritual, are the means by which human beings were able to prosper. Ritual, as such, had already been operating subtly during the era of Grand Unity; however, it became a body of named practices during the era of Modest Prosperity.[16] To borrow the terms of one commentator, ritual existed as a series of actions (*lizhishi* 禮之事) in the era of Grand Unity, but did not exist in name (*lizhiming* 禮之名) until the era of Modest Prosperity.[17]

The second comparison worthy of attention focuses on the issue of differentiation or sophistication. The era of Modest Prosperity is marked by the rise of different, and more complex, familial and social relationships, as well as more complex physical structures such as moats and city walls. No longer is just anyone from the older generation simply a "father" or "mother"; instead, fathers and mothers are differentiated from those who are not one's parents. The relationship between older brother and younger brother is delineated, as well as the relationship between ruler and minister. The creation of city walls also marks a clear distinction between insiders and outsiders. Prosperity in this more complex social setting is possible but requires a more sophisticated set of physical structures and more sophisticated rituals to properly maintain these relationships. When an aunt dies, for instance, the question now must be asked, should she be mourned for the same way that one would mourn for one's mother? As the narrative developed in the "Liyun" continues the theme of differentiation becomes more prominent.

The last significant point of comparison is between a more literal understanding of the titles "Grand Unity" and "Modest Prosperity." The terms "Grand" and "Modest" can also be rendered as "large" (*da* 大) and "small" (*xiao* 小). Many commentators, building on the fact that "Large Unity" seems intuitively better than "Small Prosperity," understand this contrast to mean that the era of Grand Unity is preferred over the era of Modest Prosperity, and humanity should, therefore, work to recreate the conditions of Grand Unity.[18] Additionally, the text is quite clear that humanity is without discord until the era of Modest Prosperity.

On the other hand, there are several reasons to reject the conclusion that Grand Unity is preferable to Modest Prosperity. For one, the figure of Confucius in the "Liyun" never advocates returning to the era of Grand Unity. Rather, throughout the text he argues for implementing the rituals created by the six rulers in the era of Modest Prosperity. Secondly, the notion of unity, or *tong* 同, in early Confucian texts is sometimes valued only in proper degree or in conjunction with other characteristics. The "Yueji" 樂記 chapter of the *Liji*, for instance, states, "Music works to unify (*tong* 同) [people] and ritual works to differentiate [them]. When unified they will love each other. When differentiated they will respect each other. If music is emphasized over [ritual] then [people] will inappropriately intermix; and if ritual is emphasized over [music] then [people] will inappropriately pull apart" 樂者為同，禮者為異。同則相親，異則相敬。樂勝則流，禮勝則離.[19] Here, the notion of unity (vis-à-vis music) must be tempered with differentiation (vis-à-vis ritual). Too much, or not enough, unity is a less-than-desirable circumstance.[20] In the case of the "Yueji," *tong* 同 is a characteristic sought after only in appropriate amounts or only when put in a kind of dynamic tension with notions of differentiation. In this light, the era of Grand Unity could be seen as an era in need of differentiation (so as to cease the inappropriate intermixing of people), or, said another way, it could be seen as an era in need of ritual.

Finally, the term I translate as "Modest Prosperity" (*xiaokang* 小康), while seldom appearing in other early Chinese texts, appears in a significant passage of the *Shijing* 《詩經》 where it refers to a period of prosperity or rest after work. The poem, in part, reads:

The people have now ceased their labors;
and are finally enjoying a season of prosperity (xiaokang 小康).
[Let us] favor this place, the middle kingdom;
and pacify the four corners of the world.
[Let us] keep it without even traces of those who seek to be deceitful;
and guard it from those who are not good.
[Let us] protect it from thieves and villains;
and destroy those who do not fear our perspicacity.
[Let us] be caring to those who are far, embrace those who are near;
and thereby [let us] establish our reign.

民亦勞止、汔可小康。
惠此中國、以綏四方。
無縱詭隨、以謹無良。
式遏寇虐、憯不畏明。
柔遠能邇、以定我王。[21]

The *Shijing* poem and the opening passages of the "Liyun" share many similar themes. They both speak about establishing a period of prosperity; dealing with thieves and deceitful schemes when creating the conditions of prosperity; and instituting a form of government—including military endeavors—that strives to continue the conditions of prosperity. As such, if the "Liyun" is drawing on the imagery of the *Shijing*, the term *xiao* 小 ("small") should not necessarily be put in contrast with *da* 大 ("large"); rather, the term *xiaokang* 小康 must be taken in its entirety, where it serves as a kind of metonym for the conditions spoken of in the poem. The era of Modest Prosperity, in this light, is not a lesser era when compared with the era of Grand Unity as much as it is a time period marked by the need for a different set of responses to create the conditions of prosperity.

In short, precisely how the "Liyun" esteems the era of Grand Unity in comparison with the era of Modest Prosperity is not entirely clear. Modest Prosperity is certainly more complex, and requires ritual to create the conditions of prosperity; but the question remains as to whether complexity should be valued, and whether it should be valued above the condition of Grand Unity where the harms described in the era of Modest Prosperity either did not exist or were effectively suppressed. Many previous interpreters have read the text as arguing against complexity, and have therefore labeled it a text influenced by "Daoists" arguing for the value of simplicity.[22]

My sense, however, given the three comparisons explained above, is to read the "Liyun" as advocating an ambivalent acceptance of the conditions of Modest Prosperity. In other words, the era of Modest Prosperity may in fact be a time where weapons, deceptive schemes, and self-interest come about, but it is also a world that supports a larger, more robust, population where, through the performance of ritual, people are able to achieve a deeper sense of self-realization. As such, the "Liyun" calls for its readers to ambivalently pursue the situation of Modest Prosperity.

The Rise of the Ritual Tradition

The "Liyun" describes the continuous development of ritual from the first organization of human society all the way through the era of Modest Prosperity. In the earliest stages of human civilization ritual was rooted in the basic needs of food and shelter. It progressed into the period of Grand Unity where, as the text states, the young were properly nourished, and males and females played distinct social roles. In the era of Modest Prosperity, ritual culminates in the intricate vessels and clothing that are employed in ritual performances. What we see here is the development of ritual in terms of a growing sophistication. Early rituals were comprised of the bare essentials of human living. They were basic and unadorned. The notion of *tong* 同 in the era of Grand Unity, as discussed above, implies a kind of undifferentiation. There was "grand undifferentiation" in the sense that people did not distinguish between their family and the families of others; their cities were also simple—lacking defense fortifications and complex forms of government. As society developed, so did ritual. As ritual became more complex, so did society. Since ritual is rooted in the everyday practices of eating, wearing clothing, and social interaction, the development of human civilization and the development of ritual are the very same process. They grow together in complexity. As such, points of tension between the emerging life of prosperity (*kang* 康) and the previous life of unity (*tong* 同) took shape in the transition from Grand Unity to Modest Prosperity.

The shift from the era of Grand Unity to Modest Prosperity, in this light, is not about the appearance of ritual; rather, what distinguishes these two time periods is a change in awareness with regards to ritual. This transition is best understood as the emergence of a discourse *about* ritual.[23] In other words, previous to the era of Modest Prosperity, ritual was simply what people did as given them by the sages. They built homes, manufactured clothing, and cooked food in accordance with the tradition established by these sages. However, in the era of Modest Prosperity ritual became an externalized (and institutionalized) discourse. It became not simply something people did, but something people thought about and had to choose to perform.[24] It became something, as we will see below, other than the facile practices of humanity. Adapting an interpretive strategy of one commentator, ritual existed in principle (*lizhili* 禮之理) during the primitive era (where the sages were the first to identify the principles of ritual), it existed in practice (*lizhishi* 禮之事) during the era of Grand Unity (where humanity did not self-consciously identify it as ritual), and it existed in name (*lizhiming* 禮之名) during the era of Modest Prosperity (where human beings labeled it to distinguish it from other practices that arose).[25]

The practices of ritual, the "Liyun" reveals, are often in tension with certain proclivities of human beings; and as society develops, these tensions become more prominent. Ritual, in other words, comes about in the era of Modest Prosperity not in terms of a new series of practices that were nonexistent in the era of Grand Unity. Instead, ritual comes about in the era of Modest Prosperity as a name for certain practices that are now in opposition to, and in competition with, other practices people are promoting and performing. The era of Modest Prosperity presents not just an added complexity in terms of ritual practices, but also a plurality of options in terms of performance. In the era of Modest Prosperity, people can perform in accordance with ritual, or they can perform a variety of nonritualized (and therefore "improper") activities, whereas in the era of Grand Unity people uniformly followed the dictates of ritual. What we have in the period of Modest Prosperity is the creation of a tradition in the sense of a series of ideas and practices that are in opposition with other competing ideas and practices.[26] It is the creation of this tradition, in tandem with people choosing to follow or reject it, that distinguishes the era of Modest Prosperity.

In short, what we see in the period of Modest Prosperity is the gradual rise of a new conceptualization of the 'self.' What we see is a self marked by the ability to reflect and determine the content of its tradition. The dispositions of this self are sometimes in tension with the demands of the ritual tradition.

This relationship between the two characters *ji* 己 ("self") and *ji* 紀 ("standard") that appear in the opening scene of the "Liyun" best captures the tension between the self and the ritual tradition. Both characters are graphically and semantically related.[27] The first *ji* (己) is usually translated as "self."[28] The second *ji* (紀), as explained above, literally refers to a knot in fabric or an abstract notion of standard—often in reference to celestial phenomena such as the sun. Later in the "Liyun" chapter, for instance, the sage is said to "take the sun and stars as his standard [*ji* 紀]" 以日星為紀.[29]

The "Liyun" explains that one fundamental difference between the era of Grand Unity and Modest Prosperity is that people were not concerned with themselves (*bubi weiji* 不必為己, literally "did not need to be for themselves") in the period of Grand Unity, whereas in the period of Modest Prosperity people were self-concerned (*weiji* 為己).[30] This opening passage suggests that in moving from the era of Grand Unity to the era of Modest Prosperity, some kind of transformation of the self (*ji* 己) took place. An alternative reading of these characters—taking *wei* 為 in the second rather than the fourth tone used in contemporary Mandarin—highlights the significance of this transformation.[31]

The character *wei* 為 in these contexts is usually understood as "for" or "in behalf of," so the phrase *bubi weiji* 不必為己 is translated character by character as "not necessary in behalf of oneself," or more fluidly as "It was not necessary for people to behave for the sake of themselves." It can also be understood, however, to mean "construct" or "become." This latter reading takes the phrase *bubi weiji* 不必為己 as "not necessary to become a self," or more loosely as "It was not necessary for people to construct a notion of the 'self.'" In other words, this alternative reading suggests that human beings in the period of Grand Unity did not yet have a developed concept of a self, or *ji* 己. This reading is supported by other concepts such as "unity," or *tong* 同, where in the period of Grand Unity human society was largely undifferentiated—there were concepts of young and old, as well as male and female, but there were no distinctions beyond these basic categories. The notion of a self, we may surmise, was one largely undifferentiated from other human beings. Translating the most famous line of the "Liyun" chapter more literally, during the era of Grand Unity "the world was one group" 天下為公.[32]

The unity of the world in the era of Grand Unity must be understood in contrast to the period of Modest Prosperity where "the world became [individual] households" 天下為家.[33] In distinction from the era of Grand Unity, people in the time of Modest Prosperity "used their labors to benefit themselves" 以功為己. Or, reading *wei* 為 as "to become," people in the era of Modest Prosperity "took the fruit of their labors as constitutive of their selves."[34] Rather than viewing the products of their labor as communal goods contributing to an undifferentiated society, people conceptualized the results of their efforts *as their own*. No longer did they work to take care of all of the older generation. Instead, they labored for their own family and for themselves. No longer did they watch after the younger generation as if they were all their children. Instead, they treated each person according to a more stratified sense of relationships. The world was no longer communal; rather, cities were divided from other cities by means of walls and moats; states were divided from other states with the creation of weapons and military troops; and the ultimate position of leadership—the role of emperor—was cut off from the public as now only those in blood relation were chosen for the position. What we see in the era of Modest Prosperity is a rise in distinctions; and in the center of this rise is a more distinctive notion of the self.

The "Liyun" chapter is not entirely clear, however, as to how this transformation of the self comes about or how it should be valued—is it a bad or good thing, for instance, that people become self-concerned?

While on the one hand, the self in the era of Modest Prosperity is able to construct a prosperous world, on the other hand, this self is also able to destroy this prosperous world. In short, the self in the era of Modest Prosperity can be understood as a *crafty* self, where the term "crafty" should be taken in its multifaceted sense meaning both skillful and devious.[35] The self in the era of Modest Prosperity is fully equipped to build housing structures that keep out the cold, to cook food in ways that nourish the body, to engage in a variety of relationships that constitute a meaningful life, and to perform complex rituals that bring the spirits down from above. This same self, though, is also fully equipped to plot and scheme against its relatives, to employ massive armies to overthrow a neighboring city, to labor for only itself, and to usurp, mis-perform, and even destroy the ritual tradition.

A close reading of the opening scene of the "Liyun" chapter reveals that the authors of the text were conflicted about the development of human society. On the one hand, human beings have become self-interested. On the other hand, the very inventions of the sages that enable self-interest were necessary for the progression of society. Therefore, at the very least, the transition from Grand Unity to Modest Prosperity is a necessary result of the continuous development of human society. The notion of *ji* 紀 plays a pivotal role in this conflicted scene.

Ji 紀 has already been discussed in several places of above. The point worth mentioning here is that the notion of *ji* 紀 appears in Confucius's description of the era of Modest Prosperity. Ritual, we are told, becomes the *ji* 紀 of the people.[36] This character—pronounced *ji* in modern Chinese—is semantically related to other characters that are also pronounced *ji* that appear in this passage. One of these characters is *ji* 己—discussed above as "the self." It appears in the descriptions of both the eras of Grand Unity and Modest Prosperity. *Ji* 紀, which we are told is ritual, acts as the mediating device between the old and new concepts of the self. Through the restraining or binding force of ritual, the new self curbs excessive self-interest and regains a semblance of its former self, being placed in proper relation with the *dao* 道. The new self, or *ji* (己), as found in the period of Modest Prosperity, must be bound together with (or by) this other *ji* (紀) in order to prosper. *Ji* 紀 in this sense represents the articulation and externalization of the practices of ritual that had been taking place in the era of Grand Unity. It is the canonization of tradition, or the accumulated recordings of past proper 'selves' that links the new self with the selves of the past.

This *ji* 紀, graphically and semantically related to yet another *ji* 記 (meaning a "record," "canon," or a "textual tradition"), is the recorded rituals of the past that serves as a standard for human beings in the era of Modest Prosperity. It is external in the sense that it is now found in the corpus of ritual texts, rather than in the innate practices of people in the era of Grand Unity. This external record is juxtaposed to alternative ways of living that other people have constructed in the era of Modest Prosperity. It is also the means by which human beings interweave themselves (*ji* 紀 also refers to thread) together with the Great Way.

The externalization of the previous practices of ritual into a discourse is problematized throughout the *Liji*. At several places the authors of the text remind its readers of the difficulty of capturing the *dao* 道 in ritual, tradition, or language. The "Tangong Shang" 檀弓上 chapter at one point notes the role of ritual in attempting to create continuity from one generation to the next:

> The mother of a man from Bian died, and [his] children wept. Confucius remarked, "The grief [of one generation] resonates with the grief [of the next generation], but it [i.e., the proper expression of grief] is hard to pass down. Rituals serve as a means of transmitting and passing down [this proper expression]. This is why wailing and leaping have defined boundaries [*jie* 節]."
>
> 弁人有其母死而孺子泣者，孔子曰：「哀則哀矣，而難為繼也。夫禮，為可傳也，為可繼也。故哭踊有節。」[37]

The "boundaries" spoken of in the last line refer to the specific number of repetitions that certain practices are performed in mourning rituals. Later, in the second half of the "Tangong" chapter, the same character, *jie* 節, is clearly employed in this sense.[38] Predetermining the number of practices serves as a means to continue the proper performances of the past in the present. Rituals serve to pattern and regulate practices so that they can be transmitted from one generation to the next. Numbering the times that one should wail, beat one's chest, or leap acts as a clear set of instructions with which one can begin to teach others how to mourn. This passage makes it clear that ritual is employed to cope with the difficulty of continuity. Implied in this passage is the idea that people naturally feel grief when a family member dies; yet, properly expressing that grief is much less natural. It requires a set of stipulations. Ritual is used as a means of stipulating expression such that sentiments of grief are not released without inhibition. Ritual, as a body of practices passed down through the generations, relates the experiences of ancestors as they grieved for the death of their predecessors with the experiences of descendants as they grieve for the death of their predecessors.

The two characters *chuan* 傳 and *ji* 繼 are particularly significant in this passage. Ritual, we are told, serves to "transmit" 傳 and "continue" 繼 the appropriate practices of the past. The character *chuan* 傳 coincidentally serves as part of the word "tradition" (*chuantong* 傳統) in contemporary Chinese. This passage also stresses the "difficulty of continuity" 難繼. Ritual is employed to offset this difficulty; yet, as the opening scene of the "Liyun" chapter demonstrates, simply creating a tradition of ritual is insufficient to overcome it. People can always construct an alternative tradition and simply choose not to perform the proper ritual script.

It is also significant that the character *chuan* 傳 can additionally mean "to record" or "to write commentary" on a text (read as *zhuan* 傳 in modern Chinese). This other meaning entails an explicit relationship with language and writing. As suggested above, ritual is an attempt to record (*ji* 記) and reproduce the standards (*ji* 紀) of the past in the present. The written text, as such, is a means of coping with the difficulty of continuity. Language, and in particular the written language, is the means by which ritual is recorded and transmitted from one generation to the next. The *Liji*, as such, is a key component of the ritual tradition. It, and other texts such as the *Yili* 《儀禮》, represent the verbal encoding of rituals that began with the civilization of humanity. They are records of the "standards" that generated the world of Modest Prosperity; but they are also the same standards that are in tension with the era of Grand Unity.

The notion of *dao* 道, rarely discussed in the *Liji*, is best understood as a process of flourishing whereby all things in the world maximize their potential for growth and development. While the authors of the *Liji* do not clearly define the concept *dao* 道, when they do discuss it they sometimes emphasize the difficulty of articulating it in language.[39] The "Tangong Xia" 檀弓下 chapter, for instance, states, "In the process of mourning there is the *dao* 道 of death. The early kings had difficulty expressing it in words" 喪有死之道焉。先王之所難言也.[40] This short passage conveys the idea that the *dao* 道 of death—perhaps referring to a way of behaving during the funerary rites—is hard to capture in words (*yan* 言). Language, in this view, does not easily represent aspects of proper performance spoken of as *dao* 道.[41] There is a suspicion of the ability of words—even the words of the exemplary kings—to capture this process. At the same time, this suspicion does not go the extent of asserting the *inability* of language to reproduce the proper way of performance. Indeed, it recognizes the possibility of such a feat, but also recognizes that such a feat is only accomplished through great difficulty. Contrary to positions such as those contained in the *Daodejing* 《道德經》, there is no ontological divide between language and the *dao* 道 in the view of the *Liji*.[42] Language is capable of adequately representing the *dao* 道. At the same time, however, the act of reproducing the *dao* 道 in language is complicated even for the early kings.

Coincidentally, other passages in the *Liji* directly relate language (*yan* 言) to ritual (*li* 禮). The "Zhongni Yanju" 仲尼燕居 chapter, for instance, defines ritual as "the act of speaking and performing what was spoken" 言而履之，禮也.[43] A similar phrase also occurs in the "Jiyi" 祭義 chapter.[44]

I presented above two passages that highlight "difficulties" associated with ritual. The first emphasizes the difficulty of continuing the proper performances of the past, and the second stresses the difficulty of expressing these performances in language. The purpose of citing these two passages is to demonstrate that the construction of a ritual tradition is set against a backdrop of difficulty and even failure. Synthesizing these perspectives leads to the following view. Proper performances that ordered human society occurred in the past. It is hard to pass these performances down from one generation to the next. It is also difficult to put them into words. Ritual, and in particular ritual as recorded in texts, is the best means available to create a tradition of proper performance.

Since this tradition is set against a backdrop of difficulty, failure is not only possible, but inevitable. As such, we should be suspicious of ritual, especially ritual reproduced by relying on the words of a text, to always be in line with the proper performance—or *dao* 道—demanded by a contemporary situation. Ritual, as a recorded tradition, will fall short of producing an ordered world. While ritual tends to succeed if competent agents perform the ritual, it is still possible for one to perform a ritual in perfect accordance with the script and have the ritual fail. Continuity between the successful performances of the past and the new context of the present is possible—and since the *Liji* contains the words of profound people it may even be probable—but this continuity is fraught with risk and great difficulty. Language (*yan* 言), the ritual tradition (*li* 禮), and contextually sensitive proper performances (*dao* 道) are sometimes in a dissonant relation with each other.

The "Liyun" as a Narrative of Dysfunction

The semantically related series of *jis*—己, 紀, 記, 繼—represent the central ideas found in the opening scene of the "Liyun" chapter. The self existed in an idyllic state in the era of Grand Unity. In the era of Modest Prosperity, people became self-interested, yet the profound people of the times employed the standards of ritual to bring about prosperity. Rituals were recorded in texts as a means of establishing continuity; yet not only is ritual an imperfect form of mediation with the Great Way, but also since it was transmitted in language its relation with the *dao* 道 is further complicated.

The significance of the "Liyun" chapter is that it provides a narrative for ritual failure. This narrative is not simply about incompetent people making mistakes in the performance of ritual—although the opening lines of the "Liyun" chapter suggest that this indeed occurs. Additionally, this is a narrative about the inevitability of ritual failure due to necessary changes in the world, as well as the tendencies of ritual to fail to adequately capture the Great Way (*dadao* 大道) of proper performance. As far as failures in efficacy are concerned, the "Liyun" argues that ritual scripts are the successful practices of the past put into language or recorded in texts. These scripts, while successful in their previous contexts, may not adequately represent the performances required by a new context. Fluent ritual agents, of course, can compensate for these changes. As explained toward the end of the "Liyun" chapter, the early kings created ritual by means of their cultivated sense of appropriateness. "Ritual," this same passage claims, "is the fruit of appropriateness" 禮，義之實也.[45] As such, rituals should change in accordance with the times. Fluent ritual agents are able to prevent most failures in efficacy.

More importantly, however, this narrative also accounts for unpreventable failures in efficacy. Ritual fails, according to the "Liyun" chapter, because the world has changed. No longer is ritual success as easy as it was in the era of Grand Unity. The era of Modest Prosperity is a period of growing complexity. The living conditions of humanity must develop in order to support a more robust population. Rituals must also grow in sophistication in order to meet the needs of the emerging society. A part of these changes entails the transformation of 'the self.' The self, in the era of Modest Prosperity, has become self-aware and self-interested—people now labor for their own benefit, or the benefit of their family, as opposed to the benefit of all of society. As relationships become more complex, and as humanity increases in numbers, various traditions emerge. Many of these traditions advocate improper ritual practices. Yet even the tradition established by the sages of the past—contained in ritual texts—cannot but fall short in reproducing the Great Way since language in general only inadequately captures the way of proper performance.

The era of Modest Prosperity is indeed a world of prosperity, but is also a world fraught with failure. Yet, the "Liyun" chapter claims, we should not turn back the clock and return to simplicity. It is notable that throughout the "Liyun" chapter Confucius makes no attempt to advocate a return to the era of Grand Unity; rather, he consistently seeks to understand and argue for the rituals of the Three Dynasties, which are part of the era of Modest Prosperity. Confucius, in short, realizes that humanity *will not*, and more importantly *should not*, return to a period of Grand Unity. Contrasting this with Mircea Eliade's notion of a "nostalgia for paradise," Confucius exhibits no "desire to live in the world as it came... fresh, pure, and strong."[46] While the era of Grand Unity is a development from the beginning of civilization where human beings lived in caves and nests, it is not simply a paradise. This is a central difference from texts usually labeled 'Daoist,' which advocate a return to or an "embracing" of simplicity. Confucius, in the "Liyun" chapter, does not believe that the era of Grand Unity represents the ideal state of humanity. Human society in the era of Modest Prosperity has become differentiated; and while a differentiated society will never be "Grand," only a differentiated society will enable large-scale human flourishing and "prosperity." As such, it is not that we cannot go back to life as it was lived in the period of Grand Unity—we have not lost this capacity nor are we ontologically separated from this era. However, our selves have been transformed in such a way that we no longer desire to live in an undifferentiated society, and instead we seek after a prosperous world. This, then, is the tragic moment as far as human civilization is concerned—humanity can go back to the era of Grand Unity, but rather than returning we choose to live in a flawed world. Carrying out the intricate practices of ritual seeks to limit these flaws, yet at the same time they also reproduce the conditions of failure.

The "Liyun" chapter encourages its readers to ambivalently work toward constructing a prosperous world. This ambivalence stems from the vulnerability of such a world. Contrary to the era of Grand Unity when people lived in accordance with the Great Way, the era of Modest Prosperity is vulnerable to deviation from the Great Way. The era of Grand Unity may have been a less sophisticated time period with rather simple homes and limited social relationships, but it was a time period where the values of trust, solidarity, and longevity were realized. People lived healthy, hard-working lives in a society led by virtuous leaders. The period of Modest Prosperity, in contrast, was a time when people more fully engaged in a variety of relationships and when the performances of ritual supported a more prosperous lifestyle, but it was also a time where deceptive schemes were hatched, military action was prevalent, and people thought more about themselves than they thought about others.

Moving to an age of Modest Prosperity meant leaving behind a way of life that worked, in exchange for one that had only a chance to work better. It meant transitioning from a safe and secure environment to one fragile and open to risk. In short, living in the age of Modest Prosperity meant living in a vulnerable world.

Unpreventable Failures Throughout the Liji

Notions of unpreventable failures in efficacy are rehearsed throughout the *Liji*. At times they are mentioned in passing. In chapter 2, for instance, I quoted a lengthy passage from the "Jiyi" chapter that discusses various purposes of ritual. It concludes by stating, "One who is able to integrate these five [uses of ritual] thereby orders the rituals of the world. While there will still be oddities, evil doings, and general disorder, they will be few" 合此五者，以治天下之禮也，雖有奇邪而不治者，則微矣.[47] The idea here is that the perfect implementation of ritual does not guarantee perfect order. There are still scenarios where disorder will occur.

Other chapters in the *Liji* take the notion of unpreventable failures in efficacy as a central theme. The "Fangji" 坊記 chapter, for instance, employs the image of a dike (*fang* 坊) as a metaphor for ritual. At one point the chapter explains, "Ritual is that which clarifies the opaque and discerns the subtle. It can be seen as a dike for people" 夫禮者，所以章疑別微，以為民坊者也.[48] Chapter 1 explored this metaphor by describing rituals as practices that serve to channel the untaught dispositions of people in a productive direction. Since I examined this metaphor in chapter 1, I will only reexamine it here as it relates to unpreventable failures in efficacy. A dominant theme throughout the "Fangji" chapter is the persistence of "overflow" (*yu* 踰), or water going beyond the confines of the dike. Literally speaking, this refers to situations where rituals fail to channel the untaught dispositions of human beings. The opening passage of the chapter immediately addresses this issue:

> The way of the profound person is like a dike—it channels the deficiencies of people. [But even if] one builds a large dike, the people will still flow beyond [*yu* 踰] it.
>
> 君子之道，辟則坊與。坊民之所不足者也。大為之坊，民猶踰之。[49]

This line likens the way of the profound person to a dike—while the way of the profound person might serve to curb the sentiments of people, it is still sometimes incapable of preventing overflow. People, it seems, have the power to overcome the curbing effects of ritual. Ritual, in this sense, is vulnerable to forces beyond the power of the ritual agents orchestrating the event. Rituals can fail regardless of how well a rite was performed.[50] This opening passage of the "Fangji" chapter sets the tone for the rest of the chapter. Nearly a dozen more times it repeats variations of the refrain "people will still flow beyond it." Put in the words of Confucius, one passage explains,

> In the funerary sacrifices there is an impersonator of the deceased; and in [the rites of] the ancestral temple there is a conductor. [These are meant to] demonstrate to people that there are those whom they should serve. Caring for the ancestral temple and reverentially offering sacrifices and oblations are meant to instruct the people to seek after filial piety. [One might] employ these practices to channel

the people [in the proper direction], yet the people will still forget their parents.

祭祀之有尸也，宗廟之主也，示民有事也。修宗廟，敬祀事，教民追孝也。以此坊民，民猶忘其親。[51]

The ancestral rites are meant to teach people filial piety; yet even when people properly carry out these rites there are still those who turn out not to be filial. Ritual, in short, cannot guarantee that people will not neglect their filial obligations. Ritual scripts, therefore, can be rendered inefficacious for fulfilling their primary purpose. Another passage states,

Be fond of virtue like [others are] fond of sex. The governors of states should not choose [a wife] from those they govern simply because the women are sexually attractive; and the ruler of a state should keep sexual encounters at a distance since he is the standard of the people. As such, men and women should not touch each other when exchanging gifts, and husbands should lead with their left hand when driving their wives in a chariot. When women return home after being married, no men should sit with them on the same mat. Widows should not wail at night; and when a wife is sick, people should ask about her, but should not ask about her sickness. All these practices can be employed as a means to channel the people [in the proper direction], yet the people will still be decadent and licentious; creating havoc in their clans.

好德如好色。諸侯不下漁色。故君子遠色以為民紀。故男女授受不親。御婦人則進左手。姑、姊妹、女子子已嫁而反，男子不與同席而坐。寡婦不夜哭。婦人疾，問之不問其疾。以此坊民，民猶淫泆而亂於族。[52]

The rituals of proper interaction between social classes and sexes serve as a dike for society; yet, despite their performance, people could still be licentious and bring chaos to the world. Ritual success, following these passages, is predicated on agencies beyond those in charge of the ritual event. While ritual agents might modify the ritual script to account for changing contexts, there are still situations where ritual will fail regardless of the changes ritual agents might make.

The "Fangji" chapter highlights the inevitability of ritual failure. Proper performance does not guarantee success. Ritual success is contingent on factors beyond the control of those directly involved in the ritual. If some people want to create a chaotic world, ritual can curb parts of these desires but it cannot completely prevent chaos. In distinction from the "Liyun" chapter, the "Fangji" chapter does not attribute ritual failure to the growing complexity of human civilization. Rather, failure is the product of people who have the power to choose to be other than instructed by ritual. At the same time, similar to the "Liyun" chapter, the "Fangji" chapter attributes failure to rituals that are incapable of generating their intended result. In the "Liyun" chapter, the ritual tradition as captured by texts and language fell short of capturing the Great Way of proper performance. In the "Fangji" chapter, on the other hand, rituals lack the power to compel people to feel and behave in predetermined ways. Both theories, of course, are not mutually exclusive.

The motif of unpreventable failures in ritual also appears in the "Zengzi Wen" 曾子問 chapter, which contains approximately two dozen questions that Zengzi is purported to have asked Confucius about performing ritual. The vast majority of these questions center on the issue of whether or not the failure of a particular ritual is preventable. The opening line, for instance, reads, "Zengzi asked, 'What happens if an heir is born shortly after the ruler dies?'" 曾子問曰：「君薨而世子生，如之何？」[53] Here, Zengzi is inquiring about how to deal with a situation where two ritual scripts conflict with each other. In the case under discussion, certain rites should be followed for the death of a ruler, but other competing rites should be held for the birth of an heir. Zengzi realizes that there are aspects of both rituals that threaten the success of each other—wailing, for instance, is prescribed for the mourning rites but it threatens the joyous activities prescribed for birth rites. Likewise, the musical performances associated with birth threaten the script of the death rites, which explicitly prohibits music. The problem, from Zengzi's perspective, is that the success of one ritual seems to entail the failure of the other. In essence, he is asking Confucius whether or not the failure of these rituals is preventable. Zengzi is wondering if it is possible to prevent the failure of the birth and death rites, or if the failure of one, or both, is inevitable.

The "Zengzi Wen" chapter contains many similar vignettes. Zengzi, for instance, asks about what to do when the day has been chosen for a wedding, but the bride's parents die shortly before it. He also asks how to handle a situation where a ruler dies, and the death of the parents of a minister shortly follows. Confucius's responses to these situations tend to be ways of mediating between the two ritual scripts such that both rituals succeed in bringing about their various purposes. If someone is a minister, for instance, and his ruler and father die in the same period of time, he should briefly return home to perform the next stage of the funerary rites for his father, then hurry back to participate in the funerary rites of his ruler. Some situations, of course, are more complex than this, but in most of the cases presented to Confucius, failure is deemed preventable.

There are other cases, however, where Confucius explains the failure of ritual to be unpreventable. Zengzi, for instance, asks, "When the feudal lords are visiting each other and the bows and courtesies are offered after entering the gate, but the ritual is not yet complete, under what circumstances should it be abandoned?" 諸侯相見，揖讓入門，不得終禮，廢者幾？ Confucius responds that there are in fact six circumstances when this ritual should be stopped. These are the emperor dying, the grand ancestral temple catching fire, an eclipse, the funerary rites of either the queen or princess, and the clothing of the feudal lords being wet from rain to the point that they lose their appropriate demeanor (天子崩，大廟火，日食，后、夫人之喪，雨霑服失容).[54] In these situations, the ritual fails for reasons that are primarily beyond the control of the ritual performers. In contrast to the other cases addressed in the "Zengzi Wen" chapter, there are no ways of mediating between the competing ritual scripts in these circumstances or altering the ritual script in jeopardy to maintain the efficaciousness of the rite (as rare as these circumstances might be). There are several other passages in the chapter that list different situations where a ritual should be "abandoned."[55]

Conclusion

Throughout the *Liji*, the theme of ritual failure is prominent. While fluent ritual agents are often able to prevent failure by recognizing threats to the success of ritual and modifying the script accordingly, other situations lead to unpreventable failures in ritual. In these scenarios, ritual success eludes even the most fluent ritual agents. Despite the fact that a ritual script might be 'open,' there is no change a ritual agent could make to prevent the ritual from failing to achieve its intended aim. The dysfunction of ritual, in these cases, is unpreventable.

The "Liyun" chapter provides a narrative for unpreventable failures in ritual. It describes the tragic situation of humanity where the performances of simple rituals related to food, housing, and basic social relations developed into sophisticated ritual events in a more complex—yet a more prosperous—world. In this era of Modest Prosperity, human beings became interested in furthering their own well-being. They also constructed cities, weapons, and a stratified system of social relationships. The practices of ritual were institutionalized in a tradition that competed with other traditions, and ritual was recorded in texts. The rituals performed in the era of Modest Prosperity necessarily fail because the growing complexity of the world creates more opportunities for extra-ritual agencies to determine the outcome of ritual and because language—especially language recorded in texts—inadequately represent the way of proper performance in a new context. The dilemma, however, is that ritual is the only means of bringing about a prosperous world. The aim of humanity, as such, is not to enact a return to the simple conditions of the era of Grand Unity; rather, its aim is to continually develop ritual in order to facilitate a more prosperous world. In short, humanity can go back to the era of Grand Unity, but the possibility of prosperity requires that we live in a flawed world. Carrying out the intricate practices of ritual seeks to limit these flaws, yet at the same time it also reproduces the conditions of failure. Similar narratives resurface in other chapters of the *Liji*. Failure, in all of these cases, is inevitable.

The next chapter of this project, chapter 6, will explore how the authors of the *Liji* struggled to differentiate between preventable and unpreventable failures in ritual.

6

Whose Fault Is Failure?

AMBIGUITY AND IMPINGING AGENCIES

When perplexed, [Confucius] passed on the perplexity [to his readers]; and as such he was careful [in arranging the Shangshu 《尚書》*].*

疑則傳疑，蓋其慎也。[1]

THE PREVIOUS CHAPTERS described and analyzed various attitudes toward failures in the rituals advocated by the authors of the *Liji*. This chapter will continue this analysis by investigating a notion of ambiguity. I will argue that we—as interpreters of the text—must remain open to the possibility that ambiguity was a deliberate rhetorical device employed by the authors or redactors of the *Liji* that served to ease the anxiety of ritual failure and consolidate the status of early Confucians as ritual authorities. In other words, this chapter argues for the possibility that ambiguity between causes of ritual failure is not only brought about by spatial, temporal, and cultural distance between the *Liji* and the contemporary interpreter (although those factors are certainly present), but can also be seen as didactic and instrumental devices used within the *Liji* to further certain arguments about the nature of ritual and the nature of the world in general. This chapter will proceed by detailing two relevant ambiguities in the *Liji*. The first is an ambiguity between failures in competency and failures in efficacy. The second is an ambiguity between preventable and unpreventable failures in efficacy. Both ambiguities result from the view held by early Confucians that the success of ritual is at least partially contingent on powers beyond those responsible for the performance of ritual. Determining where the agency of one party begins and the agency of another ends is often a difficult affair.

As far as this chapter is concerned, ritual failure is 'ambiguous' when conflicting explanations of a dysfunctional ritual, when considered independently, are similarly persuasive. Many contemporary interpreters view ambiguity as a problem that *should* be solved, or at least *could* be solved had we more knowledge of the context that produced the text. In contrast, I argue that we must remain open to the possibility that the authors of early Confucian texts sought to use ambiguity as a rhetorical device to argue for ways of rendering complex situations meaningful. My approach, therefore, will be to preserve rather than resolve points of ambiguity. This does not mean that every passage that appears ambiguous to the reader is an intentional use of ambiguity on the part of the writer (or editor). Certainly, many passages that appear ambiguous are due to our limited knowledge of the historical moment that produced the text. Additionally, the authorial intent of any passage lay beyond the ability of the reader to ascertain. Rather, my aim here is to remain open to the variety of possible intentions at play in any passage of the *Liji*—not ruling out any one reading unless there are textual or historical reasons for doing so.

At the same time, my point is to set the stage for the next chapter, which more fully entertains the question of what happens when we take the ambiguity of ritual failure as a solution to a problem rather than a problem requiring a solution. In a sense, I am posing the question of what happens when we take these ambiguities as didactic or instrumental devices for readers of the text, rather than something that is a result of a lacuna in our understanding of the situation that generated the text? I believe that when we see ambiguity as a solution to the problem of dysfunctional ritual in early China, we will gain a more robust view of the ways in which early Confucians sought to create a meaningful world. This chapter will seek to elucidate aspects of the ambiguity involved with the dysfunction of ritual.

Christoph Harbsmeier best represents a primary position among contemporary scholars. In his *Language and Logic* he states, "Private discourse must not be confused with esoteric discourse. Confucius did not speak in a deliberately obscurantist way. There is no time-honoured Chinese conspiracy to write obscurely. Confucius spoke in a familiar, in a private way."[2] Harbsmeier goes on to say that we need to interpret this discourse as if "we were eavesdropping on a stranger's conversations."[3] For Harbsmeier, ambiguity is a problem that must be solved. The issue for us, as interpreters, is to understand that the objects we interpret were never meant for us. Many of the early Confucian texts were intended as part of a curriculum for those intimately connected with Confucius. The further we are removed from this fellowship, the larger the interpretive gap. Our best route to take in facing this problem is to reconstruct the context of the discourse. Proper reconstruction of the context leads to a better understanding of the text. In the proper context, Confucius's conversations, or teachings, are not ambiguous. If a text remains ambiguous, then, it is because we have an incomplete understanding of the context.

There are several scholars who, contra Harbsmeier, argue for the use of ambiguity in early Confucian texts. David Hall and Roger Ames, for example, describe a "rhetorical skepticism" involved in writing commentaries on the classics where "the profound vagueness of these texts provided ample leeway for literati to exercise their imaginations and devise truly creative elaborations upon the original language."[4] Hall and Ames see this rhetorical skepticism as a primary point of contrast with Western philosophical discourses. They write,

> [In the Western philosophical tradition] the stipulation of terms within theoretical contexts led to the preference for clarity over vagueness, with the consequence that doctrinal differences were raised to the level of consciousness and had to be dealt with at that level. In China, by contrast, critics of a particular doctrine depended, as did its proponents, upon a cultural repository of vaguely defined concepts.[5]

For Hall and Ames, ambiguity, in terms of "vagueness," serves as a basis for the Chinese philosophical tradition. They do not, unfortunately, go on to thoroughly explain this basis.

In a more extended account, Mark Setton argues for the deliberate use of ambiguity in early Confucian material.[6] His article, "Ambiguity in the *Analects*: Philosophical and Practical Dimensions," describes three ambiguities that served as "fertile soil for [the] creative reinterpretation" of Confucianism.[7] These ambiguities, in brief, are "prescriptive," "concise," and "textual" ambiguities. The specifics of these ambiguities do not need to be recounted here. The relevant point is that Setton sees ambiguity as part of the Confucian "concept of language and the epistemological perspectives that informed it."[8] Setton, however, does not develop a full account of this concept of language or epistemology; preferring instead to provide examples of passages that can be read ambiguously.

Related to notions of ambiguity are concepts of "openness"—a belief that multiple readings of a text are permissible and possibly correct. Gu Ming Dong, a contemporary scholar, articulates a position worth noting in this regard. Gu claims that openness permeates Chinese texts from the beginning of the literary tradition. However, this openness is a result of "critical blindness" rather than "conscious insight."[9] In other words, according to Gu Chinese interpreters sought after *the real* meaning of a particular passage. As they did this, they came to contradictory, yet equally plausible, conclusions. Later interpreters drew on this diversity to create theories of reading that argued for multiple valid interpretations. Early Confucian texts, therefore, are open in the sense that no one interpretation *can* be provided for many passages. David Hall and Roger Ames, in *Thinking Through Confucius*, make a similar point in abbreviated form.[10] Gu's argument for openness bears some semblance to the argument put forth in this chapter. Ambiguity is clearly an issue in the act of interpretation. For early Confucian texts, openness is imposed on the interpreter due to the limits of their ability to recontextualize any given passage. Additionally, ambiguity can be seen as serving a didactic and instrumental function for readers of the text.

As far as Harbsmeier's position is concerned, Harbsmeier is correct in arguing that the context of a discourse is invaluable to understanding the discourse itself; and we, as contemporary interpreters, are so far removed from this particular discourse that parts of the early Confucian canon will remain permanently obscure. I see no reason, however, to ascribe a kind of intentionality to the text that excludes ambiguity as part of the rhetorical strategies available to the authors or editors. Since most issues of intentionality lie beyond the ability of the interpreter to ascertain, we should not prematurely exclude possible meanings of these texts. As we will see toward the end of this chapter, the ambiguity between unpreventable and preventable failures in ritual served to strengthen the status of early Confucians in the social landscape by relieving the burden of failure by means of what can be called "plausible deniability": Confucians could claim successful adaptations of ritual as the fruits of their own labors, but deny that failures were their fault.[11] In short, this ambiguity allowed the failure of ritual to be seen as no one's fault, the ritual agent's fault, or everyone's fault depending on the rhetorical need of the person making the claim as well as the rhetorical constraints of the situation. This ambiguity, which I will call 'the ambiguity of impinging agencies,' makes the failure of ritual the fault of no one yet everyone at the same time.

Ambiguity Between Failures in Competency and Failures in Efficacy

Chapter 2 introduced the notion of ambiguity. That chapter explained that it was sometimes difficult to distinguish between failures in competency and failures in efficacy. This was an apparent difficulty for both the interpreter of the text as well as some of the characters depicted in the text. In other words, determining whether the ritual agent failed or the ritual script failed was no easy task for the reader of the text or the actors as described in the text. Since the rituals of the past could potentially fail in the present, there is a constant tension between the script and the circumstances involved in performing a particular ritual. Early Confucians navigated this tension by opening the ritual script to include variations in ritual practice. Chapter 4 detailed several of these variations. The modification of ritual scripts by fluent agents served to navigate the tension between past and present. If a ritual is going to fail, it becomes the obligation of the ritual agent to modify it. The ritual scripts of the past, therefore, are not enough to ensure the proper performance of ritual—the presence of a fluent agent is required.

While this approach mitigates the tension between ritual scripts and their application to varying situations, it does not eliminate the ambiguity between failures in efficacy and failures in competency. Instead, it shifts the burden of properly adapting the ritual script on to the shoulders of the ritual agent. A failed ritual now becomes the fault of the ritual agent for not being competent in performing the ritual according to the script or not being fluent in making the necessary changes to the script. The ambiguity between failures in competency and failures in efficacy manifests itself in the choice and justification of the ritual agent to deviate from the ritual script, as well as the inability of the observer of the ritual and reader of the text to apprehend these justifications.

chapter 2 quoted a vignette from the "Tangong Shang" 檀弓上 chapter where Zigong, Confucius's disciple, questioned Confucius for giving a larger gift than required when coming across the funerary rites of an acquaintance whom Confucius had lived with. In this situation, it was unclear whether Confucius should have varied from the script. In Zigong's view, Confucius should have stuck to the script—bestowing the generous gift was actually a mistake on the part of Confucius. In Confucius's view, acting according to the script meant that the ritual would fail—giving a smaller gift would not properly express his sorrow. Many similar passages appear in the *Liji*. One in particular that also involves Zigong is worth recounting here:

> While in Wei Confucius happened to see someone participating in a funeral procession. Upon observing him he remarked, "How wonderful

indeed he carries out the process of mourning. He is an example sufficient [for us all]. My student, you should take note of this."

孔子在衛，有送葬者，而夫子觀之，曰：「善哉為喪乎！足以為法矣，小子識之。」

Zigong asked, "Why, Master, do you praise him?"

子貢曰：「夫子何善爾也？」

Confucius replied, "He goes as if bearing deep solitude; and he returns as if apprehensive [about how to best continue the ceremony]."

曰：「其往也如慕，其反也如疑。」

Zigong further asked, "Is it not better to return swiftly and perform the post-burial sacrifice?"

子貢曰：「豈若速反而虞乎！」

Confucius responded, "You should take note of this man. Even I have yet to be able to perform the funerary rites as he has."

子曰：「小子識之，我未之能行也。」[12]

This passage presents a situation similar to the passage mentioned above. Zigong notes that the man has deviated from the ritual script and judges this inappropriate. Confucius, on the other hand, takes this performance as a permissible deviation from the script. From the perspective of the reader, it is not obvious who is correct. Is this man an incompetent performer of ritual, or has he demonstrated an incomparable degree of fluency? Within the commentarial tradition, most interpreters, of course, side with Confucius. They take these passages as demonstrations of Confucius's uncanny ability to note proper deviations from a ritual script. Other characters in the vignette may not recognize a potential failure in efficacy, but Confucius demonstrates his unparalleled fluency. From this perspective, there is no ambiguity in Confucius's view. Many commentators also seem to presume that no such ambiguity remained on the part of the intended reader of the text, provided that he properly understood the passage. In this approach, a precondition of reading the text or being Confucius's disciple is accepting that Confucius's judgments are always correct.

On the surface this seems to support Harbsmeier's claim. The ambiguity lay at the level of interpretation, but not within the internal logic of the text—a logic that the interpreter has only glances of. Zigong and Confucius are wed to two conflicting positions, and while one position is ultimately incorrect, there is little reason to believe that either one of them saw any ambiguity in their respective position. If the contemporary interpreter only had access to the internal logic of the text, he or she would also know which position is correct. Our project, therefore, is to reconstruct this logic and apply it to this vignette. The problem confronting us as interpreters, following this line of argumentation, is that these texts are meant as didactic material for the followers of Confucius. Therefore, gaining further access into the context of these passages should provide us a better idea of how the figure of Confucius, or at least the constructed character of Confucius in the *Liji*, was able to recognize the fluency of the man in Wei. For the properly contextualized reader, this passage would provide a clear lesson as to how Confucius operates through situations that are perplexing from the perspective of the average observer.

It is worth noting that a minority of classical interpreters take the position that Confucius was occasionally wrong. They substantiate these claims by citing other passages from the *Liji* where Confucius confesses that his decision to vary from the ritual script was inappropriate.[13] In this view, even Confucius had moments of incompetency—his life of clarity is still marred by moments of uncertainty. More will be said about the failures of Confucius below; however, it is worth noting here that ambiguity has been an issue at the level of interpretation from the earliest commentaries. Indeed, commentators have arrived at equally plausible, yet contradictory, conclusions when confronted with a given passage.

These alternative positions present an interesting possibility since they tend to operate with assumptions similar to other interpreters yet they come to different conclusions. Both positions, including those of contemporary interpreters, take early Confucian texts as didactic material meant for a particular group of people. However, they disagree about the didactic purposes of certain passages. Most interpreters take vignettes of ritual performance in what can be called prescriptive terms. In this view, passages such as those presented above are understood to advocate certain performances. In the case of Confucius and Zigong, one could read these passages as recommendations to vary from the ritual script when one's dispositions conflict with it.[14] In the passage cited in chapter 2, for instance, the reason Confucius provides for giving a larger than necessary gift to the family of the man he mourned is that he "detests shedding so many tears and not following them in action" 予惡夫涕之無從也.[15] This vignette teaches the reader the kinds of circumstances under which varying from the ritual script are permissible.

Contrary to this position, but not necessarily exclusive of it, is the possibility that these passages served what can be called a descriptive didactic function.[16] In this view, rather than prescribing a kind of performance for the reader, these passages serve to illustrate the difficulties associated with demarcating the boundaries of ritual failure. In this view, passages that present two differing ritual practices—one performed in antiquity and another performed in the contemporary setting of the text—need not be taken as prescriptions to follow the rituals of antiquity. Instead, they can be understood as descriptive statements about rituals performed under different conditions—antiquity had once set of conditions, and the time of the text had another set of conditions. While many of these passages do not explore why different conditions require different ritual practices, the *Liji* as a whole does not preclude varying from the rituals of antiquity, and it moreover endorses modifying ritual from one dynasty to the next. In this light, a passage that states "In antiquity, one pace measured eight feet according to the measurement of the Zhou; but in contemporary times one pace measures six feet and four inches according to the measurement of the Zhou" 古者以周尺八尺為步，今以周尺六尺四寸為步, can be taken as a description of two equally legitimate practices of measurement rather than a value judgment on the decadence of the current state of affairs.[17] As such, the text is less interested in assigning praise and blame, and more interested in describing two divergent—yet appropriate—practices.

There are a number of similar passages that appear in the *Liji*; but rather than comparing two different ritual practices, these passages pose open-ended questions about varying from the ritual script. Noticeably lacking are any answers to these questions. The "Tangong Shang" chapter includes several of these passages. The following constitute the entirety of three of them:

> Zengzi asked, "Can [one] use whatever [one] finds in [one's] cupboards for the initial sacrifice made after someone has died?"

曾子曰：「始死之奠，其餘閣也與？」[18]

Zengzi asked, "If one is in a five-month mourning relation to the deceased, [one] does not wear mourning clothes; however, the brothers of the deceased who live far away also do not wear mourning clothes [because they hear about the death after the prescribed time for wearing them has past]. Is this permissible?"

曾子曰：「小功不稅，則是遠兄弟終無服也，而可乎？」[19]

During the mourning rites [the food offered for sacrifice] is not covered. Does this apply to all of the offerings or only the meat?

喪不剝。奠也與？祭肉也與？[20]

The *Liji* does not provide answers to these questions. As interpreters we must, of course, be careful not to overdetermine our interpretations since, in many cases, we are provided with limited information. It is in fact possible that these passages are simply fragments of larger passages that are no longer extant. In their longer form, they may have had answers. It is also possible that the answers to these questions were self-evident in the context of the construction of the text—the intended reader would immediately know the answer without having to see it. On the other hand, given that so much of the "Tangong" chapters are dedicated to the difficulties of ensuring the success of ritual, it seems plausible that these questions were not meant to have answers.[21] My suggestion, as such, is to read them as reflections of the difficulty of determining a clear course of action in every ritual circumstance. These are situations where there in fact is no one right answer. Grant Hardy proposes a similar hermeneutic with regards to the *Shiji* 《史記》: "My solution is that the *Shiji* is a 'reconstruction of the past' much more literal than that usually denoted by the phrase. It is, in fact, a textual microcosm. When we hold the *Shiji* in our hands, we are holding a model of the past itself, which intentionally replicates, though to a lesser degree, the confusing inconsistencies, the lack of interpretive closure, and the bewildering details of raw historical data."[22] The *Liji*, taken in this light, reproduces the ambivalence associated with ritual performance. The bewildering details of raw human experience produce situations of uncertainty where the ritual agent must, in essence, 'enact ambiguity.' Indeed, in some circumstances, varying from the ritual scripts of the past is worthy of *both* praise and blame. When the *Liji*, therefore, makes statements such as "[One] stops all work [of learning music] when mourning for nine months. Some, [however], say that reciting the lyrics during the nine months of mourning is permissible" 大功廢業。或曰：「大功，誦可也」, it is describing the ambiguity between failures in efficacy and failures in competency—it is a fact that some people advocate reciting the words of the songs one is studying even during the nine-month period of mourning, and this act is neither wholly blameworthy or wholly praiseworthy.[23] Said another way, the act of reciting lyrics during the nine-month mourning period seems to be either a failure of competency because the ritual script for mourning prohibits music, or a failure in efficacy because the ritual script fails to take into account the appropriate act of reciting just the lyrics; however, the reality of the situation is indeterminable—some people recite the lyrics and they are not unjustified in so doing, and others do not recite the lyrics at all. In some respects, both parties should be praised, and in other respects, both parties should be blamed. There is no indisputable way of adjudicating between competing claims.

Ambiguity Between Preventable and Unpreventable Failures in Efficacy

The "Zengzi Wen" 曾子問 chapter, as discussed in chapter 5, purports to contain approximately two dozen questions Zengzi poses to Confucius about performing rituals. The vast majority of these questions describe complex situations and center on the issue of whether or not the failure of a particular ritual is preventable. Many of these situations focus on problems caused by the death of those in one's social circle. The following are three such examples.

> Zengzi posed a question, asking, "What should be done if there are two simultaneous occasions for mourning?"
>
> 曾子問曰：「並有喪，如之何?」[24]
>
> Zengzi posed a question, asking, "What should be done if the governor's son is born shortly after [the governor dies and] is buried?"
>
> 曾子問曰：「如已葬而世子生，則如之何?」[25]

> Zengzi posed a question, asking, "What should be done if the gifts have already been exchanged and the wedding day has been determined, but the parents of the bride pass away?"
>
> 曾子問曰：「昏禮既納幣，有吉日，女之父母死，則如之何？」[26]

The responses to these questions explore how to navigate competing demands when the ritual script for funerary rites conflicts with other ritual scripts. Throughout not only the "Zengzi Wen" chapter, but also the entire *Liji*, the event of death figures as a prominent threat to the success of ritual. Since death itself is an occasion for a series of rituals, the rites required at the time of death tend to interfere with other rituals and important events in life. This problem is exacerbated by the length and complexity of death rituals—lasting for more than two years in the most extreme cases, and requiring elaborate clothing and décor at each stage of the ritual. More significantly, death is often an unpreventable event. While there are situations where one can choose the circumstances of one's death, oftentimes the external circumstances that bring about death seem to do the choosing. This appears to be the case even more so for others, over whom one has little control. The "Tangong Shang" chapter, on this note, contains a lament of Duke Ai at the passing of Confucius.

> Duke Ai of Lu eulogized Confucius, saying, "*Tian* 天 [i.e., the controlling power of the cosmos] did not let the old man stay. [Now] there is no one to assist me in my position [as duke]. Alas! Why! Elder Confucius!"
>
> 魯哀公誄孔丘曰：「天不遺耆老，莫相予位焉，嗚呼哀哉！尼父！」[27]

Confucius, according to this passage, is the passive recipient of *Tian*'s 天 actions. *Tian* 天 could have allowed Confucius to continue living. It is as if *Tian* 天 and not Confucius chose the time of death for Confucius. The loss of Confucius complicates the life of Duke Ai because in the death of Confucius he loses the advice provided by Confucius. One message the *Liji* makes clear is that the deaths of others impinge on the normal course of the lives of the living. In this sense, death can easily cause the unpreventable failure of other important events or rituals for the living.

The complexity of death rites discussed in the *Liji* cannot be overestimated. To state it generally here, death rituals, which are not portrayed uniformly in the *Liji*, usually begin with the rite of calling back the spirit of the deceased. They then proceed to the rite of coffining where the body of the deceased remains for several weeks or months while mourning and condolences take place. At that point, a funeral procession is held and the coffin is lowered into the tomb. Sacrifices are then offered and continue to be offered on the anniversary of the death of the deceased. Each of these stages calls for an elaborate display of funerary implements, performers, and various clothing worn by family and friends. Death rituals are an important sign of filial piety on the part of the living, and were believed to exert control over the spirits of the deceased. Without the funerary rites, the spiritual forces released at death could threaten the order of the world.[28] Zengzi's questions in the "Zengzi Wen" chapter should be understood in roughly this context.

In response to Zengzi's questions, Confucius advocates slight adjustments to the scripts in order to maintain the success of both rituals. If both one's parents die at the same time, for instance, one should first perform the rites for one's mother, saving the sacrifices and wailing until one performs the rites for one's father. These situations, of course, could be much more complex then this, but in most of the cases presented to Confucius failure is deemed preventable.

There are other cases, however, where Confucius explains the failure of ritual to be unpreventable. One of those passages was already discussed in chapter 5. Oftentimes these situations involve things such as catastrophes that destroy the implements needed for the ritual, the appearance of celestial phenomena such as eclipses, or the death of those in significant social positions. One such passage reads,

> Zengzi asked, "What should be done if news arrives announcing the death of the emperor, the funeral of the queen, the death of the governor, or the funeral of the governor's wife; and this be done after the ritual implements are already laid out for the feudal lords to make sacrifices to the spirits of earth and grain?"
>
> 曾子問曰：「諸侯之祭社稷，俎豆既陳，聞天子崩、后之喪、君薨、夫人之喪，如之何?」
>
> Confucius responded, "Abandon [the rite]."
>
> 孔子曰：「廢。」[29]

In these situations, the ritual fails for reasons beyond the control of the ritual performers. There are no ways, according to Confucius, of mediating the competing ritual scripts in these circumstances or altering the ritual script in jeopardy to maintain the efficaciousness of the rite. Confucius, unfortunately, provides no explicit rationale to distinguish between these unpreventable failures and the preventable failures mentioned in other passages of the "Zengzi Wen" chapter. However, the entirety of the "Zengzi Wen" chapter illustrates the backdrop against which Confucius provides answers about the preventability of ritual failure. For those posing these questions, it is certainly dubious to determine the preventability of failure. Indeed, for Zengzi, and perhaps for everyone except Confucius, knowing whether or not the failure of every ritual could be prevented is nearly impossible. While normal human beings might be able to recognize the difference in most situations, the sheer complexity of life—the myriad of relationships, roles, and powers competing with each other—renders this a tricky affair. It seems that unless one is Confucius, one will not be able to consistently recognize the preventability of ritual failure.

The fact that these situations are resolvable for Confucius suggests that at some level there may not be any ambiguity between preventable and unpreventable failures in ritual. From the perspective of the sage, there seem to be no unsolvable ritual conflicts. This, of course, is in line with Harbsmeier's analysis, and even resonates with the position of contemporary interpreters I previously called the inward turn. These views of modern scholars, it can be argued, take things from the perspective of the sage. From this view of the sage, points of failure are readily recognizable and attributable to various agencies. Every sagely teaching of the past is, in this light, clear for every other sage, and any dysfunctional situation is embraced with confidence since the sage understands the limits of his power. Ambiguity, as such, is not present for sages.

The issue worth pursuing, from this perspective, becomes primarily an epistemic one—how does one reason like a sage? Framing the question in this light reveals why so much effort of contemporary philosophers working with Confucian material is focused in the direction of deliberation and the operation of fundamental virtues. These efforts, while commendable, neglect passages in the texts that demonstrate that ambiguity still remains, even for sages. It also neglects the fact that the readers of these texts did not see themselves as sages. As such their deliberations must be made from a perspective where ambiguity is a real problem. Said another way, it may very well be the case that most, if not all, ambiguities are resolvable by a sage, but what happens when there are no sages around to resolve these ambiguities for us? Confucius might have been able to resolve the ambiguity between preventable and unpreventable failures in ritual, but we are not Confucius; neither does the text see its readers living in a world with a figure like Confucius. Indeed, from the perspective of many early Confucian texts, we are living in a post-Confucius world with no sage in sight. While the teachings of Confucius might be recorded in texts, as discussed in chapter 5, these texts cannot account for the complexities faced in an ever-changing world. In this light, it is inevitable that we will mistake preventable failures in ritual for unpreventable failures in ritual, and vice versa. As such, we, as human beings yet to be fully cultivated, cannot but act from a perspective where ambiguity is a real and impenetrable fact of life.

While the vignettes above describe a Confucius who is always ready to determine the preventability of ritual failure, other vignettes in the "Zengzi Wen" chapter reveal that Confucius sometimes struggled with this and was sometimes even wrong in his decisions about how to handle complex ritual situations. In one passage Zengzi asks Confucius about transporting the body of the deceased during an eclipse. Under normal circumstances, the funeral procession only took place during the day. But during an eclipse, day seems to turn into night. Zengzi wonders, therefore, if continuing the procession during an eclipse constitutes a failure in competency;

> Zengzi asked, "[If] during the burial rites, [the funeral procession] reaches the path to the burial ground and there is an eclipse, should [the procession] deviate [from the ritual script] or not?"
>
> 曾子問曰：「葬引至於堩，日有食之，則有變乎？且不乎？」
>
> Confucius responded, "I was previously assisting Lao Dan in the burial rites [for someone] in the village of Xiangdang, and upon reaching the path to the burial ground there was an eclipse. Lao Dan remarked, 'Confucius, stop the procession and move the right side of the road. We will stop there and wail—waiting for [things to] change.' When it was light again, we proceeded. [Lao Dan] explained, 'This is the proper ritual practice.' After returning from the burial I said to him, 'Once a funeral procession has begun it should not stop. In the event of an eclipse, we do not know how long it will last, so is it not better to continue [the procession]?' Lao Dan replied, 'When the feudal lords are going to meet the emperor at court, they travel while the sun is out. After it has set, they stop at their place of

lodging and offer up sacrifice. When ministers are on a mission they travel while the sun is out; and after it has set, they stop at their place of lodging and offer up sacrifice. The funeral procession, [on the other hand], does not set out in the morning or lodge anywhere in the evening; indeed, only criminals and those rushing home to perform the funerary rites for their parents travel while the stars can be seen. In the event of an eclipse, how does one know whether the stars will come out?'"

孔子曰：「昔者吾從老聃助葬於巷黨，及堩，日有食之，老聃曰：『丘！止柩，就道右，止哭以聽變。』既明反而后行。曰：『禮也。』反葬，而丘問之曰：『夫柩不可以反者也，日有食之，不知其已之遲數，則豈如行哉？』老聃曰：『諸侯朝天子，見日而行，逮日而舍奠；大夫使，見日而行，逮日而舍。夫柩不蚤出，不莫宿。見星而行者，唯罪人與奔父母之喪者乎？日有食之，安知其不見星也？』」[30]

In this passage, Zengzi learns that a funeral procession should not proceed during an eclipse. It is interesting to note that rather than directly answering Zengzi's question, Confucius provides an elaborate retelling of how he came to learn this lesson. For our purposes here, this account is noteworthy because it describes Confucius's initial decision to continue the procession during the eclipse—a decision he discovers is inappropriate. While he passes on the correct teaching to Zengzi, it is rooted in his attempt to mis-perform the rite in an earlier context. In that circumstance, the novelty of the situation threatened the success of the ritual, and Confucius responded inappropriately. Fortunately, Lao Dan was present to correct him.[31] Several similar passages that depict the shortcomings of Confucius appear in the *Liji*.[32] The point they make is clear—Confucius is capable of error, and even he struggles to make sense of ambiguous situations where ritual must be performed.

The idea that even sages sometimes fail to navigate the complexities of ritual practice does not only appear in the "Zengzi Wen" chapter. The "Zhongyong" 中庸 chapter actually states it more explicitly. The difficulty of achieving fluent ritual performance, spoken of in terms of *zhongyong* 中庸 (literally, "poise in all the activities of daily life"), is reiterated throughout the chapter. The reader is told, for instance, how rare it is that people actually achieve this kind of fluency (*min xiannengjiuyi* 民鮮能久矣). The text even explains that "all the states under heaven could be pacified; honors and awards could be declined; the weapons [of enemies] could be trampled on; yet fluency is not necessarily attained" 天下國家可均也，爵祿可辭也，白刃可蹈也，中庸不可能也.[33] Later, the text confronts the issue more directly and states that "there are things that even a sage does not know" 雖聖人亦有所不知焉 and "things that even a sage cannot do" 雖聖人亦有所不能焉.[34] Sages, these passages reveal, will not attain perfect fluency. There will always be situations that a sage—even a sage as great as Confucius—cannot fathom.

Theoretically, this may not be a large problem for contemporary interpreters such as Harbsmeier. It may very well be the case that, ultimately speaking, all problematic situations are resolvable. However, practically speaking this creates a significant problem for these contemporary interpreters. Not even a sage will be able to untangle the messiness of every situation. While it might be possible to escape a world of ambiguity, and while this might even happen quite often (although the "Zhongyong" chapter expresses the rarity of such an event), we cannot ignore the inevitability that we will sometimes succumb to the extremities of complication. Confucius almost always recognized the difference between preventable and unpreventable failures in ritual. Human beings in the process of self-cultivation likewise tend to recognize this difference. However, it is erroneous to think that either Confucius or human beings striving to be like Confucius will be able to consistently recognize a distinction between those failures that are in their control and those failures that are beyond their control.

Indeed, as the next section will discuss, there are many agencies that impinge on the performance of ritual. Determining where the power of one agent ends and another begins is a struggle that not even Confucius consistently overcame. The cultivated self, which advocates of the inward turn attempt to place solely within the control of the individual, is permeated in these ambiguous situations. The ambiguity of ritual failure is thereby made known—a failure can occur and leave one wondering whether or not one could have done something more to prevent it.

Impinging Agencies

The ambiguity between preventable and unpreventable failures is tied to issues of agency—who or what has control over the success of ritual? The previous chapters of this project alluded to the notion that there are multiple parties contributing to the success or failure of any given rite. It is sometimes unclear as to where one party's agency ends and another's begins.[35]

I will call this opacity between the parties that have power to determine the success of ritual 'the ambiguity of impinging agencies.' This issue is raised throughout the *Liji*. One particular passage from the "Tangong Shang" chapter illustrates this well. In this vignette, the grandson of Confucius, Zisi, experiences the passing of his mother and is warned about the number of people watching him to critique his performance of the funerary rites. It reads,

> Zisi's mother died in Wei and Liu Ruo said to him, "As a descendant of a sage [i.e., Confucius] the four corners of the world will be watching how you observe these rites. You should be cautious."
>
> 子思之母死於衛，柳若謂子思曰：「子，聖人之後也，四方於子乎觀禮，子蓋慎諸。」
>
> Zisi responded, "Why should I be cautious? I have heard that if there is an occasion for a rite, yet the material for it is lacking, the profound person does not carry it out. And if there is an occasion for a rite, and the material is present but the timing for it is wrong, the profound person does not carry it out. Why should I be cautious?"
>
> 子思曰：「吾何慎哉？吾聞之：有其禮，無其財，君子弗行也；有其禮，有其財，無其時，君子弗行也。吾何慎哉！」[36]

Zisi's response to the warning offered by Liu Ruo is that the performance of ritual depends on things other than his ability to competently enact the rite. If the proper materials were lacking or the timing was wrong, the ritual should not be carried out. While to some observers this may appear as a failure on the part of Zisi, in fact these are things that he has little or no control over; and as such they may lead to a failure of the ritual that is not the fault of Zisi.

This passage is significant for several reasons. First of all, it demonstrates the ambiguity present for at least the observers of the ritual event. The world is watching Zisi, yet an unsuccessful performance of the ritual may or may not be the fault of Zisi. There are several other factors beyond the control of Zisi that contribute to the success or failure of the rite. More importantly, this passage specifies some of these factors. Besides the performer, there are other things that determine the success of the performance. In this case, Zisi mentions the notions of material (*cai* 財) and timing (*shi* 時). Both of these were explored in greater detail in chapter 4 in terms of threats to the fluency of ritual agents. That chapter demonstrated that ritual scripts often failed to take into account the differing wealth of ritual performers or the context of the event (both the temporal and spatial context), among other things. Fluent agents, that chapter argued, are often able to alter the ritual script to account for these adaptations and ensure the success of the rite. As it relates here, things such as wealth and timing do more than contribute to the creation of a new ritual script. They turn out to be not only determinative of the context of the ritual, but also the success of the ritual itself. This is to say that Zisi is claiming that flaws or failures in the funerary rites of his mother are not entirely under his control. The ritual is vulnerable to agencies beyond the person of Zisi, and in a sense these powers have command over the ritual event.

The vulnerability of ritual is stressed throughout the *Liji*. Chapter 4 highlighted a number of these 'threats' to the success of ritual. Ritual performances are vulnerable to threats such as death, political usurpation, and natural disasters. Rather than rehearsing what was already covered in chapter 4, this section will approach the notion of threats from the perspective of vulnerability. The success of ritual, it turns out, is often contingent on factors beyond the control of the ritual performer. These factors may be things such as the sociopolitical climate of the state, the death of people in one's social circle, or, as we will see in the next chapter, the cosmic forces that control things such as rain.

Throughout the *Liji*, the agencies of other people play a significant role in determining the success of ritual. These examples are especially important because early Confucian texts are often criticized for discounting the agency of certain groups of people such as the populace of the state. Interpreters have contended that people under the influence of the profound person and his rituals—to draw from the imagery used in the *Analects*—bend like grass before the wind.[37] The populaces of the state, in this view, are merely subject to the whim of the virtuous power of the ruler. Ritual, as such, is a means of social control.

Contrary to this view, the "Fangji" 坊記 chapter continually stresses the power of the populace to resist even the perfect performance of ritual. Since several of these examples were discussed in chapter 5, I will only mention two new passages here.

> The Master explained, "[In showing] reverence, ritual implements and sacrifices are employed. As such, the profound person will not

do away with a rite in situations where [food] is meager or in situations where [food] is lavish. When food is employed in ritual, the guest will offer [a portion of it] in sacrifice if the host of the rite provides the food; but if the host does not provide the food, the guest does not offer sacrifice. This is why the profound person will not eat the food of a ritual—regardless of how lavish it is—if it is not in accord with the ritual script. . . . All these things show people [the proper course of action]; [however,] people will still fight amongst themselves for economic profit and forget what is proper."

子云：「敬則用祭器。故君子不以菲廢禮，不以美沒禮。故食禮：主人親饋，則客祭；主人不親饋，則客不祭。故君子苟無禮，雖美不食焉。。。以此示民，民猶爭利而忘義。」[38]

The Master explained, "Ascending the stairs to receive guests and accepting their condolences in the proper place is meant to teach people to seek after filial piety. Not being called 'Governor' until after the mourning [for one's father] is complete is meant to show people how not to be contentious. . . . All these things are meant to channel people [in the proper direction]; [however,] there will still be sons that murder their fathers."

子云：「升自客階，受弔於賓位，教民追孝也。未沒喪不稱君，示民不爭也。。。。以此坊民，子猶有弒其父者。」[39]

The ruler sets the example. He is the standard for the state. At the same time, he could follow the ritual script in every instance, and attempt to ensure that those in his court do likewise; yet despite his best attempts, the populace could still go astray and lead the state into chaos. The rituals of the state are vulnerable to the people of the state. What we see in this passage is that performing a ritual is partially about taking a risk. The success of the ritual is contingent on the agency of others that make up our social world. We can engage in ritual practice, but we cannot guarantee that the ritual will succeed. Other powers, and in particular other people, can determine the success of our rituals.

These passages from the "Fangji" chapter depict the relationship between the ruler and the populace. At several places in the *Liji*, the ruler is described as the father and mother of the people in a state. In a broader context, the *Liji* expresses the notion that relationships are necessary for ordering the world. In the "Daxue" 大學 chapter, for instance, the world cannot be pacified until the family unit is in accord. The good life, according to the "Daxue" chapter, does not end at the rectification of the self—one must move beyond the self to organize the family (*qiqijia* 齊其家) and order the state (*zhiqiguo* 治其國); only then will the world be at peace (*tianxiaping* 天下平).[40] The idea expressed throughout the *Liji* is that relationships are essential to self-development, but at the same time relationships also leave oneself open to the agency of the other in the relationship. To state it succinctly, the self as a relational self is also a vulnerable self. Since ritual is often performed through these relationships and for the sake of these relationships, ritual performance entails trusting those in the relationship to carry out their role. Ritual, in this sense, always brings with it a blind spot in the shape of the agency of the other. At any moment of the ritual, those involved in the ritual could choose to perform otherwise. While the fluent agent may often be able to minimize the impact of the flawed performance, there are times when this leads to the complete failure of the ritual. The lesson revealed in the *Liji* is that involvement with other people is both a necessary and a contingent affair. Other people constitute essential elements of a meaningful life, yet by implication they have a degree of latitude in determining that meaning. The proper performance of ritual and the cultivation of the self are not individual achievements; neither can they be regulated to a personal arena where only one person has the power to shape them. Ritual performance and the success of ritual is a community affair.

The Fruits of Ambiguity

In a passage quoted above, Zisi explains that factors outside his control contribute to the success or failure of the funerary rites for his mother. After being warned about the number of people monitoring his performance of these rituals, he replies with a question, "Why should I be cautious" 吾何慎哉? From Zisi's view, factors such as the materials necessary for the ritual, and the geographical and chronological situation of the event, dictate the success of the ritual. If the materials are lacking and the ritual is not carried out, it is not necessarily the fault of Zisi. The possibility of unpreventable failures in ritual provides ritual agents with an escape clause—the world is simply a place where, regardless of one's fluency, failure is sometimes inevitable. Indeed, it is possible for these early Confucians to do the best they can; yet be bound for failure.

The fact that other agencies impinge on the successful performance of ritual is both a cause of concern and a solace of relief for those invested in the outcome of ritual. It is a cause for concern for ritual performers because these agencies can at any time take control of the ritual event. In the case of Zisi, it is a solace of relief because failures in ritual are not necessarily his fault. The ambiguity between the various agencies determining the success or failure of ritual facilitates this solace. It creates what can be called a sense of "plausible deniability." In other words, utilizing the fact that observers cannot clearly recognize how other agencies contribute to the success of a ritual, the ritual agent can claim that any successful performance is a result of his own prowess. At the same time, utilizing the fact that observers cannot clearly recognize how the agency of the ritual performer contributes to the failure of a ritual, the ritual agent can ascribe any dysfunctional ritual to factors beyond his control. The ritual performer finds safety in the vagueness of competing ritual agencies.

Preserving the ambiguity between ritual agencies can benefit both the performers of a ritual as well as the observers of a ritual by masking the power relations at play in the ritual event. For the latter, this ambiguity serves as a means to check the power of ritual performers—since the fault of a dysfunctional ritual does not readily present itself, failure provides an opportunity to call into question the competency of the ritual performer. Ritual performers, in this sense, are held accountable for every performance.[41] The following passage from the "Tangong Shang" chapter illustrates this in part:

> Superintendent Ben asked Ziyou, "May I dress the deceased on the couch?"
>
> 司士賁告於子游曰：「請襲於牀。」
>
> Ziyou replied, "You may."
>
> 子游曰：「諾。」
>
> When Xianzi heard this he said, "What is Ziyou doing! He makes it his personal responsibility to permit people [to perform variations of] ritual!"
>
> 縣子聞之曰：「汰哉叔氏！專以禮許人。」[42]

In this passage, Ziyou gives Superintendent Ben permission to vary from the ritual script, which dictates the place for dressing the deceased. From Ziyou's perspective, the ritual script has failed and he makes the necessary rendition to accommodate the situation. It is not evident, however, that such a change was necessary. Indeed, the ambiguity of the situation allows Xianzi to challenge the authority of Ziyou. He, at least implicitly, demands some kind of reason for the alteration. The fact that failures in the ritual script do not readily present themselves places Xianzi in a position to question the fluency of Ziyou—the passage calls for a response to the question of *why* Ziyou agreed to the change.[43] More generally speaking, in terms of the kinds of alterations a ritual performer can make to a ritual script, the ritual performer is constrained by the persuasiveness of the reasons he provides. Alterations are accountable in the sense that ritual performers can be corralled into providing reasons for their changes. Through this process, the ritual performer is compelled into dialogue with the others parties interested in the outcome of ritual. As far as this particular passage is concerned, it is interesting to note that commentators are deeply divided as to who is right.[44]

Summarily speaking, this ambiguity functions as a means of curbing the power *of* ritual performers by demanding that they be competent. It also functions as an escape clause *for* ritual performers by allowing them to argue for the reality of unpreventable failures in efficacy. Early Confucians as ritual performers could, in this light, render this ambiguity fruitful by attempting to take credit for successful situations and avoid blame in dysfunctional situations. The same ambiguity that allows for challenging their power to perform and modify ritual also holds the potential to consolidate their authority. In many of these ambiguous situations, the ambiguity between impinging agencies may even be resolvable, but the usefulness ambiguity provides may also mean that no one wants to resolve it.

Conclusion

In this early Confucian view, living a meaningful life is partially predicated on our ability to control or shape that life. The agencies that impinge on this life both facilitate and challenge our ability to create it. Whether these agencies take the shape of the natural world, political opportunity, or familial relationships, they are always at least partially unknown and undiscovered. The point where the agency of these parties begin and our agency ends is sometimes ambiguous. As such, the success or failure of ritual events will always, at least to a certain extent, remain beyond our power to control and beyond our power to know. Since these rituals contribute to a meaningful life, this meaningful life is vulnerable to these agencies and to the ambiguity associated with them. As shown in this chapter, this ambiguity functions as both a source of anxiety as well as a source of plausible deniability in situations of dysfunctional ritual. Ambiguities in the failure of ritual mean that failures are both no one's fault and yet everyone's fault at the same time.

7

The Ancients Did Not Fix Their Graves

"[T]ragedy must always be a drowning and breaking of the dikes that separate [one from another]...."[1]

THE NARRATIVE LAID out in the "Liyun" 禮運 chapter provides an alternative paradigm with which to interpret the failure of ritual. Rather than viewing dysfunction as the result of incompetencies of the ritual agent, or the lack of fluency on the part of the ritual agent, the "Liyun" chapter argues for the possibility of unpreventable failures in ritual. Since life after the era of Grand Unity necessarily entails dysfunction, even the best efforts of profound people cannot always compensate for the failure of ritual. As such, those living after the period of Grand Unity must not only be open to the possibility of failure, but must also accept the reality of failure. Furthermore, as discussed in the previous chapter, the preventability of failure is sometimes ambiguous—one cannot always tell whether or not the failure of a ritual could have been prevented. One of the most interesting accounts to read in light of this alternative paradigm appears in the "Tangong Shang" 檀弓上 chapter of the *Liji*.

My purpose in analyzing this passage is to build on the claims of the previous chapter that described the difficulty of ritual agents to recognize a distinction between preventable and unpreventable dysfunctions in ritual. Many contemporary scholars have sought to resolve this ambiguity, and as such have neglected alternative readings of the text. In other words, my argument here is that this passage should not be read as *either* a preventable or an unpreventable failure of ritual. Instead, it should be read as a fundamentally ambiguous situation where one must remain open to both possibilities. These contemporary interpreters, in this sense, have marginalized what I consider a tragic reading of early Confucian ritual theory where one finds an inability to distinguish among the various agencies competing for ritual success (or failure), and a dissonance between an expectation of how the world should work and an experience with how the world actually works. More will be said about this tragic reading below.

The passage from the "Tangong Shang" chapter recounts the burial of Confucius's parents in the city of Fang 防. Since it deals with the collapse of their grave (*mubeng* 墓崩), I will refer to it throughout this chapter as 'the Mubeng passage.'

> Upon completing the joint burial [of his parents] in Fang, Confucius remarked, "I have heard it said that the ancients built graves but not burial mounds. But now there is me—one who travels to the north, south, east, and west. [And I] cannot afford to not recognize [the grave]."
>
> 孔子既得合葬於防，曰：「吾聞之：古也墓而不墳；今丘也，東西南北人也，不可以弗識也。」
>
> Thereupon [Confucius] built a mound four feet high. Confucius then left [Fang], with his disciples to eventually follow. Heavy rains fell. [When his disciples] finally caught up, Confucius asked, "Why did you arrive so late?"
>
> 於是封之，崇四尺。孔子先反，門人後，雨甚；至，孔子問焉曰：「爾來何遲也?」
>
> They replied, "The grave at Fang collapsed."
>
> 曰：「防墓崩。」
>
> Confucius did not respond. [They repeated this] three times. Tears welled up and fell freely [from Confucius's eyes]. He [finally] responded, "I have heard that the ancients did not fix their graves."
>
> 孔子不應。三，孔子泫然流涕曰：「吾聞之：古不修墓。」[2]

Graves are not supposed to collapse, especially graves made by those wishing to honor their parents after their death. Something obviously went wrong in the process of conducting the burial rites of Confucius's parents; but *what* went wrong, and *who* (or what) is to blame? If Confucius had done things differently—perhaps in accordance with antiquity—would the grave still have collapsed? Or, is the collapse a matter of circumstances entirely outside of his control?

There are no contemporary interpretations of this passage in the literature on Confucian ethics. As stated in the introduction of this project, other than the "Daxue" 大學 and "Zhongyong" 中庸 chapters, the *Liji* is rarely a part of the discussion in modern Confucian studies.[3] However, given the analysis provided in chapter 3, it is quite clear that some contemporary interpreters would take this passage as an account of a failure in fluency on the part of Confucius. To briefly recapitulate this view, these scholars account for what I have called failures in competency and failures in efficacy. They understand that ritual agents, for a number of reasons, often fall short in following the ritual script (i.e., failures in competency occur). They also understand that there are circumstances where the script must be altered in order for the ritual to succeed (i.e., failures in efficacy occur). Lastly, they recognize that cultivating the ability to properly deviate from a ritual script is no easy task. Ritual agents, in other words, can fail to perform fluently.

All of the failures accounted for by these interpreters are preventable failures of ritual. If the ritual agent is competent (possessing skill and knowledge in performing ritual) and is fluent (altering ritual scripts in situations where the scripts are inadequate), ritual tends not to fail. These contemporary interpreters also account for the fact that the authors of Confucian texts were aware that some failures are unpreventable. Agents with more power than the ritual agent can sometimes exercise that power, causing the ritual to fail, with no fault on the part of the ritual agent. In these circumstances, scholars such as Edward Slingerland, Philip J. Ivanhoe, and Mark Csikszentmihalyi advocate what I called 'the inward turn.' In this view, ritual agents clearly understand the successes that lie within their control and those that lie beyond their control. When faced with a failure beyond their control they "joyful[ly] accept . . . all that life may bring."[4] This joy, following Slingerland, is predicated on a "realistic and mature redirection of human energy toward the sole area of life in which one does have control—the cultivation and moral improvement of one's own self."[5] By turning inward and recognizing that which is out of the control of the ritual agent, the frustration of failure is alleviated and one enters a state where "genuine quandaries cannot arise."[6] "This inner state," according to Yu Jiyuan, "cannot be destroyed by misfortunes." Yu continues, "An excellent person enjoys peace of mind and experiences no worries, fear and inner conflict."[7] Unpreventable failures, in this reading, while providing a context for the process of self-cultivation, are not significant factors in the process of self-cultivation since they are readily recognizable as failures that are not the fault of the moral agent.

The notion of an inward turn is a dominant paradigm among contemporary interpreters. In contrast to this, this chapter will show that unpreventable failures of ritual were causes of concern for the authors of early Confucian texts because they believed that meaningful aspects of life were vulnerable to these failures, and because they found themselves occasionally unable to recognize a clear distinction between preventable and unpreventable failures of ritual. Those that advocate an inward turn are flawed in seeking to make human flourishing, self-cultivation, or joy invulnerable to agencies beyond the ritual agent. Their move is predicated on resolving the ambiguity between preventable and unpreventable dysfunctions in ritual. This is not to say that their accounts are complete misreadings of the texts—I am, of course, speaking about the *Liji*, whereas most other contemporary scholars are writing about the *Analects*, *Mencius*, or *Xunzi*; and as such I remain open to the possibility that there are significant differences between these texts. Rather, my claim is that the paradigm they have chosen to interpret the texts precludes the possibility that unpreventable dysfunctions in ritual play a role in the ethical life of early Confucians (other than, of course, learning to accept fate beyond one's control). If, following Ivanhoe, "[t]he joy of a given act marks it as right" or, following Slingerland, "[t]he aspiring gentleman focuses on what is under his control (self-cultivation), and consigns the rest to fate," there is no possibility that the virtuous agent might choose a right action but be left with lasting despair, or that he might be confronted with failure and be unable to untangle the agencies involved.[8] Rather than seeking to preserve the ambiguity and productive tension sometimes latent in a dysfunctional situation, they seek to resolve these ambiguities for the sake of providing a precise description of the process of moral reasoning. Their readings of the texts are not equipped to account for the possibility that early Confucians often saw a tragic world—tragic in the sense that the line between agency and fate can be compromised—and that the "right" choice is not always obvious, even for a sage.

The Collapse as a Preventable Failure

Reading the Mubeng passage in light of the inward turn means that Confucius's attempt to give his parents a joint burial failed either because Confucius mis-performed the ritual, or that he had yet to "talk himself out of his initial feeling of distress" when confronted with an unpreventable failure of the ritual.[9] If it is the former, then Confucius's vulnerability is his own fault—he should have better recognized a situation that called for following the ritual script. If it is the latter, then Confucius's vulnerability is only temporary—Confucius will learn to accept the failure and feel a renewed sense of joy in his own moral development in light of the failure. In either case, the truly cultivated person is invulnerable to external agencies.

There are a number of reasons to read the Mubeng passage as Confucius's mis-performance of the burial rites. Primary among these reasons is the fact that "antiquity" (*gu* 古), as discussed throughout this project, usually refers to an ideal time period in early human history where the world was perfectly ordered and ruled by sage-kings. As such, the practices and rituals of antiquity have, at the very least, normative implications for future generations. Confucius, in recognizing that he is straying from the script of antiquity in building a burial mound, foreshadows the failure of the ritual.

Other passages in the same chapter of the *Liji* also explain that the practice of joint burial (*hezang* 合葬) was not done in antiquity. One of these passages reads,

> Ji Wuzi built a house where the tomb of the Du family happened to be located at the bottom of the western stairs. [Someone from the Du family] asked him for permission to perform a joint burial [in the tomb]. [Ji Wuzi] granted them permission. However, upon entering his residence they did not dare to wail. [Seeing this] Ji Wuzi remarked, "Joint burials are not of antiquity. From the time of the Duke of Zhou onward, [however], no one has changed [back to the practice of antiquity]. How could I permit this grand [deviation from antiquity], but not a minor one?" [He then] ordered them to wail.
>
> 季武子成寢，杜氏之葬在西階之下，請合葬焉，許之。入宮而不敢哭。武子曰：「合葬非古也，自周公以來，未之有改也。吾許其大而不許其細，何居？」命之哭。[10]

In this passage, the practice of joint burial is described as being contrary to antiquity and originating with, or at least not changing since, the Duke of Zhou.[11] The Du family requests permission to perform a joint burial at Ji Wuzi's residence, and after receiving permission they proceed with the funerary rites. At first they engage in these rites without wailing, due to the fact that the rites took place at Ji Wuzi's home. Ji Wuzi, realizing that they are not wailing, orders them to wail on the basis that wailing at his residence is a minor infraction of the ritual script compared with performing a joint burial, which had already been permitted.

While this passage is difficult to interpret, two rather clear points emerge from it that relate to the discussion on the Mubeng passage. First, the practice of joint burials, although supposedly done for centuries, still had an ambivalent place in the historical context of this passage. Despite the fact that the Duke of Zhou seems to authorize, or even have started, the practice of joint burials, there still existed some unease over the rite. It is seen as a permissible, but perhaps not a preferable practice. In other words, while performing a joint burial was not de facto improper, one would be better off following the ritual script provided by antiquity. Second, and this relates to the first point, joint burials are considered "great" deviations from antiquity.

This passage, which appears only a few lines before the Mubeng passage in the "Tangong Shang" chapter, suggests that when Confucius performed a joint burial for his parents, he was already deviating from the norms of antiquity. Thus, building a mound on top of the grave was a further deviation. In contrast to the Du family whose second infraction (wailing at Ji Wuzi's home) was a minor one that they at first were willing to avoid, Confucius willingly makes a second infraction—building a mound on top of the grave. One can read these passages together to argue that Confucius's second infraction stretches beyond the bounds of permissibility. To use a contemporary idiom, he was already on thin ice by performing a joint burial. Building a mound in addition to the joint burial puts even more weight on the ice; and, as evident by the collapse of the grave, the ice could not sustain such weight. In the Mubeng passage, Confucius goes too far beyond the norms of antiquity in performing a joint burial and then constructing a mound on top of the grave. The ritual fails because the ancients knew better; thus, they did not have to fix their graves.

The notion of "excess," or *guo* 過, is a common problem for human beings as described in the *Liji*. As discussed in chapter 1, part of the purpose of ritual is to restrain the excesses of human beings. Without being deeply immersed in the ritual tradition, people constantly make mistakes. The compound *guocuo* 過錯, implying a notion of "excess," is, coincidentally, the modern word usually translated as "mistake." These mistakes in the context of the *Liji* often take the form of excessive demonstrations of untaught disposition (*qing* 情). The Mubeng passage can be read as an example of the excessiveness of Confucius. While he had a natural desire to remember his parents and therefore to recognize their grave, he allowed this desire to exceed proper practice by enacting a joint burial and then constructing a burial mound. Several classical interpreters actually interpret the Mubeng passage in precisely this light. What happens in the Mubeng passage, according to their view, is that Confucius lets his emotions get the best of him.

The description of Confucius's tears "flowing forth" (*liu* 流) implicitly supports this reading. As also discussed in chapter 1, water, and water-related objects, are central metaphors used to explain the function of ritual. In particular, dikes (*fang* 坊) as metaphors for ritual are meant to curb the flow of wild water—which is often described as *liu* 流 throughout the *Liji*. Confucius's free-flowing tears, as such, can be read as a further sign of his unrestrained emotion. Similar to the way in which turbulent water spills beyond the banks of a waterway, Confucius's emotion spills beyond the bounds of proper action. This passage, therefore, depicts the misfortune of those who allow their dispositions to become excessive.

It is worth pointing out that some classical commentators read the Mubeng passage as an example of a failure that was Confucius's fault. Du You of the Tang Dynasty, for instance, explains that the final line of the Mubeng passage—"the ancients did not fix their graves"—was a kind of self-critique made on the part of Confucius:

> "In saying that the ancients did not fix their graves, [Confucius] meant that [the ancients] originally built [their graves] such that [they] did not collapse, and did not need to be fixed.... But in this case [the grave] collapsed and was fixed. This is why [he offered] this critique.... The Master said this in order to praise antiquity and upbraid himself."

> 言古不修墓者，謂本不崩，無所修。。。今崩而後修，故譏焉。。。夫子言此者，稱古以責躬也。[12]

Du You's position is that Confucius realized that he made a mistake in constructing a tomb unlike the tombs constructed in antiquity. Because he built a mound on top of the tomb, the tomb was subject to collapse. The tomb that Confucius built required that it be fixed. The last line in the Mubeng passage—"I have heard that the ancients did not fix their graves" 吾聞之：古不修墓—in essence, is a lament for deviating from antiquity. The ancients knew how to construct sturdy graves. In adding to the practices of the ancients, Confucius weakened the grave of his parents. Confucius sheds tears of remorse for his inappropriate actions that lead to the desecration of his parent's grave.

Classical commentators interpret the minutia of this passage a multitude of different ways. Since much of this only indirectly bears on the issue of preventability, I will not go into detail except to note some of the general features of their disagreements.[13] Most commentators explain that Confucius left Fang to perform the *yu* 虞 sacrifice—a ritual done at the conclusion of burial. His disciples remained in Fang to finish the burial mound. A major point of disagreement occurs over the disciples' response when asked why they were so late in catching up to Confucius. The line is three characters long—*fangmubeng* 防墓崩. The point of disagreement between classical scholars is how to understand the first character in the phrase, *fang* 防. One could read *fang* 防 as a pronoun taking the line to mean, "The grave at Fang collapsed." Or it could be read as a verb: "[We were] preventing the grave from collapsing." At stake here is the issue of whether or not an unfilial calamity such as the collapse of the grave of Confucius's parents really occurred. Reading *fang* 防 as a verb precludes this possibility. Most classical commentators take this route in an effort to preserve Confucius's filiality and avert his involvement in the desecration of his parents' bodies. In this reading, the grave does not fully collapse, but rather the heavy rains threaten to collapse the grave and Confucius's disciples prevent it from caving in. An alternative position, which likewise seeks to preserve Confucius's filiality, advocates reading *fang* 防 as a pronoun, but argues that the burial mound was not on top of the grave; rather, it was next to the grave. Hence, what collapses is not the grave itself but the mound next to it.

The argument over how to understand *fangmubeng* 防墓崩 relates to disagreements about how to make sense of the last line in the passage—"I have heard that the ancients did not fix their graves" 吾聞之：古不修墓. There are two dominant interpretations of this line. One interpretation takes this line to mean that the ancients did not need to fix their graves.

Unlike Confucius who performed a joint burial and built a mound on top of the grave, the ancients built graves differently. They built them such that they did not collapse. Contrary to the grave built by Confucius that required maintenance, the graves of antiquity were well-constructed graves. This line is therefore a lament over the extra work required as a result of deviating from antiquity—Confucius's choices led him on a path that continues to diverge from the way of the ancients.

The second interpretation takes this line literally: the ancients, if ever confronted with a collapsed grave, did not fix it. They simply left the grave as it was. The significance of either of these views, as it relates to this project, is that the latter shifts the full blame of failure from Confucius to include his disciples. Confucius, in other words, was not necessarily wrong to perform a joint burial or erect a burial mound; instead, the major failure was in fixing the grave after it collapsed. The ancients did not fix their graves, and neither should Confucius. Hence, if this was Confucius's fault at all, it was in trusting his disciples to know that a collapsed grave should not be fixed. Confucius's tears, therefore, are primarily a lament for the mistakes made by his disciples. This view is, of course, problematic because it allows for some alterations of antiquity (i.e., the joint burial and construction of the burial mound), but does not explain why others are not allowed (i.e., fixing the grave after it collapses). Classical commentators, however, tend to latch onto it because, for the most part, it avoids the problem of explaining how someone so "grand" as Confucius could fail. The ritual fails, in this view, because Confucius's disciples are incompetent.

Classical commentators also discuss whether or not this event actually occurred. Those who take the Mubeng passage as fiction point out that Confucius's mother died when he was seventeen years old—many years before he had students and disciples. Other commentators respond to this argument with the explanation that the event must have taken place many years after the death of his mother. In this sense, it was a reburial.[14]

What we see in reading the Mubeng passage as a preventable failure is a Confucius who inappropriately alters the script of antiquity. Rather than simply following the ritual script, Confucius changes it in order to recognize the grave when he returns from his travels. It turned out, however, that the difficulty of recognizing the grave without a mound was an insufficient reason to vary from the norms of antiquity. Confucius weeps, therefore, because he realizes that he in fact failed to properly perform the ritual.

The Collapse as an Unpreventable Failure

The Mubeng passage can also be understood as an unpreventable failure in the burial rites of Confucius's parents. In this reading, Confucius is not at fault for the collapse of the grave. Instead, the situation is the inevitable result of rituals that are incapable of perfectly achieving their purported ends. Confucius cries, therefore, not because he regrets breaking from the norms of antiquity, but because he realizes (or perhaps is reminded) that such a break is necessary; and despite the fact that that the norms of his time are created by the sagely founders of the dynasty, they are still capable of failure regardless of what he does. The difference between antiquity and the era of Confucius is that in the time of Confucius, ritual is vulnerable to failure.

I noted above that other portions of the "Tangong Shang" chapter explain that joint burials were not practiced in antiquity. In the Mubeng passage, Confucius claims that burial mounds were not constructed in antiquity. Following the interpretation provided above, these were taken as signs of Confucius varying from the ritual script, for the script dictated that in accordance with antiquity neither joint burials nor burial mounds should be part of proper funerary rituals. The ritual fails, therefore, because Confucius mishandles the situation, misunderstanding it as one where varying from the script, or rewriting it, is permissible. Using the terminology developed in this project, this view understands the Mubeng passage as an example of a failure in fluency.

The practice of joint burials, while taken as a "great" deviation from antiquity, was also explained in the "Tangong Shang" chapter as originating with the Duke of Zhou. This casts the normative power of antiquity throughout the "Tangong Shang" chapter, and the *Liji* as a whole, in a perplexing light. The Duke of Zhou, at least in this case, endorsed deviating from the practices of antiquity. Other vignettes in the *Liji* also cast the Duke of Zhou as a primary figure involved with breaking from the rituals of the past.[15] When read in conjunction with the praise the Duke of Zhou receives in the "Mingtangwei" 明堂位 chapter of the *Liji*, the Duke of Zhou is portrayed as one who collected and preserved the rituals of the past that were relevant for the Zhou Dynasty—casting aside or modifying the less relevant rituals. The ambivalence, however, of breaking from antiquity is preserved in many of these vignettes.

The normative power of antiquity is also questioned when other texts such as the *Zhouli* 《周禮》—a text purported to record the ritual prescriptions of the Zhou Dynasty—prescribe constructing burial mounds for the graves of the Zhou aristocracy. While dating the *Zhouli* and the *Liji* is complex, the fact that both texts prescribe a set of practices different from earlier dynasties is a recognized fact, even within the texts themselves. In this sense, the *Zhouli* coheres with the descriptions of preventable dysfunctions provided in chapter 4. The authors of the text accepted the fact that the rituals of one dynasty would not perfectly follow the rituals of the dynasty that preceded it. Additionally, preventing the failures of the previous dynasty entailed relying on fluent agents who could recognize which rituals were out of step with the times and recreate rituals appropriate for the new era. The founders of the Zhou Dynasty were taken as fluent agents.

As noted in chapter 4, the *Liji* clearly endorses altering ritual scripts according to varying times, places, and other circumstances. It is especially aware of the need to change ritual scripts from one dynasty to the next. While the Zhou Dynasty tends to be praised for integrating the appropriate rituals of the past, it is also praised for creating new ritual scripts needed for its time. This is not to say, however, that the authors of the *Liji* always preferred the rites of the Zhou Dynasty to those of other dynasties. Occasionally the rituals of the Shang and Xia dynasties are given preference above those of the Zhou. The point, adequately demonstrated in chapter 4, is that altering ritual, if done appropriately, is necessary to ensure the continued success of ritual.

The relationship with antiquity, or *gu* 古, is of course more tenuous. There are few examples in the *Liji* that explicitly endorse varying from antiquity. Many more examples condemn it. The vast majority of references to antiquity, however, are ambiguous. As argued in chapter 5, those passages can be taken as descriptions of necessary performances due to the fact that the authors see themselves living in a world after the era of Grand Unity. In other words, straying from antiquity is not by definition bad; nor is it necessarily praiseworthy. But, in order to avoid failure, it must be done. In building on the theories of other scholars such as Michael Puett, there is a deep ambivalence about breaking from antiquity, but there is no other way to create an ordered world.[16] In the terms of the "Liyun" chapter, the era of Grand Unity was ideal in the sense that human society was perfectly in sync with the *dao* 道. However, the continued development of human society entailed a transformation of the self where people began to labor for their own interests. The rituals practiced in the era of Grand Unity became an externalized discourse, rather than the spontaneous practices people naturally performed. In short, ritual became a tradition—one set of ideas and practices in tension and competition with others. Human society, as portrayed in the "Liyun" chapter, will not return to this period of antiquity. It is not that humanity is incapable of returning to it; instead, for many good reasons, human beings will choose to live in a complex world that is dissonant with antiquity. The era of Grand Unity, therefore, is part of the past. Life after the era of Grand Unity necessarily means deviating from antiquity.

In regards to the Mubeng passage, the prescriptions of the *Zhouli* suggest that Confucius could actually have been following the ritual procedures of the Zhou Dynasty in building a burial mound. The relevant prescription reads, "The height of the burial mound should be built according to the rank [of the deceased]" 以爵等為丘封之度.[17] Beginning with the earliest classical commentators, most traditional interpreters have read the Mubeng passage in relation to this passage from the *Zhouli*. In this view, constructing a mound on top of a grave may not have been an appropriate practice in antiquity; however, it became an appropriate practice in the time of the Zhou. Confucius certainly varied from the ritual script of antiquity, but only because the ritual script of his time dictated otherwise.[18]

In this reading, Confucius realizes that following the ritual script in antiquity did not entail constructing burial mounds. However, he also understands that following the ritual script in the Zhou Dynasty is a different affair. The latter not only advocates but also requires building burial mounds. As such, the Mubeng passage does not compare two different ritual practices for the sake of making a judgment about which is orthodox; instead, it asserts that two different ritual scripts are in play—the script of antiquity and the script of the Zhou Dynasty—and for Confucius, the script of the Zhou Dynasty is authoritative.[19] In the time of the former, the appropriate thing to do is to simply build a grave; yet in the time of the latter, the appropriate thing to do is to build a mound on top of the grave. In short, the Mubeng passage depicts a Confucius who believes that he is living in an era divergent from the era of antiquity; and this new era, while in tension with antiquity, has its own legitimate series of practices.

Antiquity, in this view, was a time where simply building a grave was sufficient. Perhaps it can be said that human experience in antiquity was rooted in a stable location. People in this period of time did not need to venture very far from the graves of their ancestors in order to live in a flourishing world. They therefore easily knew where their graves were located. The "past," as such, was grounded, quite literally, in a single location, and people did not need to create additional objects to assist them in remembering this past. In Confucius's time, however, human history and contemporary human experience were ruptured. People of this time period required mediating devices such as burial mounds to assist them in recognizing the past bequeathed to them by their ancestors. Circumstances indeed dictated that Confucius travel the kingdom in an attempt to order the kingdom, but these travels came at a cost. Human beings in a world after antiquity are displaced beings. They lack the same rootedness that existed in antiquity, and therefore, out of necessity, alter the norms of antiquity to maintain a semblance of this rootedness. The burial mound on top of Confucius's parents' grave, therefore, has become a necessary connection to the past.[20] The collapse of the grave, in this light, reflects the inability, or at least the improbability, of ritual to bridge the divide between human history and contemporary human experience.

All of this is to say that Confucius, in the Mubeng passage, was following the norms of his times. He followed the ritual prescriptions of the Zhou Dynasty in performing a joint burial and in constructing a burial mound. In fact, if we take the practices advocated in the *Zhouli* as part of the repertoire of actions Confucius felt obligated to follow, he did everything according to the script. However, in spite of performing the ritual precisely as scripted, the ritual still failed. Confucius, as such, did indeed vary from the norms of antiquity, but only because he was aware that he did not live in antiquity. As a person of the Zhou Dynasty, he followed the rites of the Zhou. Undoubtedly, Confucius understood that ritual served as guides for proper comportment with the *dao* 道. Appropriate performance of a ritual, therefore, created a world of order where human beings existed in proper relation to each other and to the larger world. A world of ritual was a flourishing world. Yet in this case, the rites of the Zhou did not function as promised. Confucius's understanding of the world, and the role of ritual in that world, is shown to be dissonant with his experience in the world. The Mubeng passage, therefore, highlights Confucius's awareness of life after antiquity. He weeps because the collapse of the grave heightens his awareness of this disjuncture and the reality that ritual has become more vulnerable to failure.

When open to the possibility of unpreventable failures in ritual, numerous parts of the Mubeng passage come to life. The location of the event is a prime example. The passage begins with a statement that Confucius completed the joint burial of his parents in a place called Fang 防. Fang was the name of a city in what is now the Shandong province.[21]

The character *fang* 防, however, is also cognate with the character *fang* 坊; and is actually used interchangeably with it in many premodern texts.[22] Both terms imply a sense of protection or prevention. More concretely, they can refer to defense fortifications around a city, or barriers preventing something such as water from moving past a certain point. Chapter 5 provided a detailed look at the use of *fang* 坊 in the *Liji*. It paid particular attention to the fact that *fang* 坊 is a commonly used metaphor for ritual. It also highlighted the refrain in the "Fangji" 坊記 chapter of the *Liji* where, regardless of how well the barriers or dikes were constructed, they still could not prevent the water they channeled from occasionally overflowing its banks. One passage from the "Fangji" chapter, for instance, relates,

> Confucius explained, "Ritual dams up [*fang* 坊] the excessive desire of the people; highlighting their separate [roles], and causing them to be satisfied. [It] acts as the standard of the people. This being the case, men and women do not consort with each other if a matchmaker is not present. Without a gift of betrothal they do not visit each other for fear that the proper separation between men and women will be lost. This serves to channel [*fang* 坊] the people [in the right direction]. However there will still be people who [go contrary to this and] offer themselves [to the opposite sex]."
>
> 子云：「夫禮，坊民所淫，章民之別，使民無嫌，以為民紀者也。故男女無媒不交，無幣不相見，恐男女之無別也。以此坊民，民猶有自獻其身。」[23]

Ritual, which is meant to "channel" the excessive desire of human beings, can sometimes be overpowered. *Fang* 坊 as a metaphor for ritual is consistent with the notion that ritual occasionally fails to achieve its ends. In this case, ritual is meant to curb the excessive desire of human beings; yet, for a number of reasons, this does not always occur.

It is interesting to consider the possibility that the city of Fang was named after the prominence of dikes or waterways in the area. As such, the opening line of the Mubeng passage, which was translated above as "Confucius completed the joint burial [of his parents] in Fang" 孔子既得合葬於防, can also be rendered, "Confucius completed the joint burial [of his parents] next to a dike."[24] This reading can also be buttressed by the appearance of water in the passage. The reader is told that heavy rains fell and caused the grave to collapse. The notion of rains falling and water levels rising above the embankments of a dike is consistent with depictions of dikes throughout the *Liji*. The idea here is that the grave, being constructed next to a dike, was also susceptible to the overflow of the dike. The grave collapses, in other words, because the dike failed to hold back the water.

What we see in this interpretation of the Mubeng passage is the metaphorical become literal. Ritual is like a waterway or a dike because it curbs untaught disposition and channels it in a useful direction, similar to the way in which a dike channels and controls water. Dikes, however, sometimes fail, and so do rituals. In the Mubeng passage, rather than ritual being seen *as* a dike, the ritual itself is part of the dike. In this passage, ritual and dikes come to inhabit the same world. Metaphor and the concrete world intersect at the point of failure. Dysfunction, in this vignette, demonstrates the relationship between ideas and material objects in an early Confucian world-view. Material objects such as dikes are physically part of the landscape of a moral world.

Rhetorically speaking, *fang* 防 serves as an aptronym—the name of the object, in this case a location, 'aptly' describes certain characteristics of the object. *Fang* 防 is both the name of a place as well as a description of the place. Fang, in other words, is a city known for "prevention."[25] Building a grave in the context of a city called Prevention suggests a certain degree of protection granted by the circumstances of the location. Graves in Prevention, therefore, are not expected to collapse. However, consistent with a reading that is open to the possibility of unpreventable failures in ritual, the rituals performed in the context of Prevention will occasionally fail despite the best efforts of the ritual agents. "Prevention," following a contemporary Chinese idiom, is sometimes not enough (*fangbushengfang* 防不勝防).

When Confucius's disciples are asked why they were so late in catching up to Confucius, they respond, "The grave at Fang collapsed" 防墓崩. Many of the classical commentators, as mentioned above, read *fang* 防 in different ways. My suggestion is to interpret this *fang* 防 as an aptronym, where *fang* 防 not only refers to the physical location of the failure but also reveals important characteristics of the location. In this sense, the line would have a double meaning.[26] It would mean both "The grave at Fang collapsed," as well as "The grave in the safe location collapsed." Following this interpretation, Confucius has no response after hearing this statement because he is struck that such a thing could occur in a "safe place."

Confucius's non-response and his tears, only after being told three times of the collapse, highlight his inability to make sense of the failure.

He followed the ritual script, yet the script did not result in creating the world he imagined. He is left, literally, speechless. In chapter 5, I explored how the authors of the *Liji* were suspicious about the ability of language to accurately represent the *dao* 道. In that chapter, I argued that *yan* 言, or spoken language, was seen as precariously related to the *dao* 道. It was not that speech was incapable of representing it, but rather that such a feat could only be done through great difficulty. Chapter 5 also explained that *yan* 言 and *li* 禮 were connected throughout the *Liji* because language was seen as the primary means of transmitting the tradition of ritual. What we see in the Mubeng passage is not only the failure of ritual, but also the failure of language to render a dysfunctional situation intelligible. Where ritual falls short, language is not far behind. Language fails when it loses its explanatory power. Thus, when Confucius first learns that the grave has collapsed, there are no words to make sense of the situation. For the reader, Confucius's silence is meant as a 'screaming silence,' where he can offer no fitting first response. Confucius's second response is to weep. What we see here is a reversion to primal sound. The complexity and subtle nuance of language cannot grasp the reality of the situation. Only sobs and tears convey his perplexity.

The passage explains that "tears welled up and fell from Confucius's eyes" 孔子泫然流涕. Then, finally, he spoke. Confucius's closing comment that the ancients did not fix their graves (*gubuxiumu* 古不修墓) is, in this view, a lament over the failure of the funerary rites. However, it is not a lament of regret because he behaved inappropriately. The failure at Fang was not, in this view, his fault. He knew that he had followed the ritual script of the Zhou. As such, his lament is precisely because he *did* follow the ritual script of the Zhou, yet despite his appropriate behavior the grave still collapsed. Confucius's comprehension of the way the world *should* work collapsed along with the grave.

The Mubeng passage can be seen as a microcosm of Confucius's life in relation to the dissonance between understanding and experience. It is no coincidence that Confucius refers to himself by name, Qiu 丘, in the passage. The character *qiu* 丘 literally means a "hill" or "mound," and is often used explicitly to refer to burial mounds in early Chinese texts. The passage in the *Zhouli*—quoted above—that dictates the practice of burial mounds uses *qiu* 丘 in this very sense. In this case, *qiu* 丘 is another aptronym where two objects with the same name share related characteristics. The burial mound is similar to Confucius, and Confucius is similar to the burial mound.

This insight also prompts an alternative translation of part of the Mubeng passage with significant implications. The line translated originally as "I have heard it said that the ancients built graves but not burial mounds. But now there is me [Qiu 丘]—one who travels to the north, south, east, and west. [And I] cannot afford to not recognize [the grave]," can also be translated as,

> I have heard it said that the ancients built graves but not burial mounds. But now the world is filled with people, and high burial mounds [*qiu* 丘] are constructed so that [a grave] can be recognized.
>
> 吾聞之：古也墓而不墳；今丘也，東西南北人也，不可以弗識也。

Reading the passage in this manner changes Confucius's explanation for building the mound. Rather than needing to recognize the grave after returning from travel, Confucius instead points out the need to recognize the grave in the midst of all the other graves created in a world full of people. In this translation, the need to recognize the one from the many is the driving force behind constructing the mound. More importantly, however, this reading allows the passage to tie into more elements of Confucius's life. Confucius is the hill, meant to stand out and be recognized in a world full people.[27] He perfectly measures up to the ritual performances of his time, yet, for reasons unrelated to his stature, and despite the fact that he is supposedly "protected," he fails to meet his desired end. Confucius, just like the burial mound, crumbles through no fault of his own.

Classical commentators have also read the Mubeng passage as an unpreventable failure of ritual. Jiang Yong (ca. 1800), for instance, in his *Liji Xunyize* 《禮記訓義擇》, states, "It is not the fault of the people involved if the newly built mound collapsed because of heavy rain. As such there is no need to be suspect of either Confucius or his disciples" 若夫新墳之崩由於雨甚，此非人事之咎。不必為門人疑。亦不必為夫子疑.[28] The point here is obvious. The collapse of the grave was neither the fault of Confucius nor his disciples; as such, neither should be blamed.

Contemporary scholars such as Slingerland and Ivanhoe, as mentioned above, also account for unpreventable failures in ritual. In their view, responding to unpreventable failures in ritual is predicated on a clear understanding that the failure was not the fault of the ritual agent. While the initial reaction to such a situation might be "distress" or "doubt," the ritual agent eventually reaches a steadfast resolution. In this view, the happiness of the cultivated person is, at least in the long run, invulnerable to failures beyond their control. The Mubeng passage, therefore, if understood as an unpreventable failure, is a snapshot of Confucius's initial reaction. If the story continued we would see that Confucius was able to "talk himself out of his initial feeling of distress." The position of these contemporary scholars discounts the sorrow of Confucius in the Mubeng passage by means of an inward turn. Confucius's grief, as such, is not enduring. It is only "apparent" or "initial." The *Liji*, however, suggests something quite different. In contrast to the scholars who advocate the inward turn, I have argued that the Mubeng passage can be read in terms of ambivalence—breaking from antiquity is a necessary, yet lamentable, practice because it discontinues the tradition of an idealized past and does not guarantee ritual success. Deviating from antiquity, as such, is an ambivalent event—one cannot be dissuaded from experiencing the anxiety associated with deviation. Equally important, other parts of the *Liji* describe the way in which one's happiness is vulnerable to things such as the death of other people. The passing of one's parents, the "Tangong Shang" chapter explains, should bring about "a lifetime of unease" (*zhongshen zhiyou* 終身之憂).[29] The *Liji* is clear that we are forever penetrated by the death of our loved ones. Their death is real, and shapes us as individuals, oftentimes in ways we cannot completely control. It is not so far to claim, in this light, that Confucius's political failures were real as well. These setbacks were not just apparent points of frustration; rather, they struck him to the core.

Accounting for this vulnerability, however, is not the only problem for those who advocate the inward turn. The other issue is that their view marginalizes an openness to unpreventable failures in ritual by resolving the ambiguity between preventable and unpreventable failures, and thereby neglects the impact of this ambiguity in the moral development of the ritual agent. In other words, contemporary interpreters such as Slingerland and Ivanhoe eliminate the genuine, and uncertain, aspects of reality where the agencies of the individual and the larger world cannot be untangled. These modern scholars soothe the anxiety of the ritual agent by positing that one can know the fault of any given failure. This problem will be addressed below.

The Collapse as a Tragic Moment

Thus far in this chapter, I have provided two readings of the Mubeng passage: One took the passage as a preventable failure where Confucius was at fault for not following the norms of antiquity. The second reading argued that the Mubeng passage can be understood as an unpreventable failure in the ritual—Confucius followed the ritual script of the Zhou Dynasty, and despite his proper performance of the rite, the grave still collapsed. The remaining portion of this chapter will not attempt to mitigate these two views. Instead, I argue that the Mubeng passage indicates that the tension between these views is not resolvable. In other words, the Mubeng passage can be read as asserting a kind of descriptive ambiguity such that it reveals the uncertain and even risky nature of ritual performance. Both preventable and unpreventable failures exist, yet the actors in the passage, the authors of the passage, and the readers of the text often cannot distinguish the agencies involved in the failure. As elaborated below, I consider this a 'tragic' reading of the Mubeng passage.

Much has been said about the possibility, or impossibility, of tragedy as a genre or concept in premodern China. Some scholars presume its existence as a universal phenomenon inherent in human experience, and others exclude its existence on the basis of historically situated roots in the West. I do not intend to enter this debate.[30] Instead, my tragic reading is meant to suggest that the Mubeng passage exhibits characteristics that include a dissonance between an expectation of how the world should work and an experience with how the world actually works, an inability to distinguish among the various agencies competing for self-determination, a resignation to the need to vary from the ideals of the past, an awareness of the possibility of failure when varying from these ideals, and an anxiety born of uncertainty. Many of these themes have already emerged above in the discussion of the Mubeng passage as an unpreventable failure in ritual. I will elaborate on some of them here, but focus on the notion of ambiguity with regards to competing agencies that have the power to determine the success or failure of a ritual performance.

There are many other elements that might mark the Mubeng passage as tragic, including a reversal of fortune (accompanied with a recognition of the reversal), the possibility of a flaw or mistake, and the presence of death in the passage.[31] While the Mubeng passage undoubtedly contains tragic elements, in the end I am less interested if it actually "counts" as tragedy.[32]

The "Liyun" chapter depicts the development of society from a crude and barbaric state to a simple and peaceful state in the era of Grand Unity, then to a more complex, yet flourishing, state in the era of Modest Prosperity. There are a number of developments associated with this account, including differentiated family relationships, the rise of defense fortifications and armies, a growing sophistication of ritual, the rise of thieves and bandits, and a new mode of monarchic succession. In many regards, this is a bittersweet description of the coming forth of humanity. From certain angles it is lamentable, and perhaps no coincidence that the entire chapter begins with a sigh of Confucius after observing a failed ritual. As society forms, points of tension take shape as well. The advent of defense fortifications, while a necessary thing due to the rise of armies, also entails the need to maintain them and continually modify them as the weapons foreign armies bring against them also continue to increase in complexity. Differentiation and development foster further and even more complex differentiation and development; and this entails an ever-growing infrastructure to manage the risk associated with development. More differentiation means more points of potential failure. Ritual plays an important role in this process by both reinforcing the growing number of distinctions (*bianyi* 辨異) as well as controlling (*zhi* 治) the process of differentiation.

As pointed out in chapter 5, classical and contemporary interpreters have viewed the "Liyun" as a text heavily influenced by Daoism. Some interpreters have even discounted it altogether as a "Confucian" text. I will not engage the debate concerning what constitutes a "school" of Daoism or Confucianism in early China. However, I will note that in my reading, the "Liyun" takes the development of human society as a necessary process that entails good and bad results. In other words, contrary to some positions usually classified as "Daoist," the "Liyun" does not view differentiation negatively. It also does not advocate a return to simplicity. It is worth noting that throughout the "Liyun" chapter Confucius makes no effort to reconstruct the rites of antiquity. He recognizes that humanity will not return to an era of Grand Unity. The goal of humanity, therefore, is not to recreate the conditions of simplicity; rather, the goal is to continue to create the tools necessary to enable prosperity. Out of necessity this entails furthering the process of differentiation. Further differentiation is not in itself good, but it *must* occur to further the conditions for a good life. In the context of the "Liyun," part of the transformation of the self that occurs in the transition from the era of Grand Unity to that of Modest Prosperity is the rise of different familial and social relationships. No longer is just anyone from the older generation simply a "father" or "mother"; instead, they are "uncle," "aunt," or even "outsider." Prosperity in this more complex social setting is possible but requires a more sophisticated form of ritual to properly maintain these relationships. When an aunt dies, for instance, one should mourn differently for her than one would for one's mother. Practically speaking, more sophisticated rituals require more sophisticated ritual implements, which in turn requires more sophisticated artisans and tools to make the implements. This leads to an array of skilled and less skilled artisans, which in turn demands a more complex economy to reward the artisans according to their degree of skill.[33] The idea that prosperity is possible yet 'requires,' 'dictates,' or 'demands' a complex response, which then generates a further set of complications, can be restated by saying that only through continued differentiation is prosperity made possible for an ever-growing number of human beings. In this light, it is no coincidence that the *Shuowen Jiezi* 《說文解字》, a dictionary compiled about two hundred years after the *Liji*, glosses "distinction" (*bian* 辨) as "anxiety" (*you* 憂).[34]

Prosperity, in the era of Modest Prosperity, is therefore vulnerable in several respects. Most importantly, prosperity is dependent on the proper performance of ritual. Ritual, however, in this era is susceptible to being usurped, ignored, or otherwise mis-performed. Ritual is no longer something people unreflectively do. Rather, as a named and externalized tradition people could manipulate it, or simply not perform it. Moreover, the growing complexity of ritual entailed an increase in the number of participants required to successfully perform ritual. Each participant relied on the proper performance of the other. The officiator of a ceremony relied on artisans to construct ritual implements in proper dimension and kind, the party sponsoring the ceremony relied on those raising animals to provide them at the right time for the right sacrifice, and those offering sacrifices in the ceremony relied on those arranging the sacrificial area to equip the area with the necessary clothing and ritual instruments. If any of these people failed to properly perform their role, the ritual could fail. Ritual success, in this light, became complicated in the etymological sense of the term "complicate"—the agencies involved in the event are "entangled" or "folded together."[35]

These themes find resonance in the Mubeng passage. Confucius's time is a time of growing complexity. He can no longer remain in one location. Contrary to the time of antiquity, his political obligations now conflict with his filial obligations. Bringing order to the world entails that he travel from north to south and east to west. The necessity of his travels requires that he build a grave covered with a mound so that he can recognize it when he returns and thereby fulfill his filial obligations. This grave is markedly more complex than the graves built in antiquity. Complexity begets complication as this new grave, in contrast with the tombs of antiquity, is capable of collapsing. In order to prevent a collapse, Confucius must employ people to maintain the grave. Similar to the scene depicted in the "Liyun" chapter, the modification of ritual triggers a set of complications that must be attended to. Responding to these complications necessitates confronting the complexity of the situation. Also, more points of complication mean more points of potential failure. One reason Confucius weeps, therefore, is because he confronts the growing complexity of his times. Not only does he deviate from the norms of antiquity in conducting a joint burial and in building a burial mound, but also now he must deviate even further by maintaining the grave—the last line of the Mubeng passage reminds us that the ancients did not need to maintain their graves. There is a certain amount of longing and sorrow associated with distancing oneself even further from antiquity because antiquity was a less vulnerable time, but there is also the realization of the necessity of deviation. To simply follow the norms of antiquity ensures failure. Said another way, humanity must break from the past, but it cannot have complete faith in the new.

Confucius also weeps because the continued differentiation of ritual increases points of possible failure. Rain still fell in antiquity, but there were no mounds to be washed away in antiquity. Constructing a mound in Confucius's time meant exerting additional effort to not only build it, but also to prevent it from collapsing. Confucius must either maintain the grave himself, which would obstruct his travels, or depend on others to maintain the grave for him. The growing sophistication of ritual, as such, also entails an increase in the number of participants. More important, it demands a growing interdependence of the ritual participants. Building a proper grave for his parents in the time of Confucius is not something he could have done alone. Confucius must depend on others to plan, officiate, construct, and maintain the grave. If any of these people are incompetent or lack the fluency to properly perform their role, the ritual could fail. Confucius's successful performance of this ritual is now dependent on the successful performance of his disciples in attending to the mound. Ritual, according to the Mubeng passage, is a contingent affair.

The demands of developing ritual give way to more sophisticated rituals, and more sophisticated rituals turn out to be more vulnerable rituals. These growing points of fragility heighten the risk involved in ritual performance—the larger number of agents involved increase the number of agencies contributing to the event. They also make it more difficult to clearly determine the cause of failure (or success). In short, the complexity of the act obfuscates causality.

As far as the position of scholars such as Slingerland and Ivanhoe is concerned, the inward turn prematurely resolves the anxiety associated with an increase in the number of distinctions in the world. It also reduces the tension between preventable and unpreventable failures in ritual. As a framework of interpretation, it is not equipped to account for the possibility that early Confucians often saw a tragic world—tragic in the sense that the line between agency and fate can be compromised, and that the "right" choice is sometimes obscured by doubt, distress, and a productive anxiety.

In the Mubeng passage, who or what is to blame for the failed ritual is ultimately ambiguous. Is it Confucius's fault for straying from antiquity? Is it the fault of his disciples for fixing a grave that should not have been fixed? Is it the fault of circumstances beyond the control of Confucius and his disciples? These questions are unanswerable, and may be unanswerable for reasons other than the fact that we, living thousands of years later and communicating in a different language, lack further context about the construction of this passage. Reading it with an openness to preventable and unpreventable failures of ritual not only allows us to take the passage at face value, but it also allows us to consider the possibility that early Confucians found this a fruitful reading of the text. In the Mubeng passage, the failure of the ritual is seemingly all Confucius's fault and not his fault at the same time.

8

Productive Anxieties and the Awfulness of Failed Ritual

We dare not attack a tiger [without a weapon], and dare not cross the Yellow River without a boat.
People know this one thing, but not any other.
Be fearful and apprehensive, as if on the brink of a deep abyss, as if treading on thin ice.

不敢暴虎、不敢馮河。
人知其一、莫知其它。
戰戰兢兢、如臨深淵、如履薄冰。[1]

CHAPTER 5 EXPLORED the opening scene of the "Liyun" 禮運 in some detail. That chapter of the *Liji* begins with a sigh of Confucius upon observing the failure of a ritual in his home state of Lu. Hearing this sigh, his disciple, Ziyou, inquired after what was bothering him. Confucius responded with an account of the shift in human civilization from the era of Grand Unity to the era of Modest Prosperity—two utopian time periods in human history. The problem, according to Confucius, is that his contemporary world was incomparable to the greatness of these time periods. His sigh is an expression of angst over the decadence of his day.

As argued in chapter 5, ritual played an important role in the shift from an era of Grand Unity to an era of Modest Prosperity. It also remained the central hope in recreating the conditions of Modest Prosperity in the time of Confucius (and by implication any time period after Confucius). Chapter 7 described this scene from a tragic perspective on ritual where the success of ritual is contingent on multiple agencies, many of which are beyond the control of the individual ritual agent. Chapter 6 highlighted the difficulty of deciphering these agencies—determining where one party's agency ends and another party's agency begins was described as a complicated affair. Ritual performance, in this view, is a performance of risk. It entails rendering oneself vulnerable to the agency of others, and resigning oneself to the need to vary from the successful rituals of past, thereby moving into untested and uncertain territory. This chapter seeks to explore the anxiety associated with these uncertainties. It seeks to explain how Confucians coped with the dissonance between an understanding of ritual where ritual served to construct an ordered world and their experience with ritual as it sometimes failed to bring about such a world. This chapter will demonstrate that the anxiety associated with notions of dissonance and vulnerability functioned 'productively.' In other words, the anxiety associated with the inevitability and ambiguity of ritual failure, as well as the anxiety associated with the contingent nature of successful ritual, generated a profoundly meaningful series of opportunities valued for their creative and therapeutic power.

This notion of anxiety is captured quite well in the "Liyun" chapter. After Confucius provides his account of the eras of Grand Unity and Modest Prosperity, Ziyou asks, "Is this why ritual is so critical" 如此乎禮之急也?[2] Ziyou's question draws upon the role of ritual in the era of Modest Prosperity when it created the conditions for human flourishing. As described in the "Liyun" chapter, ritual acted as the knot (*ji* 紀) that bound human society together with the *dao* 道. Ritual is, therefore, "critical" because the world would be in chaos without it.

Translating *ji* 急 as "critical" works well to capture the nuances at play in this question. On the one hand, ritual is critical because it is decisively important to the utopic era of Modest Prosperity—without it human relationships would lack order and countries would lack sufficient governmental structure to organize society. On the other hand, ritual is critical in the sense that it is associated with uncertainty or risk, as in the contemporary colloquial statement, "The relations between the two parties have reached a critical state."[3] This latter meaning suggests a certain amount of fragility in ritual performance. Fully developed rituals are more sophisticated rituals; but more sophisticated rituals turn out to be contingent on the various agencies that contribute to their success. These areas of contingency heighten the risk involved in ritual performance—the larger number of agencies contributing to the event the larger the risk. Ritual performance, as such, is the performance of interdependence and uncertainty. Ritual, in this light, while crucial to a flourishing world, is also in a state of critical condition.

As pointed out in chapter 5, a central difference between the eras of Grand Unity and Modest Prosperity is the degree of complexity involved in human life. In the era of Grand Unity, the older generation treated all of the younger generation as their children, and the younger generation treated all of the older generation as their parents. In the era of Modest Prosperity, however, new relationships came into play. The older generation distinguished between their children and the children of other people, and the younger generation distinguished between their parents and the parents of others. No longer were there simply parent-child relationships, but a larger complex of relationships arose within human society. The era of Modest Prosperity was a time of more distinctions.

Throughout the *Liji*, ritual is discussed as a means of creating and maintaining distinctions. The opening passage of the "Aigong Wen" 哀公問 chapter, for instance, states, "If not for ritual there is nothing to distinguish [*bian* 辨] between the positions of ruler and minister, high and low, and young and old" 非禮無以辨君臣、上下、長幼之位也.[4] The prominence of ritual in the era of Modest Prosperity and its function in creating distinctions (*bian* 辨) are a primary reason for the heightened complexity of human society during the era of Modest Prosperity. A greater number of distinctions allow for a larger and more robust society, but it also entails more complexity; and with complexity come complications and the anxiety associated with these complications.

There are several reasons to connect the notion of "distinction" (*bian* 辨) with a sense of anxiety. For one, the heart radical (*xin* 心) in the character *bian* 辨 also appears in other characters that are often translated as "anxiety." In the *Liji*, these include characters such as *shen* 慎, *you* 憂, *huan* 患, *lü* 慮, *huang* 慌, *hu* 惚, *kong* 恐, and *ji* 急. The last character, *ji* 急, was already discussed in terms of the question that Ziyou posed to Confucius after Confucius recounted the transition from the era of Grand Unity to the era of Modest Prosperity. There, I translated *ji* 急 as "critical" since it expressed both the crucial role of ritual in creating a prosperous society as well as its uncertainty for success. Coincidentally, the *Shuowen Jiezi* 《說文解字》 glosses *bian* 辨 as *ji* 急 and *you* 憂.[5] Within the *Shuowen* there is a direct connection between the activity of differentiation and a sense of unease or anxiousness. The act of distinction is an apprehensive event. Other places in the *Liji* make a more direct connection between ritual and anxiety. The "Liyun" chapter, for instance, in addition to relating ritual to the notion of *ji* 急 also explains that "the early kings were concerned [*huan* 患] that ritual would not reach the people" 先王患禮之不達於下也.[6] Unfortunately, this passage does not go on to explain the nature of this concern and how it relates to ritual; however, other, more explicit examples from the *Liji* will be discussed below.

As far as this project is concerned, I will focus on three anxieties associated with the failure of ritual. These anxieties roughly correspond to issues raised in previous chapters: failures in competency and fluency, unpreventable failures in efficacy, and a sense of ambiguity between preventable and unpreventable failures in efficacy. My basic claim is that early Confucians expressed a sense of anxiety over each of these issues and that some contemporary interpreters—many of whom I have previously mentioned—mishandle the latter two.

The first anxiety is associated with shortcomings in the ritual agent. If the ritual agent lacks the necessary skills or knowledge to follow the ritual script, the ritual could fail to achieve its intended aim. The ritual could also fail if the ritual agent lacks the appropriate dispositions required by the script. Lastly, if a ritual script needs to be changed in order to ensure the success of the ritual, but the ritual agent is not sufficiently fluent, the ritual could fail. Early Confucians were concerned about themselves as competent and fluent ritual performers. For the purposes of this chapter, I will call this concern an 'anxiety of fluency.'[7] This anxiety essentially prompts the ritual agent to pose the following question to him or herself: "Am I a fluent performer of ritual?"

The second anxiety is related to unpreventable failures of ritual. When a ritual fails for reasons beyond the control of the ritual agent, it is an unpreventable failure. No degree of fluency can stop such failures. Since other agencies control aspects of a ritual performance—such as its context within a political climate—these other agencies can also dictate the success of the ritual. Unpreventable failures are not the fault of the ritual agent. However, since meaningful aspects of life are contingent on the success or failure of these rituals, the very fact that they *can* fail—with nothing one can do to stop it—creates a kind of anxiety. I will call this an 'anxiety of vulnerability.'

The third anxiety relates to the ambiguity of ritual failure. As discussed in chapter 6, identifying whether or not the failure of a ritual is preventable is not always an easy task. Occasionally, the authors of early Confucian texts present situations that are fundamentally ambiguous. In these situations, a kind of anxiety arises in the ritual agent that essentially compels him or her to ask, "Could I have done more to save this ritual; is this failure my fault?" For the sake of this chapter, I will call this an 'anxiety of accountability.' This last anxiety is undoubtedly related to the first. However, I separate them because there is also a significant difference—the first anxiety is prospective, while the last anxiety is retrospective.[8] Anxieties of accountability are retrospective in the sense that they occur after the failure of a ritual—only after the tomb collapsed could Confucius worry about whether or not the failure was his fault. It can be said that anxieties of accountability entail anxieties of fluency.

An anxiety of fluency, on the other hand, is prospective in the sense that the ritual agent experiences it before and during a ritual performance—the ritual agent should be concerned about having the required ritual implements ready before the ritual, and making sure that he follows the right steps during the ritual. In the case of a failed ritual, an anxiety of fluency becomes an anxiety of accountability once the failure occurs. In other words, when a ritual fails, the kinds of questions that concern the ritual agent transition from "Am I a fluent ritual performer?" to "Is this failure my fault?" Anxieties of accountability can be resolved if the ritual agent is able to provide sufficient justification for the failed ritual. If the justification is persuasive, the failed ritual is then accepted as an unpreventable failure. As such, if the ritual agent can explain why the failure was not his or her fault, any anxiety of accountability is resolved. This is, of course, complicated by the fact that observers of a failed ritual may not be persuaded as easily as the ritual agent is able to persuade himself that a particular failure was not his fault (or vice versa). For the sake of the argument of this chapter, however, I will not fully address this complication.

The distinction between anxieties of fluency and anxieties of accountability is significant because most contemporary interpreters give more attention to anxieties in a prospective rather than a retrospective sense. In other words, these scholars focus on how early Confucians assuaged their worries about being fluent ritual performers, but neglect their concern about being complicit in the failure of their rituals. From the perspective of these interpreters, early Confucians focused on cultivating an inner attitude of fluency, and this inner attitude gave them confidence that any failures that occurred were not their fault. This is best demonstrated in Mark Csikszentmihalyi's *Material Virtue*, which analyzes the *Wuxing* 《五行》, a text rediscovered in the 1970s. In the *Wuxing*, the notion of anxiety (*you* 憂) plays a central role in the development of virtues and human happiness. Csikszentmihalyi describes this relationship as follows: "The movement from anxiety to happiness is not a process of 'cheering up'; rather anxiety is the seed of the inner mind's pleasure, and leads to settledness, happiness, and acting out of virtue. Throughout the text, moral growth through the development of virtue is associated with a relief from externally imposed distress that allows moral decision-making to be solely an internal process, yet it originates from an attitude of anxiety and care that might be mistaken for distress."[9] While Csikszentmihalyi does not explicitly address issues of failed ritual, he is clear that anxiety serves as a kind of motivational impulse to virtuous action. Virtue is developed as one engages in an internal process of moral reasoning that begins with feelings of anxiety. By "internal process," Csikszentmihalyi seems to refer to the thinking that goes on within the individual. External factors, on the other hand, are those things beyond the body of the agent. An anxiety about these external factors is resolved as the agent engages in an internal process of moral decision-making. To other people, a virtuous person may appear distressed, but the only *real* distress of the virtuous person is an initial feeling of anxiety concerning the process of moral reasoning. As one works through this internal process, this anxiety is transformed to settledness, happiness, and virtue.

To put Csikszentmihalyi's account in the terms of this study, fluency is cultivated internally and dependent solely on the individual. It is not susceptible to external agencies, and by implication, is not predicated on the results of a ritual performance. The fluent agent, having reasoned through the situation, is able to conclusively answer the question "Am I a fluent ritual agent?" before he or she even performs a rite. Having relieved an anxiety of fluency, there will be no anxiety of accountability. Anxieties of fluency, following Csikszentmihalyi, can be resolved before the ritual event begins, so by definition anxieties of accountability cannot exist in these situations. Only if anxieties of fluency are not resolved can anxieties of accountability come about. Granted that Csikszentmihalyi is working with a very different text, but my position, in contrast to this, is that anxieties of fluency may in fact be resolved before (or during) the performance of a ritual; but a failure of the ritual may put that resolution in tension with the outcome and may cause the ritual agent to second-guess the original resolution. As such, a distinction between anxieties of fluency and anxieties of accountability highlights a significant difference between my interpretation and the interpretation of some contemporary scholars.

Coping with Anxiety

For the sake of clarity, by using the term 'anxiety' in this chapter, I mean a feeling of uncertainty or apprehension with regards to the success of a ritual.[10] So an anxiety of vulnerability, for instance, is a feeling of unease in the face of a perceived threat that lies beyond the power of the ritual agent to control, and yet could determine the success of ritual. The main point I want to make throughout this chapter is that these feelings of uncertainty or apprehension with regards to the success of ritual cannot always be resolved. This is especially true for anxieties of vulnerability—the contingency of ritual success cannot be minimized without a return to a situation similar to the one described in the "Liyun" chapter as the world of Grand Unity. Anxieties of fluency and accountability, on the other hand, can be mitigated to a certain degree in accordance with the cultivation of the ritual agent (although they cannot always be definitively resolved as contemporary interpreters such as Csikszentmihalyi suggest). Indeed, not all ritual failures are ambiguous. *Treating* or *attending to* all three anxieties often means coping with their existence rather than resolving them such that they no longer remain. Resolution, in contrast to coping with these anxieties, seeks to eliminate them, instead of seeking to live with them.

Much of the secondary scholarship, as already mentioned, has little to say about anxieties of vulnerability and accountability. However, when anxiety is discussed it tends to be in terms of resolution. The focus of this scholarship is on cultivating the ritual agent such that he becomes a mature ritual agent who is able to flawlessly perform any rite, or resolutely accept the failures that occur since they are not his fault. In this view, the more mature one is, the less anxious one is. The scholars who hold this view do not treat, and their approaches leave little room to treat, anxieties in terms other than resolution. Their attempts, therefore, as discussed in chapter 3, tend to focus on developing accounts of how the mature moral agent reasons through difficult situations. These scholars, in their accounts, seek after some method of resolving anxiety.

Part of this impulse is due to the fact that many modern scholars view Confucianism as a "locative" tradition (to borrow from J. Z. Smith). Interpreters such as Pauline Lee, working out of the paradigm developed by Smith, contrast Confucianism—as a locative tradition—with other "open" traditions (such as Daoism). Lee contrasts them in terms of their differing attitudes toward the "vast." Open traditions have an "affinity toward the vast desert and the untamed waters." For locative traditions, on the other hand, "the desert is barren, the vast waters are feared."[11] Rather than an "enthusiasm" for the vast, locative traditions express a sense of "horror" in the face of the vast. They seek to "control" and "confine" it rather than "admire" it.[12] The sage Yu demonstrates how Confucianism can be understood as a locative tradition. After several years of hard work and study, he is able to channel the floodwaters and confine them to their proper place.

When interpreters take Confucianism as a locative tradition they presume that Confucian texts necessarily seek to reduce, resolve, or eliminate tensions that threaten to destroy their sense of order. These assumptions lead to explanatory frameworks of early Confucianism that leave little room for unresolved tensions or for the possibility of coping, rather than resolving, anxiety.

Robert Eno provides a good example of this. In *The Confucian Creation of Heaven*, he lists three potential responses to the "gap" that develops between *tian* 天 as a descriptive explanation for why events occurred as they did, and *tian* 天 as a prescriptive force that provides moral reasons for acting in a certain manner. In explaining this gap, Eno states, "When good is not rewarded or evil goes unpunished, a gap occurs between *tian* 天 as a value standard and *tian* 天 as an efficient cause of amoral events." Continuing on, Eno claims, "Where such a gap develops, the three basic alternatives for bridging it are: (1) it can be ignored, (2) the ethical or the causal primacy of *tian* 天 can be compromised (which may lead to ethical relativism or determinism), (3) a new explanatory fiction can be introduced: for example, a teleological plan."[13] Eno explains that the *Analects* takes up the idea of a teleological plan: in the short term, such a gap *seems* to exist; but given a longer perspective, *tian* 天 is in fact directing a moral and just chain of events.[14] A number of other scholars make similar arguments.[15]

Eno, and other scholars who share this view, are not necessarily misguided in their interpretation of early Confucian texts—a number of strategies, including teleological strategies, are employed to resolve the anxieties described above. On the other hand, these scholars are mistaken in precluding the possibility that early Confucians sometimes took a less than definitive response to the gap between understanding and experience. Eno, for instance, presumes that the gap must be "bridged." They neglect the possibility that early Confucians believed that coping with anxiety, rather than resolving it, is not only required by the limitations of being human, but can also serve as a "productive disorientation"—a situation where one's experience in the world is dissonant with one's understanding of how the world should work, but also an opportunity valued for its creative and therapeutic power.[16]

Anxieties of Fluency

The *Liji* stresses the importance of fluent ritual performers.[17] The "Ruxing" 儒行 chapter explains,

> Confucians live within contemporary society, but study the ancients. [They know] that the actions of the current generation become the model for future generations.... [As such], they are anxious and thoughtful about their actions.
>
> 儒有今人與居，古人與稽。今世行之，後世以為楷。。。其憂思有如此者。[18]

Realizing that others are watching and that one's actions can become a paradigm for future generations is a cause for concern. Throughout the *Liji*, a sense of caution or anxiety is emphasized not only because one's current actions can become a model for future generations, but also because these actions influence the practice of current generations. This is especially true for those in leadership positions.

> When performing a ritual the profound person cannot but be cautious [*shen* 慎]. [He] is the standard of the people, and if the standard is lax the people will be disordered.
>
> 是故君子之行禮也，不可不慎也；衆之紀也，紀散而衆亂。[19]

The notion of caution or cautious-anxiety (*shen* 慎) is a prominent term in the *Liji*. It refers to not only a sense of anxiety brought about because of the observation of others, but also a concern about maintaining the integrity of the ritual, including making sure that one has the appropriate dispositions for the ritual.[20] The "Daxue" 大學 chapter, for instance, explains that the profound person is careful (*shen* 慎) about his inner dispositions (*du* 獨) because they will inevitably manifest themselves in action.[21]

Anxieties of fluency are resolvable inasmuch as the ritual agent can feel confident in his attainment of fluency. As mentioned above, many contemporary interpreters often focus on resolving anxieties of fluency because early Confucian texts tend to emphasize various programs of self-cultivation where fluently performing ritual is a central component. It is important for the ritual agent to have some sense of his or her progress in self-cultivation in terms of properly carrying out a ritual and adapting it to various circumstances. Identifying fluency, therefore, is key. The efforts of these contemporary interpreters to provide an account of fluency, as discussed in chapter 3, are commendable. As one becomes a "connoisseur" of appropriate human living, one gains a sense of confidence and ease in one's demeanor. Anxieties of fluency, therefore, are productive in the sense that they provide an initial motivation for gaining ritual competency as well as a desire to follow the ritual script. They also serve as an impulse to broadly disseminate the training necessary for all to become competent ritual performers. As mentioned above, the sage kings were concerned with extending the practice of ritual to all people because a ritually competent society is a prosperous society. The "Liyun" chapter explains that once everyone is in accord (*shun* 順) with ritual

> there will be no calamities of flood, drought, or infestation. The people will be without the afflictions of starvation and pestilence. The heavens will send down its luscious dew, the earth will send forth its sweet spring water, the mountains will provide resources for vessels and carriages, and the Yellow River will send forth its chart. The phoenixes and qilins will reside in the forests around the city, dragons and turtles will live in the palace moats, and the eggs of birds and the young of animals will all be in plain sight.
>
> 無水旱昆蟲之災，民無凶饑妖孽之疾。。。故天降膏露，地出醴泉，山出器車，河出馬圖，鳳凰、麒麟皆在郊棷，龜、龍在宮沼，其餘鳥獸之卵胎，皆可俯而闚也。[22]

Anxiety over the proper performance of ritual is the initial impetus for taking the actions necessary to recreate a world of Modest Prosperity.

Anxieties of fluency also lead to a high degree of care when altering a ritual or creating a new ritual. If a ritual script inherited from an idealized era can fail to fit current circumstances and it is the ritual agent's responsibility to recognize these circumstances and make the appropriate modifications, there is a sense of ambivalence in breaking from the idealized past to modify the ritual. This concern stems from a desire to follow the dictates of previous sages, but at the same time realizing that these dictates will not deliver the same results in a new situation. While the ritual agent is bound to the past, he is also open to the prospect of new developments for the future. As such, there is always a certain amount of tension between the past and the present manifest in the careful (i.e., anxious) modifications of ritual performers. This anxiety might be partially resolved when modified rituals are successful in their new context; however, the anxiety associated with breaking from the past is never *fully* resolved. Indeed, being able to simply disassociate oneself from for the ritual tradition of the past in circumstances where the tradition might fail in the present without some remainder of anxiety would make one a less careful and less profound ritual agent.

Borrowing from Antonio Cua, ritual agents must sometimes perform "experiments in paradigmity."[23] They must venture into untested territory in the hope that their modifications will bring about a successful ritual. The "Liyun" chapter provides the following relevant analogy of planting crops:

> Untaught human disposition is a field for the sage kings. They fashioned ritual in order to plough it, scattered appropriateness in order to sow it, discoursed on learning in order to weed it, established benevolence in order to gather its crop, and broadcast music in order to settle it. As such, ritual is the fruit of appropriateness. [When a ritual is] evaluated by one's sense of appropriateness and found in accord, then even if the early kings did not perform this ritual, [it] can be brought about by means of appropriateness.
>
> 人情者，聖王之田也。修禮以耕之，陳義以種之，講學以耨之，本仁以聚之，播樂以安之。故禮也者，義之實也。協諸義而協，則禮雖先王未之有，可以義起也。[24]

Rituals stem from appropriateness. When situations are encountered where no ritual script exists, a new ritual is created. This creation, however, as demonstrated in the following passage from the "Tangong Shang" 檀弓上 chapter, tends to be done in relation to similar rituals that are deemed less appropriate for the novel circumstance:

> At the mourning rites for Confucius, his disciples were confused about what protocol to follow. Zigong remarked, "Previously, at the mourning for Yan Yuan the Master mourned for him as if Yan Yuan were a son but did not wear the mourning clothes [normally worn when mourning for a son]. When mourning for Zilu he did the same. In mourning for the Master let us mourn for him as we

would mourn for a father, but not wear the mourning clothes [normally worn when mourning for a father]."

孔子之喪，門人疑所服。子貢曰：「昔者夫子之喪顏淵，若喪子而無服；喪子路亦然。請喪夫子，若喪父而無服。」[25]

In this vignette, Confucius's disciples are at a loss in deciding the appropriate way to mourn for Confucius. They see no ritual script that suggests a clear way of mourning for someone that was more than a friend, but not quite a father. The notion of *yi* 疑, translated in the passage as "confused," also conveys a sense of anxiety. Confucius's disciples were torn on the one hand by their desire to appropriately mourn for Confucius, and the inability of existing ritual scripts to express this desire, on the other. To navigate this tension, they constructed a new ritual script on the basis of related scripts. The creation of new rituals or ritual scripts is often based on the practice of analogous rituals. New rituals, in this sense, are not seen as coming from an extra-traditional source; rather they are seen as springing from the internal resources of the tradition. Anxieties of fluency are productive in the sense that they allow ritual agents to portray themselves as transmitters of their tradition, while at the same time modifying it to meet changing circumstances. Anxieties of fluency serve to recognize the competing needs of ritual performers to maintain tradition and to update tradition.

I have thus far discussed anxieties of fluency as mostly resolvable anxieties in light of a rigorous program of ritual training that reduces the anxiety of the ritual performer as he or she gains knowledge and skill in ritual practice. It is also resolvable in situations where an altered ritual is deemed successful, although some anxiety remains when breaking from the norms of the past. Additionally, the *Liji*, and most other early Confucian texts, often recognize the impossibility of achieving perfect fluency. As mentioned in chapter 6, the texts explain that even sages are not perfect.[26] As such, a certain degree of anxiety with regards to fluency necessarily remains. It must be coped with, since it cannot be resolved.

The chapter in the *Liji* titled "Zhongni Yanju" 仲尼燕居, translated as "Confucius at Leisure," ironically begins with a discussion between Confucius and his disciples on the necessity and difficulty of properly performing ritual. Even while at rest the figure of Confucius is depicted as someone concerned with the fluent performance of ritual. A vignette that appears in the "Dalüe" 大略 chapter of the *Xunzi* 《荀子》 also touches on the theme of not taking respite from the process of self-cultivation, and while not found in the *Liji*, this vignette seems to be in line with attitudes such as those found in the "Zhongni Yanju" chapter. In this vignette, Zigong, one of the same disciples involved in the "Zhongni Yanju" discussion of ritual, relates his desire to find rest (*xi* 息) from the hard work of learning (*xue* 學). In speaking with Confucius, he first asks if he can find rest from learning in the service of government officials. Confucius replies by explaining the difficulty (*nan* 難) such service entails, and by rhetorically asking, "How can this be rest" 焉可息哉! Zigong then proceeds to ask Confucius if he can find rest in the service of his parents, spouse, or friends. With each question Confucius responds by explaining the impossibility of finding rest in those activities. As a last attempt Zigong asks Confucius if he can find rest in plowing his own field—in essence asking if he can find rest from learning in tending to his own affairs rather than those of others. Confucius gives the same response. Frustrated, Zigong asks, "Is there then no rest for me" 然則賜無息者乎? Confucius, apparently near a freshly dug grave, replies, "Look at this grave. It is wet as a marsh, hollow as a tripod, and [has high embankments] like a plateau. In there you will [finally] know rest" 望其壙，皋如也，顛如也，鬲如也，此則知所息矣.[27] Confucius's message is clear—death is the final resolution of the work required for self-cultivation. As long as one is still living, there is still the possibility of becoming a more fluent person, and with this possibility comes the irresolvable concern over fluent performance. Being human means being anxious about one's self-development.

Recognizing the need for fluency, yet the impossibility of achieving it, could have a debilitating effect. On the other hand, early Confucians learned to cope with this anxiety in such a way that they transformed it into a productive anxiety. The possibility that Confucius, or any other sage, *could be* concerned with their own performance of ritual meant several things. First of all, it meant that these sages were real human beings—they were, in a sense, on par with everyone else. The fact that they *could be* anxious about their own self-development meant that they could also commiserate with those who were obviously not yet sages. They were also concerned about their self-development. Confucius, to state it more directly, commiserates with us in our difficulties as we commiserate with him in his difficulties. Confucius, as such, 'stands in' for other ritual agents striving to live a good life. In this light, anxieties served a therapeutic value for readers of the *Liji* in positing the achievements of the sages within the realm of human possibility. Confucius was concerned with failure, and so were the readers of the text. Anxieties of fluency, instead of being a worry that required resolution in order to attain true ease, served as a means of relating oneself to the sages of the past; all of whom experienced the same anxiety.

Anxieties of Vulnerability

Understanding that successful ritual is contingent on agencies other than the self is also a source of anxiety. As discussed in chapter 6, death, political success, and cosmic events, among other things, often lie beyond the power of the individual to control. Ritual in its role of fostering distinctions also complicates ritual success by increasing the number of parties with power to determine the success of ritual—a distinction between superior and inferior positions in government, for instance, creates two parties with sets of rituals that are dependent on the proper performance of the other party in order for their rituals to be successful. Ritual, by means of distinction, creates more points of vulnerability, and thereby furthers its own contingency. Yet because the new relationships created by ritual through acts of distinction constitute valuable components of ritual success and prosperity in human life, there is a sense of anxiety about these agencies and their power to determine the success of ritual.

The "Tangong Xia" 檀弓下 chapter contains a vignette that illustrates this notion of anxiety with regard to vulnerability:

> While passing by the side of Mount Tai, Confucius came upon a woman wailing with [great] sorrow near a grave. He stopped the cart to listen to her, and sent Zilu to speak with her. [Zilu approached the woman] saying, "You wail as one who has indeed experienced heavy sorrow [*you* 憂]."
>
> 孔子過泰山側，有婦人哭於墓者而哀，夫子式而聽之。使子路問之曰：「子之哭也，壹似重有憂者。」
>
> She responded, "Yes. A while ago my father-in-law was killed by a tiger. My husband was also killed [by this tiger], as well as my son."
>
> 而曰：「然，昔者吾舅死於虎，吾夫又死焉，今吾子又死焉。」
>
> Confucius asked, "Why don't you leave?"

夫子曰：「何為不去也?」

[She] replied, "Because there is no oppressive government here."

曰：「無苛政。」

The Master remarked [to his disciples], "You should all take note of this; an oppressive government is more fierce than a tiger."

夫子曰：「小子識之，苛政猛於虎也。」[28]

While this passage is not directly related to anxieties encountered during a ritual performance—despite the fact that the woman appears to be in the middle of the mourning rites—it demonstrates concern with elements beyond one's control. This woman, mourning at the grave of her son, weeps over the loss of her father-in-law, husband, and son, who were all mauled by a tiger. When asked by Confucius why she does not move to another location, her response is that the government of her locale is not oppressive. The main point of this passage is the comparison Confucius makes in the final line between bad government and wild animals—people would rather live in a location where their entire family might be killed by a savage tiger than in a location where the government is untamed. As it relates to the discussion of vulnerability, this passage shows that meaningful relationships, which partially constitute one's happiness in life and sense of prosperity, are subject to factors beyond one's control (whether these factors be the predatory elements of the natural world or the savage elements of human government). The natural world with its ferocious tigers, and the human world with its ferocious government, are both capable of snatching one's loved ones away and even taking one's own life. This woman's "deep sorrow" (literally, "heavy anxiety" 重憂) is an expression of anxiety over meaningful relationships that were destroyed by forces beyond her—and her family's—control.[29] It was not the case that these people incompetently performed their roles as father, husband, or son. Rather, factors greater than their powers of self-determination intruded into these roles and dictated their outcome.

While not explicitly mentioned in this passage, the concern for one's well-being includes not only an anxiety about the possible termination of meaningful relationships, but also an anxiety over the possible termination of one's own life. The notion of well-being, prosperity, or human flourishing, which is obviously predicated on human life, is vulnerable to external agencies.

These same anxieties persist in the context of ritual. The "Fangji" 坊記 chapter, as mentioned in several places in this project, highlights the vulnerability of ritual success and implies a sense of anxiety with regards to this vulnerability.

> Confucius explained, "Ritual dams up the excessive desire of the people; highlighting their separate [*bie* 別] [roles], and causing them to be satisfied. [It] acts as the standard [*ji* 紀] of the people. This being the case, men and women do not consort with each other if a matchmaker is not present. Without a gift of betrothal they do not visit each other for fear [*kong* 恐] that the proper separation [*bie* 別] between men and women will be lost. This serves to channel [*fang* 坊] the people [in the right direction]. However there will still be people who [go contrary to this and] offer themselves [to the opposite sex]."
>
> 子云：「夫禮，坊民所淫，章民之別，使民無嫌，以為民紀者也。故男女無媒不交，無幣不相見，恐男女之無別也。以此坊民，民猶有自獻其身。」[30]

This passage is significant for several reasons. First it highlights various themes that have come up in different places of this study—ritual serves to channel excess, it creates or reinforces distinctions (*bie* 別), and it serves as a metaphorical "knot" (*ji* 紀) of the people. This passage also mentions a kind of anxiety (*kong* 恐) associated with the loss of distinction, and the proclivity of people to offer themselves to the opposite sex despite the proper performance of ritual. Ritual can (and even will) fail because the success of ritual lay beyond the sole power of the ritual agent to determine. Ritual is performed out of concern for the discord associated with the lack of distinctions between male and female; yet in the end—despite the perfect enactment of ritual—discord could still ensue. While anxiety is not explicitly tied to the potential of these agencies to control the outcome of the ritual event, a fear of failed ritual and a source of failure are explicit. Ritual is meant to reinforce distinctions. A lack of distinction is a cause for concern, so one should be anxious about the proper performance of ritual (i.e., one should be concerned about one's degree of fluency). At the same time, other human beings in society can impinge on the efficacy of the rite, threatening its power to reinforce these distinctions. The vulnerability of ritual in this sense is also worthy of concern. The "Fangji" chapter, with its constant refrain of the power of the people to determine the success of ritual, suggests that human beings, with their power to determine the outcome of ritual, are causes for concern.

These passages demonstrate that early Confucians understood aspects of the self to be vulnerable to agents other than the individual because the relationships that partially constitute the self are vulnerable to these agencies. Since these relationships are sources of value for the self, the possibility that powers beyond one's control could destroy them generates a sense of anxiety within the self. One is stricken by grief at the death of someone meaningful; and while uncontrolled anxiety experienced for an extended period of time could become an 'unproductive anxiety,' the feeling of grief is nonetheless immediate and real. A passage from the "Zaji Xia" 雜記下 chapter illustrates the immediacy of sorrow experienced with the loss of a loved one:

> Zeng Shen asked Zengzi, "Should [one] use a constant pitch when wailing for one's father or mother [during their mourning rites]?"
>
> 曾申問於曾子曰：「哭父母有常聲乎？」
>
> [Zengzi] replied, "If a young child lost his [father or] mother in the middle of a journey, what constant pitch would there be [in his wailing]?"
>
> 曰：「中路嬰兒失其母焉，何常聲之有？」[31]

Zeng Shen, the son of Zengzi, is told by his father that proper wailing is not done with a constant pitch; rather, the pitch should vary. More relevantly, this passage suggests that genuine wailing extends beyond worrying about the pitch of one's voice. Indeed, one should be struck by the immediacy of the loss of one's parents, similar to the way that a young child is struck when he discovers that his parents are not by his side. One might be able to mitigate the feelings of grief by focusing on a ritual script that dictates wailing with a constant pitch. However, Zengzi explains that one's focus should be on the anxiety that one experiences in a relationship that is contingent on the wellbeing of another and not on one's personal performance. As we will see below, the vulnerability of the self, manifest in anxiety, is partially constitutive of genuine ritual performance. The tenderness of this scene depicted in the "Zaji Xia" chapter should not be missed. Zeng Shen asks his father about mourning for fathers. Zengzi, in essence, tells his son that he wants to be mourned not *as if* he were gone, but rather he wants to be mourned as someone who in actuality is gone—and is never to be seen again.

Anxieties of vulnerability function productively in several ways. First, the state of anxiety itself is valued in the performance of ritual. If one performs certain rituals without the real possibility of failure the ritual would not be properly performed. The "Jiyi" 祭義 chapter speaks of this in the context of sacrifices made after mourning for the deceased:

> Before a filial son offers up sacrifices [to his deceased parents] he is concerned [*lü* 慮] with preparing all the affairs [of the sacrifice]. If the time [for sacrifice] arrives, and all the implements are arrayed and everything is prepared, [he is able to] empty himself internally; and in the proper order, [he] performs the rite.
>
> Once the temple chamber is clean, the walls and roof are repainted, and all the ritual implements are ready, the son and his wife—having fasted and washed themselves—enter the chamber wearing the sacrificial attire and carrying the sacrifices. So engrossed and sincere, they move as if unable to bear [the weight of the sacrifices], and as if they are on the brink of dropping them. [As such], are their hearts not completely full of reverence and filial piety?
>
> The filial son displays his focus by ordering the sacrificial vessels, by arranging the rite and its accompanying music, by training the ritual participants, and by [appropriately] entering the chamber carrying the sacrifices. Because of his lost abstraction of mind [*huanghu* 慌惚] [when entering the chamber] he communes with the spirits, hoping that they might partake of the sacrifices. The aim of the filial son is to express his hope that the spirits partake of the sacrifices.
>
> 孝子將祭，慮事不可以不豫；比時，具物不可以不備；虛中以治之。宮室既修，墻屋既設，百物既備，夫婦齊戒沐浴，盛服奉承而進之。洞洞乎，屬屬乎，如弗勝，如將失之。其孝敬之心至也與！薦其薦俎，序其禮樂，備其百官，奉承而進之。於是諭其志意，以其慌惚以與神明交，庶或饗之。庶或饗之，孝子之志也。[32]

The filial son is at first concerned (*lü* 慮) with preparing for the sacrifice. He ensures that all the necessary implements are available and that the area where the sacrifice is to take place is clean. This concern is clearly an anxiety of fluency. When the ritual is performed, however, this anxiety of fluency is replaced by an attitude of *huanghu* 慌惚, translated above as "lost abstraction of mind."[33] The passage describes this attitude as "engrossed" and "sincere." It is clear that when the ritual agent is in a lost abstraction of mind he is pushed to the brink of failure—the participant brings in the sacrifices as if he cannot bear their weight and moves as if he is on the verge of dropping them. The ritual agent, this passage explains, must be in a lost abstraction of mind in order to commune with the spirits (*shen* 神).[34]

Another, more pedestrian, way of understanding the notion of *huanghu* 慌惚 is by translating it as "crazy." The ritual agent, in this scenario, is so focused on the loss of his father that he goes crazy in the multifaceted sense of the term—he is both bewildered by the circumstances of the loss and deeply dedicated to his father.[35]

The notion of *huanghu* 慌惚 can be understood in terms of anxieties of vulnerability—the death of someone meaningful is what causes the ritual agent to reach this state, and he must focus on this person, and their relationship, during the rite to ensure its success. A concern with one's performance, while appropriate before the ritual, is counterproductive during the ritual. The "Wensang" 問喪 chapter of the *Liji* describes this in relation to the rites of mourning:

> In following [the funeral procession to the grave], mourners are expectant and anxious as if seeking to follow [the deceased] but not quite able to catch up to him [i.e., they sought after the deceased as if he was living]. When returning, they wail, and are hesitant and uneasy as if they sought after [the deceased], but did not find him. As such, when mourners follow [the funeral procession to the grave] it is as if they long to see [the deceased]; and when they return it is as if they are bewildered [in not being able to find him].
>
> Regardless of where they sought him, he could not be found. They entered the door to his home, but did not find him there. They ascended up into the main hall, but did not find him there. They entered his personal quarters, but did not find him there. Alas, he was gone, only to be mourned, and never to be seen again!
>
> This is why mourners wail, shed tears, beat their chests, and falter. They stop doing these things only after they fully exhaust their sorrow. Their hearts are despondent, morose, perplexed, and

aggrieved to the point that they lose their focus and there is nothing but sorrow.

其往送也，望望然、汲汲然、如有追而弗及也。其反哭也，皇皇然若有求而弗得也。故其往送也如慕，其反也如疑。求而無所得之也，入門而弗見也，上堂又弗見也，入室又弗見也。亡矣！喪矣！不可復見矣！故哭泣辟踊，盡哀而止矣。心悵焉、愴焉、惚焉、愾焉，心絕志悲而已矣。[36]

This passage, one of the more poignant passages of the *Liji*, explains how it might feel to experience the death of a person who was meaningful to oneself. The ritual agent, in some regards, seeks to live as he did before. He visits this person's home as he had done many times previously. However, the absence of this person is obvious. The ritual agent continues to seek for him (or her), but he is not to be found. The feelings of grief and sorrow are central to the proper performance of this ritual. This is an interesting vignette because the success of these mourning rites is actually predicated on the failure of the ritual agent to find what he seeks. If he actually found the person he sought after, there would be no need for the ritual.[37]

In the death of one's family and friends, a prosperous life is revealed to be a vulnerable life. And it is this vulnerability that is valued in the proper performance of mourning rituals. If a man's happiness and sense of prosperity were invulnerable to the death of his parents, for instance, he could not truly be a "filial son" (*xiaozi* 孝子); and it is only by means of vulnerability—manifest in terms of a lost abstraction of mind—that he is able to interact with the spirits (although exactly what this entails is not entirely clear). The rituals performed after the death of a loved one must flirt with failure in order to be efficacious. The real possibility of failure enables the success of the rite. The beauty of mourning rites and sacrifices to the dead (*jisizhimei* 祭祀之美) is found in the destruction of one's relationship with the living.[38] The successful ritual is predicated on allowing the intrusion of this relationship into one's life and feeling the gravity of the loss such that "one's heart loses its focus and there is nothing but sorrow."

While experiencing this degree of sorrow for too long a period of time would jeopardize one's own well-being, the *Liji* is clear that some amount of sorrow should remain for one's entire life. The "Tangong Shang" chapter explains,

Mourning for three years is the limit [of mourning]. Although [mourning] is complete, the loss is not forgotten. As such, the pro-

> found person experiences a lifetime of anxiety, but not a morning of worry.
>
> 喪三年以為極，亡則弗之忘矣。故君子有終身之憂，而無一朝之患。[39]

Even after the completion of the mourning rites, the anxiety associated with the loss of one's parents remains, and should remain, for the rest of one's life. This loss, to use an idiom, leaves a permanent scar. Said another way, the self is never invulnerable to the relationships necessary for a flourishing life. When someone meaningful dies, in this early Confucian world-view, we lose a valuable part of ourselves.

The distinction made in this passage between anxiety and worry is significant.[40] Anxiety, the reader is told, should linger, but worry should not remain. While a full explication of this distinction lies beyond the bounds of this project, it should suffice to say that the notion of "worry" in this passage can be understood in relation to an anxiety of fluency, and the notion of "anxiety" can be understood in relation to an anxiety of vulnerability. In other words, after the completion of the mourning rites, assuming that they were performed appropriately, the ritual agent should not worry about his performance; at the same time, he should never forget the loss of his parents. The focus of this "lifetime of anxiety" is not on the self, but on the relationship that was meaningful to the self. The cultivated ritual agent, as argued above, can often resolve his anxieties of fluency; however, his anxieties of vulnerability remain.

The destruction of an ordered world due to agencies other than the self serves as a creative impulse within early Confucianism. Not only is the recognition and acceptance of vulnerability essential to the proper performance of mourning rites, but experiencing this vulnerability also leads to the creation of the mourning rites themselves. The "Liyun" chapter describes the coming forth of the *fu* 復 ceremony, where the living climb up to the roof of the house of the deceased to call back the spirit of the deceased:

> Ritual originated . . . when someone died. [The living] climbed up to the rooftop and called [after them] saying, "Alas! You [must] come back!"
>
> 夫禮之初。。。及其死也；升屋而號，告曰：「皋！某復。」[41]

Ritual began with the natural reaction of people experiencing the vulnerability of losing someone meaningful in death. Desiring the dead to remain alive leads people to take the only course of action they could think of—following after the spirit believed to ascend to the heavens and begging it to come back. The practice of climbing up to the roof of the house and calling after the deceased was a central part of Confucian mourning rites for much of Chinese history. In this account of its creation, the ritual comes about through the loss and destruction of the relationship between two people. The very destruction of the relationship, however, enables the creation of the rite—only by the loss of a loved one, and by feeling the angst associated with this loss, does the ritual come about. Moments of vulnerability, in this sense, can be turned into imaginative opportunities to (re)create ritual.

It is worth briefly mentioning that the "calling back" ceremony serves as a means of coping with the feelings of sorrow associated with leaving oneself vulnerable to relationships with others. While it is possible that the ceremony was originally created in an attempt to *resolve* an anxiety of vulnerability (i.e., they may actually have believed that the ceremony could reanimate the dead), the *Liji* makes no mention of the rite operating for reasons other than the benefit of the living to cope with the permanent loss of the dead.

Similar arguments about the creative power of destruction due to the vulnerability of human happiness and prosperity can be made with regard to the power of governmental institutions (as suggested in the vignette above about the woman who loses her family to a wild tiger). Robert Eno astutely notes that the failure of early Confucian attempts at political office fostered the creation of fellowships where Confucians could devote themselves to ritual and textual practices.[42] It is possible to take the position that Confucianism, as a tradition, only came about because of the destruction of the political ambitions of early Confucians.

In other early Confucian texts, Confucius is often portrayed as someone who turned to the work of writing and editing the Classics as the result of his inability to gain a political position. The mythical unicorn (*lin* 麟) that supposedly appeared at the birth of Confucius, only to be captured and killed shortly before his death, is often taken as a symbol of Confucius coming into the world at a time when he would not gain the prestige he deserved.[43] Yet it was the Classics, which he edited, that formed the basis of a tradition.

Confucius need not be understood as someone frustrated by his inability to gain a fitting governmental position; nevertheless, we should not neglect the possibility that these setbacks were experienced as real setbacks for him. Confucius, in other words, should be understood as a vulnerable figure whose anxiety over his inability to gain political authority was never resolved. The Confucian project sets out to order the world; yet the anxiety associated with this project's contingency on governmental structures beyond the control of Confucians is never fully resolved. Rather, it is coped with in the creation of a scholarly (i.e., *ru* 儒) tradition.

Derk Bodde famously mentioned that the burning of the books in the Qin Dynasty had the effect opposite to what was intended. Rather than destroying the past, it raised the level of consciousness of the past.[44] Something similar can be said about the failure of ritual. Failure, as it relates to vulnerability, is 'awful' in the traditional sense of the term. It is both dreadful and sublime. Failure is dreadful in that it threatens human prosperity, but sublime in that it enables the creation and proper performance of ritual upon which prosperity is founded. The vulnerability of human beings to the relationships they are involved in allows for the realization of those relationships. And the vulnerability of the "political mission" of early Confucians makes possible the articulation of the Confucian project. The awful failure of ritual does not destroy the need for ritual; quite the opposite, it raises the level of consciousness concerning the necessity of ritual.

Vulnerability, in this light, is valued because living a life without risk is a life not worth living. A vulnerable self is a permeable and precarious self, yet the self can only be cultivated by opening up to relationships with other people. A prosperous world is a vulnerable world because prosperity is contingent on factors beyond the control of the individual. Anxieties of vulnerability should not be—and cannot be—resolved; rather, they must be encountered, endured, and even embodied in ritual performance.[45]

Anxieties of Accountability

Anxieties of accountability occur when the preventability of a failed ritual is ambiguous. As argued in chapter 6, even highly refined ritual agents do not always recognize when they could have prevented a dysfunction in ritual. The fact that they *could* be to blame generates a sense of anxiety with regards to their role in ritual success. Chapter 7 described the Mubeng passage in light of this anxiety. Confucius, after hearing that the newly dug grave of his parents had collapsed, wept and remarked, "I have heard that the ancients did not fix their graves" 吾聞之：古不修墓.[46] The question, in essence, can be posed, why did Confucius cry? Was it because he foolishly varied from the ritual script of antiquity? Was it because the ritual script of the Zhou Dynasty, which he apparently followed, inevitably failed? Was it because his disciples fixed the grave, in contrast to the ancients, who did not fix their graves? Could Confucius, in short, have prevented the failure? Chapter 7 argued for a tragic reading of this passage, where the preventability of the collapse is fundamentally ambiguous. Here, the Mubeng passage reveals the uncertain and even risky nature of ritual performance. Both preventable and unpreventable failures exist, yet the actors in the passage, the authors of the passage, and the readers of the text often cannot untangle the agencies involved in ritual failure. One reason Confucius wept, therefore, was out of concern for his accountability in the process. He was anxious because he *could not* resolve the question of whether or not he was culpable for the collapse of his parents' grave. Since many of the themes related to anxieties of accountability were discussed in previous chapters (in particular, chapter 7), and many of the ways in which these anxieties function productively are similar to those discussed in previous sections of this chapter, I will not fully re-explore them here.

Besides the Mubeng passage, other passages in the "Tangong Shang" chapter depict the difficulty of distinguishing between preventable and unpreventable failures in ritual. One vignette recounts,

> Duke Zhuang of Lu fought the army of Song at Shengqiu. Xian Benfu drove the Duke's carriage and Bu Guo was the guard on the right hand side of the carriage. [At one point in the battle] the horses were spooked and the carriage fell over, tossing the Duke to the ground. The relief carriage arrived and the reigns were handed over [to Xian Benfu]. The Duke said, "I did not divine beforehand [about this battle]."
>
> 魯莊公及宋人戰于乘丘。縣賁父御，卜國為右。馬驚，敗績，公隊。佐車授綏。公曰：「末之卜也。」
>
> Xian Benfu remarked, "At no other time has the carriage ever fallen over. The fact that it fell over today was due to my lack of courage." Shortly after [saying this, Xian Benfu] died in battle.
>
> 縣賁父曰：「他日不敗績，而今敗績，是無勇也。」遂死之。

> [Later,] while bathing the horses, one of the stable boys found an arrow lodged in the inner thigh of one of the horses. [Hearing about this] the Duke exclaimed, "It was not Xian Benfu's fault!" [He] then eulogized Xian Benfu. The practice of eulogizing warriors began with this.
>
> 圉人浴馬，有流矢在白肉。公曰：「非其罪也。」遂誄之。士之有誄，自此始也。[47]

In this passage, Xian Benfu blames himself for the misfortune on the battlefield, but as it turned out, the misfortune was not his fault. The horses were not frightened because Xian Benfu had failed to adequately prepare for battle. Rather, what appeared to be fear was actually the result of unseen damage sustained in battle. Xian Benfu could not have prevented the breakdown of the carriage, but this was difficult to determine at the moment of failure. It was not until after the battle, and after he died, that those tending to the horses found an arrow lodged in one of the horses. From the perspective of the duke, Xian Benfu was not at fault for the misfortune; having a horse hit by an arrow was not something he could control. Indeed, in this view, Xian Benfu mistook this situation for a preventable failure, but in the end the failure was unpreventable.[48] There is much more that could be said about this passage, but the point worth mentioning here is that recognizing the preventability of ritual failure—and driving a chariot in battle was clearly a ritual practice—is not always a simple task.[49] It is possible to mistake an unpreventable failure for a preventable failure and a preventable failure for an unpreventable failure.[50]

Equally significant, however, is the notion that Xian Benfu's mistake became the grounds for creating a new ritual. The practice of eulogizing officers, the "Tangong Shang" chapter explains, started with Xian Benfu. The difficulty of determining preventability serves as a creative impulse within early Confucianism. Some rituals begin with the misrecognition of accountability. The ambiguity between preventable and unpreventable failures in ritual provides an imaginative space where profound ritual agents are able to bring about new rituals.

Anxieties of accountability, as in the case of Xian Benfu, are often resolvable. The "Zengzi Wen" 曾子問 chapter, discussed in several places in this project, describes countless situations where a variety of circumstances threaten the success of ritual. In this chapter of the *Liji*, Zengzi asks Confucius about each of these situations in an effort to determine the preventability of ritual failure. From Zengzi's perspective, determining which failures are preventable and which failures are unpreventable is no easy task. The entire "Zengzi Wen" chapter is shaped by his concern for accountability. Zengzi is anxious about his role in preventing ritual failure. The guidance of Confucius assists Zengzi in resolving his anxiety of accountability.

Zengzi is a prominent figure in the *Liji*, as he appears in no less than sixty passages of the text. He is consistently described as someone concerned with the proper performance of ritual. Even on his deathbed, for instance, Zengzi is worried about lying on an improper mat.

> Zengzi lay sick in his room with a serious illness. Yuezheng Zichun sat at the edge of the bed and Zeng Yuan and Zeng Shen sat at the foot of the bed. A boy sat in the corner holding a light. The boy remarked, "[The mat that Zengzi is lying on] is so elegant and smooth. Is that not a mat of an official?"
>
> 曾子寢疾，病。樂正子春坐於床下，曾元、曾申坐於足，童子隅坐而執燭。童子曰：「華而睆，大夫之簀與?」
>
> Zichun interjected, "Stop [talking]!"
>
> 子春曰：「止!」
>
> Zengzi, overhearing the conversation, was alarmed and asked, "What?"
>
> 曾子聞之，瞿然曰：「呼!」
>
> [The boy] replied, "[Your mat] is so elegant and smooth. Isn't that a mat of an official?"
>
> 曰：「華而睆，大夫之簀與?」
>
> Zengzi responded, "Yes. Ji Sun gave it to me, and I have not yet been able to change it. [Zeng] Yuan, help me up and change the mat."
>
> 曾子曰：「然，斯季孫之賜也，我未之能易也。元，起易簀。」

Zeng Yuan remarked, "Your illness is serious, so the mat cannot be changed. If you are fortunate enough to make it [through the night] I will carefully change it in the morning."

曾元曰：「夫子之病革矣，不可以變。幸而至於旦，請敬易之。」

Zengzi replied, "You honor the boy's request over mine. The profound person honors others by empowering [them], and the uncultivated person honors others by coddling [them]. What is it that I seek? I seek nothing more than to die in a proper manner." [So they] lifted [Zengzi] and changed the mat; however, he died before they could ready the new mat.

曾子曰：「爾之愛我也不如彼。君子之愛人也以德，細人之愛人也以姑息。吾何求哉？吾得正而斃焉斯已矣。」舉扶而易之。反席未安而沒。[51]

In this passage, Zengzi insists on changing his bedding despite his illness and the attempts of others in attendance to discourage the practice.[52] Zengzi, the *Liji* reveals, is someone who endeavored to perfectly follow the ritual script in any situation he confronted. Even on his deathbed Zengzi sought after what he considered to be the way of the profound person. In this vignette, Zengzi literally dies in his pursuit of competency.

Shortly after this passage in the "Tangong Shang" chapter another passage describes the scene after Zengzi's death. It states, "In the mourning rites for Zengzi, [his body] was washed in the kitchen" 曾子之喪，浴於爨室.[53] While this passage is somewhat enigmatic, when read in light of other passages that discuss how and where to wash the body of the deceased in the mourning rites, one clear point emerges: Zengzi was not washed in the location deemed proper by the ritual script.[54] Early commentators are divided as to whether or not this constituted an appropriate deviation from the script.[55] Nonetheless, it seems likely that washing Zengzi's body in the kitchen was meant as a subtle critique of his austerity.[56] While in life he strove to perfectly enact every ritual, at the conclusion of his life his body is improperly handled, and this failure in the funerary rites is done (or allowed) to make a point about ritual failure: Zengzi worked to prevent every ritual failure in his power to control; however, the degree of austerity required for this achievement can be counterproductive to other values.

Put in the terms of anxiety, Zengzi strove to resolve his anxieties of accountability: he worked to identify the failures that were in his control to prevent (as evident in the "Zengzi Wen" chapter) and sought to eliminate any concern that failure might be his fault by obsequiously following what he deemed to be the appropriate ritual script. However, in constantly striving to resolve these anxieties, he misses something significant. Namely, he misses the fact that living with some remainder of anxiety is not only a necessary condition of living in a world after the era of Grand Unity, but that coping with this anxiety is part of what constitutes a prosperous life. In other words, the attempt to absolve one's responsibility in every situation where a ritual fails creates a kind of worry that impedes one from enjoying the benefits of a prosperous life. Zengzi, rather than enjoying the relationships that ritual allowed him to engage in, worked to resolve his anxiety of accountability, and ended up more worried than anyone else.

Anxieties of accountability, as such, are productive in several ways. Most obviously, they function as encouragement for the ritual agent to be competent and fluent in ritual performance; a concerned ritual agent, in this sense, is a careful ritual agent. He works to prevent failures within his control and strives to perform every ritual appropriately. Additionally, coping with anxieties of accountability is—as demonstrated by the figure of Zengzi—valued above the total resolution of these anxieties. Living with some anxiety of accountability is preferable to living a life where one is constantly worried about following a ritual script.

Conclusion

The anxieties discussed in this chapter are part of what we can call "productive disorientations." As explored in chapter 1, the notion of managing water or ordering the flow of water is a prominent metaphor for ritual in the *Liji*. In particular, dikes or waterways (*fang* 坊) are spoken of as channeling water similar to the way in which ritual orients the flow of people's dispositions. Ritual, in this sense, provides an orientation or direction for the dispositions of human beings. The character *fang* 方, graphically and semantically related to the character for dike, is used in the sense of "guide" or "orientation" throughout the *Liji*. In several places *fang* 方 is discussed in terms of ritual. The "Jingjie" 經解 chapter, for instance, states, "[An official who] emphasizes ritual and performs ritual is considered an official with proper orientation" 隆禮由禮，謂之有方之士.[57] Ritual, in these passages, provides a sense of direction. The susceptibility of ritual to failure challenges this sense of direction. Like a boat without a bearing, a ritual agent who encounters a failed ritual is left without clear direction.[58] Ritual failure, in short, is disorienting. This disorientation, however, is productive in the sense that it provides opportunities for recreating and reinventing the ritual tradition.

These productive disorientations also function therapeutically by allowing the readers of the *Liji* to commiserate with the figures in the *Liji*, and by depicting historical figures as individuals capable of commiserating with the readers. We sympathize with Confucius because he, like us, is concerned with properly performing ritual. In situations where a ritual fails, he, like us, tends to recognize whether or not the failure was preventable, yet there are many other situations where the failure could be our fault; and he, like us, worries about these possibilities. Additionally, Confucius sympathizes with us because his life, like ours, is susceptible to the loss of something or someone meaningful. When a relationship is abruptly terminated, the grief Confucius feels is genuine grief because his self is transformed by the loss of the relationship. Confucius, in this sense, is fully human and stands in for us and we stand in for him. At the same time, Confucius provides a model of someone who successfully coped with the anxiety of ritual failure. He lived a good life in the sense of effectively turning these anxieties into productive anxieties; and in this light, Confucius is taken as a sage. Indeed, what we see here is how coping with the dissonance between one's understanding of how the world should work and one's experience with how the world actually works makes the world into a more frightening, but also a more familiar, place.

Concluding Reflections

TOWARD A TRAGIC THEORY OF RITUAL

> *Although the claims of ritual may be of an ordered, flawless system, the workings of ritual are always in the realm of the limited and the ultimately doomed.*[1]

THROUGHOUT THIS STUDY, I have focused particularly on the *Liji* and more generally on early Confucianism. In the pages that follow, I will broaden the scope of this project to situate the Confucian theory of ritual portrayed in this book within the larger context of ritual studies. In order to do this, I will first describe several relevant theories of ritual put forth by modern scholars, then I will explain how the theory of ritual delineated in this study contributes to this conversation. In short, the *Liji* articulates a tragic theory of ritual that enriches the study of change and efficacy with regards to ritual.

Correspondence and Subjunctive Theories of Ritual

Over the past century, many scholars have understood ritual in terms of 'correspondence.' Ritual, in their view, is meant to shape reality to correspond with a preexisting ideal. Oftentimes this ideal is represented in a complex system of symbols (in the case of Clifford Geertz) or in native myths of an 'eternal return' to conditions of paradise (in the case of Mircea Eliade). Ritual, as such, is meant to create an 'as is' world. It acts on reality, to change reality into a new and better place. Paraphrasing Eliade, *as was* done by the gods, *so is* done by human beings in the performance of ritual; and *as is* done in ritual, *so will be* done in the world.[2] By repeating the acts of ritual, those performing rituals believed that the profane became sacred and that the ordinary became the extraordinary. Following the views of theorists such as Arnold van Gennep, ritual enabled a kind of pivoting of the sacred where anything could be transformed into part of the sacralized world.

Often, correspondence theories of ritual are coupled with the assertion that ritual performers do not believe that their rituals change. Barbara Myerhoff, in arguing for the latter point, claims that ritual performers view ritual as part of "the underlying unchanging nature of the world."[3] In her view, ritual agents resist all implications that their rituals are anything less than representations of an immortal order. They are not the mere inventions of human hands. Myerhoff explains that if ritual performers "catch [them]selves making up rituals, [they] may recognize all [their] most precious understandings, the precepts [they] live by, as mere desperate wishes and dreams."[4]

Axel Michaels reaffirms this position in his article entitled "Ritual and Meaning" in a recent volume on ritual theory. Michaels explains, "[I]f people identify themselves in rituals with invariability and timelessness . . . they resist the uncertainty of past and future, life and death. In rituals they become 'eternal,' related to something that has always been there, never changed and detached from everyday life and profanity. Thus rituals are staged productions of timelessness, the effort to oppose change, which implies finality (and, ultimately, death)."[5] Other theorists have noted that ritual performers, in addition to claiming that their rituals do not change, also tend to introduce new ritual practices in terms of "recursivity," where the new practice is described as a return to, or rediscovery of, an older, more pure practice.[6]

When bound together, theories of correspondence and theories of changelessness lead to a significant problem for ritual performers, especially when they are compelled to explain situations where their rituals do not function as claimed. These ritual performers must attribute failure to either their own incompetence, or confront the possibility that their rituals are not able to transform the world the way they originally thought. Since ritual is supposed to bring power from some transcendent realm to bear on the world, it *should not* fail to transform the world. Where ritual does not transform the world, there necessarily arises a crisis of meaning for the performers of ritual. In short, if they did things correctly, there can be no simple, or perhaps satisfying, answer as to why their rituals were ineffective. This crisis, from the view of early theorists of ritual, becomes particularly acute in the modern world where other 'as is' discourses—such as "science" and "rationality"—compete with ritual and shape the ordinary world with more success. Ritual, as such, is outmoded for modern living.[7]

While relatively few scholars today would state this in such bald terms, scholars in the field of ritual studies continue to make sense of ritual as inheritors of this ideology. As such, ritual efficacy is a central "problem" for many parts of the academic field. Just last year (2010), both issues of the *Journal of Ritual Studies* were dedicated to the topic of ritual efficacy; and Oxford University Press published a collected volume entitled *The Problem of Ritual Efficacy*. The editor of the latter, William Sax, begins the book with the question, "Do rituals really work, and if so, then how?"[8]

This question, of course, is not new, but it is renewed when people are confronted with the fact that ritual does not seem to be disappearing from the modern world. Scholars for quite some time have answered the question posed by Sax with a series of qualified "yes's"; meaning that, in their view, ritual does succeed, but not in the way that performers of ritual claim.[9] Healing rituals, as such, do not employ a supernatural power, but they can ease the mind of the patient, thereby leading to a reprieve of certain kinds of illnesses. Ritual, in this view, is psychologically, or in other cases sociologically, efficacious, but not ontologically efficacious. The early assumptions of ritual theorists seem to be that once ritual performers realize that their rituals do not transform the world as claimed, they would then latch on to more effective means of achieving their intended aims. These new means, in the form of things such as science, could then be supplemented with other ways of attaining psychological or sociological stability. The problem for this theory, though, is that ritual remains.

The work of recent scholars, including those involved in the Sax volume, is to struggle with the persistence of ritual in light of previous interpretations of ritual as shaper of the world and as immutable ceremony.

The primary critiques of correspondence theories of ritual that I wish to focus on come from scholars such as Jonathan Z. Smith and Adam Seligman. Both Smith and Seligman provide alternative accounts of ritual efficacy—Smith highlights the awareness among ritual performers of the disjuncture between the world of ritual and the ordinary world, and Seligman explains how ritual creates a "subjunctive" reality.

In his 1980 article, "The Bare Facts of Ritual," Smith explains that "ritual represents the creation of a controlled environment where the variables (i.e., the accidents) of ordinary life have been displaced precisely because they are felt to be so overwhelmingly present and powerful. Ritual is a means of performing the way things ought to be in conscious tension to the way things are in such a way that this ritualized perfection is recollected in the ordinary, uncontrolled, course of things."[10] In Smith's view, ritual is not meant to act *on* ordinary life; rather, ritual acts *in opposition to* ordinary life.

Ritual agents perform ritual to demonstrate that they know "what ought to have been done."[11] The ritual agent, in other words, recognizes that ordinary life will not necessarily be influenced by the performance of ritual. Indeed, one of the reasons, according to Smith, the ritual agent performs ritual is to demonstrate this very fact. The "gnostic" element of ritual performance is significant for Smith. In contrast to scholars whose theories led to the crisis described above, Smith posits that ritual performers are aware of the disconnect between a ritual performance and "ordinary life." He explains, for instance, that dramatizing the kill of the hunt in pre-hunting ceremonies is done to show that "the hunter knows full well what ought to transpire if he were in control; the fact that the ceremony is held is eloquent testimony that the hunter knows full well that it will not transpire, that he is not in control."[12] In Smith's view the ritual performer is aware of the tenuous relationship between the ritualized hunt and the ordinary hunt, and is able to explain why he performs the ritual despite the rupture. Ritual, in short, does not manipulate the world; rather, it "express[es] a realistic assessment of the fact that the world *cannot* be compelled."[13]

The strength of Smith's account is that it provides a non-correspondence theory of ritual efficacy from an emic perspective. Instead of depicting primitive actors as being unaware of the constraints of changing the ordinary world, the performers are depicted as rational agents acting out because of the constraints of changing the ordinary world. In Smith's view, ritual is done to demonstrate an awareness of these constraints and to serve as a "focusing lens" with which to view the ordinary world.[14]

Adam Seligman, Robert Weller, Michael Puett, and Bennett Simon, in their book entitled *Ritual and Its Consequences*, also put forth an alternative theory of ritual efficacy. In their view, ritual creates an "as if" or a "could be" world rather than an "as is" world as argued for in correspondence theories of ritual.[15] According to Seligman and his colleagues, ritual works to build a subjunctive social world instead of a "sincere" world where "authentic" or "real" aspects of the self are sought and manifest in ritual.[16] In other words, ritual creates a kind of illusory world where performers live 'as if' they were living in a world of order, as opposed to creating a world rooted in some notion of an authentic self or an original tradition. Ritual, as such, frames the world for ritual performers so that the illusory world becomes a kind of reality, but the reality lasts only as long as performers adhere to the illusion.[17]

Similar to Smith, Seligman highlights the awareness that ritual performers have about the disjuncture between the subjunctive world and "the real world."[18] The subjunctive world, in the view of ritual performers, is the preferred world. It does not seek to transform the real world; rather, it often functions in opposition to the real world. Unlike Smith, however, Seligman does not emphasize "the cognitive aspects of incongruity."[19] Ritual, according to Seligman, is not so much about thought as it is about action. In short, ritual is not the representation of inner beliefs; rather, ritual is work; it *is* the construction of an ordered world set in the context of a real, and threatening, unritualized world.

Much of Seligman's argument is postured as an explanation for the persistence of ritual in the modern world. Instead of explaining ritual practices as attempts to return to tradition or as retrenchment to fundamentalism, Seligman explains it in terms of universal human activity. It remains because it is the work of constructing a social world; and since the social world is in constant tension with the ordinary world, ritual is in constant need of being performed. It is, stated succinctly, "among the most important things that we humans do."[20]

A Tragic Theory of Ritual

My purpose here is to bring the Confucian theory of ritual presented in this book into dialogue with the theories of ritual described above. My claim is that the *Liji* puts forth a tragic theory of ritual where ritual performers inherit the practices of the past that, in previous times, created an ordered world. When following these practices in later times, though, performers are occasionally confronted with a dissonance between an expectation of how ritual should work and their experience with how ritual actually works. In these situations, they resign themselves to the need to vary from the rituals of the past and recognize the risk they take in adapting them to new circumstances or in creating new rituals altogether. Part of this creative process entails further developing ritual in light of a continually more complex society. In antiquity, rituals worked, but the social world it created was also a simple world. In later times, a more complex social world requires more complex rituals. The growing complexity of the social world, however, leads to more interdependent rituals where successful ritual performance is contingent upon a growing number of agencies, thereby obfuscating causality in ritual success and failure.

Starting in antiquity, human beings gradually conceptualized the practices of ritual as a tradition, but this conceptualization entailed the rise of a crafty self that is also capable of constructing alternative traditions that then compete with the ritual tradition. It is also quite difficult to represent the ritual tradition in writing or words. Transmitting the ritual tradition, the *Liji* explains, is no simple affair.

In short, the world ritual is meant to construct is set against the backdrop of a dysfunctional world—a world comprised of competing ritual traditions (or social worlds), natural disasters, and death. Ritual performers project their hope onto the dysfunctional world while recognizing the loose fit between the two.

In line with Seligman and his colleagues, this Confucian theory of ritual is about the creation of a subjunctive world—a world 'wished for' or 'imagined.' But unlike Seligman, this world is not understood in terms of an "as if" world in opposition to the "real" world. Instead, the ritual world is contextualized among other competing worlds (all dysfunctional from the perspective of ritual performers), each impinging on the other. Said differently, the ritual world is not taken as an illusionary world distinct from the real world; instead, it is taken as one of many worlds competing to define reality. When it functions *as* the real world, it is in a tensive, metaphorical, sense. In other words, similar to the way that a metaphor functions by bringing two things together while preserving their individuality, ritual serves to bring the hoped-for world into contact with the real, or dysfunctional, world. So the ritual world is understood *as* the real world in the sense that ritual performers hope that the competing worlds, all of which are dysfunctional, will be ordered by ritual, while at the same time recognizing that their hope will often be in vain.

In line with correspondence theories of ritual, this tragic theory of ritual does make an ontological claim—ritual is meant to order the dysfunctional world. On the other hand, this tragic theory of ritual is not coupled with notions of changelessness. Early Confucians believed that ritual could in fact change. Since ritual performers were aware of the loose fit between the ritual world and the dysfunctional world, they turned the failures of ritual into disorienting opportunities valued for their creative and therapeutic power. The *Liji*, in this light, can be understood as a text about ritual theory.

Changing Ritual

Ritual, in creating the subjunctive world, represents itself as stable and rooted in the past, but is also dynamic in engaging the present. Confucians recognized that if they constantly performed ritual as scripted, ritual would occasionally fail to order the world. As such, they 'opened' the ritual script; thereby adapting it to different circumstances. Only a well-trained ritual specialist, however, could open the script.[21]

This meant that the failure of ritual was seen first and foremost as either the fault of an incompetent participant or the fault of a ritual agent who was insufficiently trained, before it was blamed on the ritual script. In this way, dysfunctional ritual tended to be seen as a failure, not of the ritual itself—as the ritual script accounted for or at least accommodated alterations—but of human beings in lacking the ability to properly alter the script. Confucians succeeded in turning the failure of ritual away from the ritual and on to the agent.

Ritual, in this view, is meant to be adapted. Failure to adapt is not the fault of the script, since no script can adequately take into account all the situations where a ritual might be performed. Rather, a dysfunctional ritual represents the failure of a ritual agent to be sufficiently versed in adapting the script. Reconceiving the ritual script to account for adaptations allowed early Confucians to employ a specialized discourse concerning ritual. This discourse essentially claimed that rituals rarely fail, all the while recognizing the necessity of altering them.

While ritual may have originated in the paradigmatic actions of the sages that lived in antiquity, early Confucians understood that rituals are sometimes insufficient for ordering their contemporary world. Properly performing ritual requires the presence of a well-trained ritual agent—in other words, a Confucian.

Explaining ritual in this light allowed early Confucians to affirm the value of past tradition by accounting for failures that occurred when replicating the rituals of the past in the present. In other words, a failure of a ritual from the past in the present was not the fault or the failure of the ritual tradition. Those in the past got it right. Rather, the fault for failure lies with contemporary individuals who fail to make the necessary adaptations to past rituals (and often, Confucians blame those in positions of power for not employing them to conduct the rites). In this light, the *Liji* argues for the value of the past in providing a series of effective rituals within a previous context; but at the same time it also argues for the need for authoritative figures that are well versed in the rituals of the past to lead those in the present into the future. Early Confucians postured themselves as these authority figures. This move allowed them to endorse tradition, but at the same time not be bound by tradition. It allowed them, in some sense, to use the discourse of ritual as a means of criticizing tradition.

The *Liji* justifies the performance of ritual in a changing world. Contrary to Axel Michaels, ritual is not an "effort to oppose change" nor is it a "staged production of timelessness"; and contrary to Barbara Myerhoff, ritual is not seen as part of "the underlying unchanging nature of the world." Instead, ritual constitutes a tradition that is open to new possibilities. Ironically, Confucians embraces the very view that Myerhoff sees as inimical to ritual performance—ritual, in the *Liji*, is a construct of the ritual performers; it represents their "desperate wishes and dreams."

At the same time, early Confucians were ambivalent about changing ritual. In their view, breaking from antiquity is a necessary, yet lamentable, practice because it discontinues the tradition of an idealized past and does not guarantee success in the present. This tie to the past is tragic in the sense that ritual worked in antiquity and no ontological barrier prevents humanity from returning to the conditions of antiquity. However, despite the possibility of return, humanity chooses to give up the safe, and simple, conditions of antiquity for the prosperous, yet vulnerable, conditions of a more complex ritual world. While Mircea Eliade spoke of a "terror of history" where ritual performers seek to transcend the world of change and uncertainty, early Confucians instead exhibited a tragic consciousness of history.[22] This tragic consciousness does not preclude apprehension with regard to change, yet it recognizes that if humanity wishes to live in a prosperous world, then things, including ritual, must change. As such, early Confucians took ritual as a conservative tradition, yet they reflectively advocated its change. This tragic consciousness of ritual change may be one reason for the continued performance of Confucian ritual—at least in name—throughout much of Chinese history.

Ritual and Reality

The "Liyun" 禮運 chapter of the *Liji* depicts early humanity living in savage conditions. In this period, human beings resided in caves and ate the raw flesh of animals. Eventually, sages taught people to construct simple homes and to use fire in preparing food. They also organized simple relationships such as parent in relation to child. This act of civilization marks the beginning of the ritual tradition. Society—meaning interpersonal relationships, material implements and structures, and institutions such as government—is built by means of ritual practices. As society becomes more complex, so do the ritual practices that support it.

The social world created by ritual is set amid a world of dysfunction. Other competing social worlds emerge, natural disasters occur, and people die before their time. These dysfunctional forces impinge themselves on the ritual world with a kind of brute force. The *Liji* explains that with the emergence of more social distinctions comes an awareness of those within one's social group (such as a city) and those beyond one's social group (those from another city). Defense fortifications arise, and weapons emerge in an attempt to overtake those from other social worlds. In the words of Ernest Becker, the dysfunctional world is a "gory spectacle, a science-fiction nightmare in which digestive tracts fitted with teeth at one end are tearing away at whatever flesh they can reach, and at the other end are piling up the fuming waste excrement as they move along in search of more flesh."[23]

Ritual minimizes dysfunction and projects a hope of order onto the dysfunctional world, yet it cannot prevent all dysfunction. The work of ritual is to build an ordered world. Ritual performers enact ritual over and over again to construct this world, but they never fully transform the dysfunctional world. Ritual performance understood *as* world construction is always taken in a tensive sense. The ritual world never fully becomes the only world human beings experience; rather, dysfunction continues to linger on the edges of society. Dysfunction, however, and in contrast to the view put forth by Seligman and his collaborators, is not understood as the real or true condition of the world (unless 'real' is taken as 'prior to' or 'the default condition of'). While the dysfunctional world provides the context for the creation of the ritual world, it is not any more genuine or true to human experience than the ritual world. For human beings, there is no one real world; rather, we inhabit a world occasioned by order and anomy.[24]

Chapter 8 discussed the part of the mourning rites depicted in the *Liji* where mourners seek out the dead as if they were still living—mourners follow the funeral procession to the grave as if they were about to catch up to the person on a walk, and return to the home of the person calling after him or her, hoping to find them there. The sorrow of losing a loved one reaches a heightened pitch as mourners fully confront the absence of the person. When failing to find him or her at home, mourners "exhaust their sorrow" 盡哀 by wailing and shedding tears. They are despondent to the point that they "they lose their focus and there is nothing but sorrow" 心絕志悲而已矣.[25] This particular rite is interesting because its success is predicated on the failure of mourners to find what they seek. If they found their loved one alive, there would be no need for the rite. Indeed, similar to Smith's analysis of Siberian pre-hunting ceremonies, the mourners here do not actually expect the rite to alter the course of things. They, in fact, recognize the vulnerability of their hoped-for world to forces beyond their control. In this case, the mourning rite becomes a means of confronting that vulnerability. They project their hope on to the dysfunctional world, knowing that it will not change things. They perform the rite to demonstrate their awareness of the fragility of their social world. The mourning rite, as such, becomes a means of navigating the tension between the desired world and the dysfunctional world. It becomes a kind of performative therapy for dealing with dissonance.

In this light, ritual is done to display one's understanding that one's best efforts are often frustrated by the dysfunctional world—that people do in fact die, but if it were up to us they would remain. Mourning or funerary rites are particularly apt for demonstrating this point. Death presents a kind of ambivalence for human beings.[26] Our desire to accept the finality of death conflicts with our hope for continuing a meaningful relationship with the deceased. Mourning rites, as such, become an important means of coping with ambivalence—they allow us to live in a world of hope *and* fear. The intrusion of the dysfunctional world into the social world becomes an occasion for the creation and performance of ritual. Ritual does not dissolve the tension between these worlds, but provides a way of navigating the tension. The need for ritual becomes apparent when the dysfunctional world intrudes into the social world created by ritual.

Part of what makes the world created by ritual meaningful is the possibility of intrusion. The dysfunctional world is dangerous. It kills indiscriminately and is savage. The vulnerability of the ritual world to dysfunction means that everyone living in the world of ritual lives with risk. Yet this risk itself partially renders life in the ritual world worthwhile. If relationships lasted forever, there are fewer reasons to cultivate relationships now. If ritual completely ordered the dysfunctional world, there are fewer reasons to transcend parochialism and the narrow confines of traditionalism. The threat of loss can lead to morbidity and depression, but it can also inspire the virtuous treatment of others.[27] The possibility of impingement can lead to retrenchment and fundamentalism, but it can also prompt a healthy reappraisal of tradition. The uncertainty of the ritual world, in this sense, "mobilizes [the] energies" necessary for the appropriate treatment of others and for a reflective engagement with tradition.[28]

Ritual Efficacy

Ritual is bound to fail in ordering the dysfunctional world. The inevitability of failure, as discussed in chapter 8, generates anxiety in the performers of ritual. Ritual performers are concerned with the contingent nature of the ritual world. Ritual success, in other words, is vulnerable to incompetent ritual performers, people from other social worlds wielding military or other kinds of power, natural disasters, and death. The inescapable nature of these forces elicits a kind of tragic consciousness in ritual performers. They realize that some of the work that ritual does will be done in vain. The ambiguity associated with interdependent rituals contingent on a more complex world makes it difficult to know beforehand what will work and what will fail. The obfuscation of causality and the fragility of the ritual world are two reasons for the tragic consciousness of ritual. Ritual will fail; however, ritual performers cannot always anticipate when and where failure will occur.

An additional reason for the tragic consciousness of ritual is the realization among ritual performers that ritual cannot be done as it was done in antiquity. In antiquity, ritual was simple and unadorned. It provided for basic needs such as food and shelter, and it fostered a minimal number of social relationships. It could not, however, bring about a prosperous world. Creating the conditions of prosperity entails building on, and deviating from, the foundational acts of the sages. Because of this, ritual performers are torn between desire to maintain a connection with an ordered past and desire to render ritual meaningful in the present. This ambivalence, rooted in an awareness of the necessity of enacting ritual and the necessity of varying from tradition, contributes to the tragic consciousness associated with ritual.

Stated succinctly, the tragic consciousness of ritual is an awareness of vulnerability, ambiguity, and rupture with the past. Yet this tragic consciousness, rather than working against ritual, instead secures its longevity and efficacy. It allows ritual to remain in different, and even "modern," contexts and to support claims of efficaciousness. Ritual performers can reaffirm the value of the past while looking to the present, and can mobilize the resources of vulnerability and ambiguity in enacting their rites.

In the mourning rites discussed above, for instance, the failure of the ritual world to fully transform the dysfunctional world such that death does not occur (or only occurs at the right time) is integral to the success of the mourning rites. Proper performance is a vulnerable performance where the more genuine one's hope of finding the deceased still alive when searching their home, the more genuine one's sorrow when confronting their absence. These rituals, as covered in previous chapters, must push the performer to the brink of madness (*huanghu* 慌惚). The ritual agent, as such, takes upon him or herself the risk of going beyond the brink. This kind of flirtation with failure enables the success of the rite; and it is one reason, as mentioned in chapter 1, that the theme of excess (*guo* 過) is so prevalent in the *Liji*. In performing mourning rites, a state of vulnerability is preferred over a state of invulnerability. Stated more broadly, human beings, in this view, should not render themselves invulnerable to relationships that are contingent on the erratic nature of the dysfunctional world. These relationships, at least partially, constitute a meaningful life. The real possibility of the dysfunctional world impinging itself on the ritual world opens up opportunities for deep engagement with other human beings. It provides motivation to care for others, allows one to fully experience human sentiment (*qing* 情), and creates space for continued reflection on the question of what constitutes a meaningful life.

The Mubeng passage discussed in chapter 7 is particularly apt for demonstrating the tragic consciousness of ritual performance. Confucius, in contrast to the practices of antiquity, constructs a mound on the grave of his parents. He does this because he lives in a time different from antiquity. His age is more complex, requiring him to travel around the kingdom and to employ others in completing the mourning rites. He needs the mound to help him remember the grave. Confucius is spatially and temporally displaced from the past—he cannot remain in the location of his parents, nor does he live in the same conditions as the ancients. The mound, as such, serves to bridge the displacement. The complexity of building a mound also requires him to employ his disciples in maintaining the grave. Varying from the rites of antiquity, it turns out, increases the vulnerability of the rite. Rains fall, the mound gets saturated, and the grave collapses. It is not clear who is at fault for the collapse. It may be the fault of the heavens for causing it to rain, the fault of Confucius for deviating from antiquity, or the fault of his disciples for incompetently maintaining the grave.

For its readers, this passage serves to evoke their tragic sensibilities by presenting them with issues of ambiguity, rupture, and vulnerability. Confucius is depicted as being concerned with the proper burial of his parents, and the text presumes that its readers are also concerned with the proper treatment of their parents. Confucius was concerned with deviating from tradition, and the presumed readers of the *Liji* are likewise concerned with deviating from tradition. Confucius sometimes confronted situations where the dysfunctional world overpowered the ritual world, and so do the readers of the text. The Mubeng passage connects the world of the text with the world of its readers. Confucius is shown as living in a world where an understanding of ritual does not always cohere with the experience of ritual performance. The readers of the text inhabit the same world. As such, readers feel *along with* Confucius, and he feels *for* them. Passages such as the Mubeng passage serve as reminders and comforts that the readers of the text are intimately connected with figures such as Confucius. Stated more broadly, once we, the readers, accept the proposition that understanding and experience are not always reconcilable, then we find the world we live in a more frightening, but also a more familiar, place.

The kind of justification that ritual provides for its performance need not be about the eventual triumph of the ritual world. Rather, it can sometimes justify itself by providing a kind of honesty about the world.[29] It reframes the world such that we learn to accept that there are things we do not know, and powers that we cannot control. Ritual, as such, is an embodied confession of our own limitations. It is a way of enacting our vulnerability and coming to terms with uncertainty. Depicting the failure of paradigmatic figures such as Confucius to adequately construct an ordered world allows readers of the text to establish a peculiar continuity with the past. While Confucius's failure is set in the context of breaking with the past, the readers of the text are connected with the past by means of Confucius's rupture with antiquity. His vulnerability and his difficulty in navigating his ambiguous world serve as a model for those seeking to cope with similar circumstances. Indeed, attempting to commiserate with Confucius as he commiserates with others is an important theme in many aspects of Chinese literature.

A Final Word

My hope is that this project will bring the *Liji* further into conversations about ritual and Confucian ethics. As suggested in this book, I believe that a closer look at the *Liji* will add to the ways that scholars have thought about ritual and ritual failure. I also believe that the *Liji* will challenge the ways that scholars have thought about Confucian self-cultivation.

More specifically, in this book I have engaged in a discursively informed description of the *Liji*. I have described how the authors or redactors of the text recognized, explained, and coped with dysfunctional rituals. Through examining this issue, I have demonstrated that failures in ritual were causes of acute concern for the authors of the *Liji*. In short, I have argued that early Confucians often found an ambiguous distinction between preventable and unpreventable failures in ritual, and that this gives way to a tragic reading of ritual. I offered this reading in contrast to many contemporary readings of Confucian ethics, where the ritual agent is ascribed the ability to recognize a clear distinction between preventable and unpreventable failures and thereby render his process of self-cultivation invulnerable to failures beyond his control.

The "Liyun" chapter of the *Liji* provided a recurrent theme for my tragic reading of early Confucian ritual theory. It contends that a fundamental shift occurred in the development of human civilization. While human beings originally lived in caves and ate the raw flesh of animals, they came to live as one unit—treating everyone as family, living in homes, and cooking their food with fire. In this era of Grand Unity, human civilization lived in sync with the Great Way.

Later, in the era of Modest Prosperity, human beings concerned themselves with distinctions between various members of society. The world was no longer one family. The great leaders of the time developed a ritual tradition to realign society with the Great Way. In this age, human civilization thrived, and attained a level of sophistication that could not be attained to in the previous age. Yet humanity also lost something in this transition. In the era of Grand Unity, the simple practices of ritual were efficacious—one's understanding of how ritual ordered the world cohered with one's experience in performing ritual to order the world. In the era of Modest Prosperity, on the other hand, one's understanding of how ritual ordered the world was sometimes at odds with one's experience with ritual. In the era of Modest Prosperity, ritual failure became a reality. Living in an age of prosperity, as such, means coping with the irreconcilable nature of ritual understanding and ritual experience.

Part of the tragic nature of this narrative is the fact that humanity could go back to the kind of world that existed in the era of Grand Unity; but rather than returning, we choose to live in a prosperous, yet also a flawed, world. The rituals of antiquity do not always work in the present, so living in an era of prosperity requires transforming the efficacious rituals of the past. Yet altering the rituals of antiquity does not guarantee their success.

Fluent ritual agents, in this light, perform "experiments in paradigmity" where their best efforts in altering ritual oftentimes work; however, their alterations are never guaranteed to work. Ritual is always vulnerable to those agencies that affect the situation—be it state institutions, natural forces, or co-performers of the ritual. As such, ritual performances are fraught with anxiety. The ritual agent is concerned with his attainment of fluency, and anxious over the fact that agencies other than him or her can determine the success of ritual. He is also concerned with his inability to distinguish between his agency and the agency of others that impinge on the rite.

Ritual failure, as mentioned in chapter 8, is 'awful' in the traditional sense of the term. It is both dreadful and sublime. Failure is dreadful in that it threatens human prosperity, but sublime in that it enables the creation and proper performance of rituals upon which prosperity is founded. Indeed, failure provides not only an opportunity to recreate ritual, but also provides the space for continued investigation into what constitutes a meaningful life.

APPENDIX

On the Textual Composition of the Liji

This will provide an overview of the debates surrounding the textual composition of the *Liji*. For those wanting a more in-depth look at this issue, the best source in English is Jeffrey Riegel's dissertation, "The Four 'Tzu ssu' Chapters of the *Li chi*." James Legge also retells the traditionally accepted account of the composition of the *Liji* in his 1885 translation of the text.[1] In contemporary Chinese and Japanese, the lengthy prefaces to Hong Ye's *Liji Yinde* 《禮記引得》, Wang Meng'ou's *Liji Jinzhu Jinyi* 《禮記今註今譯》, Jiang Yihua's *Xinyi Liji Duben* 《新譯禮記讀本》, and Takeuchi Teruo's *Raiki* 《禮記》 represent the state of the field previous to 1993.[2] While there are dozens of premodern commentaries on the *Liji*, the three that I have found the most helpful are Kong Yingda's *Liji Zhengyi* 《禮記正義》, Wu Cheng's *Liji Zuanyan* 《禮記纂言》, and Wang Fuzhi's *Liji Zhangju* 《禮記章句》.[3] In combination with contemporary scholarship, these commentaries provide glimpses into the study of the *Liji* at different points throughout Chinese history. Kong Yingda (574–648) wrote in the Tang Dynasty and included much of Zheng Xuan's (127–200) commentary, which is otherwise lost, but is the earliest known commentary on the *Liji*. Wu Cheng (1249–1333) wrote in the Yuan Dynasty and saw himself following after the great Neo-Confucians of the Song. Wang Fuzhi (1619–1692) wrote in the transitional period between the Ming to the Qing Dynasty—a period characterized by the call for a return to a purer understanding of the classics, which from Wang's view had been corrupted by mistaken commentators for over a millennium. I also found collected commentaries such as the *Liji Daquan* 《禮記大全》 and the *Liji Jishuo* 《禮記集說》 to be of great assistance.[4]

Since the Guodian discovery, numerous articles and several books written by Chinese scholars have taken up the project of reexamining the composition of the *Liji*.[5] The preeminent scholar in the field is Wang E 王鍔, whose *Liji Chengshu Kao* 《禮記成書考》 takes into account the recent archeological finds.[6] His work periodizes each chapter of the *Liji* by looking at things such as linguistic patterns, appearances of portions of the text in other texts with known dates of composition, and archeological evidence. This book easily provides the best summaries of modern and premodern accounts of the compilation of the *Liji*, and presents a contemporary snapshot of the field. While his general conclusion is a little specious—he claims that the entire text was written, but not redacted, before the Qin—he represents a renewed excitement in the study of the *Liji* that is eager to challenge contemporary perceptions of early China in light of recent discoveries.

Debates about the textual composition of the *Liji* focus on two issues: the question of source material (What was the source material for each chapter? Who composed it and when?), and the question of redaction (How was the source material obtained? How was it edited? When did all of this occur, and who was involved?). The general consensus, excluding a few outlying opinions, is that the text has been relatively stable since the late second century CE.

Arguments over the first issue range from claims that the entirety of source material was written in the Six Dynasties (220–589 CE) to claims that the entirety of source material was written in the Warring States and late Chunqiu periods (770–221 BCE). Most scholars take up a position between these two extremes, seeing portions of the source material written in the Warring States, and portions of it written later in the Han.

Regardless of the position one occupies on this spectrum, the theory supporting it must account for several pieces of information. Internally, some chapters in the received text purport to be the recordings of particular historical events. The "Ai Gong Wen" 哀公問 chapter, for instance, records an appearance of Confucius before Duke Ai, who presided in the state of Lu from 494–466 BCE. Other chapters in the current text contain implicit claims of authorship. The seventh chapter, "Zengzi Wen" 曾子問, for instance, presents a series of exchanges between Confucius and his disciple Zengzi. Since the authors of texts in early China rarely identified themselves, it is not always clear who composed a text. However, all interpreters must confront the prospect that in the case of chapters such as "Zengzi Wen," the text itself claims to be written by the figures described in the text.

External information that must be accounted for includes the fact that other early texts speak of a text, or texts, called *Liji* 《禮記》 (or sometimes *Li* 《禮》), or they refer to recorded discourses (*ji* 記) on the topic of *li* 禮. Some of the texts that mention a text named *Liji* date from as early as the Chunqiu period (770–476 BCE), and a few of the references parallel chapters or passages in the received text. This problem is further exacerbated by the emergence of several texts bearing the term *li* 禮 in their title—all compiled in roughly the same time period as the *Liji*. Among the most prominent are the *Da Dai Liji* 《大戴禮記》, the *Yili* 《儀禮》, and the *Zhouli* 《周禮》.[7] When early texts mention a text named *Liji*, determining which of these texts it refers to (if any), and whether or not they were discrete entities, is no simple matter.

Additionally, any theory must take into account earlier theories—in particular, the claims of early commentators who may have also assisted in the process of redaction. Ma Rong 馬融 (79–166 CE), who some scholars believe appended the "Yueling" 月令, "Mingtangwei" 明堂位, and "Yueji" 樂記 chapters in the received text, for instance, attributed authors to certain chapters in his description of the *Liji*; oftentimes without providing reasons for so doing. Other difficult theories to account for include claims from some early scholars that a *guwen Liji* 古文禮記 was found in the wall of Confucius's home during the Han Dynasty and incorporated into the received text. It is also difficult to account for material from later commentators claiming to quote earlier commentators whose work is no longer extant.

Last but not least, any contemporary theory must account for recent archeological evidence. The Guodian find in 1993 and the bamboo manuscripts acquired by the Shanghai Museum, both dating to the late third century or early fourth century BCE, contain texts that closely resemble chapters of the *Liji*. The most complete example is the "Ziyi" 緇依, which is a part of both the Guodian and Shanghai collections. The received edition has character variants, a few extra passages, and a different ordering of the passages, but otherwise this provides conclusive proof that the "Ziyi" chapter of the *Liji* is indeed a pre-Qin text.[8] Other texts in the Shanghai manuscripts such as the *Rongchengshi* 《容成氏》 and *Minzhifumu* 《民之父母》—titles assigned by modern-day editors—are contained in chapters of the received *Liji*. The "Wen Wang Shizi" 文王世子 and "Kongzi Xianju" 孔子閒居 chapters, respectively, are comprised of these texts (with slight variation) in addition to other material not found in the Shanghai manuscripts. The recently acquired Qinghua manuscripts are rumored to also contain a number of texts explicitly treating the topic of *li* 禮.

As far as the issue of redaction is concerned, scholars generally agree on the activities involved in the process of editing the current forty-nine chapters of the *Liji*. Interpreters, however, disagree as to which activities were involved in redacting each text. Wang E provides a useful list in this regard. He claims that redacting the text involved the following activities:

1. Selecting texts from original source material.[9] The Hanshu 《漢書》, for instance, mentions 131 *ji* 記 in the category of *li* 禮.[10] It otherwise makes no mention of any text entitled *Liji*, leading many interpreters to suppose that the 131 *ji* 記 were the source material.[11]
2. Adding initial or closing lines to chapters. The "Kongzi Xianju" chapter, for instance, has seven characters that begin the text and seventeen characters that close the text, which the *Minzhifumu* manuscript from the Shanghai Museum collection lacks.
3. Adding passages from other texts. The "Jiaotesheng" 郊特牲 chapter, to use an example, quotes at length from the *Yili* with practically no variation.

4. Combining similar texts into one chapter. The literary structures of the "Xiangyinjiuyi" 鄉飲酒義 and "Wen Wang Shizi" chapters, to provide an illustration, suggest that they are each made up of several sub-texts.
5. Combining passages that were previously considered commentary into the text. Everything following the first portion of the "Daxue" 大學, for instance, is a commentary on the first section.
6. Mis-transcribing the source material. The "Yanyi" 燕義 chapter quotes from the *Zhouli* but leaves out the last few characters in the sentence, leaving the line extremely difficult to interpret without presuming that it was mis-transcribed.
7. Adding new material, perhaps written by the redactor(s), in order to incorporate ideas otherwise not present in the text. The *yinyang* 陰陽 and *wuxing* 五行 theories that appear in the "Liyun" chapter are commonly thought to be such additions.[12]

While some of the examples employed in this list are debatable, the general idea that redacting the text involved these activities is widely accepted. The problem lies in determining what activity took place in which chapter; and since the *Liji* has been commented on for over 1800 years, there are about as many different interpretations as there are possible combinations of these activities in each chapter. Oftentimes, scholars will reach the same conclusion about a particular chapter or section of the *Liji*, but arrive at that conclusion by means of different arguments. This is particularly true in comparing contemporary interpreters with premodern interpreters.

Most scholars attribute the process of redaction to Dai Sheng 戴聖, a scholar that lived sometime in the first century BCE.[13] Dai Sheng and his second cousin Dai De 戴德 came from Liang 梁 and were scholars (*boshi* 博士) who served in the Han court's Office of Ritual (*Liguan* 禮官).[14] They were both the students of Hou Cang 后蒼 (73–49 BCE), a ritual specialist thought to be an authority on the *Yili*. Dai Sheng is purported to have participated in the great debate at the Stone Conduit (*Shiquge* 石渠閣) in 51 BCE, which sought to make clear several issues regarding ritual. He eventually went on to become the Grand Protector (*taishou* 太守) of Jiujiang 九江. Zheng Xuan, in his text *Liuyi Lun* 《六藝論》, which is preserved in only fragmentary form, is the first to attribute a text called the *Liji* (with 49 chapters) to Dai Sheng.[15] While some scholars have questioned whether or not the text Zheng refers to is in fact the received *Liji*, the majority of scholars tend to accept Dai Sheng as the redactor. The received *Liji* is even sometimes referred to as the *Xiao Dai Liji* 《小戴禮記》 in the centuries that follow (since Dai Sheng was the younger of the two cousins).[16]

Not all scholars believe that Dai Sheng was the redactor of the *Liji*. While this is the minority opinion, there are good reasons to challenge the theory that Dai Sheng was the redactor.[17] The problem, however, is coming up with an alternative theory that is more persuasive than the widely accepted position. In this light, some scholars have suggested that Ma Rong or Lu Zhi 盧植 (d. 192 CE), rough contemporaries of Zheng Xuan, were the redactors.[18]

To provide an example of the kinds of conclusions that can be drawn from the information and theoretical assumptions discussed above, Wang E claims that fourteen chapters were composed in the late Chunqiu or early Warring States periods. Some of these texts, in his opinion, were even authored by Confucius himself. Nineteen chapters were composed in the mid–Warring States period, seven chapters in the mid– to late Warring States, and three chapters in the late Warring States period. This source material was then redacted sometime between 51 and 21 BCE by Dai Sheng. Wang claims that the process of redaction is easily seen in most chapters.[19]

The above discussion was meant to serve as an overview of the debates surrounding the issues of the textual composition of the *Liji*. My purpose in going through this was threefold. First of all, I sought to describe the major factors that go into a theory of the textual composition of the *Liji*. Second, and related to the first, was to demonstrate the parameters of interpretation over the past two thousand years. It should be obvious here that there is no conclusive position regarding most of these issues. Last, and perhaps most important, it was to demonstrate that my reading of *Liji* was not performed unaware of these issues, although they rarely came up in the project. I do not believe that my conclusions—as far as their relation to textual composition are concerned—ignore these parameters. As a matter of fact, I would say that the factors involved in a theory of textual composition are an implicit part of the underpinnings of this project. These factors demonstrate that early Confucians were concerned with a large number of texts on a variety of interrelated topics, all of which were written over several centuries. These texts became chapters in one central text around a time when similar efforts resulted in grand claims of creating a comprehensive world view—evidenced in texts such as the *Lüshi Chunqiu* 《呂氏春秋》and the *Huainanzi* 《淮南子》. The *Liji*, in stark contrast to these texts, does not claim to present one guiding cosmological vision with which to understand the world. Rather, it presents a complex web of interrelated concepts, which were constructed and written about in a multitude of texts. These concepts were meant to create an ordered world; yet precisely how they fit together is often unclear, and indeed seems to be less of a concern for the redactor(s). The *Liji*, perhaps, represents a conscious choice not to create a grand unifying vision of the world.

Notes

INTRODUCTION

1. Other passages in the *Liji* reemphasize this metaphor. See, for instance, "Liqi," 10.20 in D. C. Lau 劉殿爵 and Fong Ching Chen 陳方正, eds., *Liji zhuzi suoyin* 《禮記逐字索引》 Chinese University of Hong Kong, Institute of Chinese Studies, Ancient Chinese Text Concordance Series 香港中文大學中國文化研究所先秦兩漢古籍逐字索引叢刊 (Taibei台北: Taiwan shangwu yinshuguan 台灣商務印書館, 1992). Hereafter, *Liji*.
2. The editors of the *Liji Zhengyi* 《禮記正義》 provide a similar interpretation of this passage: "The Five Emperors [from the era of Grand Unity] took the Great Way as their standard; and the Three Kings [from the era of Modest Prosperity] employed ritual and appropriateness as their standard" 五帝以大道為紀，而三王則用禮義為紀. From Xueqin Li 李學勤, ed., *Shisanjing zhushu* 《十三經注疏》 (Beijing 北京: Beijing daxue chubanshe 北京大学出版社, 2000), Volume 13, 772.
3. Kong Yingda interprets the title in this manner; as quoted in E Wang 王锷, "'Datong,' 'xiaokang,' yu 'Liyun' de chengpian niandai" "大同", "小康"与《礼运》的成篇年代, *Xibeishidaxuebao* 西北师大学报 43.6 (November 2006): 68. The title of a text in early China does not always reflect the content of the text. Many texts were named for the first figure or the first words to appear (such as the "Tangong" chapters of the *Liji*); and these names were often given to the text long after its creation. The "Liyun," however, appears to be named after a major theme of the text.
4. This is partially based on Jonathan Schofer's reading of *Rabbi Nathan*. "I strive to read the text with a dual interpretive commitment. On one hand, I work to identify particularity by looking for disjunctions within the text that reveal differences between its versions or conflicts between the compilers of one stage and those of another. On the other, I determine the nature and degree of regularities, such as common terminology that underlies different stances and limits in the diversity of opinion within *Rabbi Nathan*." Jonathan Wyn Schofer, *The Making of a Sage: A Study in Rabbinic Ethics* (Madison: University of Wisconsin Press, 2005), 29–30.

5. The other Classics include the *Yijing* 《易經》 (*Book of Change*), the *Shijing* 《詩經》 (*Book of Poetry*), the *Shujing* 《書經》 (*Book of History*), and the *Chunqiu* 《春秋》 (*Spring and Autumn Annals*). For more on The Five Classics, see Michael Nylan, *The Five "Confucian" Classics* (New Haven, CT: Yale University Press, 2001).
6. For a similar approach, see Michael Nylan and Thomas Wilson, *Lives of Confucius: Civilization's Greatest Sage Through the Ages* (New York: Doubeday, 2010). Borrowing from Gu Jiegang, Nylan and Wilson note that we should consider "one Confucius at a time" (26).
7. Joseph-Marie Callery, *Li-ki: ou, Memorial des Rites: Traduit pour la premiere fois du Chinois, et accompagne de notes, de commentaires et du text original* (Turin, France: Imprimerie Royale, 1853).
8. James Legge, trans., *The Sacred Books of China: The Texts of Confucianism*, Part 3–4, *The Li Ki* (Oxford: Clarendon Press, 1885). Hereafter, *Li Ki*. Large portions of the text were also translated into German by Richard Wilhelm in *Li Gi: Das Buch der Sitte des alteren und Jungeren Dai* (Jena: Eugen Diederichs, 1930). There is also a complete translation of the text into French by S. Couvreur in *Li Ki ou memoires sur les bienseances et ceremoines*, 2 vols. (Ho Kien Fou: Mission Catholique, 1913).
9. Legge, *Li Ki*, 3:12.
10. Legge, *Li Ki*, 3:13.
11. Jeffrey K. Riegel, "The Four 'Tzu ssu' Chapters of the *Li chi*: An Analysis and Translation of the *Fang chi*, *Chung yung*, *Piao chi*, and *Tzu i*" (Ph.D. diss., Stanford University, 1978).
12. Briefly, Zisizi is Confucius's grandson and is credited with writing or redacting four chapters of the *Liji*. More importantly, he is also purported to be the teacher of Mencius (thereby establishing a direct line of teaching between Confucius and Mencius). Little historical evidence, however, substantiates these claims.
13. This definition of a ritual script comes from Jens Kreinath, Constance Hartung, and Annette Deschner, eds., *The Dynamics of Changing Rituals: The Transformation of Religious Rituals within Their Social and Cultural Context* (New York: Peter Lang Publishing, 2004), 2.
14. For more on this, see Grant Hardy, "The Reconstruction of Ritual: Capping in Ancient China," *Journal of Ritual Studies* 7.2 (Fall 1993): 69–90.
15. I spend little time, for instance, taking into account the way in which material culture shapes the discourse of ritual.
16. Ronald L. Grimes makes a similar distinction in *Ritual Criticism* (Columbia: University of South Carolina Press, 1990), 208.
17. Axel Michaels, "Perfection and Mishaps in Vedic Rituals," in *When Rituals Go Wrong: Mistakes, Failure, and the Dynamics of Ritual*, ed. Ute Hüsken (Leiden: Brill, 2007), 121.

18. This is building on Schofer, *Making of a Sage*, 7: "My project is a theoretically informed descriptive analysis of late ancient rabbinic ethics centered on *The Fathers According to Rabbi Nathan*." He continues on page 8: "My analysis centers upon close literary examination of individual passages in their distinctiveness, building inductively to make broader claims about the work as a whole and framing the study of native terminology with contemporary categories of analysis."
19. Charles Wei-shun Fu, "A Creative-Hermeneutical Investigation into the Formation and Development of the *Pratitya-samutpada* Thought," *Chung-Hwa Buddhist Journal* 4 (1991): 169–199, and "Creative Hermeneutics: Taoist Metaphysics and Heidegger," *Journal of Chinese Philosophy* 3 (1976): 115–143. For a summary of this, see Sandra A. Wawrytko, "Kongzi as Feminist: Confucian Self-Cultivation in a Contemporary Context," *Journal of Chinese Philosophy* 27.2 (June 2000): 173–174.
20. Wawrytko, "Kongzi as Feminist," 173.
21. Wawrytko, "Kongzi as Feminist," 173.
22. Lee H. Yearley, "Confucianism and Genre: Presentation and Persuasion in Early Confucian Thought," in *Confucianism in Dialogue Today: West, Christianity and Judaism*, ed. John Berthrong, Shu-Hsien Liu, and Leonard Swidler (Philadelphia: Ecumenical Press, 2004), 139.
23. Wawrytko, "Kongzi as Feminist," 174.
24. Yearley, "Confucianism and Genre," 139.
25. See Lionel M. Jensen, *Manufacturing Confucianism: Chinese Traditions and Universal Civilization* (Durham, NC: Duke University Press, 1997).

CHAPTER 1

1. D. C. Lau 劉殿爵, ed., *Maoshi zhuzi suoyin: A Concordance to the Maoshi* 《毛詩逐字索引》 (Xianggang 香港: Shangwu yinshuguan 商務印書館, 1995), *Shi* 260, 137.
2. While Antonio S. Cua is probably not the first to come up with this notion of "characterization," I came across it when reading his *The Unity of Knowledge and Action: A Study in Wang Yang-ming's Moral Psychology* (Honolulu: University Press of Hawaii, 1982), 81. For a more comprehensive account of ritual in early China, see Noah Edward Fehl, *Li: Rites and Propriety in Literature and Life—A Perspective for a Cultural History of Ancient China* (Hong Kong: Chinese University of Hong Kong, 1971).
3. Scott Cook, "Unity and Diversity in the Musical Thought of Warring States China" (Ph.D. diss., University of Michigan, 1995), 29. Michael Nylan makes a similar argument in *The Five "Confucian" Classics* (New Haven, CT: Yale University Press, 2001), 197.

4. Yuri Pines, *Foundations of Confucian Thought: Intellectual Life in the Chunqiu Period, 722–453 B.C.E.* (Honolulu: University of Hawaii Press, 2002), 210.
5. Pines, *Foundations of Confucian Thought*, 102. Pages 89–104 also provide a good summary of his view.
6. Masayuki Sato, *The Confucian Quest for Order: The Origin and Formation of the Political Thought of Xun Zi* (Boston: Brill, 2003), 178–210.
7. Roger Ames, "Observing Ritual 'Propriety (*li* 禮)' as Focusing the 'Familiar' in the Affairs of the Day," *Dao: A Journal of Comparative Philosophy* 1.2 (June 2002): 147. Ames, in contrast to the other scholars discussed above, suggests that *li* 禮 has always been understood performatively.
8. William Theodore de Bary, ed., *Self and Society in Ming Thought* (New York: Columbia University Press, 1970), ix.
9. D. C. Lau 劉殿爵 and Fong Ching Chen 陳方正, eds., *Liji zhuzi suoyin* 《禮記逐字索引》Chinese University of Hong Kong, Institute of Chinese Studies, Ancient Chinese Text Concordance Series 香港中文大學中國文化研究所先秦兩漢古籍逐字索引叢刊 (Taibei台北: Taiwan shangwu yinshuguan 台灣商務印書館, 1992), "Jitong," 26.1. Hereafter, *Liji*. The commentators in the *Liji Zhengyi* claim that these five *li* 禮 can be further divided to total 36 different kinds of *li* 禮. Xueqin Li 李學勤, ed., *Shisanjing zhushu*《十三經注疏》 (Beijing北京: Beijing daxue chubanshe 北京大学出版社, 2000), 15:1570.
10. *Liji*, "Jingjie," 27.4.
11. *Liji*, "Wangzhi," 5.42 and "Hunyi," 45.4. The "Benming" 本命 chapter of the *Da Dai Liji* also speaks of nine *li* 禮. Ming Gao 高明, ed. *Da Dai Liji Jinzhu Jinyi* 《大戴禮記今註今譯》(Taibei 臺北: Taiwan shangwu yinshuguan 臺灣商務印書館, 1975), 462–463.
12. *Shisanjing zhushu*, 12:3–6.
13. Most notable is Qin Huitian's attempt in the eighteenth century. Huitian Qin 秦蕙田, *Wuli Tongkao*《五禮通考》 (Taibei 臺北: Taiwan shangwu yinshuguan 臺灣商務印書館, 1983).
14. *Liji*, "Liqi," 10.22 and "Zhongyong," 32.25.
15. *Da Dai Liji Jinzhu Jinyi*, "Weijianjun Wenzi," 225 and "Benming," 463. D. C. Lau 劉殿爵, ed., *Hanshi waizhuan zhuzi suoyin: A Concordance to the Hanshi waizhuan*《韓詩外傳逐字索引》 (Taibei 臺北: Taiwan shangwu yinshuguan 臺灣商務印書館, 1992), 4.9.27. Chunqiu Yang 羊春秋, *Xinyi Kongzi Jiayu* 《新譯孔子家語》 (Taibei 臺北: Sanmin shuju: 三民書局, 1996), "Dizi Xing," 176.
16. See, for instance, *Shisanjing Zhushu*, 12:9. For an alternative view see the commentary in *Da Dai Liji Jinzhu Jinyi*, "Benming," 463.
17. Supporting this reading is the fact that this chapter is similar in genre to other texts such as the *Yili*, which describes the specifics of ceremonial activity. Arguing against it is the fact that his actions are never described as *li* 禮, and *li*

禮 is not mentioned except for once in the chapter to refer to Confucius's actions during a particular ceremony.

18. *Liji*, "Zhongni Yanju," 29.5. A similar definition also occurs in "Jiyi," 25.35.
19. For *yan* 言 see Zhenbin Sun, "*Yan*: A Dimension of Praxis and its Philosophical Implications," *Journal of Chinese Philosophy* 24 (1997): 191–208.
20. *Liji*, "Zhongni Yanju," 29.4.
21. *Liji*, "Yueji," 19.26 and "Jiyi," 25.34. "Liqi," 10.26 also argues for an expansive notion of *li* 禮.
22. Shen Xu 許慎, *Shuowen Jiezi* 《說文解字》(Beijing: Zhonghua Shuju, 2004), 7. The entire passage reads, "*Shi* 示: The heavens hang down images to reveal fortune and misfortune, and thereby display (示) [fortune and misfortune] to people. It comes from *er* 二 [*er* 二 is the ancient character for 'up']. The three [images] that hang down are the sun, moon, and stars. Observe the patterns of the heavens to fathom the changes of the seasons. *Shi* 示 are the affairs of the spirits" 示 天垂象，見吉凶，所以示人也。从二。(二，古文上字)。三垂，日月星也。觀乎天文，以察時變。示, 神事也. Howard Wechsler also argues that the *shi* 示 radical in the character *li* 禮 could be a pictograph of reeds used in divination or a phallic symbol. Howard J. Wechsler, *Offerings of Jade and Silk: Ritual and Symbol in the Legitimation of the T'ang Dynasty* (New Haven, CT: Yale University Press, 1985) 23.
23. Following Roger Ames, this is a paronomastic definition—a "definition by phonetic and semantic associations.... Typical of paronomastic definitions is that a 'thing' reverts to an 'event', a 'noun' becomes a 'gerund', indicating the primacy and categorical nature of process." Roger Ames, "Observing Ritual 'Propriety (*li* 禮),'" 146.
24. Xu, *Shuowen Jiezi*, 7.
25. Coincedentally, Bernhard Karlgren claims that *li* 禮 and *lü* 履 were homophones in early China. As mentioned in Roger Ames, "Observing Ritual 'Propriety (*li* 禮),'" 146.
26. *Liji*, "Liyun," 9.31–32.
27. Despite the fact that most commentators take the Great One to be the subject of the second sentence, some also, following the commentary of Zheng Xuan, ascribe a kind of primordial existence to *li* 禮. The *Liji Zhengyi* commentators, for instance, state, "Before the separation of the heavens and the earth *li* 禮 was already present" 天地未分之前已有禮也. *Shisanjing zhushu*, 12:5. The Great One may be some kind of early Chinese deity.
28. *Liji*, "Xiangyinjiuyi," 46.13. Legge explains that *xiang* 鄉 is a territorial division that was originally small, but came to be about 12,500 families. The ceremony referred to in this chapter of the *Liji* occurred once every three years. The presiding officials used it to select people for government service. James Legge, trans., *The Sacred Books of China: The Texts of Confucianism*, Part 3–4, *The Li Ki* (Oxford: Clarendon Press, 1885), 3:56 and 4:442.

29. *Liji*, "Yueji," 19.1.
30. *Liji*, "Wensang," 36.1. This is in contrast to the account provided in the "Sannian Wen" chapter, which bases the three-year mourning period off the seasons of the natural world.
31. *Liji*, "Wensang," 36.1.
32. This comes from the "Liyun" chapter.
33. Legge, *Li Ki*, Part III, 13.
34. Legge, *Li Ki*, Part III, 11–12.
35. Much of my notion of "theoretical treatment" comes from Robert F. Campany, "Xunzi and Durkheim as Theorists of Ritual Practice," in *Discourse and Practice*, ed. Frank Reynolds and David Tracy (New York: State University of New York Press, 1992), 197–231. In contrast to this, scholars such as William Haines argue that early Confucians were not theorists. William A. Haines, "Confucianism and Moral Intuition," in *Ethics in Early China: An Anthology*, ed. Chris Fraser, Dan Robins and Timothy O'Leary (Hong Kong: Hong Kong University Press, 2011), 217.
36. *Liji*, "Guanyi," 44.1.
37. The characters *liqi* 禮器 translate to "ritual vessels."
38. I borrow the notion of "cultural grammar" from Chenyang Li, "*Li* as Cultural Grammar: On the Relation Between *Li* and *Ren* in Confucius' *Analects*," *Philosophy East & West* 57.3 (July 2007): 311–329.
39. In recent years there has been an outpouring of scholarship on the notion of *qing* 情 in early China. Representative works include Roger T. Ames, and Joel Marks, eds., *Emotions in Asian Thought: A Dialogue in Comparative Philosophy* (Albany: State University of New York Press, 1995). Halvor Elfring, ed., *Love and Emotions in Traditional Chinese Literature* (Leiden: Brill, 2004), and Paolo Santangelo, ed., *Love, Hatred, and Other Passions: Questions and Themes on Emotions in Chinese Civilization* (Boston: Brill, 2006).
40. *Liji*, "Liyun," 9.23.
41. *Liji*, "Liyun," 9.23.
42. *Liji*, "Liyun," 9.23.
43. *Liji*, "Zenzi Wen," 7.25 and "Tangong Xia," 4.27.
44. "Taught" and "taut" share the same etymology. See the entries for "taught" and "taut" in the *Oxford English Dictionary*, http://dictionary.oed.com.
45. *Liji*, "Liyun," 9.35.
46. *Liji*, "Liyun," 9.35, "Yueji," 19.26, and "Jiyi," 25.34.
47. *Liji*, "Zhongyong," 32.1.
48. *Liji*, "Zhongni Yanju," 29.1. A similar passage appears in *Analects* 8.2. Bingying Xie 謝冰瑩, *Xinyi sishu duben* 新譯四書讀本 (Taibei 臺北: Sanmin shuju 三民書局, 2002), 153.
49. *Liji*, "Sannian Wen," 39.1. This is also appears in the "Lilun" 禮論 chapter of *Xunzi*. D. C. Lau 劉殿爵, ed., *Xunzi zhuzi suoyin: A Concordance to the Xunzi*

《荀子逐字索引》(Xianggang 香港: Shangwu yinshuguan 商務印書館, 1996), "Lilun," 19.

50. *Liji*, "Zhongni Yanju," 29.2.
51. Xu, *Shuowen Jiezi*, 227.
52. *Liji*, "Fangji," 32.1.
53. *Shisanjing Zhushu*, 13:936.
54. Legge claims, following the Qianlong editors's comments on the *Liji*, that *fang* 坊 metaphorically act as protective barriers—keeping out what is not good. Legge, *Li Ki*, 4:284. Legge also explains that *fang* 坊 serve "the purpose of defense against peril from within, or violence from without." Legge, *Li Ki*, 3:42.
55. Fu Xu 徐復 and Wenmin Song 宋文民, *Shuowen wubaisishi bushou zhengjie* 《說文五百四十部首正解》 (Jiangsu 江蘇: Guji chubanshe 古籍出版社, 2003), 252–253.
56. This is a point reiterated in the recently discovered *Xingzimingchu* 《性自命出》. Jingmen Shi Bowu Guan 荊门市博物馆, *Guodian chu mu zhu jian* 郭店楚墓竹簡 (Beijing 北京: Wenwu chubanshe 文物出版社, 1998), 179–184.
57. *Liji*, "Yueji," 19.1.
58. See, for instance, *Liji*, "Jiyi," 25.20, "Zaji Shang," 20.12, and "Jingjie," 27.4.
59. *Liji*, "Yueji," 19.6.
60. *Liji*, "Zhongni Yanju," 29.4.
61. On the idea of ritual knowledge in ritual studies, see Theodore W. Jennings, "On Ritual Knowledge," *Journal of Religion* 62 (1982): 111–127.
62. The notion of competence in ritual performance is developed at length in Robert Lawson and Thomas McCauley, *Rethinking Religion: Connecting Cognition and Culture* (New York: Cambridge University Press, 1990), although their notion of competence is developed in light of linguistics.
63. *Liji*, "Jianzhuan," 38.1. There is some debate about what piece of clothing this refers to as well as whether this is referring to a male or female plant. For the debate, see Legge, *Li Ki*, Part IV, 385.
64. *Liji*, "Jianzhuan," 38.1.
65. *Liji*, "Jianzhuan," 38.1.
66. *Liji*, "Liyun," 9.23.
67. *Liji*, "Liqi," 10.31. See also "Wangzhi," 5.22, "Yueji," 19.8, and "Sheyi," 47.2.
68. "Want" in this sense is different from a natural desire or inclination, as this want is a decision of the mind. A helpful article on this issue is T.C. Kline III, "The Therapy of Desire in Early Confucianism: Xunzi," *Dao: A Journal of Comparative Philosophy* 5.2 (June 2006): 235–246.
69. David S. Nivison, *The Ways of Confucianism: Investigations in Chinese Philosophy* (Chicago: Open Court, 1996), 91–96.
70. This same image is also reiterated throughout the "Wensang" chapter.
71. See the entry for "fluent" in the *Oxford English Dictionary*, http://dictionary.oed.com.

72. *Liji*, "Zhongni Yanju," 29.1.
73. *Liji*, "Liqi," 10.3 and "Zhongyong," 32.8.
74. *Liji*, "Sangfu Sizhi," 50.6.

CHAPTER 2

1. Axel Michaels, "Perfection and Mishaps in Vedic Rituals," in *When Rituals Go Wrong: Mistakes, Failure, and the Dynamics of Ritual*, ed. Ute Hüsken (Leiden: Brill, 2007), 121.
2. Victor Witter Turner, *The Forest of Symbols: Aspects of Ndembu Ritual* (Ithaca, NY: Cornell University Press, 1967).
3. Catherine M. Bell, *Ritual Theory Ritual Practice* (New York: Oxford University Press, 1992), 81.
4. Clifford Geertz, *The Interpretation of Cultures* (New York: Basic Books, 2000), 142–169; originally published in *American Anthropologist* 61 (1959): 991–1012. It is worth noting here that scholars analyzed the attempts of ritual performers to prevent their rituals from failing several decades before the Geertz article. See, for instance, E. E. Evans-Pritchard, *Witchcraft, Oracles and Magic Among the Azande* (Oxford: Clarendon Press, 1937); and shortly before Geertz was also Leon Festinger, Henry W. Riecken, and Stanley Schachter, *When Prophecy Fails* (Minneapolis: University of Minnesota Press, 1956).
5. Geertz, *Interpretation of Cultures*, 146.
6. Geertz, *Interpretation of Cultures*, 146–147.
7. Geertz, *Interpretation of Cultures*, 412–453; originally published in *Daedalus* 101 (1972): 1–37.
8. Ronald L. Grimes, *Ritual Criticism* (Columbia: University of South Carolina Press, 1990), 191–209; originally published in *Semeia* 43 (1988): 103–122.
9. Grimes, *Ritual Criticism*, 204–205.
10. Grimes, *Ritual Criticism*, 193.
11. Grimes, *Ritual Criticism*, 209.
12. Grimes defines and illustrates these infelicities as follows. A Misapplication "is a legitimate rite but the persons and circumstances involved in it are inappropriate." It could also be an "ill-timed" performance such as a harvest celebration that occurs too late or a wedding that is held too soon or too late. Grimes, *Ritual Criticism*, 199–200. Flaws are "ritual procedures that employ incorrect, vague, or inexplicit formulas. . . ." This might entail a ritual agent saying the wrong formula or singing the wrong song. Grimes, *Ritual Criticism*, 200. Hitches are "misexecutions in which the procedures are incomplete." This might occur in a dedicatory ceremony where the ritual agent states, "I hereby open this library," only to have the key break in the lock. Grimes, *Ritual Criticism*, 200. Ineffectualities are "procedures that fail to bring about intended observable changes." Grimes explains, "Ineffectualities are more serious than flaws,

because the latter are partial. In the case of the former a rite may be properly performed, but it does not produce the goods." An example would be a healing ceremony that results in the death of the person supposedly being healed. Grimes, *Ritual Criticism*, 201.

13. Roy Rappaport, *Ritual in the Making of Humanity* (Cambridge: Cambridge University Press, 1999), 187.
14. Catherine M. Bell, *Ritual: Perspectives and Dimensions* (New York: Oxford University Press, 1997), 210–252.
15. Bell, *Ritual: Perspectives and Dimensions*, 210.
16. Bell, *Ritual: Perspectives and Dimensions*, 210–211.
17. Bell, *Ritual: Perspectives and Dimensions*, 224.
18. The Collaborative Research Centre on Dynamics of Ritual can be found at http://www.ritualdynamik.de/ritualdynamik/index.php.
19. Jens Kreinath, Constance Hartung, and Annette Deschner, eds., *The Dynamics of Changing Rituals: The Transformation of Religious Rituals within Their Social and Cultural Context* (New York: Peter Lang Publishing, 2004).Ute Hüsken, ed., *When Rituals Go Wrong: Mistakes, Failure, and the Dynamics of Ritual* (Boston: Brill, 2007).
20. Edward L. Schieffelin, "Introduction," in *When Rituals Go Wrong*, 16.
21. Jens Kreinath, "Theoretical Afterthoughts," in *Dynamics of Changing Rituals*, 267–268.
22. Schieffelin, "Introduction," in *When Rituals Go Wrong*, 5.
23. Jens Kreinath et al., "Introduction," in *Dynamics of Changing Rituals*, 2.
24. Matthais Jung, "Expressive Appropriateness and Pluralism: The Example of Catholic Liturgy after Vatican II," in *Dynamics of Changing Rituals*, 227.
25. Karin Polit, "Social Consequences of Ritual Failure: A Garhwali Case Study," in *When Rituals Go Wrong*, 200.
26. Axel Michaels, "Perfection and Mishaps in Vedic Rituals," in *When Rituals Go Wrong*, 121.
27. Jan Snoek, for instance, notes that "among masons, one is generally not supposed to change the rituals: they are regarded to have 'always been so'." Jan A. M. Snoek, "Dealing with Deviations in the Performance of Masonic Rituals," in *When Rituals Go Wrong*, 100.
28. D. C. Lau 劉殿爵 and Fong Ching Chen 陳方正, eds., *Liji zhuzi suoyin* 《禮記逐字索引》Chinese University of Hong Kong, Institute of Chinese Studies, Ancient Chinese Text Concordance Series 香港中文大學中國文化研究所先秦兩漢古籍逐字索引叢刊 (Taibei 台北: Taiwan shangwu yinshuguan 台灣商務印書館, 1992), "Liqi," 10.23. Hereafter, *Liji*.
29. Grimes makes a similar distinction in *Ritual Criticism*, 208.
30. *Liji*, "Tangong Shang," 3.40.
31. See, for instance, *Liji*, "Tangong Shang," 3.25, 3.27, and "Tangong Xia," 4.60.
32. *Liji*, "Yueji," 19.5.
33. *Liji*, "Quli Shang," 1.4, and "Liyun," 9.32.

34. *Liji*, "Liqi," 10.22. At face value, this passage seems extremely significant as it presents a taxonomy of rituals. However, its grammatical construction and the terms it uses are so vague that it renders the passage nearly useless beyond a few general characterizations. The classical commentaries vary widely on interpreting this passage. More contemporary interpreters have also struggled with it. See, for instance, James Legge, trans., *The Sacred Books of China: The Texts of Confucianism*, Part 3–4, *The Li Ki* (Oxford: Clarendon Press, 1885), 3:405.
35. *Liji*, "Yueling," 6.12.
36. *Liji*, "Tangong Xia," 4.35.
37. Contemporaries such as the Mohists raised similar concerns.
38. *Liji*, "Liqi," 10.3.
39. The contemporary scholar Zhang Yinshu summarizes the notion of change in the *Liji* quite well, stating that the fluent ritual agent "relies upon the times and the contours of the earth to construct what is appropriate" 因時因地而制宜. Yinshu Zhang 張銀樹, *Liji Sixiang Conglun* 《禮記思想叢論》 (Taibei 臺北: Furen Daxue Chubanshe 輔仁大學出版社, 2006), 21.
40. *Liji*, "Liyun," 9.36.
41. *Liji*, "Jiyi," 25.23.
42. See, for instance, *Liji*, "Fangji," 31.1.

CHAPTER 3

1. Antonio S. Cua, "Paradigmatic Individuals in Confucius," in *Invitation to Chinese Philosophy*, ed. Arne Naess and Alastair Hannay (Oslo: Universitetsforlaget, 1972), 53.
2. On the issue of "feelings," see T. C. Kline III, "The Therapy of Desire in Early Confucianism: Xunzi," *Dao: A Journal of Comparative Philosophy* 5.2 (June 2006): 235–246 and Manyul Im, "Emotional Control and Virtue in the *Mencius*," *Philosophy East & West* 49.1 (January 1999): 1–27.
3. The debate on "development" versus "reformation" is taken up in Philip J. Ivanhoe and T. C. Kline III, eds., *Virtue, Nature, and Moral Agency in the* Xunzi (Indianapolis: Hackett Publishing, 2000).
4. The foundational work on *yi* 義 appears in Chung-ying Cheng, *New Dimensions of Confucian and Neo-Confucian Philosophy* (Albany: State University of New York Press, 1991), 233–245 and David L. Hall and Roger T. Ames, *Thinking Through Confucius* (Albany: State University of New York Press, 1987), 89–110.
5. On connoisseurship, see Eric Hutton, "Moral Connoisseurship in Mengzi," in *Essays on the Moral Philosophy of Mengzi*, ed. Philip J. Ivanhoe and Xiusheng Liu (Indianapolis: Hackett Publishing, 2002), 163–186.
6. The language of "ruling on rules" is used throughout Antonio S. Cua, *Dimensions of Moral Creativity: Paradigms, Principles, and Ideals* (University Park: Pennsylvania State University Press, 1978). See page 74, for instance.

7. For a discussion on the language of "exceptions" and its inapplicability to Confucian ethics, see Bryan W. Van Norden, *Virtue Ethics and Consequentialism in Early Chinese Philosophy* (New York: Cambridge University Press, 2007), 238–242. Someone who does take a position of exceptions and recourse to meta-rules is Robert Eno, "Casuistry and Character in the *Mencius*," in *Mencius: Contexts and Interpretations*, ed. Alan Chan (Honolulu: University of Hawaii Press, 2002), 194–195.
8. On the topic of extension, see Philip Ivanhoe, "Confucian Self Cultivation and Mengzi's Notion of Extension," and David Wong, "Reasons and Analogical Reasoning in Mengzi," in *Essays on the Moral Philosophy of Mengzi*, ed. Philip J. Ivanhoe and Xiusheng Liu (Indianapolis: Hackett Publishing, 2002), 221–241 and 187–220. The lengthiest discussion of this topic occurs throughout Antonio S. Cua, *Ethical Argumentation: A Study in Hsün Tzu's Moral Epistemology* (Honolulu: University of Hawaii Press, 1985).
9. For more on the notion of "hard cases" in Confucianism, see John H. Berthrong, "The Hard Sayings: The Confucian Case of *Xiao* 孝 in Kongzi and Mengzi," *Dao: A Journal of Chinese Philosophy* 7.2 (June 2008): 119–123.
10. Bingying Xie 謝冰瑩, *Xinyi sishu duben* 《新譯四書讀本》 (Taibei 臺北: Sanmin shuju 三民書局, 2002), 476.
11. Cua, I should note, distinguishes between "exigencies" and "exceptions." The former are indeterminate and the latter are subsumptive.
12. Cua, *Dimensions of Moral Creativity*, 92.
13. This interpretation of the "spirit" of the rule is put forth in Yuli Liu, *The Unity of Rule and Virtue: A Critique of a Supposed Parallel between Confucian Ethics and Virtue Ethics* (Singapore: Eastern Universities Press, 2004), 148; Kwong-Loi Shun, *Mencius and Early Chinese Thought* (Stanford: Stanford University Press, 1997), 55–56 and Amy Olberding, "'Ascending the Hall': Style and Moral Improvement in the *Analects*," *Philosophy East & West* 59.4 (October 2009): 508.
14. Robert Eno, "Casuistry and Character in the *Mencius*," in Mencius*: Contexts and Interpretations*, ed. Alan K. L. Chan (Honolulu: University of Hawaii Press, 2002), 194–195.
15. D. C. Lau, trans., *Confucius: The Analects* (New York: Dorset Press, 1986), 27.
16. Arguing against this reading of *Mencius* 4A17 is the fact that Mencius seems to have this explicit argument at his disposal in terms of this being a situation where a drowning sister-in-law is not really a sister-in-law, in a way similar to a bad king not really being a king, but he does not employ this here.
17. Antonio S. Cua, *Moral Vision and Tradition: Essays in Chinese Ethics* (Washington, D.C.: Catholic University of America Press, 1998), 291.
18. Cua, *Dimensions of Moral Creativity*, 79.
19. Van Norden, *Virtue Ethics and Consequentialism*, 238–242.
20. D. C. Lau 劉殿爵 and Fong Ching Chen 陳方正, eds., *Liji zhuzi suoyin* 《禮記逐字索引》 Chinese University of Hong Kong, Institute of Chinese Studies,

Ancient Chinese Text Concordance Series 香港中文大學中國文化研究所先秦兩漢古籍逐字索引叢刊 (Taibei台北: Taiwan shangwu yinshuguan 台灣商務印書館, 1992), "Tangong Shang," 3.1. Hereafter, *Liji*.

21. For the variety of ways this term is used in the ethical discourse of early China, see Griet Vankeerberghen, "Choosing Balance: Weighing (*Quan* 權) as a Metaphor for Action in Early Chinese Texts," *Early China* 30 (2005): 47–89. See also John H. Berthrong, "Weighing the Way: Metaphoric Balance in *Analects* 9:30," in *Interpretation and Intellectual Change: Chinese Hermeneutics in Historical Perspective*, ed. Ching-I Tu, (New Brunswick, NJ: Transaction Publications, 2005), 3–18.
22. Edward G. Slingerland, "Virtue Ethics, The *Analects*, and the Problem of Commensurability," *Journal of Religious Ethics* 29.1 (2001): 104–105.
23. Philip J. Ivanhoe, *Ethics in the Confucian Tradition: The Thought of Mencius and Wang Yang-ming* (Cambridge: Hackett Publishing Company, 2002), 112. This same image also appears in early commentaries on the classics.
24. Gregory Smits, "The Intersection of Politics and Thought in Ryukyuan Confucianism: Sai On's Uses of *Quan*," *Harvard Journal of Asiatic Studies* 56.2 (December 1996): 474.
25. Lee H. Yearley, "A Confucian Crisis: Mencius' Two Cosmogonies and Their Ethics," in *Cosmogony and Ethical Order: New Studies in Comparative Ethics*, ed. Robin W. Lovin and Frank E. Reynolds (Chicago: University of Chicago Press, 1985), 316.
26. Slingerland, "Virtue Ethics," 103.
27. Chenyang Li, "*Li* as Cultural Grammar: On the Relation Between *Li* and *Ren* in Confucius' *Analects*," *Philosophy East & West* 57.3 (July 2007): 311–329.
28. Li, "*Li* as Cultural Grammar," 317 and 322.
29. Li, "*Li* as Cultural Grammar," 311.
30. Li, "*Li* as Cultural Grammar," 321.
31. Hall and Ames, *Thinking Through Confucius*, 99–100.
32. Hall and Ames, *Thinking Through Confucius*, 108.
33. An interesting correlation appears in Catherine M. Bell, *Ritual Theory Ritual Practice* (New York: Oxford University Press, 1992), 98: "A ritualized body is a body invested with a 'sense' of ritual. This sense of ritual exists as an implicit variety of schemes whose deployment works to produce sociocultural situations that the ritualized body can dominate in some way.... This 'sense' is not a matter of self-conscious knowledge of any explicit rules of ritual but is an implicit 'cultivated disposition.'" On page 107, she continues, "The ritualized social body, therefore, is one that comes to possess, to various degrees, a cultural 'sense of ritual'." On page 116, Bell calls this a "cultural sixth 'sense.'"
34. Karyn Lai employs the language of skill throughout *Learning from Chinese Philosophies: Ethics of Interdependent and Contextualised Self* (Burlington, VT: Ashgate, 2006).

35. The language of orientation appears in Adam B. Seligman et al., *Ritual and its Consequences: An Essay on the Limits of Sincerity* (New York: Oxford University Press, 2008), 4–5.
36. Gier Sigurdsson, "Learning and *Li*: The Confucian Process of Humanization Through Ritual Propriety" (Ph.D. diss., University of Hawaii, 2004), 142.
37. Amy Olberding, "The Educative Function of Personal Style in the *Analects*," *Philosophy East & West* 57.3 (July 2007): 357–374.
38. Eno "Casuistry and Character in the *Mencius*," 210.
39. Philip J. Ivanhoe, for instance, is quite direct about this: "...Kongzi is best understood as a virtue ethicist." Ivanhoe, *Ethics in the Confucian Tradition*, 4.
40. For a useful introduction to virtue ethics, see Stephen Darwall, ed., *Virtue Ethics* (Malden, MA: Blackwell Publishing, 2003).
41. The issue of skills in contrast to virtues is taken up in several places, but for an extended account see Linda Trinkaus Zagzebski, *Virtues of the Mind: An Inquiry into the Nature of Virtue and the Ethical Foundations of Knowledge* (Cambridge: Cambridge University Press, 1995), 102–137.
42. Lee H. Yearley, *Mencius and Aquinas: Theories of Virtue and Conceptions of Courage* (Albany: State University of New York Press, 1990), 13.
43. Yearley, *Mencius and Aquinas*, 70.
44. See, for instance, Van Norden, *Virtue Ethics and Consequentialism*, 39.
45. For more on potential differences between a Confucian virtue ethic and an Aristotelian virtue ethic, see Junren Wan, "Contrasting Confucian Virtue Ethics and MacIntyre's Aristotelian Virtue Theory," in *Chinese Philosophy in an Era of Globalization*, ed. Robin R. Wang (Albany: State University of New York Press, 2004), 123–149. See also Alasdair MacIntyre's response immediately following this article on pages 151–162. While Benjamin Wong and Hui-Chieh Loy in "The Confucian Gentleman and the Limits of Ethical Change," *Journal of Chinese Philosophy* 28.3 (September 2001): 209, see a virtue ethics reading of Confucianism as "non-controversial," others such as Roger Ames and Henry Rosemont have challenged the usefulness of applying virtue ethics to the study of Confucianism. See Roger T. Ames and Henry Rosemont, Jr., "Were the Early Confucians Virtuous?" in *Ethics in Early China: An Anthology*, ed. Chris Fraser, Dan Robins, and Timothy O'Leary (Hong Kong: Hong Kong University Press, 2011), 17–39.
46. Robert Merrihew Adams, *A Theory of Virtue: Excellence in Being for the Good* (Oxford: Oxford University Press, 2006), 165–168. Lisa Tessman, *Burdened Virtues: Virtue Ethics for Liberatory Struggles* (New York: Oxford University Press, 2005), 4.
47. Rosalind Hursthouse, *On Virtue Ethics* (New York, Oxford University Press, 1999), 44–51.
48. Cua is a notable exception. In *Dimensions of Moral Creativity*, 101, he develops a notion of "regret" similar to Williams's.

49. Cua summarizes this quite well: "[A]nalogical projection is not an inference from the known to the unknown, but representative of an attempt to connect items of knowledge about the present circumstance and ethical knowledge of the past." Cua, *Ethical Argumentation*, 86.
50. Cua, *Ethical Argumentation*, 82–83.
51. See, for instance, Cua, *Moral Vision and Tradition*, 286–287.
52. Wong, "Reasons and Analogical Reasoning in Mengzi," in *Essays on the Moral Philosophy of Mengzi*, 187–220.
53. Wong, "Reasons and Analogical Reasoning in Mengzi," in *Essays on the Moral Philosophy of Mengzi*, 200.
54. Wong, "Reasons and Analogical Reasoning in Mengzi," in *Essays on the Moral Philosophy of Mengzi*, 205.
55. Wong, "Reasons and Analogical Reasoning in Mengzi," in *Essays on the Moral Philosophy of Mengzi*, 212.
56. Cua and Wong seem to agree on this point. Cua uses the analogy of a "savings account in a bank." He states, "In this light, wisdom is the ability to make use of the depository of moral insights derived from the exercise of *yi* 義...." Cua, *Moral Vision and Tradition*, 286–287.
57. Philip Ivanhoe, "Confucian Self Cultivation and Mengzi's Notion of Extension," 232.
58. Van Norden, *Virtue Ethics and Consequentialism*, 236–237.
59. Cua, *Dimensions of Moral Creativity*, 18.
60. Cua, *Ethical Argumentation*, 61–87.
61. Olberding, "Educative Function of Personal Style in the *Analects*," 371.
62. Much of Cua's work on agency, it is worth noting, is situated in larger discussions about ethics and agency in the Western philosophical discourse. Ludwig Wittgenstein's *Philosophical Fragments* (New York: Macmillian, 1953) played a particularly important role in this discourse.
63. Cua, *Moral Vision and Tradition*, 5–6.
64. Cua, *Moral Vision and Tradition*, 5–6.
65. Stephen A. Wilson, "Conformity, Individuality, and the Nature of Virtue," *Journal of Religious Ethics* 23.2 (2001): 271.
66. Wilson, "Conformity, Individuality, and the Nature of Virtue," 274. Wilson unfortunately does not go on to distinguish between a "change" and a "modification"—and clarifying this kind of terminology would certainly further the debate on allowable deviation—but he does speak to the larger issue of the divide between positions of more allowable and less allowable deviation from ritual scripts. Ivanhoe shares in Wilson's critique of Hall and Ames: "[They] see Kongzi as a freewheeling, postmodern aesthete who perceives, evaluates, and responds to various actions, institutions, and events in light of his own subjective sensibilities." Ivanhoe, *Ethics in the Confucian Tradition*, 7.

67. Herbert Fingarette, *Confucius: The Secular as Sacred* (New York: Harper & Row, 1972), 57.
68. This metaphor and Fingarette's usage of it are discussed at length in Zhou Qin, "Cosmic Order and Moral Autonomy: The Rise of Confucian Ethics in Axial Age China" (Ph.D. diss., Harvard University, 2000), 2–46.
69. Randall P. Peerenboom, *Law and Morality in Ancient China: The Silk Manuscripts of Huang-Lao* (Albany: State University of New York Press, 1993), 130.
70. Olberding, "Educative Function of Personal Style in the *Analects*," 372.
71. Hall and Ames, *Thinking Through Confucius*, 159.
72. Edward G. Slingerland, "The Conception of *Ming* in Early Confucian Thought," *Philosophy East & West* 46.4 (October 1996): 567–581.
73. Slingerland, "Conception of *Ming*," 568.
74. Stephen Angle, "No Supreme Principle: Confucianism's Harmonization of Multiple Values," *Dao: A Journal of Comparative Philosophy* 7.1 (Spring 2008): 35–40.
75. Ivanhoe, "Question of Faith," 160–161. For an alternative position, see Ning Chen, "The Concept of Fate in Mencius," *Philosophy East & West* 47.4 (October 1997): 495–520. Chen's basic thesis is that in the *Mencius* moral determinism (i.e., the notion that there is a good force in the universe rewarding right and punishing wrong) functions at large, but on the small scale of the person, blind fate seems to be at play.
76. Ivanhoe, "Confucian Self Cultivation and Mengzi's Notion of Extension," 224. Yong Huang makes a similar point: "[F]or Confucians, one should be moral because it is a joyful thing to be moral." Yong Huang, "Confucius and Mencius on the Motivation to be Moral," *Philosophy East & West* 60.1 (January 2010): 66.
77. For an extended account of Ivanhoe's treatment of situations requiring sorrowful responses, see Philip J. Ivanhoe, "Death and Dying in the *Analects*," in *Confucian Spirituality*, vol. 1, ed. Weiming Tu and Mary Evelyn Tucker (New York: Crossroad Publishing Company, 2003), 220–232.
78. Ivanhoe, "Question of Faith," 158.
79. Mark Csikszentmihalyi, *Material Virtue: Ethics and the Body in Early China* (Boston: Brill, 2004), 6.
80. Csikszentmihalyi, *Material Virtue*, 7.
81. Jiyuan Yu, *The Ethics of Confucius and Aristotle: Mirrors of Virtue* (New York: Routledge, 2007), 187. Yu also states, "The fulfillment of one's original nature is within the agent's firm grasp. It can neither be enhanced by the possession of great external goods, nor be diminished by great misfortune." Yu, 187. On page 192, Yu continues, "Indeed, although Confucius acknowledges that fortune affects many aspects of human life, he does not think that it affects one's moral life. The achievement of virtue, even if it is not exercised, amounts to the fulfillment of human way which is the highest good. He realizes that virtue should be exercised, and also knows well that practicing virtue is vulnerable to

external conditions. Yet in his view, the lack of external goods is simply a matter of *ming* 命 ('what is given'). As long as an agent possesses virtue, his or her life shines even without exercising virtue."

82. Martha Nussbaum also notes similar attempts in ancient and modern philosophy to avoid the problem of vulnerability or moral luck. See Martha C. Nussbaum, *The Fragility of Goodness: Luck and Ethics in Greek Tragedy and Philosophy* (New York: Cambridge University Press, 1986), 319–322. Several other contemporary ethicists have taken up the problem of moral luck. These include Bernard Williams, *Moral Luck: Philosophical Papers, 1973–1980* (New York: Cambridge University Press, 1981) and Thomas Nagel, *Mortal Questions* (New York: Cambridge University Press, 1979). For views closer to those put forth in this article, see Margaret Urban Walker, "Moral Luck and the Virtues of Impure Agency," in *Moral Luck*, ed. Daniel Statman (Albany: State University of New York Press, 1993), 235–250. For an explicit look at the issue of moral luck in Confucianism, see Sean Drysdale Walsh, "Varieties of Moral Luck in Ethical and Political Philosophy for Confucius and Aristotle," in *Virtue Ethics and Confucianism*, ed. Steven Angle and Michael Slote, forthcoming.
83. Fingarette also takes a similar position in *Confucius: The Secular as Sacred*, 52.
84. Edward Slingerland, trans., *Confucius: Analects* (Cambridge: Hackett Publishing, 2003), 56 and 65.

CHAPTER 4

1. D. C. Lau 劉殿爵 and Fong Ching Chen 陳方正, eds., *Liji zhuzi suoyin* 《禮記逐字索引》 Chinese University of Hong Kong, Institute of Chinese Studies, Ancient Chinese Text Concordance Series 香港中文大學中國文化研究所先秦兩漢古籍逐字索引叢刊 (Taibei 台北: Taiwan shangwu yinshuguan 台灣商務印書館, 1992), "Quli Shang," 1.4. Hereafter, *Liji*.
2. *Liji*, "Tangong Shang," 3.81.
3. *Liji*, "Shaoyi," 17.30.
4. *Liji*, "Tangong Xia," 4.57.
5. *Liji*, "Jiyi," 25.9–11. I translated *huanghu* 慌惚 as "lost abstraction of mind" following James Legge, trans., *The Sacred Books of China: The Texts of Confucianism*, parts 3–4, *The Li Ki* (Oxford: Clarendon Press, 1885), 4:214.
6. *Liji*, "Tangong Xia," 4.29.
7. *Liji*, "Tangong Shang," 3.55.
8. *Liji*, "Liyun," 9.35.
9. *Liji*, "Ruxing," 42.6. While this image seems to be used in the "Ruxing" chapter in a positive sense, it is also used pejoratively in other texts to refer to the act of "cobbling things together" or making something without a mold when in fact one should be used. Some commentators also read its appearance in the "Ruxing" chapter with this pejorative meaning. See Daozhou Huang 黃道周,

Ruxing jizhuan《儒行集傳》(Taibei 臺北: Taiwan shangwu yinshuguan 臺灣商務印書館, 1983), 15–23.

10. Ronald Grimes, of course, also deals with the notion of ritual creativity in *Deeply into the Bone: Re-Inventing Rites of Passage* (Berkeley: University of California Press, 2000). See especially page 12.
11. *Liji*, "Tangong Shang," 3.74.
12. *Liji*, "Tangong Xia," 4.15.
13. *Liji*, "Yueji," 19.5.
14. *Liji*, "Tangong Xia," 4.15.
15. See, for instance, Herbert Fingarette, *Confucius: The Secular as Sacred* (New York: Harper & Row, 1972), 57.
16. *Liji*, "Tangong Shang," 3.45.
17. This is a central topic of chapters such as "Liqi," "Mingtangwei," and "Jiaotesheng."
18. *Liji*, "Tangong Shang," 3.12.
19. *Liji*, "Neize," 12.33.
20. *Liji*, "Liqi," 10.23. Some commentators read *ju* 醵 differently. See Xueqin Li 李學勤, ed., *Shisanjing zhushu* 《十三經注疏》 (Beijing北京: Beijing daxue chubanshe 北京大学出版社, 2000), 13:869.
21. *Liji*, "Mingtangwei," 14.28.
22. At the same time, however, as stated in several places of this project, the ritual scripts of the past cannot simply be abandoned. *Liji*, "Jingjie," 27.4 is worth noting in this regard. "Ritual prevents chaos like the way a dam stops up water. In this light, if [one] considers the old dams useless and destroys them, there will certainly be a flood. Likewise, if [one] considers the old rituals useless and does away with them there will certainly be chaos" 夫禮，禁亂之所由生，猶坊止水之所自來也。故以舊坊為無所用而壞之者，必 有水敗；以舊禮為無所用而去之者，必有亂患.
23. *Liji*, "Zengzi Wen," 7.18. Duke Zhao of Lu is explicitly labeled as someone who does not properly perform ritual in "Zengzi Wen," 7.7. The notion of *cimu* 慈母, translated here as "caretaker," could refer to a concubine that helps raise the king's children.
24. For a more detailed account of Jing Jiang, see Lisa A. Raphals, "A Woman Who Understood the Rites," in *Confucius and the* Analects: *New Essays*, ed. Bryan Van Norden (New York: Oxford University Press, 2002), 275–302.
25. *Liji*, "Tangong Xia," 4.14.
26. See, for instance, *Liji*, "Jiaotesheng," 11.24.
27. *Liji*, "Tangong Shang," 3.32.
28. *Liji*, "Tangong Shang," 3.49. Most commentators read *yi* 易 in this passage to refer to grass or shrubs. See, for instance, Yihua Jiang 姜義華, *Xinyi Liji duben* 《新譯禮記讀本》(Taibei 臺北: Sanmin shuju 三民書局, 1997), 100. Similar to my reading, Legge claims, "This paragraph does not seem to contain any lessons of censure or approval, but simply to relate a fact." Legge, *Li Ki*, 3:133.

29. *Liji*, "Liqi," 10.25.
30. *Liji*, "Tangong Xia," 4.65.
31. The phrase *wuwenzhi* 吾聞之 tends to be used in the sense of "hearing about the proper way things were done in the past." It usually implies a value judgment.
32. *Liji*, "Tangong Shang," 3.83.
33. *Cheng* 稱 is also used in this sense in *Liji*, "Liqi," 10.16.
34. *Liji*, "Sangfu Sizhi," 50.6.
35. For more on *quan* 權 see Griet Vankeerberghen, "Choosing Balance: Weighing (*Quan* 權) as a Metaphor for Action in Early Chinese Texts," *Early China* 30 (2005): 47–89.
36. See, for instance, *Liji*, "Zaji Xia," 21.24 and 33, "Wensang," 36.1, and "Wangzhi," 5.48.
37. *Liji*, "Liqi," 10.3.
38. See, for instance, *Liji*, "Jiaotesheng," 11.6, "Liqi," 10.27–28, "Wangzhi," 5.40, and "Quli Xia," 2.4.
39. *Liji*, "Tangong Shang," 3.44.
40. *Liji*, "Tangong Shang," 3.45 and 92.
41. This is a translation of the title.
42. *Liji*, "Tangong Shang," 3.55. This is a central theme in the "Zengzi Wen" chapter. The significance of unprecedented situations, especially cosmological anomalies, is discussed in Robert Ford Campany, *Strange Writing: Anomaly Accounts in Early Medieval China* (Albany: State University of New York Press, 1996). His comment on page 8 is worth noting: "Anomalies are 'good to think with' in at least one other respect: by their alterity they prompt individual and collective self-reflection. They are thus key vehicles for the collective fashioning of identify and the construction of society." For a discussion of the issue of anomalies in the Qing, see John B. Henderson, *The Development and Decline of Chinese Cosmology* (New York: Columbia University Press, 1984).
43. *Liji*, "Tangong Shang," 3.1.
44. See, for instance, *Liji*, "Liqi," 10.4.
45. *Liji*, "Tangong Xia," 4.60.
46. *Liji*, "Tangong Shang," 3.25.
47. See, for instance, *Liji*, "Zengzi Wen," 7.18 and "Tangong Shang," 3.53.
48. *Liji*, "Jiaotesheng," 11.10.

CHAPTER 5

1. D. C. Lau 劉殿爵 and Fong Ching Chen 陳方正, eds., *Liji zhuzi suoyin* 《禮記逐字索引》 Chinese University of Hong Kong, Institute of Chinese Studies, Ancient Chinese Text Concordance Series 香港中文大學中國文化研究所先秦兩漢古籍逐字索引叢刊 (Taibei 台北: Taiwan shangwu yinshuguan 台灣商務印書館, 1992), "Zengzi Wen," 7.4. Hereafter, *Liji*.

2. The *zha* 蜡 ceremony is a series of state-sponsored sacrifices offered in the twelfth month of the year. The "Jiaotesheng" 郊特牲 chapter of the *Liji* speaks of the *zha* 蜡 ceremony as the culmination of other similar sacrifices offered earlier in the year, with offerings made to the spirits of the harvest, the spirits associated with animals, and the spirits associated with the control of water, among others. *Liji*, "Jiaotesheng," 11.21–11.22.
3. *Liji*, "Liyun," 9.1.
4. *Liji*, "Liyun," 9.1.
5. Traditional commentaries suggest several possible reasons for why the Great Way became obscure. Sun Xidan 孫希旦 in his *Liji Jijie*《禮記集解》, for instance, attributes the shift from an era of Grand Unity to an era of Modest Prosperity to a change in the *qi* 氣 that constituted the world. *Qi* 氣 in the era of Grand Unity was more thick than in the era of Modest Prosperity. The transformation from Grand Unity to Modest Prosperity, therefore, "was caused by the times" 時為之也. This is as quoted in Lin Suwen 林素玟, *Liji Renwenxue Tanjiu* 《禮記》人文學探究 (Taibei 臺北: Wenjin chubanshe 文津出版社，2001), 236–237. Other commentators explain that people performed the rituals of antiquity (*guzhili* 古之禮), but no longer understood the reasons why they were performed (*weizu yide guren weilizhiyi* 未足以得古人為禮之意); see Shi Wei 衛湜, ed., *Liji Jishuo* 《禮記集說》(Taibei 臺北: Taiwan shangwu yinshuguan 臺灣商務印書館, 1983), 54.6a–b. Another popular explanation is the change from leaders chosen by merit to leaders chosen by lineage.
6. Liang Tao suggests that the creation of weapons correlated with the rise of rulers chosen by lineage—people now needed weapons to overthrow evil rulers. Tao Liang 梁涛, *Guodian zhujian yu simeng xuepai* 《郭店竹简与思孟学派》 (Beijing 北京: Zhongguo renming daxue chbanshe 中国人民大学出版社, 2008), 162–163.
7. *Liji*, "Liqi," 10.20.
8. Later, the "Liyun" chapter also explains, "Ritual is the means by which the early kings inherited the Way of Heaven" 夫禮，先王以承天之道. *Liji*, "Liyun," 9.2.
9. *Liji*, "Liyun," 9.5–7.
10. *Liji*, "Liyun," 9.7–9.9.
11. Chunqiu Yang 羊春秋, *Xinyi Kongzi Jiayu* 《新譯孔子家語》 (Taibei 臺北: Sanmin shuju: 三民書局, 1996), 430–450. The *Kongzi Jiayu* describes the periods of Grand Unity and Modest Prosperity but does not mention a situation where human beings lived in crude conditions. The account also does not use the label 'Modest Prosperity'; instead, it uses no label at all for the period after Grand Unity. The "Ciguo" 辭過 chapter of the *Mozi* also employs language similar to the "Liyun" in describing the coming forth of civilization. While it credits the sages with creating the implements necessary to civilize humanity, it notably does not discuss their inventions in terms of *li* 禮. Rather, a central purpose of the chapter is to critique those who have added to the inventions of

the sages—making clothing, meals, and homes ostentatious, and adding a heavy burden on society while doing this. Some interpreters of the "Liyun" have argued for a Mohist influence on the text—besides employing much of the same language in describing the precivilized state of humanity it also discusses the era of Grand Unity as largely a simple era, which can be seen as kind of a Mohist utopia. D. C. Lau 劉殿爵, ed., *Mozi zhuzi suoyin: A concordance to the Mozi* 《墨子逐字索引》 (Xianggang 香港: Shangwu yinshuguan 商務印書館, 2001), 1.6. With good reason, some scholars argue that the account of Grand Unity and Modest Prosperity actually originated in a tradition independent from the tradition that advocated early society living in deplorable conditions. Years later they were combined in the "Liyun" as found in the *Liji*. For more on this, see Chaoming Yang 杨朝明, "'Liyun' Chengpian yu xuepaishuxing deng wenti" 《礼运》成篇与学派属性等问题, *Zhongguo Wenhua Yanjiu* 《中国文化研究》 1 (2005).

12. For an alternative reading of this chronology, see Michael Puett, "Ritualization as Domestication: Ritual Theory from Classical China," in *Ritual Dynamics and the Science of Ritual*, ed. Axel Michaels et al. (Wiesbaden: Harrassowitz, 2010), 1:359–370. Puett reads the era of Grand Unity as the time where people were living in caves and nests.
13. While early commentators are not uniform in their accounts, many use labels such as "early antiquity" (*shanggu* 上古), "mid-antiquity" (*zhonggu* 中古), and "late antiquity" (*xiagu* 下古) to make sense of these various periods. See Wei, *Liji Jishuo*, 54.37b–40a, 41b–42a, and 44a–45b.
14. The second passage of the "Liyun" chapter explains, "Ritual is the means by which the early kings continued the Way of Heaven" 夫禮，先王以承天之道. *Liji*, "Liyun," 9.2.
15. The editors of the *Liji Zhengyi* 《禮記正義》 provide a similar interpretation of this passage: "The Five Emperors [from the era of Grand Unity] took the Great Way as their standard (*ji* 紀); but the Three Kings [from the era of Modest Prosperity] employed ritual and appropriateness as their standard" 五帝以大道為紀，而三王則用禮義為紀. Xueqin Li 李學勤, ed., *Shisanjing zhushu* 《十三經注疏》 (Beijing 北京: Beijing daxue chubanshe 北京大学出版社, 2000), 13:772.
16. In light of the problems discussed above concerning the textual history of the "Liyun," some traditional commentators argue that ritual only came about in the era of Modest Prosperity. See Wei, *Liji Jishuo*, 54.13b–22a.
17. Chen Yun, a contemporary scholar, builds on the account of *li* 禮 presented in the preface of the *Liji Zhengyi* to speak about three stages in the development of *li* 禮—the first stage where the "principles of ritual" 禮理 existed but people did not perform ritual, the second stage where people performed the "activities of ritual" 禮事 but did not recognize them as ritual, and the final stage where the "term ritual" 禮名 came about. Chen does not, however, explicitly situate this in

the narrative about Grand Unity and Modest Prosperity. See page 60 of Yun Chen 陈赟, "Datong, xiaokang yu liyueshenghuo de kaiqi—jianlun 'liyun' datong zhi shuo zai shenme yiyishang bushi wutuobang" 大同，小康与礼乐生活的开启——兼论《礼运》"大同" 之说在什么意义上不是乌托邦, *Fujian luntan—Renwen shehuikexueban* 福建论坛——人文社会科学版 6 (2006).

18. See, for instance, Wei, *Liji Jishuo*, 54.14a–b. This reading emerges as the dominant reading of the "Liyun" in contemporary times. Sun Yat-sen, founder of the Republic of China, even saw the Republic as the means of reinstituting the era of Grand Unity. See Renze Tang 汤仁泽, "'Datongxue' he 'Liyunzhu'" "大同学" 和《礼运注》, *Shilin* 史林 4 (1997).

19. *Liji*, "Yueji," 19.1. The *Analects*, of course, casts the notion of *tong* 同 explicitly in a pejorative light—"The profound person harmonizes [with others], but does not conform (*tong* 同) [to them]; whereas the petty person conforms [to them], but does not harmonize [with them]" 君子和而不同，小人同而不和. D. C. Lau 劉殿爵, Che Wah Ho 何志華, and Fong Ching Chen 陳方正, eds., *Lunyu zhuzi suoyin*《論語逐字索引》(Chinese University of Hong Kong, Institute of Chinese Studies, Ancient Chinese Text Concordance Series 香港中文大學中國文化研究所先秦兩漢古籍逐字索引叢刊. Xianggang 香港: Shangwu yinshuguan 商務印書館, 1995), 13.24.

20. This bears some resemblance to Otto Rank's notions of "fear of death" and "fear of life." See *Will Therapy: An Analysis of Therapeutic Process in Terms of Relationship*, translated by Julia Jesse Taft (New York: Alfred A. Knopf, 1936).

21. James, Legge, trans., *The Chinese Classics: The She King or The Book of Poetry* (Taibei: SMC Publishing Inc., 1991), 495–498. The translation is my own. The *Shijing* poem continues, replacing *xiaokang* 小康 with *xiaoxiu* 小休, *xiaoxi* 小息, *xiaokai* 小愒, and *xiaoan* 小安 in subsequent stanzas. Each of these terms refers to a period of rest. Duan Yucai claims that *kang* 康 originated from the character *kang* 穅, and defines the latter as the husk of grain. See Jianshe Jiang 姜建设, "'Datong Xiaokang' Suyuan" "大同小康"溯源, *Xinyang Shifanxueyuan Xuebao* 信阳师范学院学报 14.4 (December 1994): 59. *Xiaokang* 小康, as such, may refer to the harvest and the period of rest following the harvest. Coincidentally, the image of the harvest is central to passage 35 in the "Liyun" where *li* 禮 is likened to the plow the sages use to cultivate the field of "human disposition" 人情.

22. Fung Yu-lan states this quite succinctly in his *History of Chinese Philosophy*. In introducing the "Liyun" he explains, "Later Confucianism received considerable Daoist influence. In the political and social philosophy of one part of the Confucian school, this influence is well represented in the section entitled 'The Evolutions of *Li*' [The 'Liyun']." He then goes on to state, "This idea [of Grand Unity and Small Prosperity] is one plainly borrowed from the social and political philosophy of the Daoists." Yu-lan Fung, *A History of Chinese Philosophy*, 2 vols., translated by Derk Bodde (Princeton, Princeton University Press, 1983), 1:377–378. Liang Tao also quotes several similar statements made by earlier

commentators in *Guodian zhujian yu simeng xuepai*《郭店竹简与思孟学派》, 165. Many of these views read the "Liyun" in light of the eighteenth section of the *Daodejing*《道德經》, which explains that virtues such as rightness (*yi* 義) and filial piety (*xiao* 孝) emerge only after the Great Way has been cast aside. Guying Chen 陳鼓應, *Laozi jinzhu jinyi ji pingjie*《老子今註今譯及評介》(Taibei 臺北: Taiwan shangwu yinshuguan 臺灣商務印書館, 1997), 120–121. Themes of simplicity are also central to texts such as the *Baopuzi*《抱朴子》. Zhonghua Li 李中華, ed., *Xinyi Baopuzi*《新譯抱朴子》(Taibei 臺北: Sanmin shuju 三民書局, 1996).

23. The *Zhengyi* commentators advocate a similar view in Li, *Shisanjing zhushu*《十三經注疏》, 13:771. "The five emperors [of the era of Grand Unity] performed acts of virtue but did not consider them ritual [*li* 禮]. The three kings [of the era of Modest Prosperity] performed ritual as ritual. This is why the five emperors did not speak of ritual, while the three kings did speak of ritual" 五帝猶行德不以為禮，三王行為禮之禮，故五帝不言禮，而三王云以為禮也. This is also significant in relation to the discussion of language, or *yan* 言.
24. In some regards we can say that people began to "theorize" about ritual. For more on the notion of "theory" see Robert F. Campany, "Xunzi and Durkheim as Theorists of Ritual Practice," in *Discourse and Practice*, ed. Frank Reynolds and David Tracy (Albany: State University of New York Press, 1992), 197–231.
25. Chen, "Datong, xiaokang yu liyueshenghuo de kaiqi," 60. Chen claims to borrow this theory from Kong Yingda.
26. Alasdair MacIntyre provides a useful—although not problem free—definition of "tradition" in *Whose Justice? Which Rationality?* (Notre Dame, IN.: University of Notre Dame Press, 1988), 12. "A tradition is an argument extended through time in which certain fundamental agreements are defined and redefined in terms of two kinds of conflict: those with critics and enemies external to the tradition who reject all or at least key parts of those fundamental agreements, and those internal interpretative debates through which the meaning and rationale of the fundamental agreements come to be expressed and by whose progress a tradition is constituted."
27. Shen Xu 許慎 in *Shuowen Jiezi*《說文解字》(Beijing 北京: Zhonghua Shuju 中華書局, 2004), 271, for instance, explains that *ji* 紀 borrows the *ji* 己 radical for its sound.
28. Some critics avoid this translation because of concern with importing notions of the English word "self" into the concept of *ji* 己. For more on the issue of the self, see David L. Hall and Roger T. Ames, *Thinking from the Han: Self, Truth, and Transcendence in Chinese and Western Culture* (Albany: State University of New York Press, 1998). Xu Shen in *Shuowen Jiezi*, 309, defines *ji* 己 as a pictograph of the stomach area of a person.
29. *Liji*, "Liyun," 9.26.
30. *Liji*, "Liyun," 9.1.

31. I should point out that while this alternative reading draws attention to different conceptions of the self in the periods of Grand Unity and Modest Prosperity, this is not meant to suggest that this alternative reading is the only way to read the text. Rather, these alternative readings draw on the linguistic indeterminacy of certain characters or grammatical structures, which in turn allow for additional explanations that enrich the overall reading of the text.
32. *Liji*, "Liyun," 9.1.
33. *Liji*, "Liyun," 9.1.
34. The two characters *gong* 公 and *gong* 功 could have shared the same pronunciation in early China. One way to conceptualize the shift from the era of Grand Unity to Modest Prosperity is as a transformation from a time when "the world was comprised of public-spiritedness" 天下為公 to a time where "the world was comprised of individual effort" 天下為功.
35. This idea was sparked by reading the early commentator Jiang Junshi's 蔣君實 remark that "craft and conscious effort had not taken shape" 巧偽不形 during the early era of human society. See Wei, *Liji Jishuo*, 54.43a, see also 13a.
36. *Liji*, "Liyun," 9.1.
37. *Liji*, "Tangong Shang," 3.60.
38. *Liji*, "Tangong Xia," 4.15.
39. Some scholars have argued that capturing the ritual tradition in written language gives way to a number of problems for the tradition. See, for instance, Jack R. Goody and Ian Watt, "The Consequences of Literacy," in *Literacy in Traditional Societies*, ed. Jack R. Goody (Cambridge: Cambridge University Press, 1968), 27–68.
40. *Liji*, "Tangong Xia," 4.17.
41. David Shcaberg connects the notion of *ming* 命 (usually understood as "fate") in early Chinese texts to ritual and language, and to written language in particular, in David Schaberg, "Command and the Content of Tradition," in *The Magnitude of* Ming: *Command, Allotment, and Fate in Chinese Culture*, ed. Christopher Lupke (Honolulu: University of Hawaii Press, 2005), 23–48.
42. See, for instance, the opening line of the *Daodejing*. "The *dao* 道 that can be spoken/known/enacted is not the constant *dao* 道" 道可道，非常道. Chen, *Laozi jinzhu jinyi ji pingjie*, 47. The *Huainanzi*, commenting on this line from the *Daodejing*, states, "It is better to take the Way when it was whole rather than when it was incomplete. Hearing the actual words of the former kings is better than reciting their odes and writings. And realizing what is behind the words is better than hearing their words. What is behind the words, however, cannot be articulated. Thus 'the Way which can be spoken of is not the constant Way.'" Roger T. Ames, *The Art of Rulership: A Study in Ancient Chinese Political Thought* (Honolulu: University of Hawaii Press, 1983), 22.
43. *Liji*, "Zhongni Yanju," 29.5. "Jiyi," 25.8 also discusses the difficulty of creating a uniform standard for *yan* 言.

44. *Liji*, "Jiyi," 25.35.
45. *Liji*, "Liyun," 9.35.
46. Mircea Eliade, *The Sacred and The Profane: The Nature of Religion* (Orlando, FL: Harcourt Books, 1987), 92.
47. *Liji*, "Jiyi," 25.23.
48. *Liji*, "Fangji," 31.4.
49. *Liji*, "Fangji," 31.1.
50. The notion that rituals lack the power to dictate their purported outcomes is also expressed in the *Zhuangzi* where grave robbers are depicted quoting the *Shijing* while robbing graves. Michael Nylan makes this point in *The Five "Confucian" Classics* (New Haven, CT: Yale University Press, 2001), 104.
51. *Liji*, "Fangji," 31.9. I should also note that there are other passages that seem to argue against the position that people other than those explicitly in charge of the ritual can cause it to fail. See, for instance, "Daxue," 43.2.
52. *Liji*, "Fangji," 31.20.
53. *Liji*, "Zengzi Wen," 7.1.
54. *Liji*, "Zengzi Wen," 7.20.
55. *Liji*, "Zengzi Wen," 7.6, 19–22, and 24–25.

CHAPTER 6

1. Sima Qian 司馬遷, *Shiji* 《史記》, Qinding sikuquanshu 欽定四庫全書, 13.1, www.sikuquanshu.com (accessed August 19, 2010).
2. Christoph Harbsmeier, *Science and Civilisation in China*, vol. 7, part 1: *Language and Logic* (Cambridge: Cambridge University Press, 1998), 148.
3. Harbsmeier, *Language and Logic*, 148.
4. David L. Hall and Roger T. Ames, *Anticipating China: Thinking Through the Narratives of Chinese and Western Culture* (Albany: State University of New York Press, 1995), 210–211.
5. Hall and Ames, *Anticipating China*, 210–211. It is worth noting that Hall and Ames's analysis of "Western" and "Chinese" philosophy is often based on overgeneralizations of each tradition. Nonetheless, their point about the significance of vagueness in Confucian thought is still valid.
6. Mark Setton, "Ambiguity in the *Analects*: Philosophical and Practical Dimensions," *Journal of Chinese Philosophy* 27.4 (December 2000): 545–569.
7. Setton, "Ambiguity in the *Analects*," 545.
8. Setton, "Ambiguity in the *Analects*," 546.
9. Ming Dong Gu, *Chinese Theories of Reading and Writing: A Route to Hermeneutics and Open Poetics* (Albany: State University of New York Press, 2005), 3.
10. David L. Hall and Roger T. Ames, *Thinking Through Confucius* (Albany: State University of New York Press, 1987), 64. "One extends and deepens his understanding of the *Songs* [*Shijing*] through action and reflection. The ambiguity of

the text and the remoteness of the original intentions, far from being a failing, serve to extend its range of possibilities and make it readily adaptable to the unique circumstances of the present human condition. The Han commentators, for example, anxious to reinforce the rather stiff cultural values of their own age, were quite happy to read echoes of ribald fertility celebrations as metaphor for social solidarity. People of different ages with different concerns could use the text creatively to arrange and express their experiences, to structure their priorities and to argue for a specific point of view. In ostensibly unfolding the real meaning of the *Songs*, these interpreters would, in fact, make real their own meaning. Thus, the success of the *Songs* is in large part dependent upon the quality of its readers and the diversity of their experiences."

11. I had written this portion of the book, but lacked the term to express the concept. I came across "plausible deniability" in Grant Hardy, *Worlds of Bronze and Bamboo: Sima Qian's Conquest of History* (New York: Columbia University Press, 1999), 58.
12. D. C. Lau 劉殿爵 and Fong Ching Chen 陳方正, eds., *Liji zhuzi suoyin* 《禮記逐字索引》 Chinese University of Hong Kong, Institute of Chinese Studies, Ancient Chinese Text Concordance Series 香港中文大學中國文化研究所先秦兩漢古籍逐字索引叢刊 (Taibei 台北: Taiwan shangwu yinshuguan 台灣商務印書館, 1992), "Tangong Shang," 3.41. Hereafter, *Liji*.
13. For instance, *Liji*, "Zengzi Wen," 7.33.
14. The problem, of course, with this reading is that Confucius chastises those who alter ritual on the basis of conforming it to their dispositions in passages such as *Liji*, "Tangong Shang," 3.25 and 3.27. See also the discussion on "subsumptive" versus "indeterminate" approaches to exigencies in chapter 3.
15. *Liji*, "Tangong Shang," 3.40.
16. While I did not arrive at my analysis by reading this, Roger Ames makes a similar point: "A persistent feature of classical Confucianism corollary to the absence of 'objectivity,' is an unwillingness to separate description and prescription, reality and its interpretation." Roger T. Ames, "*Li* and the A-theistic Religiousness of Classical Confucianism," in *Confucian Spirituality*, vol. 1, ed. Weiming Tu and Mary Evelyn Tucker (New York: Crossroad Pub. Company, 2003), 175. Antonio Cua also reiterates, "This is part of the reason why Chinese thinkers, in general, do not pay attention to the distinction between normative and descriptive statements. This feature of Confucian ethics may be considered a defect or a virtue, depending on a philosopher's viewpoint. The defect lies in the Confucian neglect of the importance of conceptual clarification; the virtue, in its unwavering moral concern with man as inherently capable of responding to the world, or harmonizing his actions and intentions with things and events in the world." Antonio S. Cua, *Moral Vision and Tradition: Essays in Chinese Ethics* (Washington, DC: Catholic University of America Press, 1998), 35. David Nivison, on the other hand, argues that classical Chinese does allow for such a distinction and

demonstrates it in several texts. David Nivison, "Replies and Comments," in *Chinese Language, Thought, and Culture: Nivison and His Critics*, ed. Philip J. Ivanhoe (Chicago: Open Court, 1996), 314.

17. *Liji*, "Wangzhi," 5.56.
18. *Liji*, "Tangong Shang," 3.31.
19. *Liji*, "Tangong Shang," 3.33.
20. *Liji*, "Tangong Shang," 3.100.
21. This is similar to genres such as the "Tianwen" 天問 of the *Chuci* 《楚辭》. For more on the "Tianwen," see Stephen Field, trans., *Tian Wen: A Chinese Book of Origins* (New York: New Directions Publishing, 1986).
22. Hardy, *Worlds of Bronze and Bamboo*, 48.
23. *Liji*, "Tangong Shang," 3.29.
24. *Liji*, "Zengzi Wen," 7.4.
25. *Liji*, "Zengzi Wen," 7.2.
26. *Liji*, "Zengzi Wen," 7.11.
27. *Liji*, "Tangong Shang," 3.107.
28. *Liji*, "Tangong Shang," 3.88 makes this point.
29. *Liji*, "Zengzi Wen," 7.24.
30. *Liji*, "Zengzi Wen," 7.33.
31. There are of course a number of classical interpreters who take this passage as a "Daoist" addition to the original text.
32. See, for instance, *Liji*, "Zhongyong," 32.8 and "Tangong Shang," 3.6.
33. *Liji*, "Zhongyong," 32.5.
34. *Liji*, "Zhongyong," 32.7.
35. This resonates with Margaret Walker's notion of impure agency, which, as she describes it, is "agency situated within the causal order in such ways as to be variably conditioned by and conditioning parts of that order, without our being able to draw for *all* purposes a *unitary* boundary to its exercise at either end, nor always for *particular* purposes a *sharp* one." "Moral Luck and the Virtues of Impure Agency," in *Moral Luck*, ed. Daniel Statman (Albany: State University of New York Press, 1993), 243. In contrast, pure agency, in Walker's terms, is the kind of agency attributed to Confucian agents by proponents of the inward turn.
36. *Liji*, "Tangong Shang," 3.74.
37. Bingying Xie 謝冰瑩, *Xinyi sishu duben* 《新譯四書讀本》 (Taibei 臺北: Sanmin shuju 三民書局, 2002), 208.
38. *Liji*, "Fangji," 31.10.
39. *Liji*, "Fangji," 31.13.
40. *Liji*, "Daxue," 43.1.
41. Edward Schieffelin makes a similar point about the emergent properties of ritual authority in "On Failure and Performance: Throwing the Medium Out of the Séance," in *The Performance of Healing*, ed. Carol Laderman and Marina Roseman (New York: Routledge, 1996), 59–89.

42. *Liji*, "Tangong Shang," 3.84.
43. It is also worth questioning why the author of the passage does not include a response.
44. See, for instance, Shi Wei 衛湜, ed., *Liji Jishuo* 《禮記集說》 (Taibei 臺北: Taiwan shangwu yinshuguan 臺灣商務印書館, 1983), 19.4b–5b.

CHAPTER 7

1. W. B. Yeats, *Essays and Introductions* (New York: Macmillan, 1961), 241.
2. D. C. Lau 劉殿爵 and Fong Ching Chen 陳方正, eds., *Liji zhuzi suoyin* 《禮記逐字索引》 Chinese University of Hong Kong, Institute of Chinese Studies, Ancient Chinese Text Concordance Series 香港中文大學中國文化研究所先秦兩漢古籍逐字索引叢刊 (Taibei 台北: Taiwan shangwu yinshuguan: 台灣商務印書館, 1992), "Tangong Shang," 3.6. Hereafter, *Liji*.
3. While he does not interpret the Mubeng passage philosophically, Robert Eno does offer a prolonged reading of it in an attempt to reconstruct Confucius's early years. See Robert Eno, "The Background of the Kong Family of Lu and the Origins of Ruism." *Early China* 28 (2003): 1–42.
4. Edward G. Slingerland, "The Conception of *Ming* in Early Confucian Thought," *Philosophy East & West* 46.4 (October 1996): 568.
5. Slingerland, "Conception of *Ming*," 568.
6. Mark Csikszentmihalyi, *Material Virtue: Ethics and the Body in Early China* (Boston: Brill, 2004), 6.
7. Jiyuan Yu, *The Ethics of Confucius and Aristotle: Mirrors of Virtue* (New York: Routledge, 2007), 187.
8. Philip J. Ivanhoe, "Confucian Self-Cultivation and Mengzi's Notion of Extension," in *Essays on the Moral Philosophy of Mengzi*, ed. Philip J. Ivanhoe and Xiusheng Liu (Indianapolis: Hackett Publishing, 2002), 224. Edward Slingerland, trans., *Confucius: Analects* (Cambridge: Hackett Publishing, 2003), 65.
9. Philip J. Ivanhoe, "A Question of Faith," *Early China* 13 (1988): 158.
10. *Liji*, "Tangong Shang," 3.3.
11. The Duke of Zhou as the originator of joint burials is also reiterated in *Liji*, "Tangong Shang," 3.28.
12. You Du 杜佑, *Tongdian* 《通典》 Wenyuange Sikuquanshu Neilianwangban 文淵閣四庫全書內聯網版 (Xianggang 香港: Dizhi wenhua chuban youxiangongsi, Zhongwen daxue chubanshe 迪志文化出版有限公司, 中文大學出版社, 2002), www.sikuquanshu.com (accessed January 28, 2010). Also available in print. See: 史部·别杂史等-卷一百三·礼六十三·沿革六十三（凶礼二十五).
13. For these views, see the sections on the Mubeng passage in Shi Wei 衛湜, ed., *Liji Jishuo* 《禮記集說》 (Taibei 臺北: Taiwan shangwu yinshuguan 臺灣商務印書館, 1983), Xueqin Li 李學勤, ed., *Shisanjing zhushu* 《十三經注疏》 (Beijing 北京:

Beijing daxue chubanshe 北京大学出版社, 2000), Cheng Wu 吳澄, *Liji zuanyan* 《禮記纂言》(Jinan 濟南: Qi-Lu shushe chubanshe 齊魯書社出版社, 1997), Guang Hu 胡廣 *Liji Daquan* 《禮記大全》(Taibei 臺北: Taiwan shangwu yinshuguan 臺灣商務印書館, 1983), and Taiqu Shao 邵泰衢, *Tangong yiwen* 《檀弓疑問》(Taibei 臺北: Taiwan shangwu yinshuguan 臺灣商務印書館, 1983).

14. There is obviously much more at stake in this particular debate than simply the fact of occurrence. Taking the Mubeng passage as fiction raises a number of relevant questions: to what degree are passages such as these, or the *Liji* as a whole, products of ideological debates of the time? If the purpose of the passage is not meant to accurately describe a historical event, then what is it meant to do? What ideas, concepts, and practices are at stake in this passage, chapter, or text? Are fictional stories able to convey the same moral lessons as a historical event? In-depth answers to most of these questions fall beyond the bounds of this project. However, taking these passages as representations of debates with something other than historical accuracy at stake seems in line with the production of "historical texts" in early Confucianism. Classics such as the *Shujing* 《書經》 or the *Chunqiu* 《春秋》 are clearly meant to reproduce the lessons of actual events. Yet the details of the events are secondary to the moral import conveyed by the events. The Mubeng passage, in this view, if based on an actual event, is a retelling of the event, told with minimal detail. As such, each detail that is reported is highly relevant to the moral lessons the reader is meant to learn.
15. See, for instance, *Liji*, "Zengzi Wen," 7.35, "Tangong Shang," 3.28, and the entirety of "Mingtangwei."
16. Michael J. Puett, *The Ambivalence of Creation: Debates Concerning Innovation and Artifice in Early China* (Stanford: Stanford University Press, 2001).
17. D. C. Lau 劉殿爵, ed., *Zhouli zhuzi suoyin* 《周禮逐字索引》 Chinese University of Hong Kong, Institute of Chinese Studies, Ancient Chinese Text Concordance Series 香港中文大學中國文化研究所先秦兩漢古籍逐字索引叢刊 (Hong Kong 香港: Shangwu yinshuguan 商務印書館, 1993), 3.18.
18. Building mounds is also described as a part of the ritual script in *Liji*, "Tangong Xia," 4.59.
19. Later interpreters such as Zhu Xi (1130–1200) cite the Mubeng passage in this light: "Now I note that Confucius protected a grave with a hill four feet high at the peak. Therefore, take this as the model." As quoted in Patricia Buckley Ebrey, trans., *Chu Hsi's Family Rituals: A Twelfth-Century Chinese Manual for the Performance of Cappings, Weddings, Funerals, and Ancestral Rites* (Princeton, NJ: Princeton University Press, 1991), 124. Ebrey also notes, "In the law [of the Song Dynasty], considerably higher mounds were allowed, from eighteen feet for rank one officials down to six feet for commoners."
20. Professor Waiyee Li suggested parts of this to me in personal conversation.
21. On the location of Fang, see Robert Eno, "Background of the Kong Family," 31–34.

22. Li Wang 王力, *Wang Li gu Hanyu zidian* 《王力古漢語字典》(Beijing 北京: Zhonghua shuju 中華書局, 2000), 1578. Axel Schuessler, *ABC Etymological Dictionary of Old Chinese* (Honolulu: University of Hawaii Press, 2007), 231–232 and 418.
23. *Liji*, "Fangji," 31.17.
24. Misha Tadd suggested a literal reading of *fang* 防 and *qiu* 丘 (discussed below) in personal conversation.
25. The city of Fang is actually noted for its defense fortifications in texts such as the *Zuozhuan*. See Eno, "Background of the Kong Family," 3–4 and 31.
26. A similar notion of double meaning, or *chongzhi* 重旨, developed in premodern China. See Ming Dong Gu, *Chinese Theories of Reading and Writing: A Route to Hermeneutics and Open Poetics* (New York: State University of New York Press, 2005), 4.
27. Confucius is likened to a hill or mountain in other texts. Sima Qian, for instance, does this in the *Shiji*, which also depicts the figure of Confucius meeting infelicitous times. See Grant Hardy, *Worlds of Bronze and Bamboo: Sima Qian's Conquest of History* (New York: Columbia University Press, 1999), 120.
28. Yong Jiang 江永, *Liji xunyi zeyan* 《禮記訓義擇言》Wenyuange Sikuquanshu Neilianwangban 文淵閣四庫全書內聯網版 (Xianggang 香港: Dizhi wenhua chuban youxiangongsi, Zhongwen daxue chubanshe 迪志文化出版有限公司, 中文大學出版社, 2002), www.sikuquanshu.com (accessed January 28, 2010). In the print version, see chapter 2, 卷二.
29. *Liji*, "Tangong Shang," 3.9. This is not to say that "worry" should permeate one's entire life. This passage actually goes on to make a distinction between unease (*you* 憂) and worry (*huan* 患). The former should last a lifetime, the latter should not last a day.
30. The dominant position among scholars is that tragedy is absent in China. An exemplary statement in this regard comes from James Robert Hightower, "Chinese Literature in the Context of World Literature," *Comparative Literature* 5.2 (Spring 1953): 120. "The drama in China has nothing comparable to the great dramas of European literatures. It lacks any concept of tragedy; it is bound by a conventional morality of reward and punishment that occasionally produces melodrama but effectively prevents the development of tragic conflict." More recently this position has been reaffirmed in David N. Keightley, "Epistemology in Cultural Context: Disguise and Deception in Early China and Early Greece," in *Early China/Ancient Greece*, ed. Steven Shankman and Stephen W. Durrant (Albany: State University of New York Press, 2002): 141. "The Chinese narratives, when compared with the Greek, are remarkable for the lack of dramatic complexity. They generally provide the essence of the action; they are parables, sermons, lacking the kind of existential irony and ambiguity that flows through critical scenes, such as the slaughter of the suitors in Book 22 of the *Odyssey*." The *Encyclopedia Britannica* also has an entire entry entitled "Absence of Tragedy

in Oriental Drama": http://www.britannica.com/EBchecked/topic/601884/tragedy/51130/Absence-of-tragedy-in-Oriental-drama. Other scholars have also advocated this view in the context of comparative religion. See, for instance, John Morreall, *Comedy, Tragedy, and Religion* (Albany: State University of New York Press, 1999), 62.

31. Coincidentally, the etymological roots of *hamartia* and *zhong* 中 are both connected to the practice of archery and hitting or missing the target.
32. My point is not to read the Mubeng passage as a tragedy, but rather to provide a tragic reading of the passage. The difference between the two is significant. The former can be said to conform the material to the method, while the latter leaves the method open to the demands of the material.
33. For a historical account of the development of artisans in early China, see Anthony J. Barbieri-low, *Artisans in Early Imperial China* (Seattle: University of Washington Press, 2007).
34. Shen Xu 許慎, *Shuowen Jiezi* 《說文解字》(Beijing 北京: Zhonghua Shuju 中華書局, 2004), 219.
35. See the entry "complicate" in the *Oxford English Dictionary*, http://dictionary.oed.com.

CHAPTER 8

1. Adapted from James Legge's translation of "Xiaomin" 小旻 in the *Shijing*. James Legge, trans., *The Chinese Classics*, vol. 4 (Hong Kong: Hong Kong University Press, 1960), 333.
2. D. C. Lau 劉殿爵 and Fong Ching Chen 陳方正, eds., *Liji zhuzi suoyin* 《禮記逐字索引》Chinese University of Hong Kong, Institute of Chinese Studies, Ancient Chinese Text Concordance Series 香港中文大學中國文化研究所先秦兩漢古籍逐字索引叢刊 (Taibei 台北: Taiwan shangwu yinshuguan: 台灣商務印書館, 1992), "Liyun," 9.2. Hereafter, *Liji*.
3. See the entry for "critical" in the *Oxford English Dictionary*, http://dictionary.oed.com.
4. *Liji*, "Aigong Wen," 28.1.
5. Shen Xu 許慎, *Shuowen Jiezi* 《說文解字》(Beijing 北京: Zhonghua Shuju 中華書局, 2004), 219.
6. *Liji*, "Liyun," 9.28.
7. I use the shorter label 'anxiety of fluency' out of convenience rather than using the longer term 'anxieties of fluency and competency.'
8. I borrow these terms from Antonio Cua, who uses them in a different sense. See Antonio S. Cua, *The Unity of Knowledge and Action: A Study in Wang Yang-ming's Moral Psychology* (Honolulu: University Press of Hawaii, 1982), 22–45.
9. Mark Csikszentmihalyi, *Material Virtue: Ethics and the Body in Early China* (Boston: Brill, 2004), 72.

10. There is much more that could be said about anxiety in the context of Chinese philosophy. Xu Fuguan, for instance, believed that a kind of "concern consciousness" (*youhuan yishi* 憂患意識) was the hallmark feature of Chinese thought. Concern consciousness, for Xu, meant a kind of anxiety about one's role and responsibility in the transformation of the self and society. In contrast to religions such as Christianity, Chinese traditions do not resolve this concern by appeal to an omnipotent god. For more on Xu see Peimin Ni, "Practical Humanism of Xu Fuguan," in *Contemporary Chinese Philosophy*, ed. Chung-ying Cheng and Nicholas Bunnin (Malden, MA: Blackwell Publishers, 2002), 281–304. On the notion of concern consciousness in early Confucian texts see Dingwen Li, 李定文 "Lun Xianqin Rujia de Youhuan Yishi ji qi Xiandai Zhuanhua" 论先秦儒家的忧患意识及其现代转化, *Lanzhou Xuekan* 兰州学刊 11.182 (2008): 21–24.
11. Pauline C. Lee, "Engaging Comparative Religion: A Redescription of the *Lunyu* 論語, the *Zhuangzi* 莊子 and 'A Place on Which to Stand,'" *Journal of Chinese Religions* 35 (2007): 119.
12. Lee, "Engaging Comparative Religion," 119. "Enthusiasm" and "horror" are the words of Smith.
13. Robert Eno, *The Confucian Creation of Heaven: Philosophy and the Defense of Ritual Mastery* (Albany: State University of New York Press, 1990), 82. Michael Puett explores alternative (2) in "Following the Commands of Heaven: The Notion of *Ming* in Early China," in *The Magnitude of* Ming: *Command, Allotment, and Fate in Chinese Culture*, ed. Christopher Lupke (Honolulu: University of Hawaii Press, 2005), 49–69.
14. Eno explains, "This notion shifts the evaluative standard against which events are judged from the present into the distant future, and, in essence, subordinates the descriptive values of experience to prescriptive dogma. Regardless of the evidence, all must be for the good." Eno, *Confucian Creation of Heaven*, 88.
15. See, for instance, Grant Hardy, *Worlds of Bronze and Bamboo: Sima Qian's Conquest of History* (New York: Columbia University Press, 1999), 126–129; and Ning Chen, "The Concept of Fate in Mencius," *Philosophy East & West* 47.4 (October 1997): 495–520.
16. I borrow the term "productive disorientation" from Amy Olberding, who uses it in a different sense. Amy Olberding, "The Educative Function of Personal Style in the *Analects*," *Philosophy East & West* 57.3 (July 2007): 372. See also Volney P. Gay, "Ritual and Psychotherapy: Similarities and Differences," in *Religious and Social Ritual: Interdisciplinary Explorations*, ed. Michael B. Aune and Valerie DeMarinis (Albany: State University of New York Press, 1996), 217–234, for notions of "therapeutic" in psychotherapy and ritual.
17. Similar descriptions of anxiety (*you* 憂) appear in the *Analects* and *Mencius*. See, for instance, *Analects* 7.3 and *Mencius* 4B28. Bingying Xie 謝冰瑩, Xinyi sishu duben 《新譯四書讀本》 (Taibei 臺北: Sanmin shuju 三民書局, 2002), 137 and 504–505.

18. *Liji*, “Ruxing,” 42.5.
19. *Liji*, “Liqi,” 10.20. A similar notion of *shen* 慎 is also stressed throughout the “Ziyi” 緇衣 chapter.
20. The notion of cautious-anxiety in preparing for, and carrying out, ritual is highlighted throughout the “Jiaotesheng” 郊特牲 and “Liqi” 禮器 chapters.
21. *Liji*, “Daxue,” 43.1–2.
22. *Liji*, “Liyun,” 9.36.
23. Antonio S. Cua, *Dimensions of Moral Creativity: Paradigms, Principles, and Ideals* (University Park: Pennsylvania State University Press, 1978), 96.
24. *Liji*, “Liyun,” 9.35.
25. *Liji*, “Tangong Shang,” 3.44.
26. See, for instance, *Liji*, “Zhongyong,” 中庸32.7.
27. D. C. Lau 劉殿爵, ed., *Xunzi zhuzi suoyin: A concordance to the Xunzi* 《荀子逐字索引》(Xianggang 香港: Shangwu yinshuguan 商務印書館, 1996). 27.134–135.
28. *Liji*, “Tangong Xia,” 4.56.
29. James Legge’s translation of 重有憂者 is quite apt: “one who has suffered sorrow upon sorrow.” James Legge, trans., *The Sacred Books of China: The Texts of Confucianism*, part 3, *The Li Ki* (Oxford: The Clarendon Press, 1885), 3:190–191.
30. *Liji*, “Fangji,” 31.17.
31. *Liji*, “Zaji Xia,” 21.29.
32. *Liji*, “Jiyi,” 25.9–11.
33. I translated *huanghu* 慌惚 as “lost abstraction of mind” following James Legge, *Li Ki*, 4:214.
34. For more on the notion of sacrifice in a Confucian context see Thomas Wilson, “Sacrifice and the Imperial Cult of Confucius,” *History of Religions* 41. 3 (February 2002): 251–287.
35. The latter employs “crazy” in the sense of “being crazy about something.”
36. *Liji*, “Wensang,” 36.1.
37. This insight came when reading Susan Letzler Cole, *The Absent One: Mourning Ritual, Tragedy, and the Performance of Ambivalence* (University Park: Pennsylvania State University Press, 1985).
38. *Liji*, “Shaoyi,” 17.15.
39. *Liji*, “Tangong Shang,” 3.9.
40. The line, “Therefore the profound person has a lifetime of anxiety, but not a morning of worry” 故君子有終身之憂，而無一朝之患 is seemingly contradicted by other passages in the *Liji* such as a passage from the “Daxue” chapter, which, in elaborating on the notion of “rectifying the heart-mind” 正心, explains, “If there is any anxiety or worry, it will not be rectified” 有所憂患，則不得其正 (“Daxue,” 43.2). The “Zidao” 子道 chapter in the *Xunzi* also records a conversation between Zilu and Confucius about the anxiety of the profound person. Confucius explains, “[The profound person] has a lifetime of joy, but not a day of anxiety” 是以有終生

之樂，無一日之憂 (*Xunzi zhuzi suoyin*, 29.143). In response to this apparent contradiction, commentators have attempted to speak of two different kinds of anxieties—one productive and another unproductive. Jiao Yuanxi (1661–1736), for instance, in commenting on the productive anxiety mentioned in *Analects* 7.3 writes, "When the Master speaks of being 'joyful and forgetting worry' (7.18), this 'worry' is the sort of selfish worry that troubles the human mind—the same worry that is spoken of in the lines, 'other people could not have born such worry/hardship' (6.11), 'the Good person does not worry' (9.29), and 'the gentleman does not worry and feels no fear' (12.4). The 'worry' spoken of here [7.3], however, is the sort of worry mentioned in the line, 'the gentleman has worries his entire life' (*Mencius* 4B28)—that is, the 'trembling fear, cautiousness and discipline' spoken of in Zhu Xi's commentary to [*Mencius* 4B19]. It is this sort of 'worry,' and this alone, that allows a worthy or sage to become what they are" (Edward Slingerland, trans., *Confucius: Analects* [Cambridge: Hackett Publishing Company, 2003], 64–65). More recently, Fung Yiu-ming proposed that a productive anxiety has a specific object or focus of concern, whereas an unproductive anxiety is a general feeling of worry. "Productive" and "unproductive" are, of course, my descriptors and do not appear in Fung's article. Yiu-Ming Fung, "Disposition or Imposition? Remarks on Fingarette's *Lunyu*," *Journal of Chinese Philosophy* 37.2 (June 2010): 295–311. Amy Olberding's view is also worth contrasting with these positions, as expressed in "I Know Not 'Seems': Grief for Parents in the *Analects*," in *Mortality in Traditional Chinese Thought*, ed. Amy Olberding and Philip J. Ivanhoe, (Albany: State University of New York Press, 2011), 158–159.

41. *Liji*, "Liyun," 9.4.
42. Eno, *Confucian Creation of Heaven*, 92–93.
43. Hardy, *Worlds of Bronze and Bamboo*, 163–164 presents a good account of this.
44. As discussed in Hardy, *Worlds of Bronze and Bamboo*, 10. Jennifer Wallace makes a similar point about the genre of tragedy in relation to rules: "Tragedy, as a dramatic genre, traditionally raises questions about rules and constraints. The rules become apparent as they are blown apart by tragic events; paradoxically, constraints are desired precisely when they appear to be absent and when anything—violence, exploitation, injustice—consequently becomes possible." Jennifer Wallace, "Tragedy and Exile," in *Tragedy in Transition*, ed. Sarah Annes Brown and Catherine Silverstone (Malden, MA: Blackwell, 2007), 145.
45. This is a variation of Adrian Poole's insight found in *Tragedy: A Very Short Introduction* (New York: Oxford University Press, 2005), 90.
46. *Liji*, "Tangong Shang," 3.6.
47. *Liji*, "Tangong Shang," 3.17.
48. Or perhaps the failure was the duke's fault since he did not divine about the matter.
49. For more on charioteering and war as ritual, see Mark Edward Lewis, *Sanctioned Violence in Early China* (Albany: State University of New York Press, 1990).

50. For the latter see *Liji*, "Tangong Shang," 3.36.
51. *Liji*, "Tangong Shang," 3.18.
52. Coincidentally, Yuezheng Zichun is also depicted as someone very concerned with keeping to the ritual script. See *Liji*, "Jiyi," 25.36.
53. *Liji*, "Tangong Shang," 3.28.
54. Xueqin Li 李學勤, ed., *Shisanjing zhushu*《十三經注疏》(Beijing 北京: Beijing daxue chubanshe 北京大学出版社, 2000), 12:229–230.
55. Shi Wei 衛湜, ed., *Liji Jishuo* 《禮記集說》(Taibei 臺北: Taiwan shangwu yinshuguan 臺灣商務印書館, 1983), 16.26a–27a.
56. It is also possible that the "Tangong" chapters were edited or written by competing schools of early Confucians who had an anti-Zengzi bias.
57. *Liji*, "Jingjie," 27.3.
58. Axel Schuessler coincidentally notes that boat is an early meaning of *fang* 方. *ABC Etymological Dictionary of Old Chinese* (Honolulu: University of Hawaii Press, 2007), 231.

CONCLUDING REFLECTIONS

1. Adam B. Seligman et al., *Ritual and Its Consequences: An Essay on the Limits of Sincerity* (New York: Oxford University Press, 2008), 30.
2. Mircea Eliade, *The Myth of the Eternal Return*, trans. Willard R. Trask (New York: Pantheon Books, 1954), 21. Commenting on this idea, which comes from the Vedic tradition, Eliade states, "This Indian adage summarizes all the theory underlying rituals in all countries."
3. Barbara G . Myerhoff, "A Death in Due Time: Construction of Self and Culture in Ritual Drama," in *Rite, Drama, Festival, Spectacle: Rehearsals Toward a Theory of Cultural Performance*, ed. John J. MacAloon (Philadelphia: Institute for the Study of Human Issues, 1984), 152. Peter Berger makes a similar point in *The Sacred Canopy: Elements of a Sociological Theory of Religion* (New York: Anchor Books, 1990), 33–37.
4. Myerhoff, "Death in Due Time," 152. Eliade also states that "among primitives... any human act whatever acquires effectiveness to the extent to which it exactly *repeats* an act performed at the beginning of time by a god, a hero, or an ancestor." *Myth of the Eternal Return*, 22.
5. Axel Michaels, "Ritual and Meaning," in *Theorizing Rituals*, ed. Jens Kreinath, Jan Snoek, and Michael Stausberg (Boston: Brill, 2006), 260–261.
6. On recursivity, see Jens Kreinath, Constance Hartung, and Annette Deschner, eds. *The Dynamics of Changing Rituals: The Transformation of Religious Rituals within Their Social and Cultural Context* (New York: Peter Lang, 2004), 2. Catherine Bell makes a similar point in *Ritual: Perspectives and Dimensions* (New York: Oxford University Press, 1997), 223.
7. Ernst Cassirer is representative of this view. He speaks about the "primeval stupidity" of myth in *The Myth of the State* (New Haven, CT: Yale University Press,

1946), 4. "Many anthropologists have asserted that myth is, after all, a very simple phenomenon—for which we hardly need a complicated psychological or philosophical explanation. It is simplicity itself; for it is nothing but the *sancta simplicitas* of the human race. It is not the outcome of reflection or thought, nor is it enough to describe it as a product of human imagination. Imagination alone cannot account for all its incongruities and fantastic and bizarre elements. It is rather the *Urdummheit* of man that is responsible for these absurdities and contradictions. Without this 'primeval stupidity' there would be no myth." The American Philosophical Association Pacific Division 2009 Meeting also featured a panel entitled "Confucian Rituals, Pro and Con," which addressed this and related issues. One of the presenters, for instance, discussed liberal critiques of Confucian ritual. These presentations highlighted the fact that not all Confucian ritual can be adapted to new circumstances.

8. William Sax, Johannes Quack, and Jan Weinholded, eds., *The Problem of Ritual Efficacy* (New York: Oxford University Press, 2010).
9. For an overview of this issue, with an emphasis on Chinese rituals, see Emily M. Ahern, "The Problem of Efficacy: Strong and Weak Illocutionary Acts," *Man* 14.1 (1979): 1–17. For a more in-depth discussion in a broader context see Stanley Tambiah, *Magic, Science, Religion, and the Scope of Rationality* (New York: Cambridge University Press, 1990).
10. Jonathan Z. Smith, "The Bare Facts of Ritual," *History of Religions* 20.1–2 (1980): 124–125. Italics removed. He also makes a similar argument in *To Take Place: Toward Theory in Ritual* (Chicago: University of Chicago Press, 1987), 109–110.
11. Smith, "Bare Facts of Ritual," 125.
12. Smith, "Bare Facts of Ritual," 127.
13. Smith, "Bare Facts of Ritual," 127.
14. Smith, "Bare Facts of Ritual," 127. Smith restates this point in *To Take Place,* 109. According to Smith, ritual "provides an occasion for reflection on and rationalization of the fact that what ought to have been done was not, what ought to have taken place did not." Smith, unfortunately, does not elaborate more. He does not explain "reflection" and "rationalization," nor how they contribute to (or comprise) ritual efficacy.
15. Seligman et al., *Ritual and Its Consequences,* 7.
16. The clearest explanation of sincerity comes from Seligman et al., *Ritual and Its Consequences,* 103: "The alternatives that [sincerity] often suggests are categories that grow out of individual soul-searching rather than the acceptance of social conventions. Sincerity thus grows out of abstract and generalized categories generated within individual consciousness. The sincere mode of behavior seeks to replace the 'mere convention' of ritual with a genuine and thoughtful state of internal conviction. Rather than becoming what we do in action through ritual, we do according to what we have become through self-examination."

17. Seligman et al., *Ritual and Its Consequences*, 22.
18. Seligman et al., *Ritual and Its Consequences*, 27.
19. Seligman et al., *Ritual and Its Consequences*, 27.
20. Seligman et al., *Ritual and Its Consequences*, 182.
21. See pages 49–52 on the notion of opening the script.
22. On the notion of "terror of history" see Eliade, *Myth of the Eternal Return*, 139–162.
23. As quoted in Jonathan Wyn Schofer, *Confronting Vulnerability: The Body and the Divine in Rabbinic Ethics* (Chicago: University of Chicago Press, 2010), 185. Original in Ernest Becker, *Escape From Evil* (New York: Simon and Schuster, 1975), 1–2.
24. For more on anomy in this context see Berger, *Sacred Canopy*, 23, 26, 49–50, 90.
25. D. C. Lau 劉殿爵 and Fong Ching Chen 陳方正, eds., *Liji zhuzi suoyin* 《禮記逐字索引》 Chinese University of Hong Kong, Institute of Chinese Studies, Ancient Chinese Text Concordance Series 香港中文大學中國文化研究所先秦兩漢古籍逐字索引叢刊 (Taibei 台北: Taiwan shangwu yinshuguan: 台灣商務印書館, 1992), "Wensang" 問喪, 36.1. Hereafter, *Liji*.
26. Parts of this were inspired by Susan Letzler Cole, *The Absent One: Mourning Ritual, Tragedy, and the Performance of Ambivalence* (University Park: Pennsylvania State University Press, 1985). On page 9 she comments, "Tragedy is an imaginative model of the paradoxical demands made on human consciousness when confronted by death."
27. For more on the relationship between ethics and vulnerability see Schofer, *Confronting Vulnerability*, 183–190.
28. Schofer, *Confronting Vulnerability*, 183.
29. I adapted the notion of "honesty" from Wu Kuang-ming, *History, Thinking, and Literature in Chinese Philosophy* (Taibei: Sun Yat-Sen Institute for Social Sciences and Philosophy, 1991), 252.

APPENDIX

1. James Legge, trans., *The Sacred Books of China: The Texts of Confucianism*, parts 3–4, *The Li Ki* (Oxford: Clarendon Press, 1885), 3:1–14.
2. Ye Hong 洪業 et al., *Liji yinde* 《禮記引得》(Beiping 北平: Hafo Yanjing xue she yinde bian zuan chu 哈佛燕京學社引得編纂處, 1937). Meng'ou Wang 王夢鷗, *Liji jinzhu jinyi* 《禮記今註今譯》 (Taibei 臺北: Taiwan shangwu yinshuguan 臺灣商務印書館,1969). Yihua Jiang 姜義華, *Xinyi Liji duben*《新譯禮記讀本》(Taibei 臺北: Sanmin shuju 三民書局, 1997). Teruo Takeuchi, 竹内照夫, *Raiki* 《礼記》 (Tōkyō 東京: Meiji Shoin 明治書院, 1971–1979).

3. Xueqin Li 李學勤, ed., *Liji Zhengyi*《禮記正義》in *Shisanjing zhushu*《十三經注疏》(Beijing 北京: Beijing daxue chubanshe 北京大学出版社, 2000), vols. 12–15. Cheng Wu 吳澄, *Liji Zuanyan*《禮記纂言》(Jinan 濟南: Qi-Lu shushe chubanshe 齊魯書社出版社, 1997). Fuzhi Wang 王夫之, *Liji Zhangju*《禮記章句》(Shanghai上海: Shanghai guji chubanshe 上海古籍出版社, 1995–1999).
4. Guang Hu 胡廣, *Liji Daquan*《禮記大全》(Taibei 臺北: Taiwan shangwu yinshuguan 臺灣商務印書館, 1983). Shi Wei 衛湜, ed., *Liji Jishuo*《禮記集說》(Taibei 臺北: Taiwan shangwu yinshuguan 臺灣商務印書館, 1983).
5. Takuji Kudō 工藤卓司 provides a wonderful overview of the Japanese scholarship on the *Liji* over the last 100 years in "Jinyibainian Riben *Liji* yanjiu gaikuang 1900–2008 nian zhi huigu yu zhanwang"〈近一百年日本《禮記》研究概況——1900–2008 年之回顧與展望〉, *Zhongguo wenzhe yanjiusuo tongxun*《中國文哲研究所通訊》19.4 (2009): 53–101.
6. E Wang 王鍔, *Liji Chengshu Kao*《禮記成書考》(Beijing 北京: Zhonghua Shuju 中華書局, 2007).
7. Although the *Zhouli* did not incorporate the term *li* 禮 into its title until the Tang dynasty.
8. For more on the "Ziyi," see Edward L. Shaughnessy, *Rewriting Early Chinese Texts* (Albany: State University of New York Press, 2006).
9. Wang's original list includes six activities. I have added this one to his list.
10. Ye Hong 洪業 et al., eds., *Hanshu ji buzhu zonghe yinde*《漢書及補注綜合引得》(Beijing 北京: Hafo Yanjing daxue tushuguan yinde bian zuan chu 哈佛燕京大學圖書館引得編纂處, 1940), 30.6b, page 577.
11. The *Suishu*《隋書》notes that the *Da Dai Liji* contained eighty-five chapters. Many scholars have supposed a connection between the 131 *ji* 記 mentioned in the *Hanshu*, the eighty-five chapters of the *Da Dai Liji* noted in the *Suishu*, and the forty-nine chapters in the received text of the *Liji*. They claim the received text of the *Liji* to be a further redaction of Dai De's initial redaction of the 131 *ji* 記 into the eighty-five chapters of his book. See Huaixin Huang 黄怀信, "Guanyu *Da Dai Liji* yuanliu de jige wenti" 关于《大戴礼记》源流的几个问题, *Qilu Xuekan* 齐鲁学刊 184.1 (2005): 17.
12. These can all be found in Wang, *Liji Chengshu Kao*, 20, although I have modified number six.
13. Much of what is known about Dai Sheng comes from the *Rulinzhuan*《儒林傳》; translated in Riegel, "Four 'Tzu ssu' Chapters of the *Li chi*," 6–8.
14. Parts of this narrative are problematic as pointed out by Riegel, "Four 'Tzu ssu' Chapters of the *Li chi*," 9.
15. The *Liuyilun*《六藝論》is quoted throughout the *Liji Zhengyi*《禮記正義》. The relevant quote is found in Li, *Shisanjing zhushu*, 12:10.
16. Dai De, or Da Dai 大戴, is also credited with composing a *Liji*—the *Da Dai Liji*《大戴禮記》, which survives today in fragmentary form. Dai De 戴德, *Da Dai*

Liji《大戴禮記》(Taibei 臺北: Taiwan shangwu yinshuguan 臺灣商務印書館, 1983). For the relation between the *Xiao Dai Liji* and *Da Dai Liji*, see note 11 above.

17. For a summary of these theories, see Wang, *Liji Chengshu Kao*, 283–299.
18. Wang, *Liji Chengshu Kao*, 299.
19. Wang gives a summary of his argument for these dates in *Liji Chengshu Kao*, 19 and 321–324.

Bibliography

Adams, Robert Merrihew. *A Theory of Virtue: Excellence in Being for the Good*. Oxford: Oxford University Press, 2006.

Ahern, Emily M. "The Problem of Efficacy: Strong and Weak Illocutionary Acts." *Man* 14.1 (1979): 1–17.

Ames, Roger T. *The Art of Rulership: A Study in Ancient Chinese Political Thought.* Honolulu: University of Hawaii Press, 1983.

Ames, Roger T. "Observing Ritual 'Propriety (*li* 禮)' as Focusing the 'Familiar' in the Affairs of the Day." *Dao: A Journal of Comparative Philosophy* 1.2 (June 2002): 143–156.

Ames, Roger T., and Joel Marks, eds. *Emotions in Asian Thought: A Dialogue in Comparative Philosophy*. Albany: State University of New York Press, 1995.

Angle, Stephen C. "No Supreme Principle: Confucianism's Harmonization of Multiple Values." *Dao: A Journal of Comparative Philosophy* 7.1 (Spring 2008): 35–40.

Angle, Stephen C., and Michael Slote, eds. *Virtue Ethics and Confucianism.* Forthcoming.

Aune, Michael B., and Valerie DeMarinis, eds. *Religious and Social Ritual: Interdisciplinary Explorations.* Albany: State University of New York Press, 1996.

Barbieri-low, Anthony J. *Artisans in Early Imperial China.* Seattle: University of Washington Press, 2007.

Bell, Catherine M. *Ritual: Perspectives and Dimensions.* New York: Oxford University Press, 1997.

Bell, Catherine M. *Ritual Theory Ritual Practice.* New York: Oxford University Press, 1992.

Berger, Peter L. *The Sacred Canopy: Elements of a Sociological Theory of Religion.* New York: Anchor Books, 1990.

Berthrong, John H. "The Hard Sayings: The Confucian Case of *Xiao* 孝 in Kongzi and Mengzi." *Dao: A Journal of Chinese Philosophy* 7.2 (June 2008): 119–123.

Berthrong, John, Shu-Hsien Liu, and Leonard Swidler, eds. *Confucianism in Dialogue Today: West, Christianity and Judaism.* Philadelphia: Ecumenical Press, 2004.

Brown, Sarah Annes, and Catherine Silverstone, eds. *Tragedy in Transition*. Malden, MA: Blackwell, 2007.

Bushnell, Rebecca. *Tragedy: A Short Introduction*. Malden, MA: Blackwell Publishing, 2008.

Callery, Joseph-Marie. *Li-ki: ou, Memorial des Rites: Traduit pour la Premiere fois du Chinois, et Accompagne de Notes, de Commentaires et du Text Original*. Turin, France: Imprimerie Royale, 1853.

Campany, Robert F. *Strange Writing: Anomaly Accounts in Early Medieval China*. Albany: State University of New York Press, 1996.

Cassirer, Ernst. *The Myth of the State*. New Haven, CT: Yale University Press, 1946.

Chan, Alan K. L. ed. Mencius*: Contexts and Interpretations*. Honolulu: University of Hawaii Press, 2002.

Chen, Guying 陳鼓應. *Laozi jinzhu jinyi ji pingjie* 《老子今註今譯及評介》. Taibei 臺北: Taiwan shangwu yinshuguan 臺灣商務印書館, 1997.

Chen, Ning. "The Concept of Fate in Mencius." *Philosophy East & West* 47.4 (October 1997): 495–520.

Chen, Yun 陈赟. "Datong, xiaokang yu liyueshenghuo de kaiqi—jianlun 'liyun' datong zhi shuo zai shenme yiyishang bushi wutuobang" 大同，小康与礼乐生活的开启——兼论《礼运》"大同"之说在什么意义上不是乌托邦. *Fujian luntan—Renwen shehuikexueban* 福建论坛——人文社会科学版 6 (2006): 58–63.

Cheng, Chung-ying. *New Dimensions of Confucian and Neo-Confucian Philosophy*. Albany: State University of New York Press, 1991.

Cheng, Chung-Ying, and Nicholas Bunnin, eds. *Contemporary Chinese Philosophy*. Malden, MA: Blackwell, 2002.

Cole, Susan Letzler. *The Absent One: Mourning Ritual, Tragedy, and the Performance of Ambivalence*. University Park: Pennsylvania State University Press, 1985.

Cook, Scott. "Unity and Diversity in the Musical Thought of Warring States China." Ph.D. dissertation, University of Michigan, 1995.

Couvreur, S. trans. *Li Ki ou memoires sur les bienseances et ceremoines*. 2 vols. Ho Kien Fou: Mission Catholique, 1913.

Csikszentmihalyi, Mark. *Material Virtue: Ethics and the Body in Early China*. Boston: Brill, 2004.

Cua, Antonio S. *Dimensions of Moral Creativity: Paradigms, Principles, and Ideals*. University Park: Pennsylvania State University Press, 1978.

Cua, Antonio S. *Ethical Argumentation: A Study in Hsün Tzu's Moral Epistemology*. Honolulu: University of Hawaii Press, 1985.

Cua, Antonio S. *Human Nature, Ritual, and History: Studies in Xunzi and Chinese Philosophy*. Washington, DC: Catholic University of America Press, 2005.

Cua, Antonio S. *Moral Vision and Tradition: Essays in Chinese Ethics*. Washington, DC: Catholic University of America Press, 1998.

Cua, Antonio S. *The Unity of Knowledge and Action: A Study in Wang Yang-ming's Moral Psychology*. Honolulu: University Press of Hawaii, 1982.

Dai, De 戴德. *Da Dai Liji* 《大戴禮記》. Taibei 臺北: Taiwan shangwu yinshuguan 臺灣商務印書館, 1983.

Darwall, Stephen, ed. *Virtue Ethics*. Malden, MA: Blackwell, 2003.

de Bary, William Theodore, ed. *Self and Society in Ming Thought*. New York: Columbia University Press, 1970.

Du, You 杜佑. *Tongdian* 《通典》. Wenyuange Sikuquanshu Neilianwangban 文淵閣四庫全書內聯網版. Xianggang 香港: Dizhi wenhua chuban youxiangongsi, Zhongwen daxue chubanshe 迪志文化出版有限公司，中文大學出版社, 2002. www.sikuquanshu.com.

Ebrey, Patricia Buckley, trans. *Chu Hsi's Family Rituals: A Twelfth-Century Chinese Manual for the Performance of Cappings, Weddings, Funerals, and Ancestral Rites*. Princeton, NJ: Princeton University Press, 1991.

Elfring, Halvor, ed. *Love and Emotions in Traditional Chinese Literature*. Leiden: Brill, 2004.

Eliade, Mircea. *The Myth of the Eternal Return*. Translated by Willard R. Trask. New York: Pantheon Books, 1954.

Eliade, Mircea. *The Sacred and The Profane: The Nature of Religion*. Orlando, FL: Harcourt Books, 1987.

Encyclopedia Britannica. http://www.britannica.com (accessed June 1, 2010).

Eno, Robert. "The Background of the Kong Family of Lu and the Origins of Ruism." *Early China* 28 (2003): 1–42.

Eno, Robert. *The Confucian Creation of Heaven: Philosophy and the Defense of Ritual Mastery*. Albany: State University of New York Press, 1990.

Evans-Pritchard, E. E. *Witchcraft, Oracles and Magic among the Azande*. Oxford: Clarendon Press, 1937.

Fehl, Noah Edward. *Li: Rites and Propriety in Literature and Life—A Perspective for a Cultural History of Ancient China*. Hong Kong: Chinese University of Hong Kong, 1971.

Festinger, Leon, Henry W. Riecken, and Stanley Schachter. *When Prophecy Fails*. Minneapolis: University of Minnesota Press, 1956.

Field, Stephen, trans. *Tian Wen: A Chinese Book of Origins*. New York: New Directions Publishing, 1986.

Fingarette, Herbert. *Confucius: The Secular as Sacred*. New York: Harper & Row, 1972.

Fraser, Chris, Dan Robins and Timothy O'Leary, eds. *Ethics in Early China: An Anthology*. Hong Kong: Hong Kong University Press, 2011.

Fu, Charles Wei-shun. "A Creative-Hermeneutical Investigation into the Formation and Development of the *Pratitya-samutpada* Thought." *Chung-Hwa Buddhist Journal* 4 (1991): 169–199.

Fu, Charles Wei-shun. "Creative Hermeneutics: Taoist Metaphysics and Heidegger." *Journal of Chinese Philosophy* 3 (1976): 115–143.

Fung, Yiu-Ming. "Disposition or Imposition? Remarks on Fingarette's *Lunyu*." *Journal of Chinese Philosophy* 37.2 (June 2010): 295–311.

Fung, Yu-lan. *A History of Chinese Philosophy*. 2 vols. Translated by Derk Bodde. Princeton, NJ: Princeton University Press, 1983.

Gao, Ming 高明, ed. *Da Dai Liji Jinzhu Jinyi* 《大戴禮記今註今譯》. Taibei 臺北: Taiwan shangwu yinshuguan 臺灣商務印書館, 1975.

Geertz, Clifford. *The Interpretation of Cultures*. New York: Basic Books, 2000.

Goody, Jack R., ed. *Literacy in Traditional Societies*. Cambridge: Cambridge University Press, 1968.

Grimes, Ronald. *Deeply into the Bone: Re-Inventing Rites of Passage*. Berkeley: University of California Press, 2000.

Grimes, Ronald L. *Ritual Criticism*. Columbia: University of South Carolina Press, 1990.

Gu, Ming Dong. *Chinese Theories of Reading and Writing: A Route to Hermeneutics and Open Poetics*. Albany: State University of New York Press, 2005.

Guo, Jianxun 郭建勲, ed. *Xinyi Yijing duben* 《新譯易經讀本》. Taibei 臺北: Sanmin shuju 三民書局, 1996.

Hall, David L., and Roger T. Ames. *Anticipating China: Thinking Through the Narratives of Chinese and Western Culture*. Albany: State University of New York Press, 1995.

Hall, David L., and Roger T. Ames. *Thinking from the Han: Self, Truth, and Transcendence in Chinese and Western Culture*. Albany: State University of New York Press, 1998.

Hall, David L., and Roger T. Ames. *Thinking Through Confucius*. Albany: State University of New York Press, 1987.

Harbsmeier, Christoph. *Science and Civilisation in China*. Vol. 7, Part 1: *Language and Logic*. Cambridge: Cambridge University Press, 1998.

Hardy, Grant. "The Reconstruction of Ritual: Capping in Ancient China." *Journal of Ritual Studies* 7.2 (Fall 1993): 69–90.

Hardy, Grant. *Worlds of Bronze and Bamboo: Sima Qian's Conquest of History*. New York: Columbia University Press, 1999.

Henderson, John B. *The Development and Decline of Chinese Cosmology*. New York: Columbia University Press, 1984.

Hightower, James Robert. "Chinese Literature in the Context of World Literature." *Comparative Literature* 5.2 (Spring 1953): 117–124.

Hong, Ye 洪業 et al., eds. *Hanshu ji buzhu zonghe yinde* 《漢書及補注綜合引得》. Beijing 北京: Hafuo Yanjing daxue tushuguan yinde bian zuan chu 哈佛燕京大學圖書館引得編纂處, 1940.

Hong, Ye 洪業 et al., eds. *Liji yinde* 《禮記引得》. Beiping 北平: Hafo Yanjing xue she yinde bian zuan chu 哈佛燕京學社引得編纂處, 1937.

Hu, Guang 胡廣. *Liji Daquan* 《禮記大全》. Taibei 臺北: Taiwan shangwu yinshuguan 臺灣商務印書館, 1983.

Huang, Daozhou 黃道周. *Ruxingjizhuan* 《儒行集傳》. Taibei 臺北: Taiwan shangwu yinshuguan 臺灣商務印書館, 1983.

Huang, Huaixin 黄怀信. "Guanyu *Da Dai Liji* yuanliu de jige wenti" 关于《大戴礼记》源流的几个问题. *Qilu Xuekan* 齐鲁学刊 184.1 (2005): 15–20.

Huang, Yong. "Confucius and Mencius on the Motivation to be Moral." *Philosophy East & West* 60.1 (January 2010): 65–87.

Hursthouse, Rosalind. *On Virtue Ethics*. New York: Oxford University Press, 1999.

Hüsken, Ute, ed. *When Rituals Go Wrong: Mistakes, Failure, and the Dynamics of Ritual*. Leiden: Brill, 2007.

Im, Manyul. "Emotional Control and Virtue in the *Mencius*." *Philosophy East & West* 49.1 (January 1999): 1–27.

Ivanhoe, Philip J., ed. *Chinese Language, Thought, and Culture: Nivison and His Critics*. Chicago: Open Court, 1996.

Ivanhoe, Philip J. *Ethics in the Confucian Tradition: The Thought of Mencius and Wang Yang-ming*. Cambridge: Hackett Publishing, 2002.

Ivanhoe, Philip J. "A Question of Faith." *Early China* 13 (1988): 153–165.

Ivanhoe, Philip J., and T. C. Kline III, eds. *Virtue, Nature, and Moral Agency in the* Xunzi. Indianapolis: Hackett Publishing, 2000.

Ivanhoe, Philip J., and Xiusheng Liu, eds. *Essays on the Moral Philosophy of Mengzi*. Indianapolis: Hackett Publishing, 2002.

Jennings, Theodore W. "On Ritual Knowledge." *Journal of Religion* 62 (1982): 111–127.

Jensen, Lionel M. *Manufacturing Confucianism: Chinese Traditions and Universal Civilization*. Durham, NC: Duke University Press, 1997.

Jiang, Jianshe 姜建设. "'Datong Xiaokang' Suyuan" "大同小康"溯源. *Xinyang Shifanxueyuan Xuebao* 信阳师范学院学报 14.4 (December 1994): 59–64.

Jiang, Yihua 姜義華. *Xinyi Liji duben* 《新譯禮記讀本》. Taibei 臺北: Sanmin shuju 三民書局, 1997.

Jiang, Yong 江永. *Liji xunyi zeyan* 《禮記訓義擇言》. Wenyuange Sikuquanshu Neilianwangban 文淵閣四庫全書內聯網版. Xianggang 香港: Dizhi wenhua chubanyouxiangongsi, Zhongwen daxue chubanshe 迪志文化出版有限公司, 中文大學出版社, 2002. www.sikuquanshu.com (accessed January 28, 2010).

Jingmen Shi Bowu Guan 荊门市博物馆. *Guodian chu mu zhu jian* 《郭店楚墓竹简》. Beijing 北京: Wenwu chubanshe 文物出版社, 1998.

Kline, T. C., III, "The Therapy of Desire in Early Confucianism: Xunzi." *Dao: A Journal of Comparative Philosophy* 5.2 (June 2006): 235–246.

Kreinath, Jens, Constance Hartung, and Annette Deschner, eds. *The Dynamics of Changing Rituals: The Transformation of Religious Rituals Within Their Social and Cultural Context*. New York: Peter Lang, 2004.

Kreinath, Jens, Jan Snoek, and Michael Stausberg, eds. *Theorizing Rituals*. Boston: Brill, 2006.

Laderman, Carol, and Marina Roseman, eds. *The Performance of Healing*. New York: Routledge, 1996.

Lai, Karyn. *Learning from Chinese Philosophies: Ethics of Interdependent and Contextualised Self*. Burlington, VT: Ashgate, 2006.

Lau, D. C., trans. *Confucius: The Analects*. New York: Dorset Press, 1986.

Lau, D. C. 劉殿爵, ed. *Hanshi waizhuan zhuzi suoyin: A Concordance to the Hanshi waizhuan* 《韓詩外傳逐字索引》. Taibei 臺北: Taiwan shangwu yinshuguan 臺灣商務印書館, 1992.

Lau, D. C. 劉殿爵, ed. *Maoshi zhuzi suoyin: A Concordance to the Maoshi* 《毛詩逐字索引》. Xianggang 香港: Shangwu yinshuguan 商務印書館, 1995.

Lau, D. C. 劉殿爵, ed. *Mozi zhuzi suoyin: A Concordance to the Mozi* 《墨子逐字索引》. Xianggang 香港: Shangwu yinshuguan 商務印書館, 2001.

Lau, D. C. 劉殿爵, ed. *Xunzi zhuzi suoyin: A Concordance to the Xunzi* 《荀子逐字索引》. Xianggang 香港: Shangwu yinshuguan 商務印書館, 1996.

Lau, D. C. 劉殿爵, ed. *Zhouli zhuzi suoyin* 《周禮逐字索引》 Chinese University of Hong Kong, Institute of Chinese Studies, Ancient Chinese Text Concordance Series 香港中文大學中國文化研究所先秦兩漢古籍逐字索引叢刊. Hong Kong 香港: Shangwu yinshuguan 商務印書館, 1993.

Lau, D. C. 劉殿爵, and Fong Ching Chen 陳方正, eds., *Liji zhuzi suoyin* 《禮記逐字索引》. Chinese University of Hong Kong, Institute of Chinese Studies, Ancient Chinese Text Concordance Series 香港中文大學中國文化研究所先秦兩漢古籍逐字索引叢刊. Taibei 台北: Taiwan shangwu yinshuguan 台灣商務印書館, 1992.

Lau, D. C. 劉殿爵, Che Wah Ho 何志華, and Fong Ching Chen 陳方正, eds. *Lunyu zhuzi suoyin* 《論語逐字索引》. Chinese University of Hong Kong, Institute of Chinese Studies, Ancient Chinese Text Concordance Series 香港中文大學中國文化研究所先秦兩漢古籍逐字索引叢刊. Xianggang 香港: Shangwu yinshuguan 商務印書館, 1995.

Lawson, Robert, and Thomas McCauley. *Rethinking Religion: Connecting Cognition and Culture*. New York: Cambridge University Press, 1990.

Lee, Pauline C. "Engaging Comparative Religion: A Redescription of the *Lunyu* 論語, the *Zhuangzi* 莊子 and 'A Place on Which to Stand.'" *Journal of Chinese Religions* 35 (2007): 98–131.

Legge, James, trans. *The Chinese Classics*. Vols. 3–5. Hong Kong: Hong Kong University Press, 1960.

Legge, James, trans. *The Chinese Classics: The She King or The Book of Poetry*. Taibei: SMC Publishing Inc, 1991.

Legge, James, trans. *The Sacred Books of China: The Texts of Confucianism*. Parts 3–4, *The Li Ki*. Oxford: Clarendon Press, 1885.

Lewis, Mark Edward. *Sanctioned Violence in Early China*. Albany: State University of New York Press, 1990.

Li, Chenyang. "*Li* as Cultural Grammar: On the Relation Between *Li* and *Ren* in Confucius' *Analects*." *Philosophy East & West* 57.3 (July 2007): 311–329.

Li, Dingwen 李定文. "Lun Xianqin Rujia de Youhuan Yishi ji qi Xiandai Zhuanhua" 论先秦儒家的忧患意识及其现代转化. *Lanzhou Xuekan* 兰州学刊 11.182 (2008): 21–24.

Li, Xueqin 李學勤, ed. *Shisanjing zhushu* 《十三經注疏》. Beijing 北京: Beijing daxue chubanshe 北京大学出版社, 2000.

Li, Zhonghua 李中華, ed. *Xinyi Baopuzi* 《新譯抱朴子》. Taibei 臺北: Sanmin shuju 三民書局, 1996.

Liang, Tao 梁涛. *Guodian zhujian yu simeng xuepai* 《郭店竹简与思孟学派》. Beijing 北京: Zhongguo renming daxue chbanshe 中国人民大学出版社, 2008.

Lin, Suwen 林素玟. *Liji Renwenxue tanjiu* 《禮記人文學探究》. Taibei 臺北: Wenjin chubanshe 文津出版社，2001.

Liu, Yuli. *The Unity of Rule and Virtue: A Critique of a Supposed Parallel between Confucian Ethics and Virtue Ethics*. Singapore: Eastern Universities Press, 2004.

Lovin, Robin W., and Frank E. Reynolds, eds. *Cosmogony and Ethical Order: New Studies in Comparative Ethics*. Chicago: University of Chicago Press, 1985.

Lupke, Christopher, ed. *The Magnitude of* Ming: *Command, Allotment, and Fate in Chinese Culture*. Honolulu: University of Hawaii Press, 2005.

MacAloon, John J., ed. *Rite, Drama, Festival, Spectacle: Rehearsals Toward a Theory of Cultural Performance*. Philadelphia, PA: Institute for the Study of Human Issues, 1984.

MacIntyre, Alasdair C. *Whose Justice? Which Rationality?* Notre Dame, IN: University of Notre Dame Press, 1988.

Michaels, Axel, et al., eds. *Ritual Dynamics and the Science of Ritual*. Vol. 1. Wiesbaden: Harrassowitz, 2010.

Morreall, John. *Comedy, Tragedy, and Religion*. Albany: State University of New York Press, 1999.

Naess, Arne, and Alastair Hannay. eds. *Invitation to Chinese Philosophy*. Oslo: Universitetsforlaget, 1972.

Nagel, Thomas. *Mortal Questions*. New York: Cambridge University Press, 1979.

Nivison, David S. *The Ways of Confucianism: Investigations in Chinese Philosophy*. Chicago: Open Court, 1996.

Nussbaum, Martha C. *The Fragility of Goodness: Luck and Ethics in Greek Tragedy and Philosophy*. New York: Cambridge University Press, 1986.

Nylan, Michael. *The Five "Confucian" Classics*. New Haven, CT: Yale University Press, 2001.

Nylan, Michael, and Thomas Wilson. *Lives of Confucius: Civilization's Greatest Sage Through the Ages*. New York: Doubeday, 2010.

Olberding, Amy. "'Ascending the Hall': Style and Moral Improvement in the *Analects*." *Philosophy East & West* 59.4 (October 2009): 503–522.

Olberding, Amy. "The Educative Function of Personal Style in the *Analects*." *Philosophy East & West* 57.3 (July 2007): 357–374.

Olberding, Amy, and Philip J. Ivanhoe, eds. *Mortality in Traditional Chinese Thought*. Albany: State University of New York Press, 2011.

Oxford English Dictionary. http://dictionary.oed.com (accessed August 10, 2010).

Peerenboom, Randall P. *Law and Morality in Ancient China: The Silk Manuscripts of Huang-Lao*. Albany: State University of New York Press, 1993.

Pines, Yuri. *Foundations of Confucian Thought: Intellectual Life in the Chunqiu Period, 722–453 B.C.E.* Honolulu: University of Hawaii Press, 2002.

Poole, Adrian. *Tragedy: A Very Short Introduction*. New York: Oxford University Press, 2005.

Puett, Michael J. *The Ambivalence of Creation: Debates Concerning Innovation and Artifice in Early China*. Stanford, CA: Stanford University Press, 2001.

Qin, Huitian 秦蕙田. *Wuli Tongkao* 《五禮通考》. Taibei 臺北: Taiwan shangwu yinshuguan 臺灣商務印書館, 1983.

Rank, Otto. *Will Therapy: An Analysis of Therapeutic Process in Terms of Relationship*. Translated by Julia Jesse Taft. New York: Alfred A. Knopf, 1936.

Rappaport, Roy. *Ritual in the Making of Humanity*. Cambridge: Cambridge University Press, 1999.

Reynolds, Frank, and David Tracy, eds. *Discourse and Practice*. Albany: State University of New York Press, 1992.

Riegel, Jeffrey K. "The Four 'Tzu ssu' Chapters of the *Li chi*: An Analysis and Translation of the *Fang chi*, *Chung yung*, *Piao chi*, and *Tzu i*." Ph.D. dissertation, Stanford University, 1978.

Santangelo, Paolo, ed. *Love, Hatred, and Other Passions: Questions and Themes on Emotions in Chinese Civilization*. Boston: Brill, 2006.

Sato, Masayuki. *The Confucian Quest for Order: The Origin and Formation of the Political Thought of Xun Zi*. Boston: Brill, 2003.

Sax, William, Johannes Quack, and Jan Weinholded, eds. *The Problem of Ritual Efficacy*. New York: Oxford University Press, 2010.

Schofer, Jonathan Wyn. *Confronting Vulnerability: The Body and the Divine in Rabbinic Ethics*. Chicago: University of Chicago Press, 2010.

Schofer, Jonathan Wyn. *The Making of a Sage: A Study in Rabbinic Ethics*. Madison: University of Wisconsin Press, 2005.

Schuessler, Axel. *ABC Etymological Dictionary of Old Chinese*. Honolulu: University of Hawaii Press, 2007.

Seligman, Adam B., Robert P.Weller, Michael J. Puett, and Bennett Simon. *Ritual and Its Consequences: An Essay on the Limits of Sincerity*. New York: Oxford University Press, 2008.

Setton, Mark. "Ambiguity in the *Analects*: Philosophical and Practical Dimensions." *Journal of Chinese Philosophy* 27.4. (December 2000): 545–569.

Shankman, Steven, and Stephen W. Durrant, eds. *Early China/Ancient Greece*. Albany: State University of New York Press, 2002.

Shao, Taiqu 邵泰衢. *Tangong yiwen* 《檀弓疑問》. Taibei 臺北: Taiwan shangwu yinshuguan 臺灣商務印書館, 1983.

Shaughnessy, Edward L. *Rewriting Early Chinese Texts*. Albany: State University of New York Press, 2006.

Shun, Kwong-Loi. *Mencius and Early Chinese Thought*. Stanford, CA: Stanford University Press, 1997.

Sigurdsson, Gier. "Learning and *Li*: The Confucian Process of Humanization Through Ritual Propriety." Ph.D. dissertation, University of Hawaii, 2004.

Sima, Qian 司馬遷. *Shiji* 《史記》. Qinding sikuquanshu 欽定四庫全書, 13.1, www.sikuquanshu.com (accessed August 19, 2010).

Slingerland, Edward G. "The Conception of *Ming* in Early Confucian Thought." *Philosophy East & West* 46.4 (October 1996): 567–581.

Slingerland, Edward G., trans. *Confucius: Analects*. Cambridge: Hackett Publishing, 2003.

Slingerland, Edward G. "Virtue Ethics, The *Analects*, and the Problem of Commensurability." *Journal of Religious Ethics* 29.1 (2001): 97–125.

Smith, Jonathan Z. "The Bare Facts of Ritual," *History of Religions* 20.1–2 (1980): 112–127.

Smith, Jonathan Z. *To Take Place: Toward Theory in Ritual*. Chicago: University of Chicago Press, 1987.

Smits, Gregory. "The Intersection of Politics and Thought in Ryukyuan Confucianism: Sai On's Uses of Quan." *Harvard Journal of Asiatic Studies* 56.2 (December 1996): 443–477.

Statman, Daniel, ed. *Moral Luck*. Albany: State University of New York Press, 1993.

Sun, Zhenbin. "*Yan*: A Dimension of Praxis and its Philosophical Implications." *Journal of Chinese Philosophy* 24 (1997): 191–208.

Takeuchi, Teruo 竹内照夫. *Raiki* 《礼記》. Tōkyō 東京: Meiji Shoin 明治書院, 1971–1979.

Takuji, Kudō. "Jinyibainian Riben *Liji* yanjiu gaikuang 1900–2008 nian zhi huigu yu zhanwang" 〈近一百年日本《禮記》研究概況－－1900–2008 年之回顧與展望〉. *Zhongguo wenzhe yanjiusuo tongxun* 《中國文哲研究所通訊》 19.4 (2009): 53–101.

Tambiah, Stanley. *Magic, Science, Religion, and the Scope of Rationality*. New York: Cambridge University Press, 1990.

Tang, Renze 汤仁泽. "'Datongxue' he 'Liyunzhu'" "大同学"和《礼运注》. *Shilin* 史林 4 (1997).

Tessman, Lisa. *Burdened Virtues: Virtue Ethics for Liberatory Struggles*. New York: Oxford University Press, 2005.

Tu, Ching-I, ed. *Interpretation and Intellectual Change: Chinese Hermeneutics in Historical Perspective*. New Brunswick, NJ: Transaction Publications, 2005.

Tu, Weiming, and Mary Evelyn Tucker, eds. *Confucian Spirituality*. Vols. 1–2. New York: Crossroad Publishing Company, 2003–2004.

Turner, Victor Witter. *The Forest of Symbols: Aspects of Ndembu Ritual*. Ithaca, NY: Cornell University Press, 1967.

Van Norden, Bryan W., ed. *Confucius and the* Analects: *New Essays*. New York: Oxford University Press, 2002.

Van Norden, Bryan W. *Virtue Ethics and Consequentialism in Early Chinese Philosophy*. New York: Cambridge University Press, 2007.

Vankeerberghen, Griet. "Choosing Balance: Weighing (*Quan* 權) as a Metaphor for Action in Early Chinese Texts." *Early China* 30 (2005): 47–89.

Wallace, Jennifer. *The Cambridge Introduction to Tragedy*. New York: Cambridge University Press, 2007.

Wang, E 王锷. "'Datong,' 'xiaokang,' yu 'Liyun' de chengpian niandai" "大同", "小康" 与《礼运》的成篇年代. *Xibeishidaxuebao* 西北师大学报 43.6 (November 2006): 68–71.

Wang, E 王鍔. *Liji Chengshu Kao*《禮記成書考》. (Beijing 北京: Zhonghua Shuju 中華書局, 2007).

Wang, Fuzhi 王夫之. *Liji Zhangju*《禮記章句》. Shanghai 上海: Shanghai guji chubanshe 上海古籍出版社, 1995–1999.

Wang, Li 王力. *Wang Li gu Hanyu zidian* 《王力古漢語字典》. Beijing 北京: Zhonghua shuju 中華書局, 2000.

Wang, Meng'ou 王夢鷗. *Liji jinzhu jinyi* 《禮記今註今譯》. Taibei 臺北: Taiwan shangwu yinshuguan 臺灣商務印書館, 1969.

Wang, Robin R., ed. *Chinese Philosophy in an Era of Globalization*. Albany: State University of New York Press, 2004.

Wawrytko, Sandra A. "Kongzi as Feminist: Confucian Self-Cultivation in a Contemporary Context." *Journal of Chinese Philosophy* 27.2 (June 2000): 171–187.

Wechsler, Howard J. *Offerings of Jade and Silk: Ritual and Symbol in the Legitimation of the T'ang Dynasty*. New Haven, CT: Yale University Press, 1985.

Wei, Shi 衛湜, ed. *Liji Jishuo* 《禮記集說》. Taibei 臺北: Taiwan shangwu yinshuguan 臺灣商務印書館, 1983.

Wilhelm, Richard, trans. *Li Gi: Das Buch der Sitte des alteren und Jungeren Dai*. Jena: Eugen Diederichs, 1930.

Williams, Bernard Arthur Owen. *Moral Luck: Philosophical Papers*, 1973–1980. New York: Cambridge University Press, 1981.

Wilson, Stephen A. "Conformity, Individuality, and the Nature of Virtue." *Journal of Religious Ethics* 23.2 (2001): 263–289.

Wilson, Thomas. "Sacrifice and the Imperial Cult of Confucius." *History of Religions* 41.3 (February. 2002): 251–287.

Wittgenstein, Ludwig. *Philosophical Fragments*. New York: Macmillian, 1953.

Wong, Benjamin, and Hui-Chieh Loy, "The Confucian Gentleman and the Limits of Ethical Change." *Journal of Chinese Philosophy* 28.3 (September 2001): 209–234.

Wu, Cheng 吳澄. *Liji zuanyan*《禮記纂言》. Jinan 濟南: Qi-Lu shushe chubanshe 齊魯書社出版社, 1997.

Wu, Kuang-ming. *History, Thinking, and Literature in Chinese Philosophy*. Taibei: Sun Yat-Sen Institute for Social Sciences and Philosophy, 1991.

Xie, Bingying 謝冰瑩. *Xinyi sishu duben* 《新譯四書讀本》. Taibei: 臺北: Sanmin shuju 三民書局, 2002.

Xu, Fu 徐復, and Wenmin Song 宋文民. *Shuowen wubaisishi bushou zhengjie*《說文五百四十部首正解》. Jiangsu 江蘇: Guji chubanshe 古籍出版社, 2003.

Xu, Shen 許慎. *Shuowen Jiezi* 《說文解字》. Beijing 北京: Zhonghua Shuju 中華書局, 2004.

Yang, Chaoming 杨朝明. "'Liyun' Chengpian yu xuepaishuxing deng wenti" 《礼运》成篇与学派属性等问题. *Zhongguo Wenhua Yanjiu* 《中国文化研究》 1 (2005).

Yang, Chunqiu 羊春秋. *Xinyi Kongzi Jiayu* 《新譯孔子家語》. Taibei 臺北: Sanmin shuju: 三民書局, 1996.

Yearley, Lee H. *Mencius and Aquinas: Theories of Virtue and Conceptions of Courage.* Albany: State University of New York Press, 1990.

Yeats, W. B. *Essays and Introductions.* New York: Macmillan, 1961.

Yu, Jiyuan. *The Ethics of Confucius and Aristotle: Mirrors of Virtue.* New York: Routledge, 2007.

Zagzebski, Linda Trinkaus. *Virtues of the Mind: An Inquiry into the Nature of Virtue and the Ethical Foundations of Knowledge.* Cambridge: Cambridge University Press, 1995.

Zhang, Yinshu 張銀樹. *Liji Sixiang Conglun*《禮記思想叢論》. Taibei 臺北: Furen Daxue Chubanshe 輔仁大學出版社, 2006.

Zhou, Qin. "Cosmic Order and Moral Autonomy: The Rise of Confucian Ethics in Axial Age China." Ph.D. dissertation, Harvard University, 2000.

Index